RADICAL
PSYCHOLOGY

Radical Psychology

EDITED BY PHIL BROWN

TAVISTOCK PUBLICATIONS
London   New York   Toronto   Sydney   Wellington

First published in Great Britain in 1973
by Tavistock Publications Limited
11 New Fetter Lane London EC4P 4EE
Printed in Great Britain
by Butler & Tanner Ltd, Frome and London

SBN 422 74410 7 (*casebound*)
SBN 422 74420 4 (*paperback*)

To my parents
Sylvia and William Brown

Acknowledgments

The format of this book is partly based on the several courses I taught at Alternate U. in New York City in 1969 and 1970, and those attending were important in initial construction of a logical format for presenting radical psychology. Keith Brooks has been the most singularly important and helpful person. A co-teacher at Alternate U., a co-member in several political groups, a good friend and comrade, and an important influence on my thought in radical psychology, my debt to Keith is quite large. He has also helped by going over the preface and introductions with me, offering much helpful advice and clarifying several points. I also owe a debt to co-members of Psychologists for a Democratic Society, and, most importantly, to *The Radical Therapist*. Nancy Henley, my close friend and co-worker on *The Radical Therapist,* has provided invaluable criticism and comment on both the content of the book and the introductory statements. Craig Jackson has also made some needed suggestions. My editor, Cynthia Merman, has been available at every step, and I am most thankful to her.

Contents

Preface

"Radical psychology" is at once both an exciting new concept and an already hackneyed one. The very necessity of branding certain studies as "radical" is unsatisfactory. One would wish that all fields of study and action would be, by their very nature, radical. What, then, is this new concept of radical psychology which has grown so suddenly in the past few years?

With the growth of the antiwar movement, many changes occurred in American society. The black revolutionary movement developed out of the old civil rights struggle; new tendencies were unleashed in the antiwar movement as people took on a wider range of issues. From all of this background, people began to question seriously more aspects of their lives—while other third world groups in this country developed liberation movements, so did sexual groups—women and gays. Women's and gay libera-

tion posed questions not dealt with by the older
movements, questions of deeper feeling and significance.

At the same time, universities and their academic
oppression/nonsense were also under fire. Social
sciences in particular were heavily criticized. Yet
psychology was for the most part left out. Why?
Partly because there was no radical tradition to look
back to, as in other fields. Partly because psychology
seemed to be more "open" and "liberal." The reality
was that very few radicals were studying or working
in psychology. Students already politically aware
tended to choose other areas; students who became
politically conscious in graduate school tended to
drop out. Psychology was in fact a liberal field, but
only in that lip service was paid to liberalism while
the repressive nature actually continued.

It didn't take much reflection to see what psychologists were doing under their liberal veneer.
What made it easier was that we (I say "we," since
this was a common, shared discovery) were not
approaching the problem from the standpoint of a
professional critique. Psychology as a pseudoscience
had denied our feelings, quantified our emotions. We
thus took an approach which was tangible to us—a
gut feeling and a felt understanding. There was a
certain fear that our critique and our alternatives
would be discounted because of this antiprofessional
stance, but we struggled to get over that fear, learning much in the process.

What became clear was that there is no way to
plug radical politics into a nonradical area and ex-

pect it to be meaningful. Psychology is not just another field, one among many disciplines. *Psychological manipulation pervades all areas of society, not only through the use of "skills" and "techniques," but through the conveyance of oppressive behavior to the oppressed themselves, and through the use of psychology as an ideology for the defense of the status quo.*

In terms of so-called skills and techniques, psychological manipulation is at least overt and thus more easily identifiable. Industrial psychologists make factory workers more "comfortable," but only in ways to sap their militancy and thus insure corporate profit; fancy lounges and "counselling" services are traded off for speed-ups of the assembly line. These gimmicks are labeled as the liberal benevolence of the bosses, but the benevolence disappears when the operation of the factory is threatened by workers' organization. Advertising psychologists aid the corporations on the opposite end by brainwashing people into consuming harmful and/or meaningless products, with the promise of financial and/or sexual success if the correct products are bought. School psychologists push working class children into vocational tracks, while placing middle strata children into academic tracks. They counsel students against militancy, with thinly veiled threats of reprisal. Further, they gain students' confidence, then report their "antisocial" attitudes to the higher administration. Military psychologists polish the machinery of U.S. imperialism in Indochina and elsewhere, providing "adjustment" for antiwar GIs and counseling bomber pilots so they won't feel guilty about napalming Vietnamese. Behavior modification experts work out tortures to "cure" deviants (read: gays, political activisits, etc.); California's infamous prison system employs such experts at its Vacaville Adjustment Center for troublemakers in the prisons—the activities of the behavior modification experts at Vacaville sound remarkably like the "medical research" of Hitler's concentration camps. Social psychologists perform research for counter-insurgency plans at home and abroad, including attempts to prove sexual and racial inequality—IQ research by men such as Jensen and Herrnstein not only provides the ruling class's answer to black struggles for freedom, but also provides the rational basis for repression since it is "scientific." Community mental health centers cool out ghettos, defusing militant activities with soft-sell therapy services. State hospitals jack people up on thorazine and give electroshock or lobotomies to working class people whose behavior would never be "treated" if they were wealthy. Psychology is a class rip-off: the subjects tend to be poor; those who reap the benefits tend to be rich. The indictment is endless, and the activities of psychology professionals become more abhorrent the more we open our eyes.

But the indirect seeping down of psychological manipulation is harder to uncover. Conveyance of repressive values by private therapists has become the most obvious and discussed example. Many people put their trust in supposedly liberated shrinks, finding, however, that the same social activities were stigmatized, the same fears and hopes ridiculed as by "traditional" shrinks. From lack of recognition to rape, the person seeking help is cheated and oppressed. This is but a mirror of the larger society in which values of the ruling class seep down to the masses below because the masses of people are given no real options. Media, family, schools, and work places define antihuman values, then reward people for accepting, and punish them for transgressing these values. The attitudes of our rulers are forced on us, and we are stamped on if we reject them. Then, the body of knowledge created by psychologists concerning this value forcing is called psychological theory. I call it ideology, a codified scheme of social control. Because radical psychology is a *total* approach rather than a compartmentalized one, it can investigate the creeping manipulation of psychology in a social context.

At first there was simply a critique, as described above, radical in that it tried to get to the roots of the problem. But the difficulty remained of integrating this critique more fully with a political perspective, and then of acting on it. The essence of the future is to see that our politics and approach to psychology are unified. One interacts with the other, resulting in continual change. As we saw that this society would not accept a "new" psychology, we also saw that a people's psychology would only be possible in a new form of society—a socialist one.

Obviously we could not work within the professional organizations. Some had tried it and failed. The American Psychological Association, with an empire much like the American Medical Association, wanted to stamp out all criticism. The "liberal" associations (American Orthopsychiatric Association, Association for Humanistic Psychology, Psychologists for Social Action) were likewise of no use—they heightened the hypocrisy of professional psychology by opposing the Vietnam war, but refusing to question the values of their daily work in psychology.

We started to deal with the problem of psychology in society on many levels. We fought for community control of community mental health centers; school psychologists opposed compartmentalizing students and instead tried to help students rather than administrators; psychology students organized within their departments and presented radical views to co-students; and we taught radical and Marxist psychology at free universities. We staged guerrilla theater at professional conventions—both to desanctify their sterile, oppressive atmosphere, and to meet like-minded people. Some of us saw each other only at those times, due to distance, but we had much to tell each other about our efforts over the preceding months, much to help each other with. Some of us were in Psychologists for a Democratic Society, now defunct, but at one time having several chapters, a newspaper, and many friends and contacts who invited us to speak to various groups of people about our views and actions. Some women tried to work with the Association for Women in Psychology. Some students started independent groups in their colleges.

The movement was growing. Our understanding was becoming more substantial. Practical activities also took the form of rap centers, although not all of these were in radical places. Women set up therapy and referral services for their sisters; gay people did the same. In Berkeley the Radical Psychiatry Center spawned many different projects. Other groups experimented with radical counseling services. *The Radical Therapist,* emerging in the spring of 1970, became more than just a magazine. Friends and contacts were established all over the country. We of the RT began to provide referrals, have open house rap sessions, speak with groups of people, set up peer groups for mental health workers who wanted solidarity to fight back and to help their "clients."

But this growth was accompanied by certain problems. "Radical therapy" became a widespread term for innovative techniques that lacked real radical analysis or content. Another problem was the emphasis on therapy, which left other fields of psychology uncriticized and unchallenged. In addition, many discounted the Marxist approach of seeing psychology in its social context. A certain antistructure element within the youth culture could even see all people holding straight jobs as the enemy. Some felt that encounter groups by themselves would change society. Some radical psychologists felt that radical psychology would lead the revolution. It became necessary to separate the real from the phony. What was the cutting edge?

The growth and popularity of alternatives to mainstream psychology was best typified by the widespread acceptance of Laing's *The Politics of Experience,* but Laing was simplified and co-opted by academia in much the same manner that Cleaver's *Soul on Ice* was defused. Radical psychology grew up in the midst of a movement against sexism, particularly the women's movement (the gay movement came later and has so far been less influential, though not less important in the long run). *The women's movement gave an incredible impetus to radical psychology,* enabling it to move beyond theoretical isolation and deal with problems as political and personal at the same time. Women, particularly oppressed in therapy, had much to draw on in their critique of mainstream psychology. Also, women's groups had shown that what professionals called psychopathology in women was merely women's responses to sexist oppression. Many women realized that their problems were not individual and isolated, but social problems shared by all women. Clinical and social psychologists had stigmatized women's self-defense, had labeled them neurotic or psychotic for protecting their bodies and their personal integrity. Sex roles were probably the largest factor within psychological theory and practice which radical psychology first attacked. *Getting in touch with the reality of sex roles, particularly in the family and couple contexts, led us to learn more and feel more, to demand more of a new psychology.*

Youth culture was not the answer. Replacing housewives with earth mothers was not progress. The sexual revolution was regressive/repressive, as it was basically a coup d'état for men. Drugs and rock, while playing certain important functions in emotional release, were still not sufficient to build a social movement, much less a new society. We had to criticize even our own heroes like Laing. We had to try to live our lives as prefigurations of a postrevolutionary context, while at the same time building for that future.

Radical psychology almost becomes simply the discovery of our day-to-day life, and the transformation of it. Instead of playing with rat mazes, we ask why people run around in the mazes of "false consciousness" whereby they often act not in their own interests but in the interests of the ruling class. We replace work ethic with nonalienating work, delayed gratification with honest relationships. *In a Marxist framework, a people's psychology is the realization by the masses of people of the particularities of their existence, and the transformation of their lives through self-directed activity.*

A people's psychology is thus not merely a specialty field of social science, but an integrating factor of self-awareness within the revolutionary process. Further, as an integrating factor, it will eventually disappear, dissolving into a unified theory and practice of human existence. In the process of this ultimate negation, radical psychology will transcend the simple study, writing, and practice of its present day orientation——our understanding of mental process and emotions will include fine arts, performing arts, the changes in people's heads as they struggle for freedom, the role of people in history.

We will find that the majority of academic research and writing on what the professionals call psychology will need to be discarded. And we will discard it since we must formulate and practice our own psychology. *Radical psychology is a force of revolution, not academia.*

It has been difficult to put together *one* book to serve as an introduction to radical psychology. Some of the selections seem not so radical, but are included since they played an important role in early formulations of radical psychology. This book is not intended as an eclectic grouping of writings. Rather it has an intentional continuity. Omissions are significant. A bibliography is provided at the end of the book to aid further study. Certain topics found in the bibliography are not represented in the selections—some are covered in other sections either directly or indirectly.

RADICAL
PSYCHOLOGY

The Sociological Approach

Introduction

Although the articles in this section may seem the least politically radical in the book, they are important in that they provide an initial critique of mainstream psychology. Thomas Szasz, Erving Goffman, and Thomas Scheff stand out as three important figures who have provided sociological works on mental illness and psychology as forms of ideology. Although only Goffman and Scheff are in the field of sociology, Szasz, a psychiatrist, has explored sociological bases of mental illness. In his essay, "The Myth of Mental Illness," later expanded into a book of the same name, Szasz explored the societal context of mental illness. He perceived that mental illness was in fact a scapegoat ideology—people had problems in living, and these problems had real societal causes. Instead of dealing with those problems as real events and conditions, the psychiatric establishment was covering them up with psycho-

pathology. Psychiatric diagnosis was a way of dealing falsely with social problems; it was a way of
writing off "deviants" within a society by using the
false scientism of the medical man.

Szasz always approached the problem as one of
psychiatry—psychiatrists as specialized doctors with
the power to label certain behavior as "mental illness" and to aid the courts in committing those
exhibiting this behavior. He cites innumerable examples of involuntary commitment used as a weapon
against people by their families, the schools, the
police agencies. Speaking from a libertarian standpoint, Szasz fears an imminent 1984, with psychiatrists in the vanguard of social control. Through his
many books and articles, Szasz has explored the
legal uses of psychiatry (*Law, Liberty, and Psychiatry*) and the continuation of witch hunting and
heresy hunting into the modern era (*The Manufacture of Madness*).

The witch hunting analogy is very much to the
point. Women who acted as independent people,
refusing to bow to traditional roles assigned them,
were deviants to their society. The church, as the
dominant medieval institution, was once able to
label and persecute these women as witches. The
same behavior is now considered to be mental illness, and this ideological position persecutes women
to a much greater extent than men. "Witches," by
providing midwifery and abortions, were particularly
vulnerable to the church's oppression, since the
question of sexuality was brought to the fore. Like
the witch hunters centuries ago, what Szasz calls the

"Mental Health Movement" today refuses to deal
with the social context of behavior, and seeks
women out as agents of social evils. (I should add
that this is not Szasz's particular argument.)

Women are punished for certain sexual behavior
that is considered permissible to men, and that
punishment is often administered by the mental
health professions (*i.e.*, men). When women get
together to liberate themselves, the psychiatrists and
psychologists come out and tell these women that
they have psychological problems, not social ones.
Similar to this are the criminal activities of people
like Bruno Bettleheim, who ascribes psychological
problems to student activism—demonstrators are
acting out "unresolved oedipal complexes," etc. This
is not an accident; the mental health professions
function to funnel away the real discontent by calling
it "acting out," "father-identification," and many
other such epithets. Next, they aid the state in
attacking the opposition and, often, in committing
them to mental hospitals.

Szasz saw analogous activities in the psychiatric
profession, especially in the way it ascribed deviance
to homosexuality rather than seeing homosexuality
as a valid mode of relating. But for one who saw so
clearly the police actions of the psychiatric establishment, Szasz was still quite limited. Seeing involuntary commitment as the state's threat to personal
liberty, Szasz posited voluntary therapy as the opposite pole—good, useful, nonrepressive. Part of this
goodness, as he saw it, was that it provided a voluntary service model, involving the important aspect of

paying a fee to the therapist. Through this failure to
see the therapist's traditional role as enforcer of
social values and roles, and through his anticommu-
nist feelings, Szasz shows himself to be a *laissez
faire,* conservative theorist of the possibilities of
meliorating bad aspects of the psychiatric establishment. He cannot go beyond his limited critique, and
the contradiction between his political views and his
condemnations of psychiatry typifies the thinking of
many others who fail to integrate political analysis
with psychological theory.

Goffman, like Szasz, condemns the "medical
model." He points out the fallacy of seeing emotional problems in the same way as medical problems. The medical model involves not only the
medical orientation of psychology and psychiatry,
but also the model of mental illness as having
specific origins (etiology) and definite cures. Goffman offers the "tinkering model" as a more social
view of this medical model—an approach he sees
being utilized by society, which maintains that prob-
lems/people can be "fixed" in order to preserve the
status quo.

Goffman traces the career of the mental patient
from the moment when he is first labeled "mentally
ill." A "degradation ritual" follows, in which the
committed patient is shown his or her inferior capacity as a fixed social reality. Then follows the residency in the hospital, a "total institution" which
operates like a prison in maintaining all aspects of
the patient's life in an ordered, authoritarian manner. Goffman points out all the levels of hierarchy,

the positions of false and real power, and the manifold alienation of the patient. He strikes down the myth of neutrality among the hospital staff, showing how it is a necessary fiction (for the hospital), but at the same time an impossible one to maintain.

Thomas Scheff deals with mental illness as an ideology of the status quo. He shows how the labeling of certain behavior is a reaction to rule violations by the person, and how this labeling is vague and meaningless. As does Szasz, Scheff sees the development of religious/supernatural legitimacy into scientific/psychological legitimacy.

The work of Szasz, Goffman, and Scheff is quite useful for a partial analysis of the role of psychology in society, but falls short by failing to provide alternatives in practice. These three people question the sociological nature of psychology, but fail to phrase their questions in the total manner in which Marxist approaches do. A particular failure is the lack of a well-defined class analysis of mental illness and psychiatric commitment; later, in the section on Marxism, a beginning is made in this direction.

The selections here are provided as the best partial foundations of Szasz, Goffman, and Scheff. Szasz's "The Myth of Mental Illness" is a general survey of his indictment of the psychiatric profession. The excerpts from "Medical Model and Mental Hospitalization" from Goffman's *Asylums* illustrate his institutional and ideological approaches, although they do not deal as much with the inner society of the mental hospital as other parts of his book. Scheff's "Schizophrenia as Ideology" is a short piece outlining a critique of psychopathology, particularly as applied to schizophrenia in a social context.

1. The Myth of Mental Illness

THOMAS SZASZ

At the core of virtually all contemporary psychiatric theories and practices lies the concept of mental illness. A critical examination of this concept is therefore indispensable for understanding the ideas, institutions, and interventions of psychiatrists.

My aim in this essay is to ask if there is such a thing as mental illness, and to argue that there is not. Of course, mental illness is not a thing or physical object; hence it can exist only in the same sort of way as do other theoretical concepts. Yet, to those who believe in them, familiar theories are likely to appear, sooner or later, as "objective truths" or "facts." During certain historical periods, explanatory concepts such as deities, witches, and instincts appeared not only as theories but as *self-evident*

From *American Psychologist* 15 (1960): 113–118. Copyright 1960 by the American Psychological Association. Reprinted by permission of the publisher and author.

causes of a vast number of events. Today mental illness is widely regarded in a similar fashion, that is, as the cause of innumerable diverse happenings.

As an antidote to the complacent use of the notion of mental illness—as a self-evident phenomenon, theory, or cause—let us ask: What is meant when it is asserted that someone is mentally ill? In this essay I shall describe the main uses of the concept of mental illness, and I shall argue that this notion has outlived whatever cognitive usefulness it might have had and that it now functions as a myth.

II

The notion of mental illness derives its main support from such phenomena as syphilis of the brain or delirious conditions—intoxications, for instance—in which persons may manifest certain disorders of thinking and behavior. Correctly speaking, however, these are diseases of the brain, not of the mind. According to one school of thought, *all* so-called mental illness is of this type. The assumption is made that some neurological defect, perhaps a very subtle one, will ultimately be found to explain all the disorders of thinking and behavior. Many contemporary physicians, psychiatrists, and other scientists hold this view, which implies that people's troubles cannot be caused by conflicting personal needs, opinions, social aspirations, values, and so forth. These difficulties—which I think we may simply call *problems in living*—are thus attributed to physicochemical processes that in due time will be discovered (and no doubt corrected) by medical research.

Mental illnesses are thus regarded as basically similar to other diseases. The only difference, in this view, between mental and bodily disease is that the former, affecting the brain, manifests itself by means of mental symptoms; whereas the latter, affecting other organ systems—for example, the skin, liver, and so on—manifests itself by means of symptoms referable to those parts of the body.

In my opinion, this view is based on two fundamental errors. In the first place, a disease of the brain, analogous to a disease of the skin or bone, is a neurological defect, not a problem in living. For example, a *defect* in a person's visual field may be explained by correlating it with certain lesions in the nervous system. On the other hand, a person's *belief* —whether it be in Christianity, in Communism, or in the idea that his internal organs are rotting and that his body is already dead—cannot be explained by a defect or disease of the nervous system. Explanations of this sort of occurrence—asssuming that one is interested in the belief itself and does not regard it simply as a symptom or expression of something else that is more interesting—must be sought along different lines.

The second error is epistemological. It consists of interpreting communications about ourselves and the world around us as symptoms of neurological functioning. This is an error not in observation or reasoning, but rather in the organization and expression of knowledge. In the present case, the error lies in making a dualism between mental and physical symptoms, a dualism that is a habit of speech and not the result of known observations. Let us see if this is so.

In medical practice, when we speak of physical disturbances we mean either signs (for example, fever) or symptoms (for example, pain). We speak of mental symptoms, on the other hand, when we refer to a patient's communications about himself, others, and the world about him. The patient might assert that he is Napoleon or that he is being persecuted by the Communists. These would be considered mental symptoms only if the observer believed that the patient was *not* Napoleon or that he was *not* being persecuted by the Communists. This makes it apparent that the statement "X is a mental symptom" involves rendering a judgment that entails a covert comparison between the patient's ideas, concepts, or beliefs and those of the observer and the society in which they live. The notion of mental symptom is therefore inextricably tied to the social, and particularly the ethical, context in which it is made, just as the notion of bodily symptom is tied to an anatomical and genetic context.[1]

To sum up: For those who regard mental symptoms as signs of brain disease, the concept of mental illness is unnecessary and misleading. If they mean that people so labeled suffer from diseases of the brain, it would seem better, for the sake of clarity, to say that and not something else.

1. See T. S. Szasz, *Pain and Pleasure: A Study of Bodily Feelings* (New York: Basic Books, 1957), especially pp. 70–81; "The Problem of Psychiatric Nosology," *Amer. J. Psychiatry,* 114 (November 1957): 405–413.

III

The term "mental illness" is also widely used to describe something quite different from a disease of the brain. Many people today take it for granted that living is an arduous affair. Its hardship for modern man derives, moreover, not so much from a struggle for biological survival as from the stresses and strains inherent in the social intercourse of complex human personalities. In this context, the notion of mental illness is used to identify or describe some feature of an individual's so-called personality. Mental illness—as a deformity of the personality, so to speak—is then regarded as the cause of human disharmony. It is implicit in this view that social intercourse between people is regarded as something inherently harmonious, its disturbance being due solely to the presence of "mental illness" in many people. Clearly, this is faulty reasoning, for it makes the abstraction "mental illness" into a cause of, even though this abstraction was originally created to serve only as a shorthand expression for, certain types of human behavior. It now becomes necessary to ask: What kinds of behavior are regarded as indicative of mental illness, and by whom?

The concept of illness, whether bodily or mental, implies deviation from some clearly defined norm. In the case of physical illness, the norm is the structural and functional integrity of the human body. Thus, although the desirability of physical health, as such, is an ethical value, what health is can be stated in anatomical and physiological terms. What is the norm, deviation from which is regarded as mental illness? This question cannot be easily answered. But whatever this norm may be, we can be certain of only one thing: namely, that it must be stated in terms of psychosocial, ethical, and legal concepts. For example, notions such as "excessive repression" and "acting out an unconscious impulse" illustrate the use of psychological concepts for judging so-called mental health and illness. The idea that chronic hostility, vengefulness, or divorce are indicative of mental illness is an illustration of the use of ethical norms (that is, the desirability of love, kindness, and a stable marriage relationship). Finally, the widespread psychiatric opinion that only a mentally ill person would commit homicide illustrates the use of a legal concept as a norm of mental health. In short, when one speaks of mental illness, the norm from which deviation is measured is a *psychosocial and ethical* standard. Yet, the remedy is sought in terms of *medical* measures that—it is hoped and assumed—are free from wide differences of ethical value. The definition of the disorder and the terms in which its remedy are sought are therefore at serious odds with one another. The practical significance of this covert conflict between the alleged nature of the defect and the actual remedy can hardly be exaggerated.

Having identified the norms used for measuring deviations in cases of mental illness, we shall now turn to the question, Who defines the norms and hence the deviation? Two basic answers may be

offered: First, it may be the person himself—that is,
the patient—who decides that he deviates from a
norm; for example, an artist may believe that he
suffers from a work inhibition; and he may imple-
ment this conclusion by seeking help *for himself*
from a psychotherapist. Second, it may be someone
other than the "patient" who decides that the latter
is deviant—for example, relatives, physicians, legal
authorities, society generally; a psychiatrist may then
be hired by persons other than the "patient" to do
something *to him* in order to correct the deviation.

These considerations underscore the importance
of asking the question, Whose agent is the psychiatrist? and of giving a candid answer to it. The psychiatrist (or nonmedical mental health worker) may
be the agent of the patient, the relatives, the school,
the military services, a business organization, a court
of law, and so forth. In speaking of the psychiatrist
as the agent of these persons or organizations, it is
not implied that his moral values, or his ideas and
aims concerning the proper nature of remedial
action, must coincide exactly with those of his employer. For example, a patient in individual psychotherapy may believe that his salvation lies in a new
marriage; his psychotherapist need not share this
hypothesis. As the patient's agent, however, he must
not resort to social or legal force to prevent the
patient from putting his beliefs into action. If his
contract is with the patient, the psychiatrist (psychotherapist) may disagree with him or stop his treatment, but he cannot engage others to obstruct the

patient's aspirations.[2] Similarly, if a psychiatrist is retained by a court to determine the sanity of an offender, he need not fully share the legal authorities' values and intentions in regard to the criminal, nor the means deemed appropriate for dealing with him; such a psychiatrist cannot testify, however, that the accused is not insane, but that the legislators are—for passing the law that decrees the offender's actions illegal.[3] This sort of opinion could be voiced, of course—but not in a courtroom, and not by a psychiatrist who is there to assist the court in performing its daily work.

To recapitulate: In contemporary social usage, the finding of mental illness is made by establishing a deviance in behavior from certain psychosocial, ethical, or legal norms. The judgment may be made, as in medicine, by the patient, the physician (psychiatrist), or others. Remedial action, finally, tends to be sought in a therapeutic—or covertly medical—framework. This creates a situation in which it is claimed that psychosocial, ethical, and legal deviations can be corrected by medical action. Since medical interventions are designed to remedy only medical problems, it is logically absurd to expect that they will help solve problems whose very existence have been defined and established on nonmedical grounds.

2. See T. S. Szasz, *The Ethics of Psychoanalysis: The Theory and Method of Autonomous Psychotherapy* (New York: Basic Books, 1965).

3. See T. S. Szasz, *Law, Liberty, and Psychiatry: An Inquiry into the Social Uses of Mental Health Practices* (New York: Macmillan, 1963).

IV

Anything that people *do*—in contrast to things that *happen* to them[4]—takes place in a context of value. Hence, no human activity is devoid of moral implications. When the values underlying certain activities are widely shared, those who participate in their pursuit often lose sight of them altogether. The discipline of medicine—both as a pure science (for example, research) and as an applied science or technology (for example, therapy)—contains many ethical considerations and judgments. Unfortunately, these are often denied, minimized, or obscured, for the ideal of the medical profession as well as of the people whom it serves is to have an ostensibly value-free system of medical care. This sentimental notion is expressed by such things as the doctor's willingness to treat patients regardless of their religious or political beliefs. But such claims only serve to obscure the fact that ethical considerations encompass a vast range of human affairs. Making medical practice neutral with respect to some specific issues of moral value (such as race or sex) need not mean, and indeed does not mean, that it can be kept free from others (such as control over pregnancy or regulation of sex relations). Thus, birth control, abortion, homosexuality, suicide, and euthanasia continue to pose major problems in medical ethics.

4. R. S. Peters, *The Concept of Motivation* (London: Routledge & Kegan Paul, 1958), especially pp. 12–15.

Psychiatry is much more intimately related to problems of ethics than is medicine in general. I use the word "psychiatry" here to refer to the contemporary discipline concerned with problems in living, and not with diseases of the brain, which belong to neurology. Difficulties in human relations can be analyzed, interpreted, and given meaning only within specific social and ethical contexts. Accordingly, the psychiatrist's socioethical orientations will influence his ideas on what is wrong with the patient, on what deserves comment or interpretation, in what directions change might be desirable, and so forth. Even in medicine proper, these factors play a role, as illustrated by the divergent orientations that physicians, depending on their religious affiliations, have toward such things as birth control and therapeutic abortion. Can anyone really believe that a psychotherapist's ideas on religion, politics, and related issues play no role in his practical work? If, on the other hand, they do matter, what are we to infer from it? Does it not seem reasonable that perhaps we ought to have different psychiatric therapies—each recognized for the ethical positions that it embodies—for, say, Catholics and Jews, religious persons and atheists, democrats and Communists, white supremacists and Negroes, and so on? Indeed, if we look at the way psychiatry is actually practiced today, especially in the United States, we find that the psychiatric interventions people seek and receive depend more on their socioeconomic status and moral beliefs than on the "mental illnesses" from which they ostensibly suffer.[5] This fact should occasion no greater surprise than that practicing Catholics rarely frequent birth-control clinics, or that Christian Scientists rarely consult psychoanalysts.

V

The position outlined above, according to which contemporary psychotherapists deal with problems in living, not with mental illnesses and their cures, stands in sharp opposition to the currently prevalent position, according to which psychiatrists treat mental diseases, which are just as "real" and "objective" as bodily diseases. I submit that the holders of the latter view have no evidence whatever to justify their claim, which is actually a kind of psychiatric propaganda; their aim is to create in the popular mind a confident belief that mental illness is some sort of disease entity, like an infection or a malignancy. If this were true, one could *catch* or *get* a mental illness, one might *have* or *harbor* it, one might *transmit* it to others, and finally one could *get rid* of it. Not only is there not a shred of evidence to support this idea, but, on the contrary, all the evidence is the other way and supports the view that what people now call mental illnesses are, for the most part, *communications* expressing unacceptable ideas, often framed in an unusual idiom.

This is not the place to consider in detail the similarities and differences between bodily and men-

5. A. B. Hollingshead and F. C. Redlich, *Social Class and Mental Illness* (New York: Wiley, 1958).

tal illnesses. It should suffice to emphasize that whereas the term "bodily illness" refers to physico-chemical occurrences that are not affected by being made public, the term "mental illness" refers to sociopsychological events that are crucially affected by being made public. The psychiatrist thus cannot, and does not, stand apart from the person he observes, as the pathologist can and often does. The psychiatrist is committed to some picture of what he considers reality, and to what he thinks society considers reality, and he observes and judges the patient's behavior in the light of these beliefs. The very notion of "mental symptom" or "mental illness" thus implies a covert comparison, and often conflict, between observer and observed, psychiatrist and patient. Though obvious, this fact needs to be re-emphasized, if one wishes, as I do here, to counter the prevailing tendency to deny the moral aspects of psychiatry and to substitute for them allegedly value-free medical concepts and interventions.

Psychotherapy is thus widely practiced as though it entailed nothing other than restoring the patient from a state of mental sickness to one of mental health. While it is generally accepted that mental illness has something to do with man's social or interpersonal relations, it is paradoxically maintained that problems of values—that is, of ethics—do not arise in this process. Freud himself went so far as to assert: "I consider ethics to be taken for granted. Actually I have never done a mean thing."[6]

6. Quoted in E. Jones, *The Life and Work of Sigmund Freud* (New York: Basic Books, 1957), vol. 3, p. 247.

This is an astounding thing to say, especially for someone who had studied man as a social being as deeply as Freud had. I mention it here to show how the notion of "illness"—in the case of psychoanalysis, "psychopathology," or "mental illness"—was used by Freud, and by most of his followers, as a means of classifying certain types of human behavior as falling within the scope of medicine, and hence, by fiat, outside that of ethics. Nevertheless, the stubborn fact remains that, in a sense, much of psychotherapy revolves around nothing other than the elucidation and weighing of goals and values—many of which may be mutually contradictory—and the means whereby they might best be harmonized, realized, or relinquished.

Because the range of human values and of the methods by which they may be attained is so vast, and because many such ends and means are persistently unacknowledged, conflicts among values are the main source of conflicts in human relations. Indeed, to say that human relations at all levels—from mother to child, through husband and wife, to nation and nation—are fraught with stress, strain, and disharmony is, once again, to make the obvious explicit. Yet, what may be obvious may be also poorly understood. This, I think, is the case here. For it seems to me that in our scientific theories of behavior we have failed to accept the simple fact that human relations are inherently fraught with difficulties, and to make them even relatively harmonious requires much patience and hard work. I submit that the idea of mental illness is now being put to work to obscure certain difficulties that at present may be inherent—not that they need to be unmodifiable—in the social intercourse of persons. If this is true, the concept functions as a disguise: instead of calling attention to conflicting human needs, aspirations, and values, the concept of mental illness provides an amoral and impersonal "thing"— an "illness"—as an explanation for problems in living. We may recall in this connection that not so long ago it was devils and witches that were held responsible for man's problems in living. The belief in mental illness, as something other than man's trouble in getting along with his fellow man, is the proper heir to the belief in demonology and witch-craft. Mental illness thus exists or is "real" in exactly the same sense in which witches existed or were "real."

VI

While I maintain that mental illnesses do not exist, I obviously do not imply or mean that the social and psychological occurrences to which this label is attached also do not exist. Like the personal and social troubles that people had in the Middle Ages, contemporary human problems are real enough. It is the labels we give them that concern me, and, having labeled them, what we do about them. The demonologic concept of problems in living gave rise to therapy along theological lines. Today, a belief in mental illness implies—nay, requires—therapy along medical or psychotherapeutic lines.

I do not here propose to offer a new conception of "psychiatric illness" or a new form of "therapy." My aim is more modest and yet also more ambitious. It is to suggest that the phenomena now called mental illnesses be looked at afresh and more simply, that they be removed from the category of illnesses, and that they be regarded as the expressions of man's struggle with *the problem of how he should live.* This problem is obviously a vast one, its enormity reflecting not only man's inability to cope with his environment, but even more his increasing self-reflectiveness.

By problems in living, then, I refer to that explosive chain reaction that began with man's fall from divine grace by partaking of the fruit of the tree of knowledge. Man's awareness of himself and of the world about him seems to be a steadily expanding one, bringing in its wake an ever larger *burden of understanding.*[7] This burden is to be expected and must not be misinterpreted. Our only rational means for easing it is more understanding, and appropriate action based on such understanding. The main alternative lies in acting as though the burden were not what in fact we perceive it to be, and taking refuge in an outmoded theological view of man. In such a view, man does not fashion his life and much of his world about him, but merely lives out his fate in a world created by superior beings. This may logically lead to pleading nonresponsibility in the face of seemingly unfathomable problems and insurmount-

7. In this connection, see S. K. Langer, *Philosophy in a New Key* [1942] (New York: Mentor Books, 1953), especially chaps. 5 and 10.

able difficulties. Yet, if man fails to take increasing
responsibility for his actions, individually as well as
collectively, it seems unlikely that some higher
power or being would assume this task and carry this
burden for him. Moreover, this seems hardly a pro-
pitious time in human history for obscuring the issue
of man's responsibility for his actions by hiding it
behind the skirt of an all-explaining conception of
mental illness.

VII

I have tried to show that the notion of mental
illness has outlived whatever usefulness it may have
had and that it now functions as a myth. As such, it
is a true heir to religious myths in general, and to the
belief in witchcraft in particular. It was the function
of these belief-systems to act as social tranquilizers,
fostering hope that mastery of certain problems may
be achieved by means of substitutive, symbolic-
magical, operations. The concept of mental illness
thus serves mainly to obscure the everyday fact that
life for most people is a continuous struggle, not for
biological survival, but for a "place in the sun,"
"peace of mind," or some other meaning or value.
Once the needs of preserving the body, and perhaps
of the race, are satisfied, man faces the problem of
personal significance: What should he do with himself? For what should he live? Sustained adherence
to the myth of mental illness allows people to avoid
facing this problem, believing that mental health,
conceived as the absence of mental illness, automati-

cally insures the making of right and safe choices in the conduct of life. But the facts are all the other way. It is the making of wise choices in life that people regard, restrospectively, as evidence of good mental health!

When I assert that mental illness is a myth, I am not saying that personal unhappiness and socially deviant behavior do not exist; what I am saying is that we categorize them as diseases at our own peril.

The expression "mental illness" is a metaphor that we have come to mistake for a fact. We call people physically ill when their body-functioning violates certain anatomical and physiological norms; similarly, we call people mentally ill when their personal conduct violates certain ethical, political, and social norms. This explains why many historical figures, from Jesus to Castro, and from Job to Hitler, have been diagnosed as suffering from this or that psychiatric malady.

Finally, the myth of mental illness encourages us to believe in its logical corollary: that social intercourse would be harmonious, satisfying, and the secure basis of a good life were it not for the disrupting influences of mental illness, or psychopathology. However, universal human happiness, in this form at least, is but another example of a wishful fantasy. I believe that human happiness, or well-being, is possible—not just for a select few, but on a scale hitherto unimaginable. But this can be achieved only if many men, not just a few, are willing and able to confront frankly, and tackle courageously, their ethical, personal, and social conflicts. This means having the courage and integrity to forego waging battles on false fronts, finding solutions for substitute problems —for instance, fighting the battle of stomach acid and chronic fatigue instead of facing up to a marital conflict.

Our adversaries are not demons, witches, fate, or mental illness. We have no enemy that we can fight, exorcise, or dispel by "cure." What we do have are problems in living—whether these be biologic, economic, political, or sociopsychological. In this essay I was concerned only with problems belonging in the last-mentioned category, and within this group mainly with those pertaining to moral values. The field to which modern psychiatry addresses itself is vast, and I made no effort to encompass it all. My argument was limited to the proposition that mental illness is a myth, whose function it is to disguise and thus render more palatable the bitter pill of moral conflicts in human relations.

2. The Medical Model and Mental Hospitalization

ERVING GOFFMAN

Now, finally, we can turn to the issue posed by the title of this paper: the application of the expert servicing model, in its medical version, to institutional psychiatry.

The Western history of the interpretation of persons who seem to act oddly is a dramatic one: willful or involuntary consort with the devil, seizure by the tendencies of wild animals, etc.[1] In Britain, in the latter part of the eighteenth century, the medical mandate over these offenders began in earnest. Inmates were called patients, nurses were trained, and medically styled case records were kept.[2] Mad-

1. See, for example, Albert Deutsch, *The Mentally Ill in America* (2nd ed.; New York: Columbia University Press, 1949), pp. 12–23.

2. Kathleen Jones, *Lunacy, Law, and Conscience* (London: Routledge and Kegan Paul, 1955), pp. 55–56.

houses, which had been retitled asylums for the
insane, were retitled again, this time as mental hospitals. A similar movement was led in America by the
Pennsylvania Hospital, beginning in 1756.[3] Today
in the West there are differences in stress between
practitioners with an "organic" approach and those
with a "functional" one, but the assumptions underlying both approaches similarly support the legitimacy of applying the medical version of the service
model to asylum inmates. For example, in many
communities certification by a physician is a legal
requirement for involuntary mental hospitalization.

When a patient-to-be comes to his first admissions
interview, the admitting physicians immediately
apply the medical-service model. Whatever the
patient's social circumstances, whatever the particular character of his "disorder," he can in this setting
be treated as someone whose problem can be approached, if not dealt with, by applying a single
technical-psychiatric view. That one patient differs
from another in sex, age, race grouping, marital
status, religion, or social class is merely an item to
be taken into consideration, to be corrected for, as it
were, so that general psychiatric theory can be applied and universal themes detected behind the
superficialities of outward differences in social life.
Just as anyone in the social system can have an
inflamed appendix, so anyone can manifest one of
the basic psychiatric syndromes. A uniform professional courtesy shown to patients is matched with a
uniform applicability of psychiatric doctrine.

3. Deutsch, *The Mentally Ill,* pp. 58 ff.

There are certainly cases of mental disorder (associated with brain tumors, paresis, arteriosclerosis, meningitis, etc.) that appear beautifully to fulfill all the requirements of the service model: a randomly distributed rare event injures the client's mental functioning without anyone intending it and without his being personally to blame. After a while he and/or others sense that "something is wrong." Through a route of referrals he is brought, voluntarily or involuntarily, to the attention of psychiatrists. They gather information, make observations, provide a diagnosis, a prescription, and suggest a course of treatment. The patient then recovers, or the progress of his pathology is checked, or (a likelihood with "organic reactions") the disease follows its known and inevitable course, ending in the patient's death or his reduction to an incurable state of mere vegetative functioning. In the more benign cases, where the patient can benefit markedly from treatment, he is likely to re-evaluate his past experience so as to recognize that the psychiatric service was performed in his own interests and that he would have sought it out voluntarily had he realized what was wrong and what could be done for him. Everything ends happily ever after,[4] and if not happily then at least tidily. One can find framed case records in the hallways of the medical-surgical build-

4. A good illustration of this is provided in Berton Roueché's *New Yorker* article "Ten Feet Tall," detailing an incident of manic-depressive side effects caused by cortisone treatment. This article is available in Roueché's collection, *The Incurable Wound* (New York: Berkley Publishing Corp., n.d.), pp. 114–43.

ings of some mental hospitals that provide, in regard
to an actual case, an outline of early ("prodromal")
social signs and symptoms, documentation of the lay
failure to assess these correctly, description of the
behavior of the patient while he was sick, and drawings of the autopsy findings confirming the correctness of the diagnosis and appropriateness of the
treatment. Social misconduct and visible organic
pathology are brought together in a perfect confirmation of the applicability of the medical model.

While some psychiatric cases may be neatly
handled within the framework established by the
medical model there are very evident sources of
difficulty, especially in regard to the largest category
of mental patients, those with so-called "functional"
psychoses. Many of these difficulties have been described in the literature and are well known in psychiatry. I would like to review them briefly here,
starting with the more incidental kinds and working
up to ones that are more fundamental.

One issue in the applicability of the service model
to institutional psychiatry arises from the fact that
part of the official mandate of the public mental
hospital is to protect the community from the danger
and nuisance of certain kinds of misconduct. In
terms of the law and of the public pressures to which
the mental hospital is sensitive, this custodial function is of major importance. Within the institution
surprisingly little explicit reference is made to it,
however, the focus being on the medical-like therapeutic services the hospital supplies patients. If we
view the mentally ill as persons that others have had

a special kind of trouble with, then the custodial role of the hospital (much like the custodial role of the prison) is understandable and, many would feel, justifiable; the point here, however, is that a service to the patient's kin, neighborhood, or employer is not necessarily a service to the community at large (whatever that may be) and a service to any of these is not necessarily a service, especially not a medical service, to the inmate. Instead of a server and the served, we find a governor and the governed, an officer and those subject to him.[5]

During the patient's hospitalization he is very likely to pass from the jurisdiction of one medical person to another, and this shift is not a result of a referral system in which the practitioner suggests another server and the patient voluntarily follows the suggestion; the patient will pass from the jurisdiction of one medical person to another because of daily and weekly medical shifts, and because of the frequency with which patients are shifted from one ward to another and medical staff from one service to another. Being members of the same organization, the patient and the doctor are both subject to decisions they do not make concerning whom they will see.[6]

5. See Talcott Parsons, "The Mental Hospital as a Type of Organization," in The Patient and the Mental Hospital, ed. M. Greenblatt, D. Levinson, and R. Williams (Glencoe, Ill.: The Free Press, 1957), p. 115.
6. In research hospitals instructive attempts have been made to deal with this problem. The role of ward physician may be strictly segregated from the role of therapist, the therapist-patient relation remaining constant, regardless of a shift in ward residence of a patient. (See, for example,

Further, we must see the mental hospital in the
recent historical context in which it developed, as
one among a network of institutions designed to
provide a residence for various categories of socially
troublesome people. These institutions include nursing homes, general hospitals, veterans' homes, jails,
geriatrics clinics, homes for the mentally retarded,
work farms, orphanages, and old-folks' homes.
Every state hospital has an appreciable fraction of
patients who might better be contained in some one
of these other institutions (just as these other institutions have some inmates who might better be contained in a mental hospital), but who must be retained because no space is available, or can be
afforded, in these other institutions. Each time the
mental hospital functions as a holding station, within
a network of such stations, for dealing with public
charges, the service model is disaffirmed. All of these
facts of patient recruitment are part of what staff
must overlook, rationalize, gloss over about their
place of service.

Stewart Perry and Lyman Wynne, "Role Conflict, Role Redefinition, and Social Change in a Clinical Research Organization," *Social Forces,* XXXVIII (1959): 62–65.) In
private general hospitals which have one or two psychiatric
floors, an even closer approximation to the service relation
is found: a psychiatrist in private practice may have several "beds" and will temporarily hospitalize a patient when
he feels it is necessary. The house staff, typically residents,
will then have the job of keeping the patient fed and quiet,
and the psychiatrist will visit his patient once or twice a
day, as do the doctors who make use of beds on other
floors. Many of the forms of the service relationship are
thereby retained; how much therapy results is a different
question.

One of the most striking problems in applying the service model to mental hospitalization has to do with the largely involuntary character of admission to a mental hospital in America. As with the medical attention required by the very young and the very old, there is an effort to employ the guardian principle and assimilate action taken by a next of kin to action taken by the patient himself. It is true that treating the very young and very old as irresponsible does not seem to be violently inconsistent with or corrupting of our continued relations with them. But, though some involuntary patients do come to see the errors of their resistance to hospitalization, in general the unwilling patient's resentment seems to remain. He is likely to feel that he has been railroaded into the hospital with the help, or at least with the consent, of his close ones. While ordinarily an encounter with a server is likely to affirm the individual's belief in the rationality and good will of the society in which he lives, an encounter with hospital psychiatrists is likely to have an alienating effect.

The patient is not the only one, it seems, who declines to view his trouble as simply a type of sickness to be treated and then forgotten. Once he has a record of having been in a mental hospital, the public at large, both formally, in terms of employment restrictions, and informally, in terms of day-to-day social treatment, considers him to be set apart; they place a stigma on him.[7] Even the hospital itself

7. See, for example, Charlotte Green Schwartz, "The Stigma of Mental Illness," *Journal of Rehabilitation* (July–August 1956).

tacitly acknowledges that mental disorder is shameful; for example, many hospitals provide a code mail address so that patients can send and receive mail without having their status advertised on the envelope. Although the extent of stigmatization is declining in some circles, it is a basic factor in the life of the expatient. Unlike much medical hospitalization, the patient's stay in the mental hospital is too long and the effect too stigmatizing to allow the individual an easy return to the social place he came from.[8]

In response to his stigmatization and to the sensed deprivation that occurs when he enters the hospital, the inmate frequently develops some alienation from civil society, sometimes expressed by an unwillingness to leave the hospital. This alienation can develop regardless of the type of disorder for which the patient was committed, constituting a side effect of hospitalization that frequently has more significance for the patient and his personal circle than do his original difficulties. Here again we deal with something that does not fit the service model.[9]

8. It seems characteristic that in medical hospitals men who are laid up will joke with the nursing staff in a self-belittling hearty way, as if to say that the body lying supine for the nurses' ministrations is so uncharacteristic of the permanent self that anything can be safely said about it. In mental hospitals, on the other hand, this easy dissociation from one's current character and circumstances is much less feasible; hence, male mental patients tend to be serious, and where self-distancing expressions are introduced, these may have psychotic-like proportions.

9. In his article, "The Social Dynamics of Physical Disability in Army Basic Training," *Psychiatry*, X (1947): 323–333, David M. Schneider shows how withdrawal from

Another difficulty lies in the nature of psychiatric skills themselves. It seems fair to say that the current assumption as regards functional psychotics is that the patient has developed faulty ways of relating to persons and needs to engage in therapeutic learning experiences to correct these patterns. But the capacity to provide a patient with this experience is not quite a technical skill, nor can it be imparted as assuredly as a technical one. Further, what skills of this kind a staff may have cannot easily be broken down into the skill-status hierarchy characteristic of other service establishments, where high-placed per-

---

duties, even on medical grounds, can lead to ever-increasing isolation on the part of the sick person and increasing confirmation of his being different. The effects of separateness can then become more important than the initial causes. Operating on a somewhat similar understanding, U.S. Army research psychiatrists at Walter Reed have recently developed the notion that the more a soldier is allowed to see that he has a major psychiatric problem needful of special psychiatric treatment, the less likely is he to be quickly reassimilated into the military group in which he originally experienced his trouble. See, for example, B. L. Bushard, "The U.S. Army's Mental Hygiene Consultation Service," *Symposium on Preventive and Social Psychiatry,* 15–17 (April 1957), Walter Reed Army Institute of Research, Washington, D.C., pp. 431–443, especially p. 442:

"*These ends* [minimization of psychiatric disability] *can be accomplished through little actual, direct work with the patient himself, but do require extensive and working liaison with a variety of other agencies. Far more important than the verbal interchange with the patient is the non-verbal implication in his being seen early, listened to empathically, and restored to a duty status with dispatch. Any implication that the problem stems from remote or imponderable situations, is due to "disease" or is based upon considerations which are not immediate and amenable to mastery, will frequently lead to the undermining of such defenses as may be still intact.*"

sonnel perform the crucial brief tasks and unskilled lower levels perform routine preparatory work or merely ensure that the environment is kept benign. A ward attendant often seems to be as well equipped to offer a "good" relation to a patient as a highly trained psychiatrist, and, whether good or bad, the contribution of the attendant will impinge continuously on the patient, instead of impinging very intermittently as does the hospital psychiatrist's.[10] Menials who prepare the patient to see the psychiatrist can presumably exercise through this preparation about as much psychiatric intervention as the psychiatrist himself, the domain of face-to-face social contact being one in which every participant is equally licensed to carry and use a scalpel. This is so even though hospital administrations, operating within the medical model, give to psychiatrists the right to make crucial decisions concerning the disposition of the patient.

Operating to exaggerate the fact that little psychiatric skill is available anywhere, and where available not always distributed according to the staff hierarchy, is another issue: the usual circumspection or "functional specificity" of the server is directly denied in psychiatric service. All of the patient's actions, feelings, and thoughts—past, present, and

10. The milieu therapy movement presumably springs from a recognition that crucial hospital experience cannot be restricted to the therapeutic hour (when there is one) and that all personnel therefore can have an equal fatefulness for the patient. Sources here are Alfred H. Stanton and Morris S. Schwartz, *The Mental Hospital* (New York: Basic Books, 1954), and Maxwell Jones, *The Therapeutic Community* (New York: Basic Books, 1953).

predicted—are officially usable by the therapist in diagnosis and prescription. Current conceptions about the psychogenic character of many physical disorders even bring into the psychiatrist's domain matters otherwise apportioned to medical practitioners, with the result that the psychiatrist can indeed claim to treat "the whole person."[11] The organization of auxiliary psychiatric servers in the hospital—internist, psychologist, neurophysiologist, social worker, nursing staff—attests to the psychiatrist's diffuse mandate, feeding information to him that he alone has an official right to put together into an over-all assessment of a patient. None of a patient's business, then, is none of the psychiatrist's business; nothing ought to be held back from the psychiatrist as irrelevant to his job. No other expert server with a system to tinker with seems to arrogate this kind of role to himself.

Corresponding to this diffuse diagnostic mandate of the psychiatrist is an equally diffuse prescriptive one. Incarcerating institutions operate on the basis of defining almost all of the rights and duties the inmates will have. Someone will be in a position to pass fatefully on everything that the inmate succeeds in obtaining and everything he is deprived of, and this person is, officially, the psychiatrist. Nor need the psychiatrist exercise this right according to uniform bureaucratic rulings, as a member of the civil

11. A minor consequence of the psychogenic doctrine of physical disorders is that some mental patients are disinclined to present a claim for needed physical treatment because they fear they will be thought to be "imagining things."

service or the military might. Almost any of the living arrangements through which the patient is strapped into his daily round can be modified at will by the psychiatrist, provided a psychiatric explanation is given. Again we see that the psychiatric role is unique among servers, no other being accorded such power.

In discussing the medical model in a general hospital, it was suggested that life conditions within the hospital could be divided into an inner and outer sphere: the inner sphere contains the injured area of the organism under conditions of medically indicated control that are highly responsive to the state of the injury; the outer sphere provides, in a rougher way, housing for the inner sphere. In mental hospitals this division between a therapeutic and a housing milieu can sometimes be sustained. Where medical (as opposed to psychological) intervention is employed, there can be some effort to administer the treatment under highly controlled conditions, allowing the times between treatments to be handled with less medical attention. And there are cases, as when a patient is actively suicidal or homicidal, when his whole daily round is closely managed and constitutes an inner sphere of medical control intimately adjusted to his circumstances; life conditions can thus be assimilated to treatment. Similarly, for patients of advanced neurophysiological deterioration, backward conditions seem closely adapted to the capacities of the organism: the patient's sitting all day in one place, with a vacuous expression on his face, is, in a way, an inevitable and irremedial extension of his state.

But during the earlier stages of cerebral deterioration, and during most of the life course of some organic disorders, such as epilepsy, the absolute assurance that an organic syndrome is present is by no means clearly related to the life conditions accorded the patient in the hospital. However ultimately hopeless a condition is, there are relatively few patients so deteriorated that typical back-ward life is an accurate reflection of and response to their capacities. As to how "normal" their living arrangements could be, there is no present agreement. Diagnosis, then, may be medical, while treatment is not, the patient being treated merely with the life available for patients of his general kind. And when we turn to functional cases, ward life ceases to be a technical response to their capacities, in the sense that bed rest is an expression of the physical state of a postoperative patient. And yet, as we shall see, mental hospital staffs do argue that the life conditions of the patient are both an expression of his capabilities and personal organization at the moment and a medical response to them.

Next I want to suggest that, compared to a medical hospital or garage, a mental hospital is ill-equipped to be a place where the classic repair cycle occurs. In state mental hospitals, and to a greater extent in private and veterans' hospitals, opportunity for observing the patient is available, but staff are often too busy to record anything but acts of disobedience. Even when staff time is available for this work, the patient's conduct on the ward can hardly be taken as a sample of his conduct off it: some conduct felt to be unacceptable on the outside does not occur here (especially when this conduct was a response to disliked persons in the patient's home environment), and other forms of misconduct overlay the old in response to the inmate's current involuntary situation. A refraction of conduct thus occurs, the walls of the institution acting like a thick and faulted prism. Unless one argues for the validity of testing persons under this particular kind of stress, the ward would seem to be the worst possible place for a server's observations.

Similarly, even where diagnostic conferences are held in regard to each patient, the effort of these meetings can be directed to agreeing on which of the legally required labels will be affixed to the case record statement; and the timing of these meetings may have little to do with the presence or absence of an accumulation of data to act upon.

What is true of the difficulties of diagnosis in mental hospitals is even more true of treatment. As already suggested, the problem of easing the patient's attitude to the world is confused and exacerbated by the problem of easing his attitude to involuntary hospitalization. In any case, the treatment given in mental hospitals is not likely to be specific to the disorder, as it is, in general, in a medical hospital, garage, or radio repair shop; instead, if treatment is given at all, a cycle of therapies tends to be given across the board to a whole entering class of patients, with the medical work-up being used more to learn if there are counterindications for the standard treatments than to find indications for them.

At the same time, the patient's life is regulated and ordered according to a disciplinarian system developed for the management by a small staff of a large number of involuntary inmates. In this system the attendant is likely to be the key staff person, informing the patient of the punishments and rewards that are to regulate his life and arranging for medical authorization for such privileges and punishments. Quiet, obedient behavior leads to the patient's promotion in the ward system; obstreperous, untidy behavior to demotion. Interestingly enough, it is when the patient finds himself willing to improve his social conduct that the attendant is likely to bring him to the attention of the doctor as both worthy of consideration and able to profit from it, so that, as Ivan Belknap has described, the patient often gets a doctor's attention when he least needs it.[12]

12. Belknap, *op. cit.*, p. 144. I would like to add that since mental patients are persons who on the outside declined to respond to efforts at social control, there is a question of how social control can be achieved on the inside. I believe that it is achieved largely through the "ward system," the means of control that has slowly evolved in modern mental hospitals. The key, I feel, is a system of wards graded for degree of allowable misbehavior and degree of discomfort and deprivation prevalent in them. Whatever the level of the new patient's misbehavior, then, a ward can be found for him in which this conduct is routinely dealt with and to a degree allowed. In effect, by accepting the life conditions on these wards, the patient is allowed to continue his misbehavior, except that now he does not particularly bother anyone by it, since it is routinely handled, if not accepted, on the ward. When he requests some improvement in his lot he is then, in effect, made to say "uncle," made to state verbally that he is ready to mend his ways. When he gives in verbally he is likely to be allowed an improvement in life conditions. Should he then again

c

The period in the mental hospital is a difficult one
for the patient to assimilate to the medical model. A
very standard complaint is: "Nothing is being done
with me—I'm just left to sit." And corresponding to
this difficulty is the fact that current official psychiatric treatment for functional disorders does not, in
itself, provide a probability of success great enough
easily to justify the practice of institutional psychiatry as an expert service occupation, as here defined,
especially since the probability that hospitalization
will damage the life chances of the individiual is, as
already suggested, positive and high.

The problem, however, is not merely that of a low
probability of successful service but, for some patients, a question of the validity of applying the
whole service frame of reference in the first place.

First, we must see that the discreteness of the entity in which the disorder exists is questionable.

---

misbehave in the old way, and persist in this, he is lectured
and returned to his previous conditions. If instead of back-
sliding he states his willingness to behave even better, and
retains this line for a suitable length of time, he is advanced
further within the quick-discharge cycle through which
most first admissions are moved up and out within a year.
A point then is often reached where the patient is entrusted
to a kinsman, either for walks on the hospital grounds or
for town expeditions, the kinsman now being transformed
into someone who has the incarcerating establishment and
the law to reinforce the threat: "Be good or else I'll send
you back." What we find here (and do not on the outside)
is a very model of what psychologists might call a learning situation—all hinged on the process of an admitted
giving-in. For this reason, patient morale on the rebellious
wards seems stronger and healthier than on the discharge
wards, where there is a slight air of persons having sold
out to get out.

THE SOCIOLOGICAL APPROACH

True, in cases that are organic in character, the patient encloses within himself the world in which the damage is felt and the world in which repairs, if possible, can be made. This is not so in instances of functional psychosis. In so far as the patient's symptomatic behavior is an integral part of his interpersonal situation, the server would have to import this whole situation into the hospital in order to observe the patient's difficulty and to treat it. Instead of there being a relatively benign and passive environment and an isolated point of trouble, the figure and ground of usual service conceptions merge into one, the patient's interpersonal environment being inseparable from the trouble he is experiencing. Theoretically, it might of course be possible for a slight therapeutic change in the patient to have a benign circular effect on his environment when he gets sent back to it, and it might be possible to arrange to return him to a new environment, but in practice the patient is usually returned, when he is discharged, back into the system of which his psychotic response is a natural part.

But there is a still more fundamental issue, which hinges on the applicability of the concept of "pathology." Ordinarily the pathology which first draws attention to the patient's condition is conduct that is "inappropriate in the situation." But the decision as to whether a given act is appropriate or inappropriate must often necessarily be a lay decision, simply because we have no technical mapping of the various behavioral subcultures in our society, let alone the standards of conduct prevailing in each of them.

Diagnostic decisions, except for extreme symptoms, can become ethnocentric, the server judging from his own culture's point of view individuals' conduct that can really be judged only from the perspective of the group from which they derive. Further, since inappropriate behavior is typically behavior that someone does not like and finds extremely troublesome, decisions concerning it tend to be political, in the sense of expressing the special interests of some particular faction or person rather than interests that can be said to be above the concerns of any particular grouping, as in the case of physical pathology.[13]

For the patient, the application of the pathology concept to his conduct can have effects that are incompatible with the service ideal. In so far as he feels he has acted inappropriately at all, he may see his action as part of the normal social world of intention, responsibility, and culpability—much like the initial lay perception of his troublesome conduct. To have one's behavior defined as involuntary, nonresponsible, and nonculpable may be helpful in some cases, but this none the less involves a technical schema, not a social one, and ideally ought to disqualify the patient for any participation in the service relation even while qualifying him as an object of service. Szasz's description can be cited here:

> More precisely, according to the common-sense definition, mental health is the ability to play whatever the game of social living might consist

13. See T. S. Szasz, "Psychiatry, Ethics, and the Criminal Law," *Columbia Law Review*, I.VIII (1958): 188.

of and to play it well. Conversely, to refuse to play, or to play badly, means that the person is mentally ill. The question may now be raised as to what are the differences, if any, between social nonconformity (or deviation) and mental illness. Leaving technical psychiatric considerations aside for the moment, I shall argue that the difference between these two notions—as expressed for example by the statements "He is wrong" and "He is mentally ill"—does not necessarily lie in any observable *facts* to which they point, but may consist only of a difference in our *attitudes* toward our subject. If we take him *seriously,* consider him to have human rights and dignities, and look upon him as more or less our equal—we then speak of disagreements, deviations, fights, crimes, perhaps even of treason. Should we feel, however, that we cannot communicate with him, that he is somehow "basically" different from us, we shall then be inclined to consider him no longer as an equal but rather as an inferior (rarely, superior) person; and we then speak of him as being crazy, mentally ill, insane, psychotic, immature, and so forth.[14]

We should not overestimate this problem, however, because, in fact, there is no great danger in mental hospitals of having one's acts consistently defined in a neutral technical frame of reference. In medicine it is possible to act as if there were no right

14. T. S. Szasz, "Politics and Mental Health," *American Journal of Psychiatry,* CXV (1958): 509. See also his "Psychiatric Expert Testimony—Its Covert Meaning & Social Function," *Psychiatry,* XX (1957): 315, and "Some Observations on the Relationship between Psychiatry and the Law," *A.M.A. Archives of Neurology and Psychiatry,* LXXV (1956): 297–315.

or wrong streptococci, merely dangerous ones. In psychiatry there is a formal effort to act as if the issue is treatment, not moral judgment, but this is not consistently maintained. Ethical neutrality is indeed difficult to sustain in psychiatry, because the patient's disorder is intrinsically related to his acting in a way that causes offense to witnesses. Further, the standard way of dealing with such offenses in our society is to sanction the offender, negatively and correctively. Our whole society operates on this assumption in every item and detail of life, and without some functional equivalent it is hard to see how we could maintain a social order without it.

It is understandable, then, that even occasions set aside to demonstrate that professional nonmoralistic psychotherapy is taking place in the institution will be invaded by a moralistic perspective, albeit a modified one. It is understandable that a large part of psychotherapy consists of holding the sins of the patient up to him and getting him to see the error of his ways. And in a sense, I do not see how it can or should be otherwise. The interesting point here is that psychiatric staff are in a position neither to forego the fiction of neutrality nor actually to sustain it.

When applied to the mental hospital, the service model leads to a very characteristic ambivalence of action on the part of staff. Psychiatric doctrine requires ethical neutrality in dealing with patients, for what others see as misbehavior the staff must see as pathology. The law even underwrites this position, a mental patient having the privilege of committing crimes without having to face legal action. And yet, in the actual management of patients, ideals of proper conduct must be held up as desirable, infractions inveighed against, and the patient treated as a "responsible" person, that is, one capable of a personal effort to behave himself. Psychiatric staff share with policemen the peculiar occupational task of hectoring and moralizing adults; the necessity of submitting to these lectures is one of the consequences of committing acts against the community's social order.

3. Schizophrenia as Ideology

THOMAS J. SCHEFF

In lieu of beginning this paper with a (necessarily) abstract discussion of a concept, *the public order,* I shall invite the reader to consider a *gedanken* experiment that will illustrate its meaning. Suppose in your next conversation with a stranger, instead of looking at his eyes or mouth, you scrutinize his ear. Although the deviation from ordinary behavior is slight (involving only a shifting of the direction of gaze a few degrees, from the eyes to an ear), its effects are explosive. The conversation is disrupted almost instantaneously. In some cases, the subject of this experiment will seek to save the situation by rotating to bring his eyes into your line of gaze; if you continue to gaze at his ear, he may rotate through a full 360 degrees. Most often, however, the conversation is irretrievably damaged. Shock, anger, and

From *Schizophrenia Bulletin,* 2 (Fall 1970): 15–19. Reprinted by permission of the author.

vertigo are experienced not only by the "victim" but, oddly enough, by the experimenter himself. It is virtually impossible for either party to sustain the conversation, or even to think coherently, as long as the experiment continues.

The point of this experiment is to suggest the presence of a public order that is all-pervasive, yet taken almost completely for granted. During the simplest kinds of public encounter, there are myriad understandings about comportment that govern the participants' behavior—understandings governing posture, facial expression, and gestures, as well as the content and form of the language used. In speech itself, the types of conformity are extremely diverse and include pronunciation; grammar and syntax; loudness, pitch, and phrasing; and aspiration. Almost all of these elements are so taken for granted that they "go without saying" and are more or less invisible, not only to the speakers but to society at large. These understandings constitute part of our society's assumptive world, the world that is thought of as normal, decent, and possible.

The probability that these understandings are, for the most part, arbitrary to a particular historical culture (is shaking hands or rubbing noses a better form of greeting?) is immaterial to the individual member of society whose attitude of everyday life is, *whatever is, is right*. There is a social, cultural, and interpersonal status quo whose existence is felt only when abrogated. Since violations occur infrequently, and since the culture provides no very adequate vocabulary for talking about either the presence or abuse of its invisible understandings, such deviations are considered disruptive and disturbing. The society member's loyalty to his culture's unstated conventions is unthinking but extremely intense.

The sociologist Mannheim referred to such intense and unconscious loyalty to the status quo as *ideological*. Ideology, in this sense, refers not only to the defense of explicit political or economic interests but, much more broadly, to a whole world view or perspective on what reality is. As a contrast to the ideological view, Mannheim cited the *utopian* outlook, which tends "to shatter, either partially or wholly, the order of things prevailing at the time."[1] The attitude of everyday life, which is ideological, is transfixed by the past and the present; the possibility of a radically different scheme of things, or revolutionary changes in custom and outlook, is thereby rejected. The utopian perspective, by contrast, is fixed on the future; it rejects the status quo with abrupt finality. *Social change* arises out of the clash of the ideological and utopian perspectives.

Residual Rule Violations

It is the thesis of this paper that the concepts of mental illness in general—and schizophrenia in particular—are not neutral, value-free, scientifically precise terms but, for the most part, the leading edge of an ideology embedded in the historical and cultural present of the white middle class of Western

1. K. Mannheim, *Ideology and Utopia* (London: Routledge and Kegan Paul, 1936).

societies. The concept of illness and its associated vocabulary—symptoms, therapies, patients, and physicians—reify and legitimate the prevailing public order at the expense of other possible worlds. The medical model of disease refers to culture-free processes that are independent of the public order; a case of pneumonia or syphilis is pretty much the same in New York or New Caledonia. (For criticism of the medical model from psychiatric, psychological, and sociological perspectives. see footnotes 2–7.)

Most of the "symptoms" of mental illness, however, are of an entirely different nature. Far from being culture-free, such "symptoms" are themselves offenses against implicit understandings of particular cultures. Every society provides its members with a set of explicit norms—understandings governing conduct with regard to such central institutions as the state, the family, and private property. Offenses against these norms have conventional names; for example, an offense against property is called "theft," and an offense against sexual propriety is called "perversion." As we have seen above, how-

2. E. Goffman, *Asylums* (New York: Doubleday, Anchor, 1961).

3. R. D. Laing, *The Politics of Experience* (New York: Pantheon Books, 1967).

4. E. M. Lemert, *Social Pathology* (New York: McGraw-Hill, Inc., 1951).

5. T. J. Scheff, *Being Mentally Ill: A Sociological Theory* (Chicago: Aldine Publishing Company, 1966).

6. T. S. Szasz, *The Myth of Mental Illness* (New York: Hoeber-Harper, 1961).

7. L. P. Ullman, and L. Krasner, *A Psychological Approach to Abnormal Behavior* (Englewood Cliffs, N.J.: Prentice-Hall, Inc., 1969).

ever, the public order also is made up of countless unnamed understandings. "Everyone knows," for example, that during a conversation one looks at the other's eyes or mouth, but not at his ear. For the convenience of the society, offenses against these unnamed residual understandings are usually lumped together in a miscellaneous, catchall category. If people reacting to an offense exhaust the conventional categories that might define it (*e.g.,* theft, prostitution, and drunkenness), yet are certain that an offense has been committed, they may resort to this residual category. In earlier societies, the residual category was witchcraft, spirit possession, or possession by the devil; today, it is mental illness. The symptoms of mental illness are, therefore, violations of residual rules.

To be sure, some residual-rule violations are expressions of underlying physiological processes; the hallucinations of the toxic psychoses and the delusions associated with general paresis, for example. Perhaps future research will identify further physiological processes that lead to violations of residual rules. For the present, however, the key attributes of the medical model have yet to be established and verified for the major mental illnesses. There has been no scientific verification of the cause, course, site of pathology, uniform and invariant signs and symptoms, and treatment of choice for almost all of the conventional, "functional" diagnostic categories. Psychiatric knowledge in these matters rests almost entirely on unsystematic clinical impressions and professional lore. It is quite possible, therefore, that many psychiatrists' and other mental-health workers' "absolute certainty" about the cause, site, course, symptoms, and treatment of mental illness represents an ideological reflex, a spirited defense of the present social order.

Residue of Residues

Viewed as offenses against the public order, the symptoms of schizophrenia are particularly interesting. Of all the major diagnostic categories, the concept of schizophrenia (although widely used by psychiatrists in the United States and in those countries influenced by American psychiatric nomenclature) is the vaguest and least clearly defined. Such categories as obsession, depression, and mania at least have a vernacular meaning. Schizophrenia, however, is a broad gloss; it involves, in no very clear relationship, ideas such as "inappropriateness of affect," "impoverishment of thought," "inability to be involved in meaningful human relationships," "bizarre behavior" (*e.g.,* delusions and hallucinations), "disorder of speech and communication," and "withdrawal."

These very broadly defined symptoms can be redefined as offenses against implicit social understandings. The appropriateness of emotional expression is, after all, a cultural judgment. Grief is deemed appropriate in our society at a funeral, but not at a party. In other cultures, however, such judgments of propriety may be reversed. With regard to thought disorder, cultural anthropologists have long been at pains to point out that ways of thought are fundamentally different in different societies. What constitutes a meaningful human relationship, anthropologists also report, is basically different in other times and places. Likewise, behavior that is bizarre in one culture is deemed tolerable or even necessary in another. Disorders of speech and communication, again, can be seen as offenses against culturally prescribed rules of language and expression. Finally, the notion of "withdrawal" assumes a cultural standard concerning the degree of involvement and the amount of distance between the individual and those around him.

The broadness and vagueness of the concept of schizophrenia suggest that it may serve as the residue of residues. As diagnostic categories such as hysteria and depression have become conventionalized names for residual rule breaking, a need seems to have developed for a still more generalized, miscellaneous diagnostic category. If this is true, the schizophrenic explores not only "inner space" (Ronald Laing's phrase) but also the normative boundaries of his society.

These remarks should not be taken to suggest that there is no internal experience associated with "symptomatic" behavior; the individual with symptoms *does* experience distress and suffering, or under some conditions, exhilaration and freedom. The point is, however, that public, consensual "knowledge" of mental illness is based, by and large, on knowledge not of these internal states but of their overt manifestations. When a person goes running down the street naked and screaming, lay and professional diagnosticians alike assume the existence of mental illness within that person—even though they have not investigated his internal state. Mental health procedure and the conceptual apparatus of the medical model posit internal states, but the events actually observed are external.

Labeling Theory

A point of view which is an alternative to the medical model, and which acknowledges the culture-bound nature of mental illness, is afforded by labeling theory in sociology.[8] Like the evidence supporting the medical model, which is uneven and in large measure unreliable, the body of knowledge in support of the labeling theory of mental illness is by no means weighty or complete enough to prove its correctness.[9-13] But even though labeling theory is hypothetical, its use may afford perspective—if only because it offers a viewpoint that, along a number of different dimensions, is diametrically opposed to the medical model.

The labeling theory of deviance, when applied to

8. H. Becker, *Outsiders* (New York: Free Press, 1963).
9. M. Balint, *The Doctor, the Patient, and the Illness* (New York: International Universities Press, Inc., 1957).
10. R. D. Laing and A. Esterson, *Sanity, Madness and the Family* (London: Tavistock, 1964).
11. Lemert, *Social Pathology*.
12. T. J. Scheff, *Mental Illness and Social Processes* (New York: Harper & Row, Publishers, 1967).
13. S. P. Spitzer and N. K. Denzin, *The Mental Patient: Studies in the Sociology of Deviance* (New York: McGraw-Hill, Inc., 1968).

mental illness, may be presented as a series of nine hypotheses:

1. Residual rule breaking arises from fundamentally diverse sources (*i.e.,* organic, psychological, situations of stress, volitional acts of innovation or defiance).

2. Relative to the rate of treated mental illness the rate of unrecorded residual rule breaking is extremely high.

3. Most residual rule breaking is "denied" and is of transitory significance.

4. Stereotyped imagery of mental disorder is learned in early childhood.

5. The stereotypes of insanity are continually reaffirmed, inadvertently, in ordinary social interaction.

6. Labeled deviants may be rewarded for playing the stereotyped deviant role.

7. Labeled deviants are punished when they attempt the return to conventional roles.

8. In the crisis occurring when a residual rule breaker is publicly labeled, the deviant is highly suggestible and may accept the label.

9. Among residual rule breakers, labeling is the single most important cause of careers of residual deviance.

The evidence relevant to these hypotheses is reviewed in the author's *Being Mentally Ill.*

According to labeling theory, the societal reaction is the key process that determines outcome in most cases of residual rule breaking. That reaction may be either denial (the most frequent reaction) or labeling. Denial is to "normalize" the rule breaking by ignoring or rationalizing it ("boys will be boys"). The key hypothesis in labeling theory is that, when residual rule breaking is denied, the rule breaking will generally be transitory (as when the stress causing rule breaking is removed; *e.g.,* the cessation of sleep deprivation), compensated for, or channeled into some socially acceptable form. If, however, labeling occurs (*i.e.,* the rule breaker is segregated as a stigmatized deviant), the rule breaking which would otherwise have been terminated, compensated for, or channeled may be stabilized; thus, the offender, through the agency of labeling, is launched on a career of "chronic mental illness." Crucial to the production of chronicity, therefore, are the contingencies (often external to the deviants) that give rise to labeling rather than denial; *e.g.,* the visibility of the rule breaking, the power of the rule breaker relative to persons reacting to his behavior, the tolerance level of the community, and the availability in the culture of alternative channels of response other than labeling (among Indian tribes, for example, involuntary trance states may be seen as a qualification for a desirable position in the society, such as that of shaman).

"Schizophrenia"—A Label

On the basis of the foregoing discussion, it would seem likely that labeling theory would prove particularly strategic for facilitating the investigation of schizophrenia. Schizophrenia is the single most widely used diagnosis for mental illness in the United States, yet the cause, site, course, and treatment of choice are unknown, or the subject of heated and voluminous controversy. Moreover, there is some evidence that the reliability of diagnosis of schizophrenia is quite low. Finally, there is little agreement on whether a disease entity of schizophrenia even exists, what constitutes schizophrenia's basic signs and symptoms if it *does* exist, and how these symptoms are to be reliably and positively identified in the diagnostic process. Because of the all but overwhelming uncertainties and ambiguities inherent in its definition, "schizophrenia" is an appellation, or "label," which may be easily applied to those residual rule breakers whose deviant behavior is difficult to classify.

In this connection, it is interesting to note the perfectly enormous anomaly of classification procedures in most schizophrenia research. The hypothetical cause of schizophrenia, the independent variable in the research design—whether it is a physiological, biochemical, or psychological attribute—is measured with considerable attention to reliability, validity, and precision. I have seen reports of biochemical research in which the independent variable is measured to two decimal places. Yet the measurement of the dependent variable, the diagnosis of schizophrenia, is virtually ignored. The precision of the measurement, obviously, is virtually nil, since it represents at best an ordinal scale, or, much more likely, a nominal scale. In most studies, the reliability and validity of the diagnosis receives no attention at all; An experimental group is assembled by virtue of hospital diagnoses—leaving the measurement of the dependent variable to the mercy of the obscure vagaries of the process of psychiatric screening and diagnosis. Labeling theory should serve at least to make this anomaly visible to researchers in the field of schizophrenia.

More broadly, the clash between labeling theory and the medical and psychological models of mental illness may serve to alert researchers to some of the fundamental assumptions that they may be making in setting up their research. Particular reference should be made to the question of whether they are unknowingly aligning themselves with the social status quo; for example, by accepting unexamined the diagnosis of schizophrenia, they may be inadvertently providing the legitimacy of science to what is basically a social value judgment. For the remainder of this paper, I wish to pursue this point—the part that medical science may be playing in legitimating the status quo.

As was earlier indicated, there is a public order which is continually reaffirmed in social interaction. Each time a member of the society conforms to the stated or unstated cultural expectations of that society, as when he gazes at the eyes of the person with whom he is in conversation, he is helping to maintain the social status quo. Any deviation from these expectations, however small and regardless of its motivation, may be a threat to the status quo, since most social change occurs through the gradual erosion of custom.

Since all social orders are, as far as we know,

basically arbitrary, a threat to society's fundamental customs impels its conforming members to look to extrasocial sources of legitimacy for the status quo. In societies completely under the sway of a single, monolithic religion, the source of legitimacy is always supernatural. Thus, during the Middle Ages, the legitimacy of the social order was maintained by reference to God's commands, as found in the Bible and interpreted by the Catholic Church. The Pope was God's deputy, the kings ruled by divine right, the particular cultural form that the family happened to take at the time—the patrilocal, monogamous, nuclear family—was sanctified by the church, and so on.

In modern societies, however, it is increasingly difficult to base legitimacy upon appeals to supernatural sources. As complete, unquestioning religious faith has weakened, one very important new source of legitimacy has emerged: In the eyes of laymen, modern science offers the kind of absolute certainty once provided by the church. The institution of medicine is in a particularly strategic position in this regard, since the physician is the only representative of science with whom the average man associates. To the extent that medical science lends its name to the labeling of nonconformity as mental illness, it is giving legitimacy to the social status quo. The mental health researcher may protest that he is interested not in the preservation of the status quo but in a scientific question: "What are the causes of mental illness?" According to the argument given here, however, his question is loaded—like, "When did you stop beating your wife?" or, more to the point, "What are the causes of witchcraft?" (For a comparison of the treatment of witches and the mentally ill, see Szasz's *The Manufacture of Madness*.[14]) Thus, a question about causality may also be ideological, in Mannheim's sense, in that it reaffirms current social beliefs, if only inadvertently.

14. T. S. Szasz, *The Manufacture of Madness* (New York: Harper & Row, Publishers, 1970).

II

Antipsychiatry

Introduction

Antipsychiatry, the informally constituted British group best known through the work of R. D. Laing, has been a decisive influence on radical psychology. Laing, David Cooper, and Aaron Esterson were the founders of this approach over a decade ago, but the group has since been enlarged by Joe Berke, Mary Barnes, and Morty Schatzman. There is no way to synopsize the antipsychiatrists' writings—their work speaks to us quite on its own. What I wish to do is provide a little background to antipsychiatry and stress a few of its major points.

Laing's first book, *The Divided Self* (1959), was the culmination of the European school of existential/phenomenological psychology, best represented by Ludwig Binswanger (see bibliography). Binswanger was a friend of Freud who broke with him on many levels, creating an existential/phenomenological framework that attempted to understand people's felt experiences rather than fitting those experiences into preconceived, rigid molds. It was radical in the sense that it broke with the biological determinism and positivistic category of psychoanalysis and offered a larger level of freedom to the individual's existence. *The Divided Self* went further than the European existentialists, seeing a social context for mental illness, although that context was not yet clearly explained. Laing showed how psychological classification is a way of not dealing with people's problems, how the mystifications of professionals could never clarify the world of a psychotic episode. Psychological manipulation and self-fulfilling prophesies had to be ended. As he stated in *The Divided Self*, a therapist would have to

> have the plasticity to transpose himself into another strange and even alien view of the world. In this act he draws on his own psychotic possibilities without foregoing his sanity. Only thus can he arrive at an understanding of the patient's existential position.

In this lay the germ for Laing and Cooper's future theoretical framework, as yet undeveloped. Laing still clung to certain classifications, but they were certainly much less repulsive than the Freudian ones. "Ontological insecurity," "engulfment," "implosion," and "petrification" would be criticized by Laing himself three years later. A large amount of credit for this self-criticism lay in the book he wrote with Cooper, *Reason and Violence* (1964), an attempt to explicate Sartre's developing Marxist existentialism. Both of these antipsychiatrists had begun to grasp the social context more clearly through the light of Marxism, particularly as approached by Sartre. Unfortunately there was no immediate way for them to develop this understanding, although Laing and Cooper found another mode of practice.

Cooper set up Villa 21 in 1962, an experimental ward of a mental hospital where patients, professionals, paraprofessionals, and workers joined together to deal with emotional problems in a nonrepressive, nonstructured environment. Laing was the impetus behind the Kingsley Hall experiment a couple of years later, which established a place where people could come and work out their emotional problems in a free community setting. The necessity of such counterinstitutions had been forced, in a sense, by antipsychiatry's development in the period between *The Divided Self* and *Reason and Violence*.

Laing's *The Self and Others* (1961) had isolated problems of communication between people in a brilliant analytical method which showed how social roles were destructive: "Other people become a sort of identity kit whereby one can piece together a picture of oneself." Laing showed how children took upon themselves the symptoms of mental illness in order to escape their social roles and to find their real identity, since they found it unbearable to live in situations in which "we learn to be whom we are told to be," as a young patient expressed it to Laing. *Sanity, Madness, and the Family* (1964), written with Esterson, was the result of years of family studies, and developed the view of social context and family connection further than before. The book contains eleven case histories of women who were diagnosed as schizophrenic by other psychiatrists. Laing and Esterson observed them as *real* people, also observing their parents, brothers, sisters, and occasionally other relatives. Sara Danzig, who fit the usual diagnosis of paranoia, was ridiculed by her parents for claiming that she was being plotted against. Laing and Esterson, however, noticed that in fact Sara's parents did spy on her, listen to her phone calls, and intrude on her life in many aspects. They claimed that their daughter spent too much time in the privacy of her room. This is a social example of the existential necessity for integrity and autonomy that is denied by social institutions, in this case the family. Maya Abbot was a similar case, claiming parental intrusion. Investigating her family context, Laing and Esterson noticed actual gestures between parents at family sessions, by means of which the parents presented a united front against their labeled daughter.

As well as seeing the need for counterinstitutions to provide a line of defense against this oppression by the family, antipsychiatry saw further levels. Counterinstitutions were initially founded on principles of reform of current psychiatric principles and practice—they would later be transformed into more direct opposition. Part of this was that by 1967 Laing's *The Politics of Experience* and Cooper's *Psychiatry and Anti-Psychiatry* were criticizing the very concept of mental illness. Psychosis was seen as a mode of existence which offered real communication and provided real alternatives and benefits. It was a way of living in an untenable situation, and it explored the possibilities of different ways of living. Laing asked who was crazier, the paitent who claimed to have an atom bomb inside himself or the government leader who actually had the capacity to drop the bomb. The new idea was to transcend the death culture, to journey to the inner recesses of one's being, from birth to present, returning through all possible futures. Cooper posed a similar concept:

> There is, relatively speaking, something remarkable about the chronic schizophrenic preoccupied with his inner world, spending the day hunched over the central heating fitting in a decrepit back ward. If he does not have the solution to the riddle of life, at least he has fewer illusions.

This was the advent of the "madness revolution," a term Cooper utilizes in his recent *The Death of the Family*. Cooper sees a true revolution as requiring the abolition of the family in order that true love can be attained between people. This true love is not a required social bond, but rather "that paring away of feeling, falsely transposed onto the new presence, which leaves one free to love—and that mutually recognized freedom to love *is* love." Cooper sees the family as preventing such love because the family is society's primary socializer and cannot tolerate "subversive" love:

> The family, over the last two centuries, had mediated an evasiveness into the lives of individuals that is essential to the continued operation of imperializing capitalism. The family, definitionally, can never leave one alone, as it is the hypostisiza-

tion of the ultimately perfected mass medium. The family is the television box replete with color, touch, taste, and smell effects that has been taught to forget how to turn off.

Cooper sees the death of the family and the growth of freedom as inextricably related to social revolution. There are, of course, large elements of male-orientation in Cooper's view, but the possibilities for further development remain greater in Cooper than in Laing, whose recent *Knots* seems little more than complicated vignettes of verbal logic. Both, however, are somewhat romantic, though less so than many of their young adherents to whom schizophrenia has become very much of a cool thing to talk about (and to do?). Mary Barnes came through the madness revolution at Kingsley Hall. She speaks of the beginning and end points, and the lack of these points. Her recent book with Joe Berke, *Mary Barnes: Two Accounts of a Journey Through Madness,* speaks of the total experience of going through a rebirth via psychosis. Yet even with the concrete reality of her "therapeutic" residency at Kingsley Hall, there remains a certain utopianism that cannot be translated into a social movement. Antipsychiatry still deals mainly with individual solutions, although it contains the possibilities of greater social applications. Transcendence is important, but only if it incorporates the destruction of the old and the building of the new. We must also be wary of turning emotionally troubled people into "noble savages," for the antipsychiatrists are talking about *all* of us.

Counterinstitutions, as antipsychiatry and radical

psychology wish to see established, are incredibly important. Radical psychology owes much, including this, to the antipsychiatrists. But we must go further into revolutionary situations, enlarging the scope of our analysis and our practice, opening up counter-institutions to everyone and making them part of an overall movement.

The selections here offer a variety of antipsychiatry's work. "The Ghost of the Weed Garden" is an existential/phenomenological study of a young woman, Julie, from Laing's *The Divided Self*. Laing has given us an experiential record of her life, pointing out the destructiveness of Julie's parents' socially "correct" approach to child-rearing. Julie tells us her mother is trying to kill her—from listening to her life-script we see that she is right. In "The Mystification of Experience," from Laing's *The Politics of Experience,* the categories and classifications are toppled, as Laing offers us perhaps his best social context, although in nonanalytic terms. He approaches war, families, and other everyday mystifications/oppressions with the intent of offering us a world view in which to see mental illness. Cooper's "Violence and Psychiatry," from his *Psychiatry and Anti-Psychiatry,* explores many levels of social violence perpetrated by psychiatrists in the service of the status quo. Underlying his answers to the problems Cooper includes the Sartrean "project," a self-intentional battle for survival and freedom. In "On Being Born into a Family," from his *The Death of the Family,* Cooper takes the matter further, detailing incidents and matrices of family structure which destroy people, and proposes revolutionary restructuring of that and all other destructive institutions. Mary Barnes's "Flection/Reflection" offers a poetical prose description of her life before, after, and during her stay at Kingsley Hall. She speaks of the reality of her "voyage" with Laing, Berke, and others. And she speaks of her "return." It is a beautiful account of the actualization of antipsychiatry's theoretical approach.

4. The Ghost of the Weed Garden: A Study of a Chronic Schizophrenic

R. D. LAING

> . . . *for the Truth is past all commiseration*
> *Maxim Gorky*

Julie, at the time I knew her, had been a patient in a
ward of a mental hospital since the age of seventeen,
that is, for nine years. In these years, she had
become a typical "inaccessible and withdrawn"
chronic schizophrenic. She was hallucinated, given to
posturing, to stereotyped, bizarre, incomprehensible
actions; she was mostly mute and when she did
speak it was in the most "deteriorated" "schizo-
phrenese." On admission, she had been diagnosed as
a hebephrenic and given a course of insulin, without

From *The Divided Self* by R. D. Laing (London: Tavistock,
and New York: Pantheon, 1960), pp. 178–205. Copyright
© 1960 by Tavistock Publications, © 1969 by R. D.
Laing. Reprinted by permission of Pantheon Books and
Tavistock Publications.

improvement, and no other specific attempts had been made to recall her to sanity. Left to herself, there is little doubt she would quickly have become physically entirely "dilapidated," but her outward appearance was maintained by the almost daily attentions of her mother, in addition to the work of the nursing staff.

On account of various odd and somewhat alarming things she said and did at the time, her parents had taken her to see a psychiatrist when she was seventeen. In her interview with the psychiatrist, he recorded that there was nothing particularly unusual about her nonverbal behavior in itself but that the things she said were enough to establish the diagnosis of schizophrenia. In clinical psychiatric terminology, she suffered from depersonalization; derealization; autism; nihilistic delusions; delusions of persecution, omnipotence; she had ideas of reference and end-of-the-world phantasies; auditory hallucinations; impoverishment of affects, etc.

She said the trouble was that she was not a real person; she was trying to become a person. There was no happiness in her life and she was trying to find happiness. She felt unreal and there was an invisible barrier between herself and others. She was empty and worthless. She was worried lest she was too destructive and was beginning to think it best not to touch anything in case she caused damage. She had a great deal to say about her mother. She was smothering her, she would not let her live, and she had never wanted her. Since her mother was prompting her to have more friends, and to go out to

dances, to wear pretty dresses, and so on, on the face
of it these accusations seemed palpably absurd.

However, the basic psychotic statement she made
was that "a child had been murdered." She was
rather vague about the details, but she said she had
heard of this from the voice of her brother (she had
no brother). She wondered, however, if this voice
may not have been her own. The child was wearing
her clothes when it was killed. The child could have
been herself. She had been murdered either by herself or by her mother, she was not sure. She proposed to tell the police about it.

Much that Julie was saying when she was seventeen is familiar to us from the preceding pages. We
can see the existential truth in her statements that
she is not a person, that she is unreal, and we can
understand what she was getting at when she said
that she was trying to become a person, and how it
may have come about that she felt at once so empty
and so powerfully destructive. But beyond this point,
her communications become "parabolic." Her accusations against her mother, we suspect, must relate
to her failure to become a person but they seem, on
the surface, rather wild and far-fetched (see below).
However, it is when she says that "a child has been
murdered" that one's common sense is asked to
stretch further than it will go, and she is left alone in
a world that no one will share.

Now, I shall want to examine the nature of the
psychosis, which appeared to begin about the age of
seventeen, and I think this can best be approached
by first considering her life until then.

Clinical Biography of a Schizophrenic

It is *never* easy to obtain an adequate account of a schizophrenic's early life. Each investigation into the life of any single schizophrenic patient is a laborious piece of original research. It cannot be too strongly emphasized that a "routine" or even a so-called dynamically oriented history obtained in the course of several interviews can give very little of the crucial information necessary for an existential analysis. In this particular case, I saw the mother once a week over a period of several months and interviewed (each on a number of occasions) her father, her sister, three years older, who was her only sibling, and her aunt (father's sister). However, no amount of fact-gathering is proof against bias. Searles, for instance, is I think absolutely correct to emphasize the existence of positive feelings between the schizophrenic and his mother, a finding that has been singularly 'missed' by most other observers. I have no illusions that the present study is immune from bias which I cannot see.

Father, mother, sister, aunt were the effective personal world in which this patient grew up. It is the patient's life in her own interpersonal microcosmos that is the kernel of any psychiatric clinical biography. Such clinical biography is therefore self-consciously limited in scope. The socio-economic factors of the larger community of which the patient's family is an integral part are not *directly* relevant to the subject matter that is our concern.

D

This is not to say that such factors do not profoundly influence the nature of the family and hence of the patient. But, just as the cytologist puts, *qua* cytologist, his knowledge of macroanatomy in parentheses in his description of cellular phenomena, while at the same time being in possession of this knowledge, so we put the larger sociological issues in parentheses as not of direct and immediate relevance to the understanding of how this girl came to be psychotic. Thus I think the clinical biography that I shall present could be of a working-class girl from Zürich, of a middle-class girl from Lincoln, or of a millionaire's daughter from Texas. Very similar human possibilities arise in the interpersonal relationships of people as differently placed within society as these. I am, however, describing something that occurs in our twentieth-century Western world, and perhaps not, in quite the same terms, anywhere else. I do not know what are the essential features of this world that allow of such possibilities to arise. But we, as clinicians, must not forget that what goes on beyond our self-imposed horizons may make a great difference to the patterns to be made out within the boundaries of our clinical interpersonal microcosmos.

I have felt it necessary to state this briefly here because I feel that clinical psychiatry in the West tends towards what a schizophrenic friend of mine called "social gaucherie," whereas Soviet psychiatry seems to be rather gauche in the interpersonal sphere. Although a clinical biography must, I believe, focus on the interpersonal sphere, this should be in such a way as not to be a closed system which excludes the relevance in principle of what one may temporarily place in parentheses for convenience.

Now, although each of the various people interviewed had his or her own point of view on Julie's life, they all agreed in seeing her life in three basic states or phases. Namely, there was a time when,

1. The patient was a *good,* normal, healthy child; until she gradually began

2. to be *bad,* to do or say things that caused great distress, and which were on the whole "put down" to naughtiness or badness, until

3. this went beyond all tolerable limits so that she could only be regarded as completely *mad.*

Once the parents "knew" she was mad, they blamed themselves for not realizing it sooner. Her mother said,

> I was beginning to hate the terrible things she said to me, but then I saw she couldn't help it . . . she was such a good girl. Then she started to say such awful things . . . if only we had known. Were we wrong to think she was responsible for what she said? I knew she really could not have meant the awful things she said to me. In a way, I blame myself but, in a way, I'm glad that it was an illness after all, but if only I had not waited so long before I took her to a doctor.

What is meant precisely by good, bad, and mad we do not yet know. But we do now know a great deal. To begin with, as the parents remember it now,

of course, Julie acted in such a way as to appear to
her parents to be everything that was right. She was
good, healthy, normal. Then her behavior changed
so that she acted in terms of what *all* the significant
others in her world unanimously agreed was "bad"
until, in a short while, she was "mad."

This does not tell us anything about what the child
did to be good, bad, or mad in her parents' eyes, but
it does supply us with the important information that
the original pattern of her actions was entirely in
conformity with what her parents held to be good
and praiseworthy. Then, she was for a time "bad,"
that is, those very things her parents most did not
want to see her do or hear her say or to believe
existed in her, she "came out with." We cannot at
present say why this was so. But that she was
capable of saying and doing such things was almost
incredible to her parents. All that emerged was
totally unsuspected. They tried at first to discount it,
but as the offence grew they strove violently to repudiate it. It was a great relief, therefore, when,
instead of saying that her mother wouldn't let her
live, she said that her mother had murdered a child.
Then all could be forgiven. "Poor Julie was ill. She
was not responsible. How could I ever have believed
for one moment that she meant what she said to me?
I've always tried my best to be a good mother to
her." We shall have occasion to remember this last
sentence.

These three stages in the evolution of the idea of
psychosis in members of a family occur very commonly. Good–bad–mad. It is just as important to

discover the way the people in the patient's world have regarded her behavior as it is to have a history of her behavior itself. I shall try to demonstrate this conclusively below, but at this point I would like to observe one important thing about the story of this girl as told me by her parents.

They did not suppress facts or try to be misleading. Both parents were anxious to be helpful and did not deliberately, on the whole, withhold information about actual facts. The significant thing was the way facts were discounted, or rather the way obvious possible implications in the facts were discounted or denied. We can probably best present a brief account of this girl's life by first grouping the events together within the parents' framework. My account is given predominantly in the mother's words.

Phase I: A normal and good child

Julie was never a demanding baby. She was weaned without difficulty. Her mother had no bother with her from the day she took off nappies completely when she was fifteen months old. She was never "a trouble." She always did what she was told.

These are the mother's basic generalizations in support of the view that Julie was always a "good" child.

Now, this is the description of a child who has in some way never come alive: for a really alive baby is demanding, is a trouble, and by no means always does what she is told. It may well be that the baby was never as "perfect" as the mother would like me

to believe, but what is highly significant is that it is
just this "goodness" which is Mrs. X's ideal of what
perfection is in a baby. Maybe this baby was not as
"perfect" as all that; maybe in maintaining this the
mother is prompted by some apprehensiveness lest I
blame her in some way. The crucial thing seems to
me to be that Mrs. X evidently takes just those
things which I take to be expressions of an inner
deadness in the child as expressions of the utmost
goodness, health, normality. The significant point,
therefore, if we are thinking not simply of the patient
abstracted from her family, but rather of the whole
family system of relationships of which Julie was a
part, is not that her mother, father, aunt all describe
an existentially dead child, but that none of the
adults in her world know the difference between
existential life and death. On the contrary, being
existentially dead receives the highest commendation
from them.

Let us consider each of the above statements of
the mother in turn:

1. *Julie was never a demanding baby.* She never
cried really for her feeds. She never sucked vigor-
ously. She never finished a bottle. She was always
"whinie and girnie"; she did not put on weight very
rapidly. "She never wanted for anything but I felt
she was never satisfied."

Here we have a description of a child whose oral
hunger and greed have never found expression. Instead of a healthy vigorous expression of instinct in
lusty, excited crying, energetic suckling, emptying the

bottle, followed by contented satiated sleep, she
fretted continually, seemed hungry, yet, when presented with the bottle, sucked desultorily, and never
satisfied herself. It is tempting to try to reconstruct
these early experiences from the infant's point of
view, but here I wish to restrict myself only to the
observable facts as remembered by the mother after
over twenty years, and to make our constructions
from these alone.

As stated above, and this is I believe an important
point when thinking of etiological factors, one of the
most important aspects of this account is not simply
that we get the picture of a child who, however
physically alive, is not existentially becoming alive,
but that the mother so far misunderstands the situation that she continues to rejoice in the memory of
just those aspects of the baby's behavior which were
most dead. The mother is not alarmed that the baby
did not cry "demandingly" nor drain the bottle. That
Julie did not do so, is not sensed by her as an
ominous failure of basic oral instinctual drives to
find expression and fulfilment but solely as token of
"goodness."

Mrs. X repeatedly emphasized that Julie had
never been a "demanding" baby. This did not mean
that she was not a generous person herself. In fact,
she had "given her life" for Julie, as she put it. As
we shall see, Julie's sister had been a demanding,
greedy baby. Her mother had never had much hope
for her: "I just let her go her own way." However, it
was just the fact that Julie from the start had never
been demanding that seemed largely to have encour-

aged her mother to give her so much, as she had done. It was therefore a terrible thing for her when, in her teens, Julie, instead of displaying some gratitude for all that had been done for her and given to her, began to accuse her mother of *never having let her be*. Thus, although it seems to me quite possible that, owing to some genetic factor, this baby was born with its organism so formed that instinctual need and need-gratification did not come easily to it, put in the most general way, added to this was the fact that all the others in its world took this very feature as a token of goodness and stamped with approval the absence of self-action. The combination of almost total failure of the baby to achieve self-instinctual gratification, along with the mother's total failure to realize this, can be noted as one of the recurrent themes in the early beginnings of the relation of mother to schizophrenic child. More research is needed to establish how specific this combination is.

2. *She was weaned without any trouble*. It is in feeding that the baby for the first time is actively alive with another. By the time of weaning the ordinary infant can be expected to have developed some sense of itself as a being in its own right, it has a "way of its own," and some sense of the permanence of the mother as prototypical other. On the basis of these achievements, weaning occurs without much difficulty. The baby at this stage is given to playing "weaning games" in which he drops, say, a rattle, to have it returned to him; drops it again, to have it returned; drops it, and so on, interminably.

The baby seems here to be playing at an object going away, returning, going away, returning, the central issue of weaning in fact. Moreover, the game has usually to be played *his* way so that we find it "natural" to collude with him in maintaining the impression that he is in control. In Freud's case, the little boy kept his reel of string attached to him when he threw it away, in contrast to the fact that he could not keep his mother thus under control by an attachment to her "apron strings." Now, if, as we have inferred, this girl was, in early months, not achieving the autonomy that is the prerequisite for the ability to go one's own way, to have a mind of her own, then it is not surprising that she should appear to be weaned without difficulty, although it could hardly be called weaning when the infant is giving up something it has never had. In fact, one could hardly speak of weaning having occurred at all in Julie's case. Things went so smoothly at this time that her mother could recall very few actual incidents. However, she did remember that she played a "throwing away" game with the patient. Julie's elder sister had played the usual version of this game and had exasperated Mrs. X by it. "I made sure that *she* (Julie) was not going to play that game with me. *I* threw things away and she brought them back to *me*," as soon as she could crawl.

It is hardly necessary to comment on the implications of this inversion of roles for Julie's failure to develop any real ways of her own.

She was said to have been precocious in walking (just over one year), and would scream if she could not get to her mother across the room quickly enough. The furniture had to be rearranged because "Julie was terrified of any chairs that came between her and me." Her mother interpreted this as a token of how much her daughter had always loved her. Until she was three or four, she "nearly went crazy" if her mother was out of her sight for a moment.

This seems to lend confirmation to the suggestion that she was never really weaned because she had never reached a stage when weaning, in any more than a physical sense, could take place. Since she had never established an autonomous self-being, she could not begin to work through the issues of presence and absence to the achievement of the ability to be alone by herself, to the discovery that the physical presence of another person was not necessary for her own existence, however much her needs or desires may have been frustrated. If an individual needs another in order to be himself, it presupposes a failure fully to achieve autonomy, *i.e.,* he engages in life from a basically insecure ontological position. Julie could be herself neither in her mother's presence nor in her absence. As far as her mother remembers, she was never actually physically out of earshot of Julie until she was almost three.

3. *She was clean from the moment that nappies were taken off at fifteen months.* One may note at this point that it is not unusual to find in schizophrenics a precocious development of bodily control although it is not known how they compare with others in this respect. One is certainly often told by parents of schizophrenics of how proud they were of their children because of their precocious crawling,

walking, bowel and bladder functioning, talking, giving up crying, and so on. One has to ask, however, in considering the conjunction between what the parent is proud to tell about and what the child has achieved, how much of the infant's behavior is an expression of its own will. The question is not how good or how naughty a child is, but whether the child develops a sense of being the origin of his own actions, of being the source from which his actions arise: or whether the child feels that his own actions are generated not from within himself, but from within the mother, despite possibly giving every appearance of being the agent of his acts (cf. the person in hypnosis who is under orders to *pretend* to be autonomous). It can happen that the body may perfect its skills and thus do all that is expected of it; yet genuine self-action seems never to have become established to any extent, but instead all action is in almost total compliance and conformity with outside directives. In Julie's case, her actions appear to have been trained by her mother, but "she" was not "in" them. This must have been what she meant by saying that she had never become a person and in her constant reiteration as a chronic schizophrenic that she was a "tolled bell" (or "told belle"). In other words, she was only what she was told to do.

4. *She always did what she was told.* As we remarked earlier about telling the truth and lying, there are good reasons for being obedient, but being unable to be disobedient is not one of the best reasons. So far, in Mrs. X's account one is unable to see that the mother recognized in Julie any possibilities

other than her being what Julie herself called "the told belle." She "gave her life" to the tolled bell, but she totally denied, and still did twenty-five years later, the possibility that this good, obedient, clean little girl, who so loved her that she nearly went crazy when separated from her if only by a chair, was petrified into a "thing," too terror-stricken to become a person.

5. *She was never a "trouble."* It was now clear that from the time that this patient emerged beyond the early months of life she was without autonomy. She had never, as far as can be judged from what her mother remembers, developed ways of her own. Instinctual needs and gratifications had never found any expression through channels of bodily activity.

Real satisfaction arising from real desire for the real breast had not occurred in the first instance. Her mother regarded the consequences of this with the same approval as she did its first manifestations.

"She would never take too much cake. You just had to say, 'That's enough, Julie,' and she wouldn't object."

We noted earlier how it may come about that hatred is expressed only in and through the very complianee of the false-self system. Her mother commended her obedience, but Julie began to carry her obedience to such lengths that it became "impossible." Thus, she had a spell, at about the age of ten, when she had to be told everything that was going to happen in the course of the day and what she was to do. Every day had to begin with such a catalogue. If her mother refused to comply with this ritual she would start to whimper. Nothing would stop this whimpering, according to her mother, but a sound thrashing. A she grew older, she would not use any money she was given herself. Even when encouraged to say what she wanted or to buy a dress herself or to have friends like other girls, she would not express her own wishes; she had to have her mother to buy her clothes, and she showed no initiative in making friends. She would never make a decision of any kind.

Besides the whimpering mentioned above, there were a few other occasions in childhood when Julie upset her. She had a spell during the years from five to seven when she bit and tore at her nails; from the first beginnings of speech she had a tendency to turn words round back to front. Suddenly, at the age of eight, she started to overeat, and continued in this for some months before reverting to her usual half-hearted way of eating.

Her mother, however, discounted such things as transitory phases. One has in them, nevertheless, sudden glimpses of an inner world of violent destructiveness with a short-lived desperate access of manifest greed which, however, soon became curbed and submerged again.

II: The "Bad" Phase.

From about fifteen, her behavior changed, and from being such a "good" girl, she became "bad." At this time also, her mother's attitude had begun to change towards her. Whereas, previously, she had thought it right and proper that Julie should be with her as much as possible, now she began to urge her to get out more, have friends, go to the pictures and even to dances, and have boy friends. All these things the patient "obstinately" refused to do. Instead, she would sit and do nothing, or wander the streets, never telling her mother when she would be back. She kept her room extravagantly untidy. She continued to cherish a doll which her mother felt she should now have "grown out of." We shall have occasion to return to this doll later. Julie's diatribes against her mother were endless and were always on the same theme: she would accuse her mother of not having wanted her, of not letting her be a person, of never having let her breathe, of having smothered her. She swore like a trooper. Yet to other people she could be charming, when she wanted.

So far we have considered only the relationship of Julie with her mother. But now, before we can go further, we must say a word about the total family constellation.

In recent years, the concept of a "schizophrenogenic" mother has been introduced. Fortunately an early "witch-hunt" quality about the concept has begun to fade. This concept can be worked out in various rather different ways, but it can be stated in the following terms: there may be some ways of being a mother that impede rather than facilitate or "reinforce" any genetically determined inborn tendency there may be in the child towards achieving the primary developmental stages of ontological security. Not only the mother but also the total family situation may impede rather than facilitate the child's capacity to participate in a real shared world, as self-with-other.

It is the thesis of this study that schizophrenia is a possible outcome of a more than usual difficulty in being a whole person with the other, and with not sharing the common-sense (*i.e.,* the community sense) way of experiencing oneself in the world. The world of the child, as of the adult, is "*a unity of the given and the constructed*" (Hegel), a unity for the child of what is mediated to it by the parents, the mother in the first instance, and of what he makes of this. The mother and father greatly simplify the world for the young child, and as his capacity grows to make sense, to inform chaos with pattern, to grasp distinctions and connections of greater and greater complexity, so, as Buber puts it, he is led out into "a feasible world."

But what can happen if the mother's or the family's scheme of things does not match what the child can live and breathe in? The child then has to develop its own piercing vision and to be able to live by that—as William Blake succeeded in doing, as Rimbaud succeeded in stating, but not in living—or else become mad. It is out of the earliest loving bonds with the mother that the infant develops the beginnings of a being-for-itself. It is in and through these bonds that the mother "mediates" the world to the infant in the first place. The world he is given may be one he can manage to *be* in; it is possible, on the contrary, that what he is given is just not feasible for him at the time. Yet, despite the importance of the first year of life, the nature of the milieu in which the child has to exist throughout its infancy, childhood, and adolescence may still have great effect one way or the other. It is at these subsequent stages that the father or other significant adults may play a decisive role in the child's life, either in direct relation with the child or, indirectly, through effects on the mother.

These considerations suggest that one might do better to think of schizophrenogenic families, rather than too exclusively of schizophrenogenic mothers. At least, doing so might encourage more reports of the dynamics of the family constellation as a whole, instead of studies of mothers, or fathers, or siblings, without sufficient reference to the whole family dynamics.[1]

Julie's sister, three years older, was a rather forthright assertive married woman, not, however, without femininity and charm. According to her mother, she had been "difficult" from birth: demanding and always "a trouble." In short, she seems to have been a relatively "normal" child of whom her mother never very much approved. But they appeared to get on well enough together. The sister regarded her mother as a rather dominating person if one did not stand up to her. But "she's done everything for Julie, and Julie was always her favorite." It was quite clear that this sister had early on achieved integral auton-

1. See particularly Laing and Esterson, *Sanity, Madness, and the Family*.

omous status. If one cared to look closely into her personality, there were many neurotic elements to be found in her, but there seemed little doubt that at least she had achieved the primary ontological status that Julie had never reached. When she was a child, she had friends of her own age, just too old for Julie, and Julie did not appear to have come close to her. Julie, however, had built into her scheme of phantoms a big sister who was one of the few predominantly good figures in her "world," "a Sister of Mercy."

The father had a more obviously significant part to play. In her mother's eyes, he was a "sexual beast." In his, her mother was cold and unsympathetic. They spoke to each other no more than was absolutely necessary. He found sexual satisfaction elsewhere. However, although they had many accusations to make against each other, neither built into these accusations any allegations about mistreating their daughter. The father, indeed, as he said, had not much to tell me, because he had "withdrawn himself emotionally" from the family before Julie was born.

The patient's sister told me two incidents, both of which must have been of very great importance to Julie. The first her mother probably did not know about; the second she could not bring herself to tell me of. We shall return to the second incident later. The first occurred when Julie was fourteen or fifteen. Despite her father's distance from her and his relative inaccessibility, Julie had seemed fond of him. He occasionally took her for a walk. On one occa-

sion Julie came home from such a walk in tears. She
never told her mother what had happened. Her
mother mentioned this to me to say that she was sure
that something awful had taken place between Julie
and her husband but she had never discovered what.
After this, Julie would have nothing to do with her
father. She had, however, confided to her sister at
the time that her father had taken her into a call-box
and she had overheard a "horrible" conversation
between him and his mistress.

Mrs. X did not hesitate to miscall her husband to
her daughters, and in piling up innumerable instances of injustices she tried to get them on her side.
However, the elder sister took a middle way, and
Julie apparently would never openly collude with her
mother against her father: after the telephone-box
incident, she simply cut herself off from him but
would not supply the information for grist to her
mother's mill. The father, however, had, as he said,
withdrawn himself from the family. He did not make
accusations against his wife to his daughters, since
he did not need their support against her. Although
he regarded her as a useless wife, "To be fair to
her," as he put it, "she was a good mother. I have to
grant her that." The elder sister saw faults on both
sides but tried as far as possible to be reasonable and
balanced, and not to take one side more than another. But if she had to, she took her mother's side
against her father, and her mother's side against
Julie. In this latter respect, it was not unreasonable
that she should do so. Julie's accusations against her
mother were, from a matter-of-fact, common-sense

point of view, wild and fantastic from the first. They must have sounded from the start rather mad. To "rant and rave" about being smothered and not being allowed to live and be a person seemed to this ordinary common-sense family to make no sense at all. She said her mother had never wanted her, and yet she was the favorite; her mother had done everything for her and given her everything. She said her mother was smothering her, and yet her mother was urging her to grow up. She said her mother did not want her to become a person, and yet her mother was urging her to make friends, go to dances, etc.

It is remarkable that, despite the radical disruption of the relationship between husband and wife, in one respect at least they maintained a collusion. Both accepted the patient's false self as good and rejected every other aspect of her as bad. But in the "bad" phase, a corollary to this was perhaps even more important. Not only did they reject as bad all of Julie apart from the compliant lifeless shadow which passed in their eyes for a real person, they completely refused to "take to heart" any of the reproaches that Julie had against them.

Julie and her mother were at this time both desperate people. Julie in her psychosis called herself Mrs. Taylor. What does this mean? It means "I'm tailor-made." "I'm a tailored maid; I was made, fed, clothed, and tailored." Such statements are psychotic, not because they may not be "true" but because they are cryptic: they are often quite impossible to fathom without the patient decoding them for us. Yet even as a psychotic statement this seems a very cogent point of view and it gives in a nutshell the gist of the reproaches she was making against her mother when she was fifteen and sixteen. This "ranting and raving" was her "badness." What I feel must have been the most schizophrenogenic factor of this time was not simply Julie's attack on her mother, or even her mother's counterattack, but the complete absence of anyone in her world who could or would see some sense in her point of view, whether it was right or wrong. For various reasons, neither her father nor her sister could see that there was any validity in Julie's side of the argument. Like our group patient she was not fighting to win an argument, but to preserve her existence: in a way, Julie was not simply trying to preserve her existence, she was trying to achieve existence. We can see, I think, that by fifteen or sixteen, Julie could hardly have developed what one might call "the ability of common sense." The common family sense accorded "her" no existence. Her mother had to be right, totally right. When her mother said she was bad, Julie felt this as murder. It was the negation of any autonomous point of view on her part. Her mother was prepared to accept a compliant, false self, to love this shadow, and to give it anything. She even tried to order this shadow to act as though it were a person. But she had never recognized the real disturbing presence in the world of a daughter with her own possibilities. The existential truth in Julie's delusions was that her own true possibilities were being smothered, strangled, murdered. To exist, to be able to breathe, Julie felt that her mother had to admit that she could have been wrong about some things, that she could have made mistakes, that there was a sense in which what her daughter said could be right and have weight. Putting it in one way, one might say that Julie needed to be allowed to project some of her bad-self into her mother, and to be allowed to take some goodness out of her mother, not merely to be given it all the time. But, to the whole family, Julie was trying to prove white was black. Reality did not yield. She began to convert existential truth into physical facts. She became deluded. If she began by accusing her mother of never having let her live, in an existential sense, she ended by talking and acting more than half as though her mother had, in a legal sense, actually murdered an actual child, and it was quite clearly a relief to the family when they could then pity her and no longer have to vindicate themselves by condemning her. Only her father, in a curious way, treated her as a responsible person. He never admitted that she was mad. To him she was wicked.

He was not "taken in" by her game. It was all an expression of spite and ingratitude. He regarded what we called her catatonic negativism as sheer "thrawn-ness," her hebephrenic symptoms as vindictive silliness. He was the only one of the family who did not pity her. On some of his occasional visits, he was known to have shaken and pinched her and twisted her arm to get her to "stop it."

Phase III: Mad.

Julie's basic accusation was that her mother was trying to kill her. When she was seventeen, an incident occurred that was probably the efficient cause in the transition from being bad to being mad.

This is the second circumstance told me by the sister. Until the age of seventeen, Julie had a doll. She had had this doll from infancy; she dressed and clothed it, played with it in her room, no one knew quite in what way. It was a secret enclave in her life. She called it Julie Doll. Her mother became more and more insistent that she should give up this doll, because she was a big girl now. One day the doll was gone. It was never known whether Julie had thrown it out, or whether her mother had put it away. Julie accused her mother. Her mother denied that she had done anything to the doll and said that Julie must have lost it herself. It was shortly after this that Julie was told by a voice that a child wearing her clothes had been beaten to pulp by her mother, and she proposed to go to the police to report this crime.

I said that either Julie or her mother disposed of the doll because it seems highly probable that at this stage her "mother" for Julie was already more an archetypal destroyer than her real mother outside. When Julie said that her "mother" killed the doll, it is quite possible that "she" did so, that is, that her "internal" mother had done so. However it happened, in fact the action was catastrophic; for Julie was evidently closely identified with the doll. In her play with the doll, the doll was herself and she was its mother. Now it is possible that in her play she became more and more the bad mother who finally killed the doll. We shall see later that in her psychosis the "bad" mother acted out and spoke through her a good deal. If the doll had been destroyed by her actual mother, who had admitted it, the event might even have been less catastrophic. Julie's shreds of sanity at this stage depended on the possibility of being able to lodge some bad in her actual mother. The impossibility of doing this, in a sane way, was one of the factors that contributed to a schizophrenic psychosis.

The Ghost of the Weed Garden

> . . . at some stage a machine which was previously assembled in an allover manner may find its connexions divided into partial assemblies with a higher or lower degree of independence.
> NORBERT WIENER: *Human Use of Human Beings*

The remarks that follow apply to Julie and to other chronic schizophrenics of the hebephrenic-catatonic type. They are not intended to encompass all forms of chronic psychotic states where splitting in one form or other is very evident. In particular, they are least applicable to paranoid psychoses where there is a much greater integration of the personality, of a kind, than that found in Julie and those like her.

Julie's self-being had become so fragmented that she could best be described as living *a death-in-life existence in a state approaching chaotic nonentity*.

In Julie's case, the chaos and lack of being an identity were not complete. But in being with her one had for long periods that uncanny "praecox[2] feel-

2. From the term dementia praecox formerly used to denote what we now generally call a form of schizophrenia occurring in young people which was thought to go on to

ing" described by the German clinicians, *i.e.*, of being in the presence of another human being and yet feeling that there was no one there. Even when one felt that what was being said was an expression of someone, the fragment of a self behind the words or actions was not Julie. There might be someone addressing us, but in listening to a schizophrenic, it is very difficult to know "who" is talking, and it is just as difficult to know "whom" one is addressing.

In listening to Julie, it was often as though one were doing group psychotherapy with the one patient. Thus I was confronted with a babble or jumble of quite disparate attitudes, feelings, expressions of impulse. The patient's intonations, gestures, mannerisms, changed their character from moment to moment. One may begin to recognize patches of speech, or fragments of behavior cropping up at different times, which seem to belong together by reason of similarities of the intonation, the vocabulary, syntax, the preoccupations in the utterance or to cohere as behavior by reason of certain stereotyped gestures or mannerisms. It seemed therefore that one was in the presence of various fragments, or incomplete elements, of different "personalities" in operation at the one time. Her "word-salad" seemed

---

a conclusion of chronic psychosis. This "praecox feeling" should, I believe, be the audience's response to Ophelia when she has become psychotic. Clinically she is latterly undoubtedly a schizophrenic. In her madness, there is no one there. She is not a person. There is no integral selfhood expressed through her actions or utterances. Incomprehensible statements are said by nothing. She has already died. There is now only a vacuum where there was once a person.

to be the result of a number of quasi-autonomous partial systems striving to give expression to themselves out of the same mouth at the same time.

This impression is strengthened, though hardly made the less confusing, by the fact that Julie seemed to speak of herself in the first, second, or third person. One requires an intimate knowledge of the individual patient before one can be in a position to say anything about the significance of this (this is true in all other aspects of schizophrenic activity).

Janet has differentiated dissociation or splitting into molar splits and molecular splits. The hysterical split personality is a molar split. Schizophrenia consists of molecular splitting. In Julie's case, there seemed to be both. The overall unity of her being had broken up into several "partial assemblies" or "partial systems" (quasi-autonomous "complexes," "inner objects"), each of which had its own little stereotyped "personality" (molar splitting). In addition, any actual sequence of behavior was fragmented in a much more minute manner (molecular splitting). Even the integrity of words, for instance, would be disrupted.

It is not surprising therefore that we speak of the "inaccessibility" and "praecox feeling" in such a case as this. With Julie it was not difficult to carry on a verbal exchange of a kind, but without her seeming to have any overall unity but rather a constellation of quasi-autonomous partial systems, it was difficult to speak to "her." However, one must not think primarily in terms of any mechanical analogy since even this state of near-chaotic nonentity was by no means irreversible and fixed in its disintegration. She would sometimes marvellously come together again and display a most pathetic realization of her plight. But she was terrified of these moments of integration, for various reasons. Among others, because she had to sustain in them intense anxiety; and because the process of disintegration appeared to be remembered and dreaded as an experience so awful that there was refuge for her in her unintegration, unrealness, and deadness.

Julie's being as a chronic schizophrenic was thus characterized by lack of unity and by division into what might variously be called partial "assemblies," complexes, partial systems, or "internal objects." Each of these partial systems had recognizable features and distinctive ways of its own. By following through these postulates, many features of her behavior become explicable.

The fact that her self-being was not assembled in an all-over manner, but was split into various partial assemblies or systems, allows us to understand that various functions which presuppose the achievement of personal unity or at least a high degree of personal unity could not be present in her, as indeed they were not.

Personal unity is a prerequisite of reflective awareness, that is, the ability to be aware of one's own self acting relatively unselfconsciously, or with a simple primary nonreflective awareness. In Julie, each partial system could be aware of objects, but a system might not be aware of the processes going on in another system which was split off from it. For example, if, in talking to me, one system was "speaking," there seemed to be no overall unity within her whereby "she" as a unified person could be aware of what this system was saying or doing.

In so far as reflective awareness was absent, "memory," for which reflective awareness would seem to be prerequisite, was very patchy. All her life seemed to be contemporaneous. The absence of a total experience of her being as a whole meant that she lacked the unified experience on which to base a clear idea of the "boundary" of her being. Such an *overall* "boundary" was not, however, entirely lacking. Thus Federn's term, *ego* boundary, is unsatisfactory. One needs another term for the total of which the ego is a part. Rather, *each system seemed to have a boundary of its own.* That is to say, to the awareness that characterized one system, another system was liable to appear outside itself. Within an overall unity, a diverse aspect of her being, if sufficiently "dystonic" to the rest, would set up painful conflict. In her, however, conflict of this kind could not arise. It was only "from the outside" that one could see that different conflicting systems of her being were active at the same time. Each partial system seemed to have within it its own focus or center of awareness: it had its own very limited memory schemata and limited ways of structuring percepts; its own quasi-autonomous drives or component drives; its own tendency to preserve its autonomy, and special dangers which threatened its autonomy. She would refer to these diverse aspects as "he," or "she," or address them as "you." That is, instead of having a reflective awareness of those aspects of herself, "she" would *perceive* the operation of a partial system as though it was not of "her," but belonged outside. She would be hallucinated.

Together with the tendency to perceive aspects of her own being as not-her, was the failure to discriminate between what "objectively" was not-her and what was her. This is simply the other aspect of the lack of an overall ontological boundary. She might for instance feel that rain on her cheek was her tears.

William Blake in his description of split states of being in his Prophetic Books describes a tendency to *become what one perceives*. In Julie all perception seemed to threaten confusion with the object. She spent much of her time exercising herself with this difficulty. "That's the rain. I could be the rain." "That chair . . . that wall. I could be that wall. It's a terrible thing for a girl to be a wall."

All perception seemed to threaten mergence and all sense of being perceived by the other threatened her similarly. This meant that she was living in a world of constant persecution and felt herself to be doing to others what she dreaded as happening to her. Almost every act of perception appeared to involve a confusion of self with not-self. The ground was prepared for this confusion by the fact that, since large aspects of her person were partially outside her "self," it was easy to confuse those split-off aspects of her being with other people, *e.g.,* her confusion of her "conscience" with her mother, and her mother with her "conscience."

To love was therefore very dangerous. To like =
to be like = to be the same as. If she likes me, she is
like me, she is me. Thus she began by saying that she
was my sister, my wife, she was a McBride. I was
life. She was the Bride of Life. She developed my
mannerisms. She had the Tree of Life inside her. She
was the Tree of Life. Or again:

She is thinking thoughts a, b, c.

I express closely similar thoughts a^1, b^1, c^1.

Therefore, I have stolen her thoughts.

The completely psychotic expression of this was
to accuse me of having her brains in my head.

Conversely, when she copied or imitated me, she
was liable to expect retribution from me for "coming
out" with a bit of me which she felt she had stolen.
Of course, the degree of mergence fluctuated from
moment to moment. Stealing, for instance, presupposes some boundary between self and not-self.

We shall now illustrate and elaborate the above
points by examples.

One of the simplest instances of the operation of a
split of her being into two partial "assemblies" is
seen when she issued herself an order and proceeded
to obey it. She was doing this continually, either
under her breath, out loud, or by hallucinations.
Thus "she" would say, "Sit down, stand up," and
"she" would sit down and stand up; or an hallucinated voice, the voice of one partial system, would
issue the order and "she," the action of another
partial system, would obey it.

Another common simple instance was when "she"
would say something which "she" would greet with

derisive laughter (incongruity of thought and affect).
Let us suppose that the statement emanates from
system A and the laughter from system B. Then A
says to me, "She's a Royal Queen," while B laughs
derisively.

A good deal of what appeared to be something
akin to "jamming" went on. A would say something
relatively coherently and then it would become
jumbled up and B would start to speak. A would
break in again to say: "She (B) has stolen my
tongue."

These various partial systems could be identified,
at least to some extent after getting to know her, by
reason of the consistency of the role each played in
what one might call the intrapersonal "group" they
comprised.

For instance, there was the peremptory bully who
was always ordering her about. The same peremptory voice would make endless complaints to me
about "this child": "this is a wicked child. This child
is wasted time. This child is just a cheap tart. You'll
never do anything with this child. . . ." The "you"
here might be referring directly to me, or to one of
her systems, or I could be embodying this system.

It was evident that this bullying figure within her
was for much of the time "the boss." "She" did not
think much of Julie. "She" did not think Julie would
get well, nor that she was worth getting better. She
was neither on her side, nor on my side. It would be
appropriate to call this quasi-autonomous partial
system a "bad internal mother." She was basically

an internal female persecutor who contained in concentrated form all the bad that Julie ascribed to her
mother.

Two other partial systems could be readily identified. One fulfilled the role of an advocate on her
behalf to me, and a protector or buffer against
persecution. "She" frequently referred to Julie as her
little sister. Phenomenologically, therefore, we may
refer to this system as "her good sister."

The third partial system that I shall introduce was
an entirely good, compliant, propitiating little girl.
This seemed to be a derivative of what some years
before was probably a system very similar to the false-
self system I have described in schizoid cases. When
this system spoke, she said, "I'm a good girl. I go to
the lavatory regularly."

There were derivations also of what seemed to
have been an "inner" self, which had become almost
completely volatilized into pure possibility. Finally,
as I remarked earlier, there were periods of precarious sanity in which she spoke in a pathetically
scared, barely audible tone, but seemed to be more
nearly speaking "in her own person" than at any
other time.

Let us now consider these various systems operating together. The examples I give are of her more
coherent utterances.

> I was born under a black sun. I wasn't born, I
> was crushed out. It's not one of those things you
> get over like that. I wasn't mothered, I was smoth-
> ered. She wasn't a mother. I'm choosey who I
> have for a mother. Stop it. Stop it. She's killing

me. She's cutting out my tongue. I'm rotten, base.
I'm wicked. I'm wasted time . . . .

Now, in the light of the foregoing discussion, I
would offer the following interpretation of what is
happening.

She starts by talking to me in her own person to
level the same accusations against her mother as she
has persisted in for years. But in a particularly clear
and lucid way. The "black sun" (*sol niger*) appears
to be a symbol of her destructive mother. It was a
frequently recurring image. The first six sentences
are spoken sanely. Suddenly she appears to be subject to some terrifying attack, presumably from this
bad mother. She breaks off in an intrapersonal crisis.
"Stop it, stop it." Addressing me briefly again she
exclaims, "She's killing me." Then follows a defensive denigration of herself, couched in the same
terms as her bad mother's condemnations of her, "I'm
rotten, base. I'm wicked. I'm wasted time. . . ."

Accusations against her mother were always liable
to precipitate some such catastrophic reaction. On a
later occasion she made her usual accusations
against her mother and the bad mother interrupted
with her customary accusations against "that child":
"That child's bad, that child's wicked. That child's
wasted time." I interrupted these remarks to say,
"Julie's frightened of being killed by herself for saying these things." The diatribe did not continue, but
"she" said very quietly, "Yes, that's my conscience
killing me. I've been frightened of my mother all my
life and always will be. Do you think I can live?"
This relatively integrated statement makes clear the

remaining *con-fusion* of her "conscience" and her real mother. Her bad conscience was a bad persecuting mother. As stated above, it may have been one of the schizophrenogenic elements in her life that she could not get her real mother in a real sense to accept her need to project part of her bad conscience into her. That is, for her mother really to admit some validity to Julie's accusations and thus, by allowing her to see some imperfections in her mother, to relieve some of the internal persecution from her "conscience."

> This child doesn't want to come here, do you realize that? She's my little sister. This child does not know about things she shouldn't know about.

Here her "big sister" is speaking, making clear to me that Julie is innocent and ignorant and therefore blameless and irresponsible. The "big sister" system, in contrast to the innocent and ignorant "little sister" system, was a very knowing and responsible "person," rather patronizing though kindly and protective. However, "she" is not on the side of Julie, the little sister, growing up, and is always speaking "for" the little sister. She wishes to maintain the *status quo*.

> This child's mind is cracked. This child's mind is closed. You're trying to open this child's mind. I'll never forgive you for trying to open this child's mind. This child is dead and not dead.

The implication of this last sentence is that, by remaining in a sense dead, she can be not dead in a sense, but if she takes responsibility for being "really" alive, then she may be "really" killed.

E

However, this "sister" could also speak in this way:

> You've got to want this child. You've got to make her welcome . . . you've got to take care of this girl. I'm a good girl. She's my little sister. You've got to take her to the lavatory. She's my little sister. She doesn't know about these things. That's not an impossible child.

This big sister contained experience, knowledge, responsibility, reasonableness, in contrast to the little sister's innocence, ignorance, irresponsibility, and waywardness. We see here also that Julie's schizophrenia consisted in the *all-over* lack of integration, not simply in the absence of a locus in her of "sanity." This "big sister" component of her being could speak in a reasonable, sane, and balanced way, but it was not *Julie* who was speaking; her sanity was, if you like, split off and encapsulated. Her real sanity depended not on being able to speak sanely in the person of a "big sister" but in achieving an overall integration of her total being. The schizophrenia is betrayed by her reference to herself as a third party, and in the sudden intrusion of the little sister while the big sister is speaking ("I'm a good girl").

When she did present words or actions to me as her own, this "self" that was so presented was completely psychotic. Most of the really cryptic condensed statements seemed to belong to the remnants of her self system. When decoded they reveal that this system was probably the derivative of the phantasticized inner self that we described in sane schizoid states.

We have already attempted to give an account of how it comes about that the experience of this self involves such extreme paradoxes of phantastic omnipotence/impotence and so on, at the same time. The phenomenological characteristics of the experience of this self seem in Julie to be in principle similar. However, one must be prepared to paraphrase her schizophrenia into sane speech before one can attempt a phenomenological construct of the experience of this "self." I must make it clear once more that in using the term "self" in this context, I do not mean to imply that this was her "true" self. This system did, however, seem to comprise a rallying point around which integration could occur. When disintegration occurred this seemed to be "the center" which could not hold. It seemed to be a central reference for centripetal or centrifugal tendencies. It appeared as the really mad kernel of her being, that central aspect of her which, so it seemed, had to be maintained chaotic and dead lest she be killed.

We shall attempt to characterize the nature of this "self" by statements made not only by this "self" directly but also by statements that appear to originate in other systems. There are not a great many of these statements, at least by the "self" in person as it were. During her years in hospital, many of them probably had become run together to result in constantly reiterated short telegraphic statements containing a great wealth of implications.

As we saw above, she said she had the Tree of Life inside her. The apples of this tree were her

breasts. She had ten nipples (her fingers). She had
"all the bones of a brigade of the Highland Light
Infantry." She had everything she could think of.
Anything she wanted, she had and she had not,
immediately, at the one time. Reality did not cast its
shadow or its light over any wish or fear. Every wish
met with instantaneous phantom fulfilment and
every dread likewise instantaneously came to pass in
a phantom way. Thus she could be anyone, anywhere, anytime. "I'm Rita Hayworth, I'm Joan
Blondell. I'm a Royal Queen. My royal name is
Julianne." "She's self-sufficient," she told me. "She's
the self-possessed." But this self-possession was
double-edged. It had also its dark side. She was a girl
"possessed" by the phantom of her own being. Her
self had no freedom, autonomy, or power in the
real world. Since she was anyone she cared to mention, she was no *one*. "I'm thousands. I'm an in
divide you all I'm a no un" (*i.e.,* a nun: a noun: no
one single person). Being a nun had very many
meanings. One of them was contrasted with being a
bride. She usually regarded me as her brother and
called herself my bride or the bride of "leally lovely
lifely life." Of course, since life and me were sometimes identical for her, she was terrified of Life, or
me. Life (me) would mash her to pulp, burn her
heart with a red-hot iron, cut off her legs, hands,
tongue, breasts. Life was conceived in the most violent and fiercely destructive terms imaginable. It was
not some quality about me, or something I had (*e.g.,*
a phallus=a red-hot iron). It was what I was. I was
life. Notwithstanding having the Tree of Life inside

her, she generally felt that she was the Destroyer of Life. It was understandable, therefore, that she was terrified that life would destroy her. Life was usually depicted by a male or phallic symbol, but what she seemed to wish for was not simply to be a male herself but to have a heavy armamentarium of the sexual equipment of both sexes, all the bones of a brigade of the Highland Light Infantry and ten nipples, etc.

> She was born under a black sun.
> She's the occidental sun.

The ancient and very sinister image of the black sun arose quite independently of any reading. Julie had left school at fourteen, had read very little, and was not particularly clever. It was extremely unlikely that she would have come across any reference to it, but we shall forgo discussion of the origin of the symbol and restrict ourselves to seeing her language as an expression of the way she experienced being-in-her-world.

She always insisted that her mother had never wanted her, and had crushed her out in some monstrous way rather than give birth to her normally. Her mother had "wanted and not wanted" a son. She was "an occidental sun," *i.e.*, an accidental son whom her mother out of hate had turned into a girl. The rays of the black sun scorched and shrivelled her. Under the black sun she existed as a dead thing. Thus,

> I'm the prairie.
> She's a ruined city.

The only living things in the prairie were wild beasts. Rats infested the ruined city. Her existence was depicted in images of utterly barren, arid desolation. This existential death, this death-in-life was her prevailing mode of being-in-the-world.

She's the ghost of the weed garden.

In this death there was no hope, no future, no possibility. Everything had happened. There was no pleasure, no source of possible satisfaction or possible gratification, for the world was as empty and dead as she was.

The pitcher is broken, the well is dry.

She was utterly pointless and worthless. She could not believe in the possibility of love anywhere.

She's just one of those girls who live in the world. Everyone pretends to want her and doesn't want her. I'm just leading the life now of a cheap tart.

Yet, as we saw from earlier statements, she did value herself if only in a phantom way. There was a belief (however psychotic a belief it was, it was still a form of faith in something of great value in herself) that there was something of great worth deeply lost or buried inside her, as yet undiscovered by herself or by anyone. If one could go deep into the depth of the dark earth one would discover "the bright gold," or if one could get fathoms down one would discover "the pearl at the bottom of the sea."

5. The Mystification of Experience

R. D. LAING

It is not enough to destroy one's own and other people's experience. One must overlay this devastation by a false consciousness inured, as Marcuse puts it, to its own falsity.

Exploitation must not be seen as such. It must be seen as benevolence. Persecution preferably should not need to be invalidated as the figment of a paranoid imagination; it should be experienced as kindness. Marx described mystification and showed its function in his day. Orwell's time is already with us. The colonists not only mystify the natives, in the ways that Fanon so clearly shows,[1] they have to mystify themselves. We in Europe and North

From *The Politics of Experience* by R. D. Laing (London: Penguin, 1967), pp. 57–76. Copyright © 1967 by R. D. Laing. Reprinted by permission of the publisher.

1. Frantz Fanon, *The Wretched of the Earth* (London: MacGibbon and Kee, 1965); also Frantz Fanon, *Studies in a Dying Colonialism* (New York: Monthly Review Press, 1965).

America are the colonists, and in order to sustain our amazing images of ourselves as God's gift to the vast majority of the starving human species, we have to interiorize our violence upon ourselves and our children and to employ the rhetoric of morality to describe this process.

In order to rationalize our industrial-military complex, we have to destroy our capacity to see clearly any more what is in front of, and to imagine what is beyond, our noses. Long before a thermonuclear war can come about, we have had to lay waste our own sanity. We begin with the children. It is imperative to catch them in time. Without the most thorough and rapid brainwashing their dirty minds would see through our dirty tricks. Children are not yet fools, but we shall turn them into imbeciles like ourselves, with high IQ's if possible.

From the moment of birth, when the Stone Age baby confronts the twentieth-century mother, the baby is subjected to these forces of violence, called love, as its mother and father, and their parents and their parents before them, have been. These forces are mainly concerned with destroying most of its potentialities, and on the whole this enterprise is successful. By the time the new human being is fifteen or so, we are left with a being like ourselves, a half-crazed creature more or less adjusted to a mad world. This is normality in our present age.

Love and violence, properly speaking, are polar opposites. Love lets the other be, but with affection and concern. Violence attempts to constrain the other's freedom, to force him to act in the way we desire, but with ultimate lack of concern, with indifference to the other's own existence or destiny.

We are effectively destroying ourselves by violence masquerading as love.

I am a specialist, God help me, in events in inner space and time, in experiences called thoughts, images, reveries, dreams, visions, hallucinations, dreams of memories, memories of dreams, memories of visions, dreams of hallucinations, refractions of refractions of refractions of that original Alpha and Omega of experience and. reality, that Reality on whose repression, denial, splitting, projection, falsification, and general desecration and profanation our civilization as much as on anything is based.

We live equally out of our bodies and out of our minds.

Concerned as I am with this inner world, observing day in and day out its devastation, I ask why this has happened?

One component of an answer, suggested in Chapter I, is that we can *act* on our *experience* of ourselves, others, and the world, as well as take action on the world through behavior itself. Specifically this devastation is largely the work of *violence* that has been perpetrated on each of us, and by each of us on ourselves. The usual name that much of this violence goes under is *love*.

We act on our experience at the behest of the others, just as we learn how to behave in compliance with them. We are taught what to experience and what not to experience, as we are taught what movements to make and what sounds to emit. A child of two is already a moral mover and moral talker and moral experiencer. He already moves the "right" way, makes the "right" noises, and knows what he should feel and what he should not feel. His movements have become stereometric types, enabling the specialist anthroplogist to identify, through his rhythm and style, his national, even his regional, characteristics. As he is taught to move in specific ways out of the whole range of possible movements, so he is taught to experience out of the whole range of possible experience.

Much current social science deepens the mystification. Violence cannot be seen through the sights of positivism.

A woman grinds stuff down a goose's neck through a funnel. Is this a description of cruelty to an animal? She disclaims any motivation or intention of cruelty. If we were to describe this scene "objectively," we would only be denuding it of what is "objectively," or better, ontologically present in the situation. Every description presupposes our ontological premises as to the nature (being) of man, of animals, and of the relationship between them.

If an animal is debased to a manufactured piece of produce, a sort of biochemical complex—so that its flesh and organs are simply material with a certain texture in the mouth (soft, tender, tough), a taste, perhaps a smell—then to describe the animal *positively* in those terms is to debase oneself by debasing being itself. A *positive* description is not "neutral" or "objective." In the case of geese-as-raw-material-for-*pâté,* one can only give a negative description if the description is to remain underpinned by a valid ontology. That is to say, the description moves in the light of what this activity is a brutalization of, a debasement of, a desecration of: namely, the true nature of human beings and of animals.

The description must be *in light of* the fact that the human beings have so brutalized themselves, have become so banal and stultified, that they are unaware of their own debasement. This is not to superimpose onto the "neutral" description certain value judgments that have lost all criteria of "objective" validity, that is to say, any validity that anyone feels needs to be taken really seriously. On "subjective" matters, anything goes. Political ideologies, on the other hand are riddled with value judgments, unrecognized as such, that have no ontological validity. Pedants teach youth that such questions of value are unanswerable, or untestable, or unverifiable, or not really questions at all, or that what we require are metaquestions. Meanwhile Vietnam goes on.

Under the sign of alienation every single aspect of the human reality is subject to falsification, and a positive description can only perpetuate the alienation which it cannot itself describe, and succeeds only in further deepening it because it disguises and masks it the more.

We must then repudiate a positivism that achieves its "reliability" by successfully masking what is and what is not, by serializing the world of the observer, by turning the truly given into *capta* which are *taken as given,* by denuding the world of being and relegating the ghost of being to a shadow land of subjective "values."

The theoretical and descriptive idiom of much

research in social science adopts a stance of apparent "objective" neutrality. But we have seen how deceptive this can be. The choice of syntax and vocabulary is a political act that defines and circumscribes the manner in which "facts" are to be experienced. Indeed, in a sense it goes further and even creates the facts that are studied.

The "data" (given) of research are not so much given as *taken* out of a constantly elusive matrix of happenings. We should speak of *capta* rather than data. The quantitatively interchangeable grist that goes into the mills of reliability studies and rating scales is the expression of a processing that we do *on* reality, not the expression of the processes *of* reality.

Natural scientific investigations are conducted on objects, or things, or the patterns of relations between things, or on systems of "events." Persons are distinguished from things in that persons experience the world, whereas things behave in the world. Thing-events do not experience. Personal events are experiential. Natural scientism is the error of turning persons into things by a process of reification that is not itself part of true natural scientific method. Results derived in this way have to be dequantified and dereified before they can be reassimilated into the realm of human discourse.

Fundamentally, the error is the failure to realize that there is an ontological discontinuity between human beings and it-beings.

Human beings relate to each other not simply externally, like two billiard balls, but by the relations of the two worlds of experience that come into play when two people meet.

If human beings are not studied as human beings, then this once more is violence and mystification.

In much contemporary writing on the individual and the family there is assumed some not-too-unhappy confluence, not to say pre-established harmony, between nature and nurture. Some adjustments may have to be made on both sides, but all things work together for good to those who want only security and identity.

Gone is any sense of possible tragedy, of passion. Gone is any language of joy, delight, passion, sex, violence. The language is that of a boardroom. No more primal scenes, but parental coalitions; no more repression of sexual ties to parents, but the child "rescinds" its Oedipal wishes. For instance:

> The mother can properly invest her energies in the care of the young child when economic support, status, and protection of the family are provided by the father. She can also better limit her cathexis of the child to maternal feelings when her wifely needs are satisfied by her husband.[2]

Here is no nasty talk of sexual intercourse or even "primal scene." The economic metaphor is aptly employed. The mother "invests" in her child. What is most revealing is the husband's function. The provision of economic support, status and protection, in that order.

There is frequent reference to security, the esteem

2. T. Lidz, *The Family and Human Adaptation* (London: Hogarth Press, 1964), p. 54.

of others. What one is supposed to want, to live for, is "gaining pleasure from the esteem and affection of others."[3] If not, one is a psychopath.

Such statements are in a sense true. They describe the frightened, cowed, abject creature that we are admonished to be, if we are to be normal—offering each other mutual protection from our own violence. The family as a "protection racket."

Behind this language lurks the terror that is behind all this mutual back-scratching, this esteem-, status-, support-, protection-, security-giving and getting. Through its bland urbanity the cracks still show.

In our world we are "victims burning at the stake, signaling through the flames," but for some, things go blandly on. "Contemporary life requires adaptability." We require also to "utilize intellect," and we require "an emotional equilibrium that permits a person to be malleable, to adjust himself to others without fear of loss of identity with change. It requires a basic trust in others, and a confidence in the integrity of the self."[4]

Sometimes there is a glimpse of more honesty. For instance, when we "consider society rather than the individual, each society has a vital interest in the *indoctrination* of the infants who form its new *recruits*."[5]

What these authors say may be written ironically, but there is no evidence that it is.

3. Ibid., p. 34.
4. Ibid., pp. 28–29.
5. Ibid., p. 19.

Adaptation to what? To society? To a world gone mad?

The family's function is to repress Eros; to induce a false consciousness of security; to deny death by avoiding life; to cut off transcendence; to believe in God, not to experience the Void; to create, in short, one-dimensional man; to promote respect, conformity, obedience; to con children out of play; to induce a fear of failure; to promote a respect for work; to promote a respect for "respectability."

Let me present here two alternative views of the family and human adaptation:

> Men do not become what by nature they are meant to be, but what society makes them. . . . Generous feelings . . . are, as it were, shrunk up, seared, violently wrenched, and amputated to fit us for our intercourse with the world, something in the manner that beggars maim and mutilate their children to make them fit for their future situation in life.[6]

and:

> In fact, the world still seems to be inhabited by savages stupid enough to see reincarnated ancestors in their newborn children. Weapons and jewelry belonging to the dead men are waved under the infant's nose; if he makes a movement, there is a great shout—Grandfather has come back to life. This "old man" will suckle, dirty his straw and bear the ancestral name; survivors of his ancient generation will enjoy seeing their com-

6. E. Colby, ed., *The Life of Thomas Holcroft, Continued by William Hazlitt* (London: Constable & Co., 1925), vol. 2, p. 82.

rade of hunts and battles wave his tiny limbs and bawl; as soon as he can speak they will inculcate recollections of the deceased. A severe training will "restore" his former character, they will remind him that "he" was wrathful, cruel or magnanimous, and he will be convinced of it despite all experience to the contrary. What barbarism! Take a living child, sew him up in a dead man's skin, and he will stifle in such senile childhood with no occupation save to reproduce the avuncular gestures, with no hope save to poison future childhoods after his own death. No wonder, after that, if he speaks of himself with the greatest precautions, half under his breath, often in the third person; this miserable creature is well aware that he is his own grandfather.

These backward aborigines can be found in the Fiji Islands, in Tahiti, in New Guinea, in Vienna, in Paris, in Rome, in New York—wherever there are men. They are called parents. Long before our birth, even before we are conceived, our parents have decided who we will be.[7]

In some quarters there is a point of view that science is neutral, and that all this is a matter of value judgments.

Lidz calls schizophrenia a failure of human adaptation. In that case, this too is a value judgment. Or is anyone going to say that it is an objective fact? Very well, let us call schizophrenia a successful attempt not to adapt to pseudo-social realities. Is this also an objective fact? Schizophrenia is a failure of ego functioning. Is this a neutralist definition? But what is, or who is, the "ego"? In order to get back to

7. J.-P. Sartre, Foreword to *The Traitor* by André Gorz (London: Calder, 1960), pp. 14–15.

what the ego is and what actual reality it most nearly relates to, we have to desegregate it, de-depersonalize it, de-extrapolate, de-abstract, de-objectify, de-reify, and we get back to you and me, to our particular idioms or styles of relating to each other in social context. The ego is by definition an instrument of adaptation, so we are back to all the questions this apparent neutralism is begging. Schizophrenia is a successful avoidance of ego-type adaptation? Schizophrenia is a label affixed by some people to others in situations where an interpersonal disjunction of a particular kind is occurring. This is the nearest one can get at the moment to something like an "objective" statement, so called.

The family is, in the first place, the usual instrument for what is called socialization, that is, getting each new recruit to the human race to behave and experience in substantially the same way as those who have already got here. We are all fallen Sons of Prophecy, who have learned to die in the Spirit and be reborn in the flesh.

This is also known as selling one's birthright for a mess of pottage.

Here are some examples from Jules Henry, an American professor of anthropology and sociology, in his study of the American school system:

> The observer is just entering her fifth-grade classroom for the observation period. The teacher says, "Which one of you nice, polite boys would like to take (the observer's) coat and hang it up?" From the waving hands, it would seem that all would like to claim the honor. The teacher chooses one

child, who takes the observer's coat. . . . The teacher conducted the arithmetic lessons mostly by asking, "Who would like to tell the answer to the next problem?" This question was followed by the usual large and agitated forest of hands, with apparently much competition to answer.

What strikes us here are the precision with which the teacher was able to mobilize the potentialities of the boys for the proper social behavior, and the speed with which they responded. The large number of waving hands proves that most of the boys have already become absurd; but they have no choice. Suppose they sat there frozen?

A skilled teacher sets up many situations in such a way that a *negative attitude can be construed only as treason*. The function of questions like, "Which one of you nice, polite boys would like to take (the observer's) coat and hang it up?" is to blind the children into absurdity—to compel them to acknowledge that it is better to exist absurd than not to exist at all. The reader will have observed that the question is not put, "Who *has* the answer to the next problem?" but "Who *would like to tell* it?" What at one time in our culture was phrased as a challenge in skill in arithmetic, becomes an invitation to group participation. The essential is *that nothing is but what it is made to be by the alchemy of the system*.

In a society where competition for the basic cultural goods is a pivot of action, people cannot be taught to love one another. It thus becomes necessary for the school to teach children how to hate, and without appearing to do so, for our culture cannot tolerate the idea that babes should hate each other. How does the school accomplish this ambiguity?[8]

8. J. Henry, *Culture Against Man* (New York: Random House, 1963), p. 293.

Here is another example given by Henry:

Boris had trouble reducing 12/16 to the lowest terms, and could only get as far as 6/8. The teacher asked him quietly if that was as far as he could reduce it. She suggested he "think." Much heaving up and down and waving of hands by the other children, all frantic to correct him. Boris pretty unhappy, probably mentally paralyzed. The teacher quiet, patient, ignores the others and concentrates with look and voice on Boris. After a minute or two she turns to the class and says, "Well, who can tell Boris what the number is?" A forest of hands appears, and the teacher calls Peggy. Peggy says that four may be divided into the numerator and the denominator.[9]

Henry comments:

Boris's failure made it possible for Peggy to succeed; his misery is the occasion for her rejoicing. This is a standard condition of the contemporary American elementary school. To a Zuni, Hopi or Dakota Indian, Peggy's performance would seem cruel beyond belief, for competition, the wringing of success from somebody's failure, is a form of torture foreign to those noncompetitive cultures.

Looked at from Boris's point of view, the nightmare at the blackboard was, perhaps, a lesson in controlling himself so that he would not fly shrieking from the room under enormous public pressure. Such experiences force every man reared in our culture, over and over again, night in, night out, even at the pinnacle of success, to dream not of success, but of failure. In school the external nightmare is internalized for life. Boris was not learning arithmetic only; he was learning the

9. Ibid., p. 27.

> *essential nightmare also. To be successful in our*
> *culture one must learn to dream of failure.*[10]

It is Henry's contention that in practice education
has never been an instrument to free the mind and
the spirit of man, but to bind them. We think we
want creative children, but what do we want them to
create?

> If all through school the young were provoked
> to question the Ten Commandments, the sanc-
> tity of revealed religion, the foundations of patri-
> otism, the profit motive, the two-party system,
> monogamy, the laws of incest, and so on . . .[11]

. . . there would be such creativity that society
would not know where to turn.

Children do not give up their innate imagination,
curiosity, dreaminess easily. You have to love them
to get them to do that. Love is the path through
permissiveness to discipline; and through discipline,
only too often, to betrayal of self.

What school must do is to induce children to want
to think the way school wants them to think. "What
we see," in the American kindergarten and early
schooling process, says Henry, "is the pathetic sur-
render of babies." You will, later or sooner, in the
school or in the home.

It is the most difficult thing in the world to recognize this in our own culture.

In a London class, average age ten, the girls were
given a competition. They had to bake cakes and the

10. Ibid., pp. 295–296.
11. Ibid., p. 288.

boys were to judge them. One girl won. Then her "friend" let out that she had bought her cake instead of baking it herself. She was disgraced in front of the whole class.

Comments:

1. The school is here inducting children into sex-linked roles of a very specific kind.

2. Personally, I find it obscene that girls should be taught that their status depends on the taste they can produce in boys' mouths.

3. Ethical values are brought into play in a situation that is at best a bad joke. If coerced into such game-playing by adults, the best a child can do is to play the system without getting caught. I most admire the girl who won and hope she will choose her "friends" more carefully in future.

What Henry describes in American schools is a strategy that I have observed frequently in British families studied by my colleagues and myself.

The double action of destroying ourselves with one hand, and calling this love with the other, is a sleight of hand one can marvel at. Human beings seem to have an almost unlimited capacity to deceive themselves, and to deceive themselves into taking their own lies for truth. By such mystification, we achieve and sustain our adjustment, adaptation, socialization. But the result of such adjustment to our society is that, having been tricked and having tricked ourselves out of our minds, that is to say, out of our own personal worlds of experience, out of that unique meaning with which potentially we may

endow the external world, simultaneously we have
been conned into the illusion that we are separate
"skin-encapsuled egos." Having at one and the same
time lost our *selves* and developed the illusion that
we are autonomous *egos,* we are expected to comply
by inner consent with external contraints, to an almost unbelievable extent.

We do not live in a world of unambiguous identities and definitions, needs and fears, hopes, disillu-
sions. The tremendous social realities of our time are
ghosts, specters of murdered gods and our own
humanity returned to haunt and destroy us. The
Negroes, the Jews, the Reds. *Them.* Only you and I
dressed differently. The texture of the fabric of these
socially shared hallucinations is what we call reality,
and our collusive madness is what we call sanity.

Let no one suppose that this madness exists only
somewhere in the night or day sky where our birds
of death hover in the stratosphere. It exists in the
interstices of our most intimate and personal
moments.

We have all been processed on Procrustean beds.
At least some of us have managed to hate what they
have made of us. Inevitably we see the other as the
reflection of the occasion of our own self-division.

The others have become installed in our hearts,
and we call them ourselves. Each person, not being
himself either to himself or the other, just as the
other is not himself to himself or to us, in being
another for another neither recognizes himself in the
other, nor the other in himself. Hence being at least
a double absence, haunted by the ghost of his own

murdered self, no wonder modern man is addicted to other persons, and the more addicted, the less satisfied, the more lonely.

Once more there is a turn of the spiral, another round of the vicious circle, another twist of the tourniquet. For now love becomes a further alienation, a further act of violence. My need is a need to be needed, my longing a longing to be longed for. I act now to install what I take to be myself in what I take to be the other person's heart. Marcel Proust wrote:

> How have we the courage to wish to live, how can we make a movement to preserve ourselves from death, in a world where love is provoked by a lie and consists solely in the need of having our sufferings appeased by whatever being has made us suffer?

But no one makes us suffer. The violence we perpetrate and have done to us, the recriminations, reconciliations, the ecstasies and the agonies of a love affair, are based on the socially conditioned illusion that two actual persons are in relationship. Under the circumstances, this is a dangerous state of hallucination and delusion, a mishmash of fantasy, exploding and imploding, of broken hearts, reparation and revenge.

Yet within all this, I do not preclude the occasions when, most lost, lovers may discover each other, moments when recognition does occur, when hell can turn to heaven and come down to earth, when this crazy distraction can become joy and celebration.

And, at the very least, it befits Babes in the Wood

to be kinder to each other, to show some sympathy and compassion, if there is any pathos and passion left to spend.

But when violence masquerades as love, once the fissure into self and ego, inner and outer, good and bad occurs, all else is an infernal dance of false dualities. It has always been recognized that if you split Being down the middle, if you insist on grabbing *this* without *that,* if you cling to the good without the bad, denying the one for the other, what happens is that the dissociated evil impulse, now evil in a double sense, returns to permeate and possess the good and turn it into itself.

When the great Tao is lost, spring forth benevolence and righteousness.

When wisdom and sagacity arise, there are great hypocrites.

When family relations are no longer harmonious, we have filial children and devoted parents.

When a nation is in confusion and disorder, patriots are recognized.

We must be very careful of our selective blindness. The Germans reared children to regard it as their duty to exterminate the Jews, adore their leader, kill and die for the Fatherland. The majority of my own generation did not or do not regard it as stark raving mad to feel it better to be dead than Red. None of us, I take it, has lost too many hours' sleep over the threat of imminent annihilation of the human race and our own responsibility for this state of affairs.

In the last fifty years, we human beings have

slaughtered by our own hands coming on for one hundred million of our species. We all live under constant threat of our total annihilation. We seem to seek death and destruction as much as life and happiness. We are as driven to kill and be killed as we are to let live and live. Only by the most outrageous violation of ourselves have we achieved our capacity to live in relative adjustment to a civilization apparently driven to its own destruction. Perhaps to a limited extent we can undo what has been done to us and what we have done to ourselves. Perhaps men and women were born to love one another, simply and genuinely, rather than to this travesty that we call love. If we can stop destroying ourselves we may stop destroying others. We have to begin by admitting and even accepting our violence, rather than blindly destroying ourselves with it, and therewith we have to realize that we are as deeply afraid to live and to love as we are to die.

6. Violence and Psychiatry

DAVID COOPER

At the heart of our problem is violence. The sort of violence that I shall consider here, however, has little to do with people hitting each other on the head with hammers and will not much be about what crazy mental patients are supposed to do. If one is to speak of violence in psychiatry, the violence that stares out screaming, proclaiming itself as such so loudly that it is rarely heard, is the subtle, tortuous violence that other people, the "sane ones," perpetrate against the labeled madmen. In so far as psychiatry represents the interests or pretended interests of the sane ones, we may discover that, in fact, violence in psychiatry is preeminently the violence *of* psychiatry.

But who are these sane people? How do they define themselves? Definitions of mental health pro-

From *Psychiatry and Anti-Psychiatry* by David Cooper (London: Tavistock, 1967), pp. 17–40. Reprinted by permission of the publisher.

pounded by the expert usually amount to the notion
of conformism to a set of more or less arbitrarily
posited social norms, or else they are so conveniently
general—for example, "the capacity to tolerate and
develop through conflict"—that they deprive themselves of operational significance. One is left with the
sorry reflection that the sane ones are perhaps those
who fail to gain admission to the mental observation
ward. That is to say, they define themselves by a
certain absence of experience. But then the Nazis
gassed tens of thousands of mental patients, and tens
of thousands more in this country have their brains
surgically mutilated or battered by successive
courses of electroshock and, above all, their personalities systematically deformed by psychiatric institutionalization. How can such very concrete facts
emerge on the basis of an absence, a negativity—the
compulsive nonmadness of the sane?

In fact, this whole area of definition of sanity and
madness is so confused and those who venture into it
so uniformly terrified (whether they are "professionally qualified" or not) by the hint of what they might
encounter, not only in "the others" but also in
themselves, that one must seriously consider relin-
quishing the project. One cannot proceed, I believe,
without challenging the basic classification of clinical
psychiatry of people into "psychotic," "neurotic,"
and "normal." But then, since the history of psychiatry has consisted very largely in the elaboration of an
immense public convenience that takes the form of
large mental hospitals, outpatient clinics, general-
hospital psychiatric units, and, sometimes, unfortunately, the psychoanalytic couch, one should not let

this deter one from attempting what might seem to be a radical and possibly dangerous reevaluation of the problem of madness.

The essence of this necessary reevaluation of madness, as I see it, is perhaps most aptly and economically expressed in the diagram. In this schematic representation, which for present purposes restricts itself to a very conventional terminology, we discover first the point of insertion of the individual person at point alpha. From this point the person develops in the sense of progressively taking into himself, registering, and then acting on the things his parents are taught, feel, and then teach him to be the "correct" things. Along with this he learns his "masculine-instrumental" or she learns her "feminine-expressive" social role. If all progresses "well" in his family and school, he attains the point of adolescent "identity crisis" where he, in effect, sums up everything that has conditioned him so far, all the early identifications he has made, all the things that he has been "made of," everything he has been stuffed full of. (This constitutes "normality"—a statistical concept that most of us live by as a golden rule.) Then, more or less successfully, he projects himself into an independent future, but one which must of necessity, unless there has been some fortunate error, reduce him to what is conventionally accepted. From this point on he lives forty or fifty years in what remains virtually the same state, although by a process of accretion he becomes more "experienced," "wise," develops a greater capacity to adjust to altering circumstances, knows what is

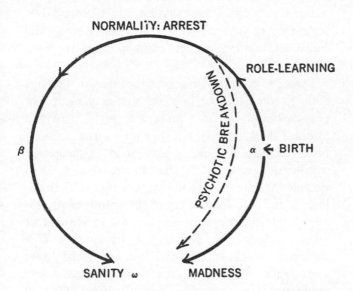

From the moment of birth most people progress through the social learning situations of family and school until they achieve social normality. Most people are developmentally arrested in this state of normality. Some others break down during this progress and regress to what is called madness in the diagram. Others, very few, manage to slip through the state of inertia or arrest represented by alienated, statistical normality and progress to some extent on the way (β) to sanity, retaining an awareness of the criteria of social normality so that they may avoid invalidation (this is always a dicey game). One should note that normality is "far out" at an opposite pole not only to madness but also to sanity. Sanity approaches madness but an all-important gap, a difference, always remains. This is the omega point (ω).

"best" for him and probably for most other people. He lives in this way and then dies. He is known, remembered, and then forgotten. These latter periods may vary chronologically but on the cosmic time scale they do not matter at all. This is surely the career and the fate of most of us, particularly if we are "mentally healthy."

Perhaps, however, this need not be so. Perhaps there is some manner in which we may escape or liberate ourselves into a more real, less stereotyped future. I think there is, but then one runs the risk of being thought mad and one is then in danger of psychiatric treatment. Psychiatric treatment is often ridiculed in terms of its failure, but this is most unjust. If one is to speak truly of the failure of psychiatric treatment one must be prepared to see that its failure resides most precisely in its success. This treatment in either its official or unofficial guise (nonmedical therapeutic conditioning) usually succeeds in producing a requisite conformism either on the level of the chronic back ward or on the (higher or lower) level of the all-commanding captain of industry. There are many species and genera of vegetables but all of them, by our principles of classification, lie in the mud. They grow there and they are gathered there. Potatoes, Tomatoes, Chicory, and Turnips. Nonhuman ones and human ones. To alter the analogy, one might say that we live lives that are boxed in[1] from birth to death. From the womb we

1. Compare Pete Seeger's well-known folk-song "Little Boxes, on the Hillside"; this expresses very well the nature of the "boxed-in" condition.

are born into the box of the family from which we
progress into the box of the school. By the time we
leave school we have become so conditioned to being
in a box that from then on we erect our own box,
prison, bin around us—until, finally with relief, we
are put into the coffin or the oven. I shall return
later in this volume to the prospect of liberation but
in the meantime there are other tasks. Let us simply
note the possible connection between socially prescribed sanity, psychiatric treatment, and boxes.

We must look at the Sane a little more closely.
Despairing of connotation, we see that denotatively
they include the families of the patients, employers
at work, general practitioners, mental welfare officers, the police, magistrates, social workers, psychiatrists, mental nurses, and many others. All these
people, some of whom may be most sincere and
devoted to the patient, are implicated more or less
deeply, but inexorably albeit despite themselves, in a
subtle violence against the objects of their care. I do
not have the intention of denigrating certain psychiatrists and other mental health workers who are
struggling quite genuinely, and often against formidable institutional obstacles, to provide authentic help
for their patients. But, of course, we have also to
remember that good intentions and all the trappings
of professional respectability very often cover a truly
cruel human reality. We recall, for instance, that
Boger of Auschwitz had ideas for dealing with teen-
age delinquents not dissimilar from those expressed
by many respected and eminent members of *our*
society, and that Dr. Capesius has been noted since

the war to be particularly considerate and kindly towards animals and children.

To comprehend my present usage of the term "violence," we shall have to understand it as the corrosive action of the freedom of a person on the freedom of another. It is not direct physical assaultiveness, although this may issue from it. The free action (or praxis) of a person can destroy the freedom of another or at least paralyze it by mystification. Human groups are formed in relation to some real or illusory menace outside the group, but as this external menace becomes more remote, the group, which has literally or metaphorically become a pledged group, is faced with the necessity to reinvent fear to ensure its own permanence.[2] This secondary fear, which is a free product of the group determined to prevent its internal dissolution, is *terror* induced by the *violence* of common freedom. Violence in this sense, in the psychiatric field, commences in the family of the mental patient-to-be. But it does not end there.

In the mental hospital there are people with widely differing problems. In some cases behavior that is regarded socially as disturbed is explicable in

2. The pledged group displays a form of reciprocity that Sartre has called the pledge (*serment*). A multiplicity of freedoms produce a common praxis aimed at securing some basis for permanence of the group. The resulting form of reciprocity is the pledge. Only occasionally is this reciprocity expressed in words or ritual acts.

The original account of this is in Sartre, *Critique de la raison dialectique* (1960). An exposition in English is available in R. D. Laing and D. G. Cooper, *Reason and Violence* (1964), part 3, pp. 129 ff.

terms of biological processes such as brain disease, pathological ageing of the brain, epilepsy, and so on. But in other cases, the majority, this behavior is different in nature, cannot be explained in terms of any known biological process, but is intelligible in terms of what concrete other persons in actual relationship to the patient do to him in interaction with him doing things to them. What we must do to avoid a fatal confusion is to distinguish between behavior presenting in terms that are most appropriately seen as *explicable* process, and, on the other hand, behavior that is *intelligible* in terms of what people are actually doing to each other. These differently presented problems imply a corresponding difference in method of approach. The fact that these totally different sorts of problems are contained within the same institution is one reason why the myth of disease process, with all its implicit violence, has been perpetuated in the case of schizophrenia. "Schizophrenics," "neurotics," "psychopaths" have been placed in wards next to people with actual brain diseases. This dubious disease called "schizophrenia" accounts for the great majority of mental hospital beds, and mental hospital beds constitute about half the hospital beds in this country.

In the popular mind the schizophrenic is the prototypical madman, he is the author of the totally gratuitous crazy act, the act that always has overtones of violence to others. He is the one who mocks the sane ones ("mannerism," "grimacing," "buffoonery," subtle forms of withdrawal), but at the same time concedes to them the ground for his

F

own invalidation. He is the illogical man, the man whose logic is "ill." Or so they say. But perhaps we can discover some nuclear sense lying at the heart of this apparent nonsense. Where does he come from, this lunatic? Where does he come from and how does he get here in the midst of us? Is there just possibly a secret sanity concealed in this madness?

First, he is born into a family and this, some would say, is the highest common factor in his relation to the rest of us. But let us examine his family, assuming for the moment that this family is significantly different from most others.

In the family of the person destined to be designated schizophrenic we discover a peculiar sort of extremism. Even the most seemingly trivial issues are hinged around the polarities sanity/madness, life/death. The family group laws that regulate not only behavior but also permissible experience are both confusing and inflexible. A child in such a family has to learn a mode of relating to, say, his mother upon which, he is taught, her very mental and physical integrity depends. He is taught that if he breaks the rules, and the most apparently innocuous autonomous act may constitute such a breach, he will cause both the fatal dissolution of the family group and the personal disintegration of his mother and possibly others. In this way, as R. D. Laing and A. Esterson (Laing, *The Self and Others;* Laing and Esterson, *Sanity, Madness, and the Family*), have so clearly shown, he is progressively placed in an untenable position. His choice at the final critical point is ony that between, on the one hand, total submission, the total abandonment of his freedom, and, on the other hand, departure from the group, which entails the anguish of witnessing the prophesied devastation of the others and contending with the guilt that has with such affectionate care been planted in him. Most destined schizophrenics find a synthetic answer to this dilemma which often coincides in the present state of affairs with that which their families find for them, namely to leave the family but to leave it to enter the mental hospital.

In the mental hospital, society has, with unerring skill, produced a social structure that in many respects reduplicates the maddening peculiarities of the patient's family. In the mental hospital he finds psychiatrists, administrators, nurses, who are his veritable parents, brothers, and sisters, who play an interpersonal game which only too often resembles in the intricacies of its rules the game he failed in at home. Once again he is perfectly free to choose. He may decide to vegetate his days away in a chronic back ward or he may decide to oscillate between his family hell and the not dissimilar hell of the conventional psychiatric admission ward—the latter course being the usual present day idea of psychiatric progress. That is to say, schizophrenic patients may be discharged from hospitals in less than three months, but about half of them are readmitted in less than a year. A course between these alternatives has yet to be discovered.

But how does a person get into so unfortunate a position in which such violence is done to him? Basically, the situation is like this: mother and child form an original biological unit which persists some time after the physical fact of the child's birth. Then, bit by bit, the actions of the mother, if these are correct in a certain definable sense, engender a field of praxis with the possibility of reciprocity. There are two people who can do things with and to each other. The child then initiates action that affects the mother as the other to whom he is another. This beginning of action which affects another, or personal beginning, is the second birth or existential birth that dialectically transcends the original organismal reflect level and by attaining a new level of synthetic organization initiates a dialectic between persons. But the mother, for various reasons, may fail to generate on her side this field of reciprocal action, and it is in this sense that some people, in fact very many people, have never been born or, more usually, their birth has been only a shadow event and their lives represent only a marginal form of existence. Finally, even their death may be appropriated from them and become merely an event "for others"—that is to say, the person lacks awareness of the direction of his life towards his personal death: he will never die *his* death since death for him is merely a statistical inevitability in the anonymous future. The job of a mother is to produce not only a child, but a field of possibilities in which her child may become someone else, another person.

So, the process of becoming a person may go wrong, and it may go wrong within the first few months of a life. If the mother fails to generate the field of reciprocal action so that the infant learns how to affect her as another, the child will lack the precondition for the realization of his personal autonomy. He will forever be a thing, an appendage, something not quite human, a perfectly animated doll. This never happens absolutely but relatively to a widely varying degree it is common; in fact, a degree of failure is universal.

But the beginning of personal development is never a pure passivity. The acts of the mother are its precondition but never its cause. From the first moment of mother-child interaction, where each is another to the other, the child is in the position of having to initiate the project to become whoever he is to be, and this is, in principle, a free choice, his free creation of his essential nature.

For some people, however, not only is there a failure of the preconditional basis of their separate human existence, but once they have some precarious foothold on autonomy they are confused by others in their family with regard to the true nature of each intention they entertain and each act they perform. If such confusion is intensive and extensive enough, their position in the family may become untenable, and when this is the case violence is revealed quite naked.

Sometimes a person is fixed in the position where the only possible move he can make in the interpersonal game is one which is most likely to be termed "violent" by *others*. Such is the case, for example, with the young man who has never been able to realize himself as a separate person from his mother. All the stratagems employed in the interest of love

fail, because love demands reciprocation and there
can be no real reciprocation in this case, since in the
mother's view, and this view totally regulates the
field, there can be no reciprocal field of action, no
lover and no loved one. There is a perfect symbiosis
where the symbiotic couple lose sight of the difference (parasite/host) and become, almost in fact and
certainly in fantasy, *one person*. For example, the
fifty-year-old man in a chronic ward in the mental
hospital who is dutifully taken home each weekend
by his mother. She looks after him very well, of
course. Like his ward charge nurse, she strips him,
bathes him, inspects his body for signs of injury or disease, and then writes letters to his doctor expressing
concern about the swelling on his left big toe which
needs specialist attention. *She* usually gets it. In such
a case the only move left to play seems to be that of
apparently arbitrary, sudden, gratuitous, aggressive
self-assertion on the part of the child. The child,
who may be twenty, thirty, forty, or fifty years old is
aggressive towards his mother as a means, the only
means left, of breaking away from her. The rigorous
logic of this situation is: "If I hit you I am not
you . . . *I* am *me* since I hit *you* . . . You are
yourself since by hitting you I am another person
. . . You are another person . . . you . . . I
am . . . me." Q.E.D.[3] In the clinical record a note
is then made to the effect that his behavior on this

3. This, needless to say, applies also to certain surrogate
murders such as those done by Raskolnikov in *Crime and
Punishment*.

occasion was bizarre, irrational, and purposelessly violent.

It is only in the last ten years or so that some psychiatrists have begun to take into account the other side of the story of violence. It has been noted that the labeled schizophrenic patient is repeatedly confronted by contradictory demands in his family and sometimes in the psychiatric ward. This has been termed the "double bind" by some Amercian workers. I shall consider this notion in its theoretical context in the next chapter but can exemplify it here with the simple case where the mother makes a statement which she contradicts by gestures: She tells her son, "Go away, find your own friends and don't be so dependent on me," but, at the same time, indicates nonverbally that she will be very upset if he does leave her, even in this limited way. Or, while signalling anxiety about any physical closeness, she says, "Come and kiss your mother, dear!" Unless her child can discover a ruthlessness, a counterviolence, in himself with which he can demolish the whole absurd interchange, his response can only be muddle and ultimately what is called psychotic confusion, thought disorder, catatonia, and so on.

It is something like the situation expressed in certain Zen Buddhist koans where one is *fixed* in the position of having to make a response but each of the stated, alternative responses is predefined as wrong. This cannot be worked out rationally or analytically: the only answer must be an act that carries one from the false existential position in which one has been placed, a position in which one cannot exist, to a true self-centered rather than other-centered position. But if one attempts to break out of the system of false rationality of the family, particularly when this system is reinforced by the collusion with the family of agents of the wider society, then one runs the risk of being called irrational. One might even have some "disease" that has led to this madness. The fact that this irrationality is really a necessary anti-logic and not ill-logic and that the patient's violence is a necessary counter violence may only too easily be overlooked. To a quite remarkable extent the "illness" or the illogicality of the schizophrenic has its origin in the illness of the logic of other people.

So the family, then, in order to preserve itself in its inauthentic manner of living invents a disease. Medical science, sensitive to such widespread social needs, has provided a special discipline, psychiatry, to conceptualize, formalize, classify, and provide treatment for this disease.[4] The notion of disease-

4. The medical establishment tends to regard psychiatry with condescension. This is only partly without justification. The justification resides in the fact that many psychiatrists have totally lost themselves in the intricacies of organic medicine, they take examinations in higher medicine, learn how to inspect the fundus of the eye and how to ascertain the exactly correct proportion of substances in our various excreta. They gradually and painstakingly acquire a requisite ignorance concerning the other person (patient) whom they confront or, more usually, refuse to confront. In fact, many psychiatrists are second-rate doctors—people who could not "make it" in general medicine, but this fact does not limit the possibilities of pretense. The pretense breaks down, however, in certain cases—cases where the psychiatrist has actually tried to understand his patient on the basis of an understanding he has tried to achieve of himself—perhaps

entity implies symptoms and the family prepares a formidable list of these. Schizophrenic symptoms are virtually whatever makes the family unbearably anxious about the tentatively independent behavior of one of its offspring. These behavioral signs usually involve issues such as aggression, sexuality, and generally any form of autonomous self-assertion. These signs may well be the customary expression of the needs of an adolescent person, but, in certain families, even these are quite unacceptable and must, if necessary by some desperate means, be invalidated. A most respectable and readily available form of invalidation is to call such behavior "ill." The ill patient is then removed from the family, with the co-operation of various social and medical agents, and the family is left to mobilize all its resources into pitying itself for the tragedy that has befallen it. Befallen it, of course, due to the hand of God which moves inexplicably and without relation to the actual needs of other people in the family.

I shall at this point refer to an actual case of this sort of thing. A patient was admitted to a mental hospital on a Detention Order (that is to say, a form of certification under the Mental Health Act of 1959 which removes from the patient his rights to leave

---

through lengthy and costly psychoanalytic training. This is a halting and imperfect course, perhaps, but one which the medical establishment and its hand-picked selection committees (for psychiatric jobs) show little sign of comprehending. For this reason, people who are humanly, technically, and professionally ill-equipped are thrust into positions of sociomedical power as consultants, superintendents, and even, sometimes, professors of psychiatry.

hospital of his own accord, and if he does so provides for his forcible return to hospital by either police or hospital staff). The story was that this young man had, among other things which remained unspecified, behaved aggressively and violently towards his parents and that he, as the order stated, had to be removed for the protection of others to an institution for observation of his mental state. His parents had referred their problem to the general practitioner who, with the assistance of the Mental Welfare Officer, had issued the Detention Order. However, when one probed deeply enough into the circumstances of the family crisis one discovered that the aggressive and violent behavior consisted in (a) breaking one tea cup, (b) slamming the front door, and (c) stamping his foot once, but rather emphatically, on the garden path. In the course of the assessment of the family situation, which included a staged reenactment of the "crisis," it was discovered that the patient's mother had been struggling for many years with feelings of severe depression. At a certain moment in the history of the family when father, who was himself a depressed, totally withdrawn person, became crippled by a stroke, it became necessary for mother to rid herself of her intense feelings of guilt in order to cope with her new and difficult role of nurse, and the only person available for her as a receptacle for these feelings was her twenty-five-year-old son. Her son had, successfully enough, been conditioned to be such a receptacle. This situation, now at crisis point, had developed over three to four years. Her son, at the age of twenty-one, had had the usual feelings of extreme sensitivity about himself. He had projected unacceptable sexual and aggressive bits of himself into others and had experienced the return of these aspects of himself as ridicule and even persecution. This had led to an earlier admission to hospital in which he had proclaimed the delusional idea that he was Jesus Christ. At that time, as on the present occasion, he was bearing vicariously the full load of his mother's guilt, and in the microsocial family world he was dying in order that the others, principally his mother, might be saved. We all repeatedly die partial deaths in order that the others, for whom we are the sacrificial offerings, may live. The archetypal Christ, in so far as he has any reality at all, is in each of us. In this sense the patient's delusional proclamation was quite true, but it was a truth that no one else could allow himself to see. If one reads the score this way, one appreciates the dictum of the American psychiatrist who defined delusion as a true idea held by the patient which the psychiatrist deludes himself into accepting literally. But the opposite of the literal is not necessarily the metaphorical. The existential reality of a person transcends this opposition.

When this young man comes into the mental observation ward we find that these obvious facts are either excluded from consideration or that they are distorted in a uniformly peculiar way, and if we are to understand the reality of psychiatric violence we shall have to get some idea of what the distortion is.

The mental patient, once he has been so labeled, is obliged to take a sick role. Essential to this role is a certain passivity. There is supposed to be a disease which, coming somehow from outside the person, is a process that alters him. The patient is affected, altered in such a manner that his own affecting and altering become relatively inessential. He is reified to become the object in which the disease process works itself out. The process is suffered, undergone. No one, it is supposed, does anything at all until the *mise en scène* of the psychiatrist who (sometimes, and usually disastrously) cures the rot. The disease happens to the person who, in so far as this is a mere happening, becomes quite literally no one at all. As the bearer of symptoms that result from a process, he is dispensable as a person and, therefore, is dispensed with. One is left with the doctor who confronts an inert nonhuman field of symptoms (which must always be removed or suppressed) and disease process (which must, if possible, be eliminated). This prestructuring of the situation that arises when someone enters the mental hospital immediately implies that what has gone on between the elected patient and other persons has a significance (if it has any at all) that is only secondary to the supposed disease. To say this by no means implies malevolence or even a lack of "human warmth" in the doctor.

The recognition of such violence finds its closest parallel in current psychiatric thinking in the concept of "institutionalization" in the mental hospital. But it is ironic that this critique of institutionalization has itself fallen into the trap of institutionalized thinking, in particular when it produces ideas such as that of "institutional neurosis." The invention of this curious disease (yet another disease) has led one of its protagonists to list causal factors, symptoms, diagnosis, prognosis, and treatment. If one cannot find a real virus, one invents a social virus.

On the ground that it does violence to human reality, we must question this whole way of thinking, centered on the notion of passivity, of being altered by a disease process, biological and/or psychological and/or social.

This disease (or diseased) way of thinking, however, is firmly rooted in the medical tradition in which the work that psychiatrists do, for certain historical reasons, has become enmeshed. But whereas the disease idea functions reasonably and serviceably in general medicine and its other specialties, its wholesale transplantation into a field where problems are presented in terms of relationships between persons has produced confusion and formidable contradictions on every level of theory and meta-theory—although the latter level is rarely attained and never sustained in the clinical psychiatric literature, for the very reason that one cannot make a theoretical study, within a continuous framework of reference, of a theory which is self-contradictory in its most basic elements. The most advanced and radical critique of psychiatric theory in terms of its false conceptual model must propose an analysis of psychiatry and psychoanalysis in their historical origins.[5]

In concrete fact, there is very little explicit awareness about what is really happening when someone goes into a mental hospital ward. Not only does the patient's physical bed await him in the ward, but there is also a Procrustean bed of staff preconceptions into which he must be fitted at whatever cost in terms of mutilation of his personal reality. The violence that commences in his family is perpetuated in the conventional psychiatric ward. Most apparent psychiatric progress expressed in the catchwords "open doors," "permissiveness," "informality," "friendly staff-patient relations," serves to obscure this far more central area in which the traditional psychiatric hospital has not advanced one inch since the days of Kraepelin in the last century.

It is a truism to say that the patient's relationships with his family, his doctor, and other significant persons must be taken into consideration when we have to decide how best to act in relation to him to be "therapeutic." Of course, this is done, at least in principle, in all but the most backward psychiatric institutions. It is, however, still almost revolutionary to suggest that the problem lies not in the so-called ill person but in the interacting network of persons,

5. See Szasz, *Myth of Mental Illness.* Szasz deals paradigmatically almost exclusively with hysteria, showing what violence is done to the existence of the hysterical person by construing the main aspects of his behavior as symptoms of a mysterious disease process; but while his examination of this pseudo-disease amply supports his thesis, I believe that a similarly oriented examination of the whole field of psychiatric madness does so even more strongly.

particularly his family, from which the admitted patient, by a piece of conceptual sleight of hand, has already been abstracted. Madness, that is to say, is not "in" a person but in a system of relationships in which the labeled "patient" participates: schizophrenia, if it means anything, is a more or less characteristic mode of disturbed group behavior. There are no schizophrenics. The usual abstraction of an "ill person" from the system of relationships in which he is caught up immediately distorts the problem and opens the way to the invention of pseudo-problems which are then quite seriously classified and analyzed causally—all genuine problems having vanished unnoticed through the hospital gates (along with the departing relatives).

Attributions of strangeness, queerness, oddity, craziness, incongruity or absence of feelings, purposeless acts, impulsiveness or unreasoning aggression, are not unquestionable, absolute, or even (in ordinary clinical experience) reasonably objective judgments about the patient-to-be when they are made by other members of his family. These attributions are highly functional and they function in relation to a system of needs in the family at a certain point in its history. Nor are attributions of madness made by agents of the extra-familial society, in particular general practitioner and Mental Welfare Officer, occasionally the police, necessarily more objective than those made by the family. Only too often they fall into a rather subtle, skillfully (albeit unconsciously) prepared collusion with the family attitudes.

This collusive relation between family and the agents of society is the basis of real as opposed to mythical violence in psychiatry. It has not been nor will it remain an eternal characteristic of the social system. In medieval times the present boundaries between family and extra-familial community did not exist. Not only was the family "out" in the community far more than it is today, but also the household, especially in the case of the upper classes, included many extra-familial others—servants, nursemaids, guests. As soon as the child emerged from early infantile dependence he became, in the eyes of the adults, as the iconography of the period confirms, a "miniature adult." In the sixteenth, seventeenth, and particularly the eighteenth century the situation began to change: the *rites de passage* which from neolithic times had initiated the child into his adult identity (often through symbolic death, or the partial death of symbolic castration and reversal of sexual identity, and the conferring of a new name), these and the Hellenistic *paideia* had all disappeared in medieval Europe; in the eighteenth century a preoccupation with the nature of childhood and the transition into adult life reappeared.[6]

Henceforth it was recognized that the child as a special sort of person, a special, rather disturbing presence, should have a special preparation, and education, for his adult role in life. The child was segregated from the life of the adult community by

6. This thesis is expounded and amply documented by Philippe Ariès in *Centuries of Childhood* (New York: Random House, 1962).

family and school, often in a harshly monastic manner in the claustrating total institution of the boarding-school. The attendant brutalities, however, reflected not the medieval indifference to the child as a child but an obsessive, imprisoning family love. Here indeed we see love as violence.

The widely proclaimed contemporary evidence for the loosening of family bonds (*e.g.,* the divorce rate and weakening of paternal authority) does little but transparently mask a peculiar sort of intensification of family cohesion in our society—a cohesion for which we may discover the historical intelligibility. The concept of "a family," which differs significantly from the demographic institution, implies a family-community boundary-line and is a phenomenon of modern history; before the sixteenth to eighteenth century, class divisions, although always objectively definable, were often blurred in the actual processes of social intercourse and the denumerable members of each family were all very much part of the total community; after the eighteenth century the early development of the basic contradictions of capitalist society limited the blurring of class distinctions, which became less tolerable to the upper classes, who began to withdraw socially, geographically (to special districts), and in terms of the upbringing of children. Henceforth values of privacy, the immuration of the family, reigned—to some extent imitatively reproduced in working-class life in so far as this was conditioned by the values imposed by the ruling upper and middle classes.

We can think this out in terms of the categories

suggested by Claude Lévi-Strauss in *Tristes Tro-
piques* (1955). There are societies which swallow
people up, namely anthropophagic societies, and
societies which vomit people out—anthropoemic societies. We then see a transition form, on the one
hand, the medieval "swallowing up" of the child-per-
son in the community, a mode of assimilative acceptance relating to ritualistic cannibalism in "primitive" societies in which the ritual enabled people to
accept the unacceptable—particularly death—to, on
the other hand, the anthropoemic modern society
which ejects from itself all that it cannot draw into
accepting the artfully invented rules of its game. On
this basis it excludes facts, theories, attitudes, and
people—people of the wrong class, the wrong race,
the wrong school, the wrong family, the wrong sexuality, the wrong mentality. In the traditional psychiatric hospital today, despite the proclamation of
progress, society gets the best of both worlds—the
person who is "vomited" out of his family, out of
society, is "swallowed up" by the hospital and then
digested and metabolized out of existence as an
identifiable person. This, I think, must be regarded
as violence.

The process of getting rid of someone is, of
course, denied, usually by some form of assertion of
the inherent peculiar badness and madness of certain
individuals. This denial, which operates both in the
family and in the wider society, is that most sterile,
tortuous, and yet all-pervasive piece of social illogic,
the negation of the negation. The steps of the process are as follows: First, there is a negative act, an
act of invalidation of a person by others; this may

involve diagnostic labeling, passing sentence, physically removing the person from his social context: second (concurrently, rather than chronologically after), this negative act is denied in various ways; it is held that the person has invalidated himself or has been invalidated by his inherent weaknesses or disease process, other persons have nothing much to do with the matter. By means of this double negation the social group conceals its praxis from itself. The "good," "sane" people, who define themselves as such by defining certain of their number as "mad" and "bad" and then extruding them from the group, maintain a safe and comfortable homeostasis by this lie about a lie. The elected scapegoats often collude with this process, often finding that the only way they can feel needed by others or confirmed in a definite enough identity is by taking a mad or bad social role. The "delusion" of being Christ, of sacrificing oneself for the sake of humanity, as we saw in the earlier example, finds its intelligibility in terms of this inauthentic social praxis.

When society is a little less dishonest about what it is up to one discovers analogous forms of practice expressed much more obviously and concretely. In illustrating his thesis that all social evil is projection, Sartre in his book on Jean Genet (1952, p. 29), describes an industry which once flourished in Bohemia. The "normal" adults took little children, split their lips, compressed their skulls and imprisoned them day and night in boxes to prevent growth. By this means they were able to produce "monsters" which could be publicly exhibited at a profit. Today, in the case of labeled lunatics, society is developing a

rudimentary awareness of guilt in connection with
the production and maintenance of a segregated mad
subcommunity. This guilt is manifested in contradictory efforts to improve the status of mental patients
by promoting them to the rank of ordinary sick
people, and by greater permissiveness in psychiatric
institutions, but, on the other hand, to keep them in
their mad role by the whole pseudo-medical system
of patient identification and confirmation and by a
host of difficulties of obscure origin in the rehabilitation process. In the setting of this quasi-medical
mystique the periodic bursts of frenetic therapeutic
activity directed by some psychiatrists against their
schizophrenic patients does little but perpetuate the
irrationality of the system.

Antonin Artaud, the eminent writer and theorist
of the "theatre of cruelty," has written some very
relevant things about this. There were long dialogues
between Artaud and his psychiatrists in which
Artaud defended his belief that he was the victim of
voodoo spells and defended his right to withdraw
from other people. In opposition to this, the psychiatrist would painstakingly spell out the need for him
to conform with society. And so it would go on. But
at the final critical moment of the dialogue the rub
was always this: "If you speak of bewitchment
again, M. Artaud, you shall have sixty-five electro-
shocks." There is a sense in which Artaud's "delusional statements" represented a profound reality in
life, a reality which, seventeen years after his death,
we are only just beginning to appreciate; he had
more to say relevant to madness than all the text-

books of psychiatry, but the trouble was that Artaud saw too much and spoke too much of the truth. He had to be cured. It is perhaps not too absurd to say that it is very often when people start to become *sane* that they enter the mental hospital.

If we are to advance from the present position in psychiatry where the violence of which I have been speaking is so widely prevalent, we shall have to recognize the dialectical complexity of human reality and refuse to reduce all human action and experience to process terms. We shall have to seek the vital moment of praxis, the intentional core of each human existence, the project by which each person defines himself in the world. This has always been difficult to accomplish in the large traditional psychiatric institution and, in practical terms, our experience suggests that what is needed is a small community of about thirty or forty people which will function without the usual clinical preconceptions and prejudices, without rigid, externally imposed staff-patient hierarchization, and with full and active involvement of families of people in the community. In such an "experimental" community a person will not have to contend with the alienated desires of others who try to beat him into shape, to cure him of trying to become the person he really is. He will at last have the chance to discover and explore authentic relatedness to others. Such a community does not yet exist but may be created.

In the meantime, if one has to go mad, the tactic to learn in our society is one of discretion.

7. Being Born into a Family

DAVID COOPER

The family is not only an abstraction, that is, a false existence, an essence, but also exists as a challenge to "go beyond" all the conditioning one has undergone in it. The way one effects this going-beyond seems always to be blocked, however. There are numerous taboos in the family system that reach much further than the incest taboo and taboos against greed and messiness. One of these taboos is the implicit prohibition against experiencing one's aloneness in the world. There seem to be very few mothers indeed who can keep their hands off their child long enough to allow the capacity to be alone to develop. There is always a need to try to arrest the wailing desperation of the other—for one's own

From *The Death of the Family* by David Cooper (London: Penguin Books, and New York: Pantheon Books, 1970), pp. 13–26. Copyright © 1971 by David Cooper. Reprinted by permission of the publishers.

sake, not for theirs. This leads to a violation of the temporalization, that is to say the personal time-making as distinct from time-keeping, of the other, so that the mother's need-time system (more or less passively mediating the need-time system of the wider society) gets imposed on the infant's. The infant may need, in *her* or *his* time, to experience frustration, desperation and finally a full-scale experience of depression. In my experience any respect for the time of the other, or the time the other needs to take in their relationship to oneself, is very rare indeed. One of the main, perhaps the most important contributions of Freudian psychoanalytic technique has been the systematic and disciplined development in the analyst of this sort of respect for the natural unfolding of the interplay of temporalizations—without interference, but with total attentiveness. In this sense the psychoanalytic situation can, ideally, become a sort of anti-family—a family that one can enter by choice and leave by choice when one has done what one has to do in it. The analytic situation is not a family transference situation in which one, in some sort of unknowing simplism, converts the other into bits of one's totality of impressions of past family experience. This is only "by the way," although it is a *voie galactique* that one has to traverse. That sort of milk is already spilled, and there is no good in crying over it. So one goes through all this with a proleptic impulse that penetrates one's self with past intimations of the self, that that self would penetrate itself by. What one has to do in it is to discover a fluent dialectic that moves all the time on the shifting antithesis between *being-alone* and *being-with-the-other*. It is this antithesis that we must examine further if we are to discover how a person, deprived of the lifeblood of his solitude in the first year of his life, later, in a moment of great anguish, invents his separateness in the world.

A boy called Philip, at the age of six years, lived with his parents in a hotel owned by relatives. All his life he had been assiduously cared for. He had never been left alone for a moment. But then one day, playing in the gardens, he rested his hands on a whitewashed birdbath and looked into the mossy water reflecting the sky. With a shock, he looked up at the sky, seeing it for the first time as if initiated into awareness of its reality by its reflection. Then he realized in a moment of suffocation, which was also a moment of liberation, his total contingency and aloneness in the world. He knew that from that moment onward he could call to no one, and that no one could call to him in any way that would deflect the trajectory of his life project, which he now knew he had already chosen—although of course the details would have to be filled in. His mother called out that supper was ready. He went in to eat, but for the first time he knew that he was no longer his mother's child but was, in fact, his own person. The point is that Philip could not say one word about his experience to anyone else in his family that would not be contorted into *their* terms or into some joke about *their* boy.

If one does not discover one's autonomy in one's first year of life, and if one does not discover it by this anguished moment in later childhood, one is either driven mad in late adolescence, or one gives up the ghost and becomes a normal citizen, or one battles one's way through to a freedom in the working out of subsequent relationships, whether these be spontaneously originated or planned, analytic relationships. In any case, one has to leave home one day. Maybe the sooner the better.

This is all about communication and the failure of reception of communication that characterizes the family system. Take a very ordinary situation between parent and child. Parent walks down the high street holding his child's hand. At a certain point there is a necessary breakdown of reciprocity—the parent holds the child's hand, but the child no longer holds the parent's hand. By a subtle kinesic alteration in hand pressure, the child of three or four years indicates to the parent that she wants to make her own way down the high street in her own time. The parent either tightens his grip or takes what he has been taught to experience as a fearful risk—to let his child leave him, not in his time, or in socially prescribed time, but in the child's time.

How do we learn to mind our own business—as did the Japanese *haiku* poet Bashō? In his journal, *The Narrow Road to the Deep North,* Bashō describes how, shortly after setting out, he saw on the other side of a river an abandoned child, small, desolate and weeping. He could have gone back to the child and found some sort of home for it in a nearby village, but he chose to continue his elected, solitary voyage. Bashō's compassion was fully expressed in

verse, but his voyage had to come first—he knew he
could do nothing for the child until he knew what he
had to do for himself. The hardest lesson of all is to
know what one has to do for oneself.

The main task to be accomplished, if we are to
liberate ourselves from the family in both the external sense (the family "out there") and the internal sense (the family in our heads), is to *see
through* it. To make this phenomenologically real,
one might meditate on this visualization—the visualization of a *family queue*. Imagine one looks through
a series of veils—the first veil may bear an image of
one's mother in a certain mood that one spontaneously remembers, the second veil bears the imprint
of one's father in a similar characteristic mood, then
one sees through successive veils including siblings,
grandparents and all other significant persons in
one's life until, at the end of the queue, one sees a
veil with one's own image. All one has to do then,
having seen through the family, is to see through
oneself into a nothingness that returns one to oneself, insofar as this nothingness is the particular
nothingness of one's being. After a sufficient view
through this nothing, the entailed terror rings with an
incidental note only.

To put it another way, the superego (our internalized parents, primitive loved and hated bits and
pieces of their bodies, fragments of minatory utterances and confusing life-or-death injunctions that
ring through our mental ears from the first year to
the last of our lives) has to be transformed from a
theoretical abstraction, which we can merely under-

stand, into a phenomenal reality. The superego is *nothing* (the theoretical abstraction) but a series of sensory impressions, images that must be seen, heard, smelled, tasted and touched in our consciousness. For reasons that we may explore later, I shall condense all these sensory modalities into vision, into seeing and seeing through. The object, I think, must be to concretize the superego into real, phenomenal components so that one can *use it* as a sort of social shield, burglar alarm and submachine gun —rather than be used and possibly destroyed by it. The techniques one may find or invent to do this are multifarious.

Apart from interpretations in therapy, one can recall stories and myths and, more importantly, conjure up one's own personal mythology. Lots of us, for instance, talk about the golem myth. Let us remember the original Kabbalistic story. Jewish households erected an effigy of clay and on its brow wrote the word "Aemaeth," meaning "Truth." This monster could be used as a servant doing all manner of household tasks, until it became incompetent or disobedient or simply too big. Then the householder had to reach up to the brow of the golem and erase the first two letters from "Aemaeth"—this left the word "maeth," which meant "he is dead." The monster would then die and be swept away. One householder, however, let the golem grow so big that he could no longer reach the brow of the obstreperous creature. So he thought a bit, and then, knowing that all golems or superegos are essentially obedient, he ordered the creature to bend down and remove his

boots. As the golem obeyed him, he erased the first
two letters from "Aemaeth"—but forgetting the size
of the creature, he was suffocated to death by the
mass of original mud that fell onto him. It's all like
dying prematurely of coronary thrombosis or cancer
or getting shot up by riot police. So how do we be-
friend our golems—which is all "they" probably
want, anyhow.

Then again, to illustrate the power of the internal
family, the family that one can separate from over
thousands of miles and yet still remain in its clutches
and be strangled by those clutches. Someone I saw
was trying desperately to free himself from a complex family situation that seemed to invade every
move he made in relation to his work and in his
relationship with his wife and child. Then one day
his mother told him a well-known Jewish story. It
was about a young man who fell in love with a
beautiful princess in the next town, several miles
away. He wanted to marry her, but she made the
condition that he would have to cut out the heart of
his mother and bring it to her. He went home, and
while his mother was sleeping he cut out her heart.
Joyously (but secretly only joyfully) he ran back
over the fields to the princess, but at one point he
stumbled and fell. The heart fell out of his pocket.
As he lay there, the heart spoke and asked him,
"Have you hurt yourself, my darling son?" By being
too obedient to the internal mother, projected in one
form into the princess, he became totally enslaved by
this internal mother whose omnipresent, immortal
love he could never escape again.

Recently a child who had been diagnosed schizophrenic, in "autistic withdrawal," was brought to see me. This beautiful boy of eight was brought into my room by his mother and father, and he wore a badge saying, "It's wrong to eat people." He grimaced and gesticulated and could not (or perhaps more relevantly, did not want to) sit in one place and take part in the discussion. His mother, obviously engaged in some sort of overeating spree, was consuming the child in terms of an orientation of her whole mind and body to his "welfare"—protecting him from rough friends at school and an overly punitive headmaster who smelled out a "wrong one." But she was erecting this abdominal wall around her son because she was being starved, in terms beyond the sexual, by her husband, who taught at a university west of London. He was starving her because he was being starved of any sort of real intercourse with others by the academic bureaucracy, which mediated to him the first-world famine situation (which seems to be hardly recognized by university administrators, but which is protested with increasing frequency by radical students—with increasing effect). After a few sessions in therapy, in which she got a good feed (talking out, in the mode of drinking in), she tended to "eat up" her son less and less. He went back to school and formed his first friendships with other boys. A month later I saw him again, and this time he bore none of the psychiatric stigmata—this time he wore a badge saying, "Eat me up, I'm delicious." The "clinical problem" was resolved. Beyond that there is only politics.

A Tibetan monk, engaged in a long solitary meditative withdrawal, began to hallucinate a spider. Every day the spider appeared, growing larger each time, until finally it was as big as the man himself and appeared very threatening. At this point the monk asked his guru for advice and obtained the following: "Next time the spider comes, draw a cross on its belly and then, with due reflection, take a knife and plunge it into the middle of the cross." The next day the monk saw the spider, drew the cross and then reflected. Just as he was about to plunge the knife into the spider's belly, he looked down and in amazement saw the mark chalked across his own umbilicus. It is evident that to distinguish between the inner and the outer adversary is literally a matter of life or death. The spider was the internal family that could only harm him in fantasy.

Families are about the inner and the outer.

Families are about life or death or ignominious flight.

One very obvious manifestation of the operation of unseen, or insufficiently seen, internalized family structures is in political demonstrations where the organizing group is lacking in vision of this sort of reality in themselves. So we find demonstrators getting unnecessarily hurt because they unknowingly project bits of their parents in their negative, punishing, powerful aspect onto the police. This leads to an attack "from the rear," insofar as they are defending themselves not only against the attack from the police "out there" but also against the internal attack from the family policeman in their heads. The *people* most vulnerable to this twofold attack are, significantly, smelled out by the police and the judges; significantly those demonstrators who dutifully get beaten up most severely also get the heaviest sentences in the courts. The revolutionary objective is, needless to say, forgotten.

If we are to regard paranoia as a morbid state of existence in any sense any more, I think that the only place in which we find this as a social problem is in the minds of policemen, administrators of the law, and the consensus politicians of the imperialist countries. These unfortunate people embody the projected superegos of the rest of us to such an extent that their internalizations of the self-punitive bits of our minds squeeze them out of any sort of human existence of their own. Any compassion that *we* achieve in relation to *them,* however, need not stultify the effective force of our anger against the real persecution unknowingly embodied by them— against the third world that is situated in Africa, Asia and Latin America as well as against the unrecognized and self-unrecognizing third world that resides in the heart of the first world. I shall define this secret third world later—for the moment, suffice it to say that it is black (whatever one's literal color), hippy, orientated to local seizure of power in factories, universities, schools. It's deprived not *of* education but *by* education, it breaks the cannabis laws and more often than not gets away with it, and it knows how to burn cars and make bombs that sometimes work. This secret third world gets put down as suffering, for instance, from "infantile omnipotence"—a malady which, one psychiatric colleague suggested, afflicted the Red Guards in the Cultural Revolution. The emerging question, however, is whether this so-called psychopathological category may now elude the amateur diagnostics of the family and some of their psychiatric colleagues, all of whom are so imbued with the frightened archaeo-ideology of the bourgeois watchdog that in terror would evade its reality as a lapdog. Having eluded this invalid possibility, the people so stigmatized may find a social revolutionary use for their "aberrations" instead of letting them sink into a private neurosis which always confirms "the system" and plays endless, joyless games with it.

Through considerations of this sort, one begins to sense a rumbling, deep-toned possibility asserting itself—perhaps fearfully, certainly terrorizing in its intent: the possibility of a destructuring of the family on the basis of a full realization of the destructiveness of that institution. A destructuring that will be so radical—precisely because of the lucidity that finally points the way to it—that it demands a revolution in the whole society. All the time now we have to differentiate between prerevolutionary and postrevolutionary forms and possibilities. In concrete terms, all we can do in a prerevolutionary context is to lay down certain isolated prototypes that may be developed on a mass social scale in a postrevolutionary context.

Let us sum up on some of the factors that operate within the family, often with lethal but always with humanly stultifying consequences. Later we shall explore the possibilities of reversing them.

Firstly, there is the gluing together of people based on the sense of one's own incompleteness. To take one classical form of this, let us consider the mother who feels incomplete as a person (owing to a complex set of reasons that usually includes, with contrality, her relationship with her mother, and the general suppression of extrafamilial social effectiveness in women). So in the whole colloidal system of the family she glues, say, her son onto herself, to be that bit of her self that she feels to be missing (the bit her mother "taught" her was missing) and the bit that actually is missing (the factor of objective social suppression). The son, even if he "succeeds" in leaving home and getting married, may never become more personally complete than her, because he has experienced himself during the most critical years of his "formation" as an appendage to her body—(her penis)—and to her mind—her mind-penis, or socially prescribed effectiveness. In the most extreme form of this symbiosis, his only exit might be by a series of acts that lead him to be designated schizophrenic (about one percent of the population are hospitalized at some point in their lives with this label), and transferred to the replica family of the mental hospital. Probably the only way that people, glued to each other in the family and in the replica families of social institutions, can unglue themselves is by using the warmth of love. The irony here is that love gets warm enough to accomplish this ungluing only if it traverses a region usually experienced as arctic: the region of total respect for one's own autonomy and for that of each other person one knows.

Secondly, the family specializes in the formation of

G

roles for its members rather than in the laying down
of conditions for the free assumption of identity. I do
not mean identity in the congealed, essentialist[1] sense,
but rather a freely changing, wondering but highly
active sense of who one is. Characteristically in a
family a child is indoctrinated with the desired desire
to become a certain sort of son or daughter (then
husband, wife, father, mother), with a totally enjoined, minutely prescribed "freedom" to move within
the narrow interstices of a rigid lattice of relationship.
Instead of the feared possibility of acting from the
chosen and self-invented center of oneself, being
self-centered in a good sense, one is taught to submit, or else, to live in an eccentric way of being in
the world. Here, "eccentric" means being normal
or located in the normal—way off the center of
oneself, which becomes a forgotten region from which
only our dream voices address us, in a language that
we have equally forgotten. Most of our conscious
use of language amounts to little more than a pale,
squeaking fascimile of the strange, deeper-resonating
tongues of our dreams and prereflective modes of
awareness ("unconscious").

Being a well-brought-up, eccentric, normal person
means that one lives all the time relatively to others,
and this is how the falsely splitting system originates
in family indoctrination, so that one functions all the
time in social groups in later life as one side or other
of a duality. Essentially, this is collusion on the

1. By "essentialist" I mean the interposition across the
line of one's vision of general categories of thought that
make it difficult to see the concrete individual being.

parameter,[2] refusal/acceptance, of one's freedom. One refuses certain possibilities of one's own and deposits these refused possibilities in the other, who in turn deposits his possibilities of an opposite sort in oneself. In the family there is the built-in antithesis of the bringer-up (parents) and the brought-up (children). All possibilities of children bringing up their parents are relegated. The socially imposed "duty" of parents suppresses, finally, any joy that might shatter the division of roles. This obligation structure is then transported into every other institutional system subsequently entered by the person brought up in the family (I include, of course, adoptive families and orphanages, which follow the same model). One of the saddest scenes I know is when a child of six or seven plays school with desks and lessons arranged, under the parents' view, in precisely the same form that exists in the primary school. How might we reverse this abdication, and stop stopping the child teaching her or his secret wisdom that we make them forget because we forget that we have forgotten it?

Thirdly, the family, in its function as primary socializer of the child, instills social controls in its children that are patently more than the child needs to navigate his way through the obstacle race laid down by the extrafamilial agents of the bourgeois state, whether these be police, university adminis-

2. By "parameter" I mean implicitly or explicitly defined lines of argument about where a person is at in relation to each other person in a situation of meeting.

trators, psychiatrists, social workers, or his "own" family that passively re-creates his parents' family model—although the television programs these days are a bit different, of course. The child, in fact, is taught primarily not how to survive in society but how to submit to it. Surface rituals like etiquette, organized games, mechanical learning operations at school replace deep experiences of spontaneous creativity, inventive play, freely developing fantasies and dreams. These forms of life have to be systematically suppressed and forgotten and replaced by the surface rituals. It may take therapy, in the best sense, to revalue one's experience highly enough to register one's dreams properly, and to sequentially develop one's dreams beyond the point of dream stagnation that most people reach before the age of ten. If this happens on a wide enough scale, therapy becomes dangerous to the bourgeois state and highly subversive because radically new forms of social life are indicated. Suffice it to say for the moment, however, that every child, before family indoctrination passes a certain point and primary school indoctrination begins, is, germinally at least, an artist, a visionary and a revolutionary. How do we recover this lost potential, how do we start stepping backward on the inexorable march from the truly *ludic,* joyful play that invents its autonomous discipline, to the *ludicrous*—that is, normal, games-playing social behavior, obedient to a narrow set of rules?

Fourthly, and this again we shall explore in subsequent chapters, there is an elaborate system of taboos that is instilled in each child by its family. This, like the teaching of social controls more generally, is achieved by the inplantation of guilt—the sword of Damocles that will descend on the head of anyone who prefers his own choices and his own experiences to those enjoined on him by the family and the wider society. If one loses one's head enough to openly disobey these injunctive systems, one is, poetically enough, decapitated! The "castration complex," far from being morbid, is a social necessity for bourgeois society, and it is when they are in danger of *losing* it that many people, in perplexity, search for therapy—or a new form of revolution.

The taboo system that the family teaches extends well beyond the obvious incest taboos. There is a restriction of the sensory modalities of communication between people to the audio-visual, with quite marked taboos against people in the family touching, smelling or tasting each other. Children may romp with their parents, but demarcation lines are very firmly drawn around the erotogenic zones on both sides. There has to be a very carefully measured obliquity and stiltedness in, say, the way that growing-up sons have to kiss their mothers. Transexual hugging and holding are rapidly precipitated, in the minds of family members, into a zone of "dangerous" sexuality. Above all, there is the taboo on tenderness that Ian Suttie (in *Origins of Love and Hate*) wrote so well about. Tenderness in families may be felt, certainly, but not expressed unless it is formalized almost out of existence. One is reminded of the young man, quoted by Grace Stuart,[3] who, on seeing his father in his coffin, bent over him and kissed his brow, saying, "There, father, I never dared do that while you were alive!" Perhaps if we realized how dead "alive" people are we might be prepared, goaded by despair, to take more of a risk.

Throughout this chapter I have, perforce, used a language that I find archaic, essentially reactionary and certainly discrepant with my thinking. Family words like "mother," "father," "child" (in the sense of "their" child), "supergo." The connotation of "mother" takes in a number of biological functions, primary protector functions, a socially overdefined role and a certain legal "reality." In fact, the maternal function can be diffused into other people beyond the mother: the father, siblings, and above all, other people outside the biologically grouped family. There seems to me to be no sense in reducing complex but intelligible social relationships to purely contingent and circumstantial biological facts—facts that are mere facts, facts that precede acts which initiate a true sociality. I remember a conjoint session with a mother and her daughter described to me by a colleague. At one point the mother, with deep sadness and not a little courage, said that she had begun to feel a tremendous and decisive sense of loss and envy on realizing that the therapist (a man) was now her daughter's mother far more than she was.

3. Grace Stuart, *Narcissus, A Psychological Study of Self-Love* (New York: Macmillan Co., 1955; London: George Allen & Unwin Ltd., 1951).

The boundary between "tranference" relationship and "real" relationship can never be—and I believe never should be—all that clear. It's a matter of living a necessary ambiguity, with a requisite sense of difference between the projected (altering) image and the unaltered perception of the other.

Anyhow, with this grumble against the language one has to use, I shall not suggest a new language now but simply underline the fatuity and danger of the fetish of consanguinity.

Blood is thicker than water only in the sense of being the vitalizing stream of a certain social stupidity.

The family, for want of a capacity for producing holy Idiots, becomes moronic.

8. Flection / Reflection

MARY BARNES

Flection

Flection: the act of bending or the state of being bent. That's how I was at Kingsley Hall, bent back into a womb of rebirth. From this cocoon I emerged, changed to the self I had almost lost. The buried me, entangled in guilt and choked with anger as a plant matted in weed, grew anew, freed from the knots of my past.

That was Kingsley Hall to me, a backward somersault, a breakdown, a purification, a renewal. It was a place of rest, of utter stillness, of terrible turmoil, of the most shattering violence, of panic and of peace, of safety and security, and of risk and reckless joy. It was the essence of life. The world, caught, held, contained, in space and time. Five

From *The Radical Therapist,* vol. 1, no. 4 (October–November 1970). Reprinted by permission of the author.

years as five seconds; five seconds as five hundred years.

Kingsley Hall, my "second" life, my "second" family, may it ever live within me. My life, within a life. It was a seed, a kernel of the time to come. How can I know what will come. As I write, as I paint, the words, the colors they emerge, grow, take shape, blend, and part; a sharp line, darkness; light. The canvas, a paper, a life, is full; complete, whole. We are at one with God. Through the half-light, the blessed blur of life, we stumble to the God we sense within.

Knowing, yet unknowing. Seeing, yet blind. Striving yet yielding; we reach out, from our own depth to the height of heaven, and in our stretch all life is held, bubbling and breaking with joy; still as deep water, moving as the clouds. Thousands, millions of lives. A word, a color, alone yet a part. One life seeking to live, expanded consciousness, participation in the "sight of God." How would I be in a new place? God knows.

I would let everything "be"; all the "Johns" and "Janets" and "Peters" and "Pamelas" I would let "be." We should be alone, yet in communion, in communication, with each other. In order to come to the light we have to germinate in the dark.

We must go the way we are made, an oak cannot be bent as a willow.

To lay down, to pray; to draw in to the core of one's being, is to "start a place." What place? A house, a community, a group of people? You have to wait and see what will happen, and let it happen.

The place that you start is there already, inside the people that will come. It's as white as heaven and black as hell and the background is gray, because that's the mixture we mainly are. How to build heaven on earth, how to save souls. That's what it's all about.

"Don't be too 'spiritual,' " says Joe. "No," I replied, "I'll try to express it in psychological terms."

"Dark night of the soul," deep despair, desperate depression; schizophrenia, split mind, tormented with distractions; cut off from God; division of the self; "to die to the self to live in God"; to get free from the self in the mother to live in God within the self; "our life as a bird has escaped from the snare," from the bonds, or rather the emotional ties, of the past have I through psychotherapy been released.

Different ages, different terms, the world moves, in the eternal breath of God.

Reflection

Ronnie (Dr. R. D. Laing) told me "What you need is analysis twenty-four hours out of twenty-four." I was one of those people who just cannot be healed through spasmodic help, whilst living in an ordinary situation. I just had to be in a special place, a house for madness.

It's the inner state that matters. But it's less sick people than I was who can get free, whole, through the ordinary course of life. Extreme states help to "bring it up," to uncover the real self, but to go further in extreme conditions is very rare. How many, in a prison, physically living with the family one was born into, or in a contemplative convent, reach through to integration, wholeness, sanctity? It's what we are all made for, given time in this life to achieve.

Yet, never, for one moment, do we "make it" of ourselves. God, through other people reaches out to us and draws us on. It's a question of suffering but the suffering for many of us means madness before sanity—sanctity—wholeness. We go from false self, to madness, to sanity.

Mother Mary of Jesus early in this century spent two years alone in her cell, in a sense sick, yet not physically ill, before she was able to participate in the life of her community. Many years later she founded thirty-three Carmelite convents in England, Scotland, and Wales before she died in 1942.

A convent day school in London is boarding one of their older pupils, because she is in mental distress. But it is rare for an established community to accommodate itself to the needs of such people, and if these people were in psychotherapy as such, with all the tremendous emotional upheaval that entails, it would probably be well nigh impossible to accommodate them within "so-called" sane living conditions.

A very twisted-up person cannot get free without being allowed extremes of behavior. Regression is a safety valve. Playing, bashing about, screaming, sucking, messing with shit, lying naked, wetting the bed, are all ways of getting the anger into the body without hurting the body.

Lying in a painful position, being alone for a day, will resolve anger. But resolution through bodily pain, fasting, and isolation as all religious orders of all religions through all ages practice is *not* possible, at least at *first,* for people who are very twisted up, as I was. They have to be allowed, encouraged, to *be* as "baby" as they feel and emotionally regrown until they can participate in what might be termed a more "spiritual" level of development.

Just as one doesn't give a one-year-old baby tranquilizers or kneel him down to meditate, so must one *not* have expectations of a person in madness utterly beyond his state. Otherwise, there is danger of just shaking him (a modern way of doing this is electric shocks) or shutting him away in a cupboard (the chronic ward of a mental hospital).

The person must be seen and understood as the baby he is—and allowed to live that way, through it.

He is dying to be loved, to be wanted, to be accepted. He has within himself to emotionally accept, to feel, all the anger, the anguish of the past, to go through periods of deadness when nothing at all can be felt, to be green with envy and hating with jealousy. Still, he must be loved, totally, for what he is, as a baby needs love.

Important as understanding is, it is love and trust that matter most. As a mother knows her baby, so can one "know" another person. Immediate response of feeling is not in the head. It's the heart, the feeling that counts. Intellect and feeling come together later. Madness is the nursery, not the library. Babies suck and mothers love. Let therapists beware of too much thought and lettered words. (Madness and the understanding of it is more akin to contemplation than intellectual activity, as such.)

As a "little baby" with eyes tight shut I lay together "whole" on the floor. Anything more was "too much." Too much for my "wholeness." It was better to be "very baby" and whole than pretending and talking or walking and split.

Truth wells up from within, and living growing life brings changing forms and structures to suit the needs of one's being. (After psychotherapists the people I seemed most able to "meet" in madness, or "felt" nearest to, were contemplative nuns.)

The fear of coming out of a straitjacketed, stereotyped existence to a consciously unknown, long-forgotten life, is very great. Not iron bars or padded cells, not injections or tablets, but *people,* who love and accept, and know how and when to leave you alone, are what's needed. Given the soil, a plant will grow.

How to let go, lie down, break, be held, be beyond words, float, is a matter of trust. It's trusting God, through another person and no matter if so-called "mistakes" are made, God doesn't "drop us." Through every shattering, smashing explosion our life is still there, more whole than before. Our will submitted we are yet free, and every happening is a growing step. When in a mad state one is "without words," in touch with the "hidden underneath" of another person. Very sensitive and fragile you respond or withdraw as a snail with a shell. The other person may have no idea what he is hiding, but you pick it up—like a magnet.

Madness is purification. To go through it needs a

guide, in the terms of our world today, a psychotherapist. It has to be gone *through,* not round, and only someone else can keep us there. "You're a slippery eel; the more you suffer, the more free you get." So Joe (Dr. Joseph Berke) would tell me.

When of ourselves we would give all, we must take half, and when of ourselves we would take half, we must give all.

Joe taught me a lot about this through food. If in the course of going through madness, the baby regressed state is at times "leapt above," the baby as it were sensing, seeing, as a "wise old man," and what might be termed mystical experience is encountered, this should not be "wallowed in." It's a drink, a refreshment, a shady tree, a magnificent view, before again going down through the woods.

Going through madness is a matter of right *discipline* and *control.* So *feeling frees* and *serves* us, instead of *binding* and *killing.* A saint feels evil as fire on flesh. Many of us feel much that is not evil as if it was. Something is amiss, we are astray, off track.

The feeling of shame, guilt, that brings us to a dead stillness, makes all giving and receiving of love impossible, is a barrier to all creativity, causes us to feel as ghosts and bury our souls and bodies in "living death," is a *very* great sickness.

When very twisted up so the feelings, the emotions, are not true, the impulse of the being is to break down.

To resist is "screaming agony" or "living death."

To be helped, to make the break, to go *through* madness, *is* salvation.

III

The Marxist Foundation

Introduction

Marxism is a method of social analysis, not a simple scientism. It gives us a framework and an approach to society as a whole, rather than as a series of facts and postulates. We learn from Marx that history is primarily the history of class struggle, revolving around an economic *base,* but with a noneconomic *superstructure* which includes the state, religion, beliefs, behavior, etc. We learn that history is not an arbitrary progression of events, but a dialectical struggle wherein opposing forces clash and yield new forms. We also learn that society is a totality, and that we cannot understand it by simply breaking it down into its components. The whole is not simply an agglomeration of its parts, and cannot be understood as such. This does not mean that there is no Marxist manner with which to approach a particular problem, but rather that there *is* such a way if we see that problem in the light of its social context.

Particularly integral to the Marxist approach to psychology is class-orientation, the ability to perceive certain institutions, behavior, and problems as related to social classes. It is clear that working class people represent the largest group of people committed to mental hospitals. Given that, it is impossible to see the true nature of mental hospitals without understanding their class basis.

Values, ethics, religion, psychology, the arts, education, recreation all have their origins in the class basis of society. Often this is not direct or apparent, since forms frequently lag behind their social foundations. People do not always understand the context in which they act or the end results of their activity. Marx attributed this to "false consciousness," the mystification of reality and experience which arises from the oppression of the majority of people by the small ruling class, an oppression usually conducted through the various institutions of society rather than by direct force. For instance, the worker who is paid in one year what his boss spends on a two week vacation is taught in the schools that thrift and personal perseverance will reward him with financial status and social prestige. All those who fail do so because of a personal lack, rather than the realities of the social system. As the cartoonist Cobb put it, "Poverty is God's way of punishing those who have little or no faith in capitalism."

Marx did not know what mass media and advertising could accomplish in impressing values on people. Nor did he envision that many of the working class would go to college in this country, attend-

ing junior colleges which provide them with
a minimal amount of training so that they can function as minor technicians, while feeling a step above
those still doing manual labor. Marx did not see the
"cultural revolution" as we see it; he had no idea of
a black or women's or gay movement, no inkling of
a "counterculture." But he did understand that the
interpersonal relationships within capitalist society
were alienating, and that the *origins* of that alienation occurred as a result of work relations.

Marx's *Economic and Philosophic Manuscripts*
(also called the *Paris Manuscripts* or *1844 Manuscripts*) was the main work in which he formulated
a theory of consciousness and alienation. Marx
traced three types of alienation which arise from the
worker's relation to production. First, the laborer
produces goods, being paid only a fraction of their
worth and having no decision over their distribution.
The worker thus relates to his product as to an alien
object. Second, the wages paid the worker are little
more than enough to live on and reproduce more
workers. (This is less so today, overall, but still
holds true for many, especially in light of the current
recession.) The work is forced labor, since without
working the person will starve. But the work process
is alienating—the worker's life is not his own, since
it is preoccupied with producing the world's wealth.
The third type of alienation is a synthesis of the first
two. The human worker becomes, unlike other animals, one who lives only as a means of existence,
rather than as a person who is "at one with its life
activity." The worker's reflection is in a world he has

created, but of which he shares no part. He is separated from his co-workers as well, since all share in the alienating work process which divides individuals from each other. This is "species alienation," the social estrangement that divides the people and makes them feel as fragmented atoms.

These may seem like abstract categories, but they still hold true in the present world. Most of us hold jobs which are noncreative, dull, boring, often dangerous. We have no control over those jobs, or even over the manner in which we transport ourselves to work. We produce objects or services which more often than not provide benefits only to our bosses. Further, we are often afraid to complain and take action to change the situation since we are atomized from each other, as well as fearful of losing our livelihood. The workplace is also the arena of society in which racism and sexism come out very overtly, the part of our lives where color and sex relegate people to inferior jobs where they are treated worse than other workers and made to feel like simple cogs in a machine.

Marx also saw the "fetishism of commodities," an attitude in which "Private property has made us so stupid and partial that an object is only ours when we have it." People learn to buy everything, without thinking of how it would be easier to share. This is a reflection of the bourgeois values which are handed down through social institutions: "The ideas of the ruling class are in every epoch the ruling ideas, i.e., the class, which is the ruling material force of society, is at the same time its ruling intellectual force"

(*The German Ideology,* with Engels). Taking that approach further, Marx related consciousness to people's role in the production process:

> In the social production which men carry on they enter into definite relations that are indispensable, and independent of their will; these relations of production correspond to a definite stage of development of their material powers of production. The sum total of these relations of production constitute the economic structure of society—the real foundations on which rise legal and political superstructures and to which correspond definite forms of social consciousness. The mode of production in material life determines the general character of the social, political, and spiritual processes of life. It is not the consciousness of men that determines their existence, but, on the contrary, their social existence determines their consciousness ("Preface" to *A Contribution to the Critique of Political Economy*).

This approach to consciousness, furthered by Antonio Gramsci (see bibliography), is incredibly important to an understanding of radical psychology. Many would-be Marxists claim that only the young and "immature" Marx spoke of alienation as a major force in society, but they are disproven by the recent publication of Marx's *Grundrisse,* a series of manuscripts and outlines for his complete lifework in which both political economy and consciousness were integrated.

Wilhelm Reich, the German psychoanalyst, in the period of his life when he was a Marxist revolutionary, tried to integrate material conditions and consciousness. He concentrated mainly on the role of sexuality in society, seeing it as capable of causing authoritarian personality when dammed up. Slighting the major economic and political questions, Reich dealt with repressed sexuality in the masses as responsible for fascism in Germany. As he saw it, the German Communist Party had approached sexuality in the same way as the bourgeois ethic dictated—that sexuality was a taboo, that children should be prevented from engaging in mutually-desired sexual relations, and that tight family control was necessary even for revolutionaries. Reich felt that types of consciousness, particularly sexual, could become strong enough to themselves act as "material forces," shaping society. He believed that the German left failed to stop fascism largely because it failed to understand this and to correct its attitudes toward sexuality.

Although Reich's view of the sexual revolution was male-oriented and antihomosexual, he prefigured much of the revolutionary upsurge that we see today. Young people have severely questioned sexual roles as agents of oppression, and have begun to fight that sexual oppression within the revolutionary movement. Reich offered a specific view of false consciousness, based on Marx's foundations, relating it largely to personal problems. This is the sort of theory which modern Marxism needs to expand.

Frantz Fanon dealt with a similar problem, although more completely. A black psychiatrist from the French colony of Martinique, Fanon became a revolutionary and a Marxist while working in Algeria during the Algerian struggle for independence from France. While an active freedom fighter, Fanon grew to understand that the oppressed Algerians were so divided among themselves that they often fought each other rather than the French. This, as he saw it, was one of the terrible ways in which lack of autonomy led to self-destruction.

A guiding principle that Fanon utilized was that the mental illness he treated in Algerians was a direct function of oppression. The Algerians were seen as less than human by the French. From constantly being treated as such, they developed symptoms of persecution and worthlessness. Further, the French attributed to them the "pathological" problems of laziness and dependency, attributions which the French attempted to turn into actualities. For Fanon, the revolutionary process was the most "therapeutic" environment for the Algerians. In addition to personal autonomy gained through the revolutionary process, the struggle began to break down the paternal family relationships and sexual repression of the Algerian people. As we know, Algeria is not now a liberated nation, and the processes of liberation have been arrested. But it was the beginnings of struggle, which shall again arise, that brought about personal changes in the people. This does not mean that as soon as revolt triumphs anywhere, all emotional problems will disappear; simply that struggle is the necessary but not sufficient condition.

What is so important about Fanon is the lucidity of his theory of revolution and mental health, and his nearly singular ability to integrate the theory and practice of Marxist revolutionary psychology. Others have been unable to provide this integration, either because of a failure to put theory into practice, or because of having a faulty theory. Particularly I refer to attempts to synthesize Marx and Freud. Many would-be Marxists feel that Marx did not provide enough of a framework in which to understand psychology. They also have a very shallow understanding of Marxism, seeing it as a theory of economic determinism. In addition, they think that people can bypass historical reality in making a revolution. Thus they turn to Freud for the psychological approach and expect that they can plug Freud and Marx into the same outlet to come up with the right answer. Such people do not understand that the two are incompatible—Freud was the apostle of bourgeois values of sexual repression, delayed gratification, and social control via psychology. I will not dwell further on this matter, as we have two fine articles written expressly for this book on the subject.

Of all sections of this book, this one will be the most incomplete. The reason is that a Marxist approach toward developing a people's psychology cannot be incorporated into a few pages. This is a similar problem to other areas covered in the book, but in terms of Marxism the problem is greater since *Marxism cannot exist without practice,* and there has been pathetically little Marxist activity in the various fields of psychology.

Marx's "Alienated Labor" ("Estranged Labor") presents the basis for his views on alienation as related to social structure. The chapter of Reich's "The Sexual Struggle of Youth," only recently translated, provides his most coherent analysis of the relationship of sexuality, psychology, and class structure. My article on Reich, "Civilization and Its Dispossessed," attempts to place Reich in a greater perspective and to investigate the usefulness of his approach to the present struggle. "The So-Called Dependency Complex in Colonized Peoples," from Fanon's *Black Skins, White Masks,* shows the reality of psychological destruction of oppressed colonial people, and the manner in which the dynamics of that destruction takes place. The excerpt from "Concerning Violence," from Fanon's masterpiece, *The Wretched of the Earth,* is the most brilliant and moving example of the relationship of mental health and revolution. Keith Brooks, in a most insightful article, investigates the impossibility of a Marx/Freud synthesis in light of building a Marxist psychology. He stresses the reactionary implications of Freudian theory, going beyond the more overt statements of Freud. Terry Kupers traces the attempts at the Marx/Freud synthesis, showing that all failures to achieve it are due to a faulty Marxism.

9. Alienated Labor

KARL MARX

We have proceeded from the premises of political economy. We have accepted its language and its laws. We presupposed private property, the separation of labor, capital and land, and of wages, profit of capital and rent of land—likewise division of labor, competition, the concept of exchange-value, etc. On the basis of political economy itself, in its own words, we have shown that the worker sinks to the level of a commodity and becomes indeed the most wretched of commodities; that the wretchedness of the worker is in inverse proportion to the power and magnitude of his production; that the necessary result of competition is the accumulation of capital in a few hands, and thus the restoration of monopoly in a more terrible form; and that finally

From *Economic and Philosophic Manuscripts of 1844* by Karl Marx (New York: International Publishers, 1964), pp. 106–19. Copyright © 1964 by International Publishers Co., Inc. Reprinted by permission of the publisher.

the distinction between capitalist and land rentier, like that between the tiller of the soil and the factory worker, disappears and that the whole of society must fall apart into the two classes—the property *owners* and the propertyless *workers*.

Political economy starts with the fact of private property, but it does not explain it to us. It expresses in general, abstract formulas the *material* process through which private property actually passes, and these formulas it then takes for *laws*. It does not *comprehend* these laws, *i.e.,* it does not demonstrate how they arise from the very nature of private property. Political economy does not disclose the source of the division between labor and capital, and between capital and land. When, for example, it defines the relationship of wages to profit, it takes the interest of the capitalists to be the ultimate cause, *i.e.,* it takes for granted what it is supposed to explain. Similarly, competition comes in everywhere. It is explained from external circumstances. As to how far these external and apparently accidental circumstances are but the expression of a necessary course of development, political economy teaches us nothing. We have seen how exchange itself appears to it as an accidental fact. The only wheels which political economy sets in motion are *greed* and the war *amongst the greedy— competition.*

Precisely because political economy does not grasp the way the movement is connected, it was possible to oppose, for instance, the doctrine of competition to the doctrine of monopoly, the doctrine of the freedom of the crafts to the doctrine of the guild, the doctrine of the division of landed property to the doctrine of the big estate—for competition, freedom of the crafts and the division of landed property were explained and comprehended only as accidental, premeditated and violent consequences of monopoly, of the guild system, and of feudal property, not as their necessary, inevitable and natural consequences.

Now, therefore, we have to grasp the essential connection between private property, greed, and the separation of labor, capital and landed property; between exchange and competition, value and the devaluation of men, monopoly and competition, etc.—the connection between this whole estrangement and the *money* system.

Do not let us go back to a fictitious primordial condition as the political economist does, when he tries to explain. Such a primordial condition explains nothing; it merely pushes the question away into a gray nebulous distance. It assumes in the form of a fact, of an event, what the economist is supposed to deduce—namely, the necessary relationship between two things—between, for example, division of labor and exchange. Theology in the same way explains the origin of evil by the fall of man; that is, it assumes as a fact, in historical form, what has to be explained.

We proceed from an economic fact *of the present*.

The worker becomes all the poorer the more wealth he produces, the more his production increases in power and size. The worker becomes an ever cheaper commodity the more commodities he creates. With the *increasing value* of the world of things proceeds in direct porportion the *devaluation* of the world of men. Labor produces not only commodities: it produces itself and the worker as a *commodity*—and this in the same general proportion in which it produces commodities.

This fact expresses merely that the object which labor produces—labor's product—confronts it as *something alien,* as a *power independent* of the producer. The product of labor is labor which has been embodied in an object, which has become material: it is the *objectification* of labor. Labor's realization is its objectification. In the sphere of political economy this realization of labor appears as *loss of realization* for the workers; objectification as *loss of the object* and *bondage to it;* appropriation as *estrangement,* as *alienation.*

So much does labor's realization appear as loss of realization that the worker loses realization to the point of starving to death. So much does objectification appear as loss of the object that the worker is robbed of the objects most necessary not only for his life but for his work. Indeed, labor itself becomes an object which he can obtain only with the greatest effort and with the most irregular interruptions. So much does the appropriation of the object appear as estrangement that the more objects the worker produces the less he can possess and the more he falls under the sway of his product, capital.

All these consequences result from the fact that the worker is related to the *product of his labor* as to an *alien* object. For on this premise it is clear that the more the worker spends himself, the more powerful becomes the alien world of objects which he creates over and against himself, the poorer he himself—his inner world—becomes, the less belongs to him as his own. It is the same in religion. The more man puts into God, the less he retains in himself. The worker puts his life into the object; but now his life no longer belongs to him but to the object. Hence, the greater this activity, the greater is the worker's lack of objects. Whatever the product of his labor is, he is not. Therefore the greater this product, the less is he himself. The *alienation* of the woker in his product means not only that his labor becomes an object, an *external* existence, but that it exists *outside him,* independently, as something alien to him, and that it becomes a power on its own confronting him. It means that the life which he has conferred on the object confronts him as something hostile and alien.

Let us now look more closely at the *objectification,* at the production of the worker; and in it at the *estrangement,* the *loss* of the object, of his product.

The worker can create nothing without *nature,* without the *sensuous external world.* It is the material on which his labor is realized, in which it is active, from which and by means of which it produces.

But just as nature provides labor with the *means of life* in the sense that labor cannot *live* without objects on which to operate, on the other hand, it also provides the *means of life* in the more restricted sense, *i.e.,* the means for the physical subsistence of the *worker* himself.

Thus the more the worker by his labor *appropriates* the external world, hence sensuous nature, the more he deprives himself of *means of life* in a double manner: first, in that the sensuous external world more and more ceases to be an object belonging to his labor—to be his labor's *means of life;* and secondly, in that it more and more ceases to be *means of life* in the immediate sense, means for the physical subsistence of the worker.

In both respects, therefore, the worker becomes a slave of his object, first, in that he receives an *object of labor, i.e.,* in that he receives *work;* and secondly, in that he receives *means of subsistence.* Therefore, it enables him to exist, first, as a *worker;* and, second, as a *physical subject.* The height of this bondage is that it is only as a *worker* that he continues to maintain himself as a *physical subject,* and that it is only as a *physical subject* that he is a *worker.*

(The laws of political economy express the estrangement of the worker in his object thus: the more the worker produces, the less he has to consume; the more values he creates, the more valueless, the more unworthy he becomes; the better formed his product, the more deformed becomes the worker; the more civilized his object, the more barbarous becomes the worker; the more powerful labor becomes, the more powerless becomes the worker; the more ingenious labor becomes, the less ingenious becomes the worker and the more he becomes nature's bondsman.)

Political economy conceals the estrangement inherent in the nature of labor by not considering the direct relationship between the worker (labor) *and production.* It is true that labor produces for the rich wonderful things—but for the worker it produces privation. It produces palaces—but for the worker, hovels. It produces beauty—but for the worker, deformity. It replaces labor by machines, but it throws a section of the workers back to a barbarous type of labor, and it turns the other workers into machines. It produces intelligence—but for the worker stupidity, cretinism.

The direct relationship of labor to its products is the relationship of the worker to the objects of his production. The relationship of the man of means to the objects of production and to production itself is only a *consequence* of this first relationship—and confirms it. We shall consider this other aspect later.

When we ask, then, what is the essential relationship of labor we are asking about the relationship of the *worker* to production.

Till now we have been considering the estrangement, the alienation of the worker only in one of its aspects, *i.e.,* the worker's *relationship to the products of his labor.* But the estrangement is manifested not only in the result but in the *act of production,* within the *producing activity,* itself. How could the worker come to face the product of his activity as a stranger, were it not that in the very act of production he was estranging himself from himself? The product is after all but the summary of the activity, of production. If then the product of labor is alienation, production itself must be active alienation, the alienation of activity, the activity of alienation. In the estrangement of the object of labor is merely summarized the estrangement, the alienation, in the activity of labor itself.

What, then, constitutes the alienation of labor?

First, the fact that labor is *external* to the worker, *i.e.,* it does not belong to his essential being; that in his work, therefore, he does not affirm himself but denies himself, does not feel content but unhappy, does not develop freely his physical and mental energy but mortifies his body and ruins his mind. The worker therefore only feels himself outside his work, and in his work feels outside himself. He is at home when he is not working, and when he is working he is not at home. His labor is therefore not voluntary, but coerced; it is *forced labor*. It is therefore not the satisfaction of a need; it is merely a *means* to satisfy needs external to it. Its alien character emerges clearly in the fact that as soon as no physical or other compulsion exists, labor is shunned like the plague. External labor, labor in which man alienates himself, is a labor of self-sacrifice, of mortification. Lastly, the external character of labor for the worker appears in the fact that it is not his own, but someone else's, that it does not belong to him, that in it he belongs, not to himself, but to another. Just as in religion the spontaneous activity of the human imagination, of the human brain and the human heart, operates independently of the individual—that is, operates on him as an alien, divine or diabolical activity—so is the worker's activity not his spontaneous activity. It belongs to another; it is the loss of his self.

As a result, therefore, man (the worker) only

feels himself freely active in his animal functions—
eating, drinking, procreating, or at most in his dwelling and in dressing-up, etc.; and in his human
functions he no longer feels himself to be anything
but an animal. What is animal becomes human and
what is human becomes animal.

Certainly eating, drinking, procreating, etc., are
also genuinely human functions. But abstractly
taken, separated from the sphere of all other human
activity and turned into sole and ultimate ends, they
are animal functions.

We have considered the act of estranging practical
human activity, labor, in two of its aspects. (1) The
relation of the worker to the *product of labor* as an
alien object exercising power over him. This relation
is at the same time the relation to the sensuous external world, to the objects of nature, as an alien
world inimically opposed to him. (2) The relation of
labor to the *act of production* within the *labor* process. This relation is the relation of the worker to
his own activity as an alien activity not belonging to
him; it is activity as suffering, strength as weakness,
begetting as emasculating, the worker's *own* physical
and mental energy, his personal life indeed, what is
life but activity?—as an activity which is turned
against him, independent of him and not belonging
to him. Here we have *self-estrangement,* as previously we had the estrangement of the *thing.*

We have still a third aspect of *estranged labor* to
deduce from the two already considered.

Man is a species being, not only because in practice and in theory he adopts the species as his object

(his own as well as those of other things), but—and this is only another way of expressing it—also because he treats himself as the actual, living species; because he treats himself as a *universal* and therefore a free being.

The life of the species, both in man and in animals, consists physically in the fact that man (like the animal) lives on inorganic nature; and the more universal man is compared with an animal, the more universal is the sphere of inorganic nature on which he lives. Just as plants, animals, stones, air, light, etc., constitute theoretically a part of human consciousness, partly as objects of natural science, partly as objects of art—his spiritual inorganic nature, spiritual nourishment which he must first prepare to make palatable and digestible—so also in the realm of practice they constitute a part of human life and human activity. Physically man lives only on these products of nature, whether they appear in the form of food, heating, clothes, a dwelling, etc. The universality of man appears in practice precisely in the universality which makes all nature his *inorganic body*—both inasmuch as nature is (1) his direct means of life, and (2) the material, the object, and the instrument of his life activity. Nature is man's *inorganic body*—nature, that is, in so far as it is not itself the human body. Man *lives* on nature—means that nature is his *body,* with which he must remain in continuous interchange if he is not to die. That man's physical and spiritual life is linked to nature means simply that nature is linked to itself, for man is a part of nature.

H

In estranging from man (1) nature, and (2) himself, his own active functions, his life activity, estranged labor estranges the *species* from man. It changes for him the *life of the species* into a means of individual life. First it estranges the life of the species and individual life, and secondly it makes individual life in its abstract form the purpose of the life of the species, likewise in its abstract and estranged form.

Indeed, labor, *life-activity, productive life* itself, appears in the first place merely as a *means* of satisfying a need—the need to maintain physical existence. Yet the productive life is the life of the species. It is life-engendering life. The whole character of a species—its species character—is contained in the character of its life activity; and free, conscious activity is man's species character. Life itself appears only as a *means to life.*

The animal is immediately one with its life activity. It does not distinguish itself from it. It is *its life activity.* Man makes his life activity itself the object of his will and of his consciousness. He has conscious life activity. It is not a determination with which he directly merges. Conscious life activity distinguishes man immediately from animal life activity. It is just because of this that he is a species being. Or rather, it is only because he is a species being that he is a conscious being, *i.e.,* that his own life is an object for him. Only because of that is his activity free activity. Estranged labor reverses this relationship, so that it is just because man is a conscious being that he makes his life activity, his *essential* being, a mere means to his *existence.*

In creating a *world of objects* by his practical activity, in *his work upon* inorganic nature, man proves himself a conscious species being, *i.e.,* as a being that treats the species as its own essential being, or that treats itself as a species being. Admittedly animals also produce. They build themselves nests, dwellings, like the bees, beavers, ants, etc. But an animal only produces what it immediately needs for itself or its young. It produces one-sidedly, whilst man produces universally. It produces only under the dominion of immediate physical need, whilst man produces even when he is free from physical need and only truly produces in freedom therefrom. An animal produces only itself, whilst man reproduces the whole of nature. An animal's product belongs immediately to its physical body, whilst man freely confronts his product. An animal forms things in accordance with the standard and the need of the species to which it belongs, whilst man knows how to produce in accordance with the standard of every species, and knows how to apply everywhere the inherent standard to the object. Man therefore also forms things in accordance with the laws of beauty.

It is just in his work upon the objective world, therefore, that man first really proves himself to be a *species being*. This production is his active species life. Through and because of this production, nature appears as *his* work and his reality. The object of labor is, therefore, the *objectification of man's species life:* for he duplicates himself not only, as in consciousness, intellectually, but also actively, in reality, and therefore he contemplates himself in a world that he has created. In tearing away from man the object of his production, therefore, estranged labor tears from him his *species life,* his real objectivity as a member of the species and transforms his advantage over animals into the disadvantage that his inorganic body, nature, is taken away from him.

Similarly, in degrading spontaneous, free, activity, to a means, estranged labor makes man's species life a means to his physical existence.

The consciousness which man has of his species is thus transformed by estrangement in such a way that species life becomes for him a means.

Estranged labor turns thus:

(3) *Man's species being,* both nature and his spiritual species property, into a being *alien* to him, into a *means* to his *individual existence.* It estranges from man his own body, as well as external nature and his spiritual essence, his *human* being.

(4) An immediate consequence of the fact that man is estranged from the product of his labor, from his life activity, from his species being is the *estrangement of man* from *man.* When man confronts himself, he confronts the *other* man. What applies to a man's relation to his work, to the product of his labor and to himself, also holds of a man's relation to the other man, and to the other man's labor and object of labor.

In fact, the proposition that man's species nature is estranged from him means that one man is estranged from the other, as each of them is from man's essential nature.

The estrangement of man, and in fact every relationship in which man stands to himself, is first realized and expressed in the relationship in which a man stands to other men.

Hence within the relationship of estranged labor each man views the other in accordance with the standard and the relationship in which he finds himself as a worker.

We took our departure from a fact of political economy—the estrangement of the worker and his production. We have formulated this fact in conceptual terms as *estranged, alienated* labor. We have analyzed this concept—hence analyzing merely a fact of political economy.

Let us now see, further, how the concept of estranged, alienated labor must express and present itself in real life.

If the product of labor is alien to me, if it confronts me as an alien power, to whom, then, does it belong?

If my own activity does not belong to me, if it is an alien, a coerced activity, to whom, then, does it belong?

To a being *other* than myself.

Who is this being?

The *gods?* To be sure, in the earliest times the principal production (for example, the building of temples, etc., in Egypt, India and Mexico) appears to be in the service of the gods, and the product belongs to the gods. However, the gods on their own were never the lords of labor. No more was *nature.* And what a contradiction it would be if, the more man subjugated nature by his labor and the more the miracles of the gods were rendered superfluous by the miracles of industry, the more man were to renounce the joy of production and the enjoyment of the product in favor of these powers.

The *alien* being, to whom labor and the product of labor belongs, in whose service labor is done and for whose benefit the product of labor is provided, can only be *man* himself.

If the product of labor does not belong to the worker, if it confronts him as an alien power, then this can only be because it belongs to some *other man than the worker*. If the worker's activity is a torment to him, to another it must be *delight* and his life's joy. Not the gods, not nature, but only man himself can be this alien power over man.

We must bear in mind the previous proposition that man's relation to himself only becomes for him *objective* and *actual* through his relation to the other man. Thus, if the product of his labor, his labor *objectified,* is for him an *alien,* hostile, powerful object independent of him, then his position towards it is such that someone else is master of this object, someone who is alien, hostile, powerful, and independent of him. If his own activity is to him related as an unfree activity, then he is related to it as an activity performed in the service, under the dominion, the coercion, and the yoke of another man.

Every self-estrangement of man, from himself and from nature, appears in the relation in which he places himself and nature to men other than and differentiated from himself. For this reason religious self-estrangement necessarily appears in the relationship of the layman to the priest, or again to a mediator, etc., since we are here dealing with the intellectual world. In the real practical world self-estrangement can only become manifest through the real practical relationship to other men. The medium through which estrangement takes place is itself *practical*. Thus through estranged labor man not only creates his relationship to the object and to the act of production as to men that are alien and hostile to him; he also creates the relationship in which other men stand to his production and to his product, and the relationship in which he stands to these other men. Just as he creates his own production as the loss of his reality, as his punishment; his own product as a loss, as a product not belonging to him; so he creates the domination of the person who does not produce over production and over the product. Just as he estranges his own activity from himself, so he confers to the stranger an activity which is not his own.

We have until now only considered this relationship from the standpoint of the worker and later we shall be considering it also from the standpoint of the nonworker.

Through *estranged, alienated labor,* then, the worker produces the relationship to this labor of a man alien to labor and standing outside it. The relationship of the worker to labor creates the relation to it of the capitalist (or whatever one chooses to call the master of labor). *Private property* is thus the product, the result, the necessary consequence, of *alienated labor,* of the external relation of the worker to nature and to himself.

Private property thus results by analysis from the concept of *alienated labor, i.e.,* of *alienated man,* of estranged labor, of estranged life, of *estranged* man.

True, it is as a result of the *movement of private property* that we have obtained the concept of *alienated labor (of alienated life)* from political economy. But on analysis of this concept it becomes clear that though private property appears to be the source, the cause of alienated labor, it is rather its consequence, just as the gods are *originally* not the cause but the effect of man's intellectual confusion. Later this relationship becomes reciprocal.

Only at the last culmination of the development of private property does this, its secret, appear again, namely, that on the one hand it is the *product* of alienated labor, and that on the other it is the *means* by which labor alienates itself, the *realization of this alienation.*

This exposition immediately sheds light on various hitherto unsolved conflicts.

(1) Political economy starts from labor as the real soul of production; yet to labor it gives nothing, and to private property everything. Confronting this contradiction, Proudhon has decided in favor of labor against private property. We understand, however, that this apparent contradiction is the contradiction of *estranged labor* with itself, and that political economy has merely formulated the laws of estranged labor.

We also understand, therefore, that *wages* and *private property* are identical: since the product, as the object of labor pays for labor itself, therefore the wage is but a necessary consequence of labor's estrangement. After all, in the wage of labor, labor does not appear as an end in itself but as the servant of the wage. We shall develop this point later, and meanwhile will only derive some conclusions.

An enforced increase of wages (disregarding all other difficulties, including the fact that it would only be by force, too, that higher wages, being an anomaly, could be maintained) would therefore be nothing but *better payment for the slave,* and would not win either for the worker or for labor their human status and dignity.

Indeed, even the *equality of wages* demanded by Proudhon only transforms the relationship of the present-day worker to his labor into the relationship of all men to labor. Society is then conceived as an abstract capitalist.

Wages are a direct consequence of estranged labor, and estranged labor is the direct cause of private property. The downfall of the one must involve the downfall of the other.

(2) From the relationship of estranged labor to private property it follows further that the emancipation of society from private property, etc., from servitude, is expressed in the *political* form of the *emancipation of the workers;* not that *their* emancipation alone is at stake, but because the emancipation of the workers contains universal human emancipation—and it contains this, because the whole human servitude is involved in the relation of the worker to production, and every relation of servitude is but a modification and consequence of this relation.

Just as we have derived the concept of *private*

property from the concept of *estranged, alienated labor* by *analysis,* so we can develop every *category* of political economy with the help of these two factors; and we shall find again in each category, *e.g.,* trade, competition, capital, money, only a *definite* and *developed expression* of these first elements.

Before considering this aspect, however, let us try to solve two problems.

(1) To define the general *nature of private property,* as it has arisen as a result of estranged labor in its relation to *truly human* and *social property.*

(2) We have accepted the *estrangement of labor,* its *alienation,* as a fact, and we have analyzed this fact. How, we now ask, does *man* come to *alienate,* to estrange, *his labor?* How is this estrangement rooted in the nature of human development? We have already gone a long way to the solution of this problem by *transforming* the question of the *origin of private property* into the question of the relation of *alienated labor* to the course of humanity's development. For when one speaks of *private property,* one thinks of dealing with something external to man. When one speaks of labor, one is directly dealing with man himself. This new formulation of the question already contains its solution.

As to (1): The general nature of private property and its relation to truly human property.

Alienated labor has resolved itself for us into two elements which mutually condition one another, or which are but different expressions of one and the same relationship. *Appropriation* appears as *estrangement,* as *alienation;* and *alienation* appears as *ap-*

propriation, estrangement as true introduction into society.

We have considered the one side—*alienated* labor in relation to the *worker* himself, *i.e.,* the *relation of alienated labor to itself.* The *property relation of the nonworker to the worker and to labor* we have found as the product, the necessary outcome of this relationship. *Private property,* as the material, summary expression of alienated labor, embraces both relations—the *relation of the worker to work and to the product of his labor and to the nonworker,* and the relation of the *nonworker to the worker and to the product of his labor.*

Having seen that in relation to the worker who *appropriates* nature by means of his labor, this appropriation appears as estrangement, his own spontaneous activity as activity for another and as activity of another, vitality as a sacrifice of life, production of the object as loss of the object to an alien power, to an *alien* person—we shall now consider the relation to the worker, to labor and its object of this person who is *alien* to labor and the worker.

First it has to be noted that everything which appears in the worker as an *activity of alienation, of estrangement,* appears in the nonworker as a *state of alienation, of estrangement.*

Secondly, that the worker's *real, practical attitude* in production and to the product (as a state of mind) appears in the nonworker confronting him as a *theoretical* attitude.

Thirdly, the nonworker does everything against

the worker which the worker does against himself; but he does not do against himself what he does against the worker.

Let us look more closely at these three relations.

[*At this point the first manuscript breaks off unfinished.*]

10. The Sexual Struggle of Youth

WILHELM REICH

Introduction by Lee Baxandall

This article is the final chapter of Wilhelm Reich's small book *The Sexual Struggle of Youth*, which he published in Germany in 1932 as part of his sex-political work with various Communist youth groupings.

The book consisted largely of straightforward information regarding the sexual organs and reproduction, contraception, sexual maturity, masturbation, intercourse, venereal disease, homosexuality. In simple language, the problem of orgastic satisfaction was introduced as an aspect of the oppression of sexual life in capitalism. And because his theories

From *The Radical Therapist*, vol. 2, no. 4 (Dec. 1971), and *Sex-Pol* by Wilhelm Reich, edited by Lee Baxandall. (New York: Random House, 1972). Copyright © 1972 by Lee Baxandall. Reprinted by permission of the publisher.

and practice were stirring considerable unease in the more sexually-orthodox German Communist circles, Reich attached these remarks, which take up the objections one after another, only to expose their illogic.

As his later wife Ilse Ollendorff Reich has written: "The German Communist Party agreed to the organization of an association on the basis of Reich's sex-political platform, the Deutscher Reichsverband für Sexual-politik (German Association for Proletarian Sexual Politics) which had a membership of more than 20,000. The platform contained the following demands as its main points:

a) better housing conditions for the masses of people;

b) abolition of laws against abortion and homosexuality;

c) change of marriage and divorce laws;

d) free birth-control advice and contraceptives;

e) health protection of mothers and children;

f) nurseries in factories and in other large employment centers;

g) abolition of laws prohibiting sex education;

h) home leave for prisoners.

"Reich traveled a great deal all over Germany, giving lectures and helping to establish hygiene centers in key industrial cities under the auspices of the Reichsverband."

The rapid growth of Reich's organization alarmed Communist functionaries who believed that interest and energies would be diverted from essential party goals. After he fled from Hitler into Scandinavian exile, Reich's membership in the party came to an end; even before March 1933 however, official pressures were applied to decrease the sales of his books and his general influence among party members.

Not the least interest of this article is the proof that it gives of how politically responsible Reich found it possible to be. We see him speaking plainly, in the context of broad party concern and debate; relating his special contribution to the questions of the political economy and the expected revolution. He does not fear to deal directly with Lenin's attitudes, affirming some, raising a question about the emphasis of others. He offers an example of audacity and reasoning which, we must agree, situates him as a peer among the leading revolutionary theorists of his time.

*　*　*

We must be quite clear in our minds about the possibilities open to working youth in a capitalist society. Since the Young Communist League is adopting the clear political line of social revolution, it should aim at being the leader of youth in the field of sexual problems, too. And working youth would recognize it as such, if only its approach to this question—this urgent and delicate question—were the right one of ruthless candor; if only they could feel that the YCL really understands their plight, and is defending their cause.

Translation by Anna Bostock. Copyright 1971 by Lee Baxandall.

We must practice genuine self-criticism. We must ask ourselves why it is that, on this of all problems, we have until now been so mealy-mouthed, why we have not dared to consider the only opportunities open to working youth. As a first step, we must admit that on this question of sex we have behaved like the man asleep who keeps trying to chase a fly away by vainly flapping a hand in its direction.

It has been pointed out again and again in the revolutionary youth organizations that the "sex question" disturbs and impedes the struggle for revolution. And the conclusion has been drawn, again and again, that we must leave the sex question aside, because we have no time to deal with it and because we have more important things to do. But if the issue has come up again and again, more and more urgently, more and more pressingly; if, as a matter of fact, many youth organizations have collapsed, owing to the sexual difficulties of their members (a fact we must openly admit)—then, we must ask ourselves *why* the question is so disturbing, and we must not, just because it is disturbing, declare that we have no time for it and we have more urgent things to do, that sex life is a private affair, etc. *Sex life is not a private affair if it preoccupies you, and, in the form in which it has existed hitherto, it interferes with the political struggle.*

What other problem that causes similar difficulties would we dismiss in the same way? What would we say to such an attitude towards any other issue? We should rightly say that it was an evasive attitude.

We should rightly condemn anyone who resorted to such excuses. We ought to be consistent with ourselves. Our view should be that, for Bolsheviks, there is no such thing as an insurmountable difficulty and therefore, the attitude that I have described is a bourgeois and opportunist one.

When such problems arise, they do not fall from the sky, but come out of the very real contradictions of our social system; and, as such, they demand an answer. We have found time in our class struggle to deal with sport, the theatre, religion, the radio. Why are we not equally consistent when it comes to the sexual problem of youth? However, if we agree that we have been evading the issue, we must become clear about why this is so.

A superficial reason is the fact that by ignoring the problem of sex, we hope to be able to devote ourselves entirely to revolutionary work, thus emphasizing the difference between us and the bourgeois types whose interest is centered on the problem of sex and who do nothing but chatter about it. This has led us into serious error. Many of us have wanted to dismiss sexuality altogether, as something inessential or even "bourgeois." We were wrong: that is the lesson of reality. We must solve the sex problem in a revolutionary way, by evolving a clear sexual-political theory; proceeding from it to a sexual-revolutionary praxis; and integrating both these in the proletarian movement as a whole. That, we are convinced, is the *right* way towards a definitive solution.

Many comrades justify their negative attitude by invoking Lenin's conversation with Clara Zetkin where he sharply criticized the discussions and debates on sex taking place in workers' and youth associations, and said that there were more important things to be done. We completely endorse the point of view which Lenin adopted at the time. He was attacking superficial, woolly chatter about sex which merely took people's minds off more essential things, and we, too, are against that. These "sex discussions" are generally nothing other than a substitute for sexual activity, intellectual masturbation of the most common kind. But we shall understand at once how the problem ought to be treated if, at the same time, we quote a second remark of Lenin's made in the course of the same conversation with Clara Zetkin: "Communism will not bring asceticism, but joy of life, power of life, and a satisfied love life will help to do that."

If Communism is to bring about the enjoyment of sexual life, surely this has to be fought for.

The point of the matter, therefore, is this: we must not indulge in empty discussions about sex, but neither must we ignore the sex problem. Without talking about it, we cannot solve it. What is left for us to do? We must talk about it *politically*. Then we shall be discussing it in the right way and taking the right action as a result. However, before we go into further detail and produce evidence to show that this is the only possible way out, we must still define the *deeper* reason for our avoidance of this question.

Where were we all brought up? Under what conditions did we grow up? We grew up in families, and were brought up under the capitalist system. The

objection will be raised that there is a great difference between proletarian and bourgeois families. But
it isn't as simple as that. We don't have to think for
very long before coming up with a response; we need
only consider some of the elements of our way of
thinking and living.

Have we freed ourselves from the bourgeois ideology concerning property? Yes, to a considerable extent; for there is a marked difference between
bourgeois and working-class families as regards
property relations. Have we completely freed ourselves from religion? Here, things are no longer as
simple. There are many thousands of proletarian
families that are religious. The further we penetrate
into the petty-bourgeois proletariat, the more deep-
seated we find religion to be. And what about sexual
morality? Isn't it rooted in the very nature of the
family—which proletarians, too, are forced to maintain, due to the conditions of life under capitalism?

Doesn't sexual oppression and the implanting of
bourgeois morality form part and parcel of bourgeois
marriage and the bourgeois family? Of course, the
contradictions between the worker's way of life and
bourgeois family morality are very great. The contradictions are different too in the middle and upper
bourgeoisie. But bourgeois sexual morality nevertheless exists in the proletariat; and of all bourgeois
ideologies it is the most deeply anchored, because it
is most strongly implanted from earliest childhood.
It is one of the bourgeoisie's strongest ideological
props within the oppressed class.

We see all the time that even class-conscious youth

find it very difficult to liberate themselves from this. Bourgeois sexual morality whose most essential feature is that it does not view sexual life as natural, self-evident, and also connected with the particular social order of the time, but denies it and is afraid of it—is more deeply embedded in the very marrow of us Communists than we all realize. We should not allow ourselves to be deceived either by sexual showing-off, which is the counterpart of sexual timidity. This is simply the same bourgeois sexuality, with a different mathematical sign in front of it. Lenin was perfectly right, therefore, when he described the "glass of water" theory as a "good bourgeois theory."

What matters are the sexual deformations that every one of us bears inside himself, as a result of sexual oppression, and that are connected with unconscious repressed attitudes, so that in our sex life we are not quite masters of ourselves. These are the deeper reasons for our reluctance to deal openly and consistently with the problem of sex—the reasons why all of us without exception, even those who have the best insight into the problem, do not dare to include sexual liberation slogans in the rest of our propaganda. We must learn to understand why so many Communists get that funny smile and start pulling that special face as soon as sex is mentioned. We must seriously put an end to all that, however hard it will be for us to overcome our own inhibitions.

The further we reach into the unenlightened, not class-conscious strata of youth, the greater the inhibitions we shall meet. But practice will show, as it has already shown in individual cases, that our work

of bringing political knowledge to these young
people—the political knowledge they need so
badly—will be made easier to the extent that we
succeed in overcoming their sexual inhibitions and
moral prejudices. We shall be successful in our
political work of enlightenment only if we propose
an openly and clearly sex-affirming ideology in place
of the hypocritical and negative ideology of the
bourgeoisie. Many reactionary attitudes will come to
grief on this front, first because the Christian and
National Socialist youth have no tenable argument
against us, and secondly, and more importantly,
because although they deny their sexuality, they also
affirm it—in secret.

Let us now consider the question as it stands
within the Young Communist League—using as our
basis a discussion which took place at an evening or
mass criticism of A. A. Bogdanov's *The First Girl,*
held in Berlin on April 21st, 1931. If we succeed in
gaining a little clarity on this issue, it will make it
easier for us to tackle other problems in the Fichte
groups and in the Christian, petty-bourgeois and
National Socialist youth groups.

A Red Scout, Comrade Hermann, said among
other things:

There isn't a book in which the questions that
affect the German youth are treated—the position of
young men and girls in the proletarian organizations,
in the youth movement in general, and questions of
sexual relations of young people among themselves
and with the responsible Party officials. These ques-

tions naturally play an important role for us and they have to be discussed here. The question has been raised how the sexual difficulties of German youth can be overcome, and what we can try to do about it. I am sure there can be no overcoming of sexual difficulties for youth under the present system in any satisfactory sense. Because the greatest hang-ups for young people are economic; for example, if a girl wants to have a child but she hasn't got the money. Another thing is that most questions are still seen from the bourgeois point of view, even among ourselves, and moral bullying is still practiced not only by parents but even by party comrades, and is by no means a thing of the past. My own view is that an active Communist, an active party member, has very little time for love affairs and can't obtain one hundred per cent satisfaction in this respect. Generally speaking we still have to get the girls into the movement and see to it that they really become comrades with equal rights. Girls are still too inhibited by their bourgeois upbringing; they still have too many feelings of inferiority to fight side by side with the men as we'd like them to. That is why we have to make them realize that they enjoy equal rights in the organization.

Sex is always more of a problem for the girls. They feel these things much more than a young man, who goes with one girl one day and with another girl another day. The girls are always much more attached to a particular comrade; I'd say that was the norm, even if there are exceptions. I'm of the opinion that relations should be much healthier in this respect. Sexual tensions take up too much room in the lives of proletarian youth, who ought to regard the class struggle as their first task. These things are too much of a distraction. They really have lost us many a good comrade who's just got swallowed up and disappeared from sight. Useful people who could certainly have helped build the organization have let themselves be diverted from the struggle by all that personal stuff.

This young comrade put the problem in the right way on the most essential points. The sexual troubles of youth really can't be solved in a satisfactory way, within the present system. But let us go further with our self-criticism. Let us examine the reason which the comrade gave for this—and see how we are still imprisoned in a bourgeois mentality in sexual matters, even when our political ideas are perfectly correct. The example he gives is that of a girl who for economic reasons can't satisfy her desire to have a child. This is doubtless true of many girls. But it is *not a central problem*.

Let us not deceive ourselves: Very many girls think first and foremost of how they can have sexual intercourse *without* getting pregnant. Young people feel bad because they cannot cope with their turbulent sexuality as a result of material poverty and a lack of opportunities, of money and contraceptives. For the moment then, let us leave psychological disturbances aside. And so I think comrade Ernst was right, when he said:

Of course there is a big sex problem in Germany, like there is in all capitalist countries. It stems from the fact that young people live at home, because they can't get a place of their own to live. Many are unemployed, haven't the money to keep themselves and therefore can't live with whoever they want to live with. Many relationships which would be good under more or less secure material conditions simply break down, or can't even properly come into existence. Why? Simply because the necessary conditions are not available.

If we were to put the question of girls wanting to have babies at the top of the list, then, even if the question does play some part, we are side-tracking the issue. The typical bourgeois way of evading the problem of sex has been to put mother love and the desire for children on a pedestal and in that way to obscure everything else. It is a fact that the desire to have a child generally occurs only when the needs of the senses have been more or less satisfied. What young people are concerned about, to put it bluntly, isn't reproduction but contraception and sexual gratification at the time of their youthful ripening. They're concerned with *putting their love life in order*.

And the preconditions for this are really totally lacking under capitalism. Housing construction is in the hands of real-estate speculators, who have a vested interest in mass poverty. Only the socialization of housing construction, the transfer of housing into public ownership, as is the case in the Soviet Union today, can solve this problem. The precondi-

tion is and remains the abolition of private ownership of real estate. But this can only be the result of
a social revolution. Making the best contraceptives
available to the young as soon as they wish to begin
having sexual intercourse is a further precondition
for an ordered and satisfactory sex life. But political
reaction is just as sharply opposed to this, just as
terroristic, as it is in every other area which the
bourgeoisie considers important. The possibility of
having an unwanted pregnancy terminated at a public clinic is another fundamental precondition.
Hungry, wretched young people excluded from every
kind of culture, hanging about the streets and the
bars, are not capable of having an ordered, satisfying
sex life, because they are either sexually deprived—
which isn't their fault but the fault of society—or
sexually disturbed.

Since the cause of sexual disturbances and brutalization is bourgeois sexual oppression in the parental
home and at school, what is needed to remove them
is—once again—a complete reorganization of economic and social existence, in the sense that women
become materially independent and free from the
power of their husbands, and that parents lose the
right to oppress and dominate their children. Yet
another precondition for this is free public education
of children and a complete change of outlook in the
matter of infantile sexuality.

Comrade Hermann pointed out that moral bullying is practiced by party comrades as well as by
parents. That is absolutely true. Many older comrades who have had to live in a marriage and a

family are not behaving correctly towards youth. We have to admit to ourselves that this is a form of counterrevolutionary activity in our camp, and that in the last analysis it only serves the interests of the ruling class.

A great deal can be done in this field by organizing large-scale public debates between the young people and parents, where the young people, who daren't protest when they are alone at home, or who fritter away their energies in futile squabbles with their parents, could bring out their problems and grievances in public at meetings controlled by the mass of youth and parents. We can be sure (for this has already been proved in practice) that parents will not be able to maintain for long in public the point of view they represent at home. And so the young people will come out victorious and new forces will be released for the youth organizations. And the parents, too, in many cases for the first time, will come into contact with the proletarian movement and will get their first clear view of themselves and their position. Now, is the sex problem of youth a politically important problem? We cannot deny it.

Comrade Hermann also said that an active party member has very little time for love affairs and can't obtain one hundred per cent satisfaction in that respect. That is no doubt true, but put in this way it is incomplete and can lead to false generalizations. A Communist youth leader plays an immensely important part in the movement as a whole. He ought therefore to be an example for others, in matters of sexual behavior as well as in everything else. At the present time we are called upon to make great personal sacrifices and to subordinate our private lives to the class struggle. Yet in approaching this problem we must distinguish who we are dealing with— with a young person who is completely class-conscious or one who is indifferent, with a bourgeois or with a proletarian who still thinks in a reactionary way about certain things.

But let us for the moment stay with the party official. It is quite true that our officials are terribly overloaded with urgent party work and have no time for "love affairs." In the proletarian youth movement there are three types of officials: first, the one that has no sex life at all and has dedicated all his energies to party work; then the second type who, without anyone hearing or seeing much of it, leads an ordered sexual life with some girl comrade and at the same time also devotes all his strength to the party; and, lastly, we have the third type who is constantly involved in conflict (which may be more or less acute) between his party duties and his love life. If we do not just glance in passing at these comrades but if we consider their careers as a whole, we shall find that the best official—that is to say the one who not only does his work most thoroughly, but also has the greatest staying power and sticks with the movement through thick and thin—is the one with an ordered love life. For him, sexuality has stopped being a problem. The first type is also a good official, but experience shows that often he can only last for a limited time. This is because he at first

tries to drown his personal difficulties in work, but
later he breaks down in one way or another and is
lost to the movement. Medical and political experience of such party workers shows very clearly that
the cause of the eventual breakdown is not only (or
primarily) overwork, but, rather, that the comrade
concerned has been made unfit for the struggle by
the difficulties of "private life" in conjunction with
the great demands made on him by the party. One
just can't survive a complete lack of sex life without
serious disturbances in the long run. We adopt this
point of view not only for health reasons but also in
the interests of revolutionary work, which is harmed
by the continually high turnover rate of party
workers. We have an interest in every party worker
remaining fit for his task for the longest possible
time, and one of the most important preconditions
for this is a modicum of order in sexual matters.

Some people believe that by excluding sex altogether they gain strength. That is a fallacy. The fact
is that if your sex life is too restricted, then your
working intensity, at least, is bound to suffer; while if
you have a sex life that is more or less satisfactory,
then the freshness with which you tackle your work
will more than make up for time lost on a "private
life."

Of course there are times in party life—sometimes
weeks, sometimes months—when the tasks are so
great that comrades are obliged to restrict or sacrifice even the necessary minimum of sexual satisfaction. We have to reckon with this. However this
cannot be made the rule in ordinary times. And even

in the periods I am talking of, some relief can be found for healthy comrades, in the sense that, given these circumstances, they can enter comradely relationships of shorter duration; this need not harm the permanent relationships provided the matter is discussed and settled quite openly. And so we see that we must not consider these questions abstractly but always in relation to the situation in which they occur.

A further point is to be made about the third type of party worker we have described. Comrades who are constantly involved in a conflict between party work and private life are usually those who have not rid themselves of an unnecessarily complicated bourgeois attitude towards sex. This is especially true of the women comrades; and in most cases some sort of sexual disturbance is also present. In such cases, it isn't sexuality that makes difficulties for them; on the contrary an existing sexual disturbance makes them suffer. Good advice is very precious in such instances, since very few people can afford to have their bourgeois deformations and sexual disturbances removed by prolonged psychological treatment. For the masses, such treatment is impossible. But here, too, we must not fall into skepticism. We must realize that by creating a more open, freer sexual atmosphere within the organization, we can aid many of these comrades, as well, to find a way out of their difficulties and to do a better job for the party.

Comrade Hermann also said, and very rightly, that one of our most important tasks is to get the

girls into the movement and see to it that they really
become comrades with equal rights. But it was Comrade Lotte who, on the same occasion, hit the nail on
the head when she said:

What do things look like in practice inside the
YCL? It would be more to the point to say: How
can we get more girls into the YCL? Because when
there's a group of thirty-eight boys and only two
girls, then everything looks quite different. Last night
we held the first conference of Young Women
Workers of Germany. The girls of the YCL met in
Berlin last night and there were some wonderful girls
among them. Of course compared with the total
number of women, far too few are organized, but
once they're in, they work with much more staying-
power and more enthusiasm than the boys. If we
take a look inside the groups, the usual ratio is about
twenty boys to two girls. Just because there are only
two girls there, their position is pretty funny and
complications certainly do arise. The boys go with
other girls who aren't in the group and whom they
can't immediately get to join the group, and in that
way the boys often drop out too.

From all this we are bound to conclude the following:

1. It is more difficult to get girls to join the organization than boys.

2. The numerical ratio of girls to boys inside the
organization is extremely harmful to our work, since

the boys go with other girls and leave the organization.

3. The important practical question facing us is therefore this: how can we get more girls to join the organization so as to correct this state of affairs?

Comrade Lotte also discussed the question why we cannot get the girls to join. She thought the reason was that our methods are not always such that a young person can feel at home among us for long. She said the Young Communists were trying to find new methods. One of the reasons was that the papers read at meetings are too long, too learned and generally such that "nobody understands a word." She said very rightly: "If our methods were livelier, all relations would be improved, including the relationship between the boys and girls. But first we must have methods which sweep the young people along, so that they get really involved in the cause. Delivering a political talk and then allowing five minutes for personal matters is doing things the wrong way round."

Let us consider the first question: Why are girls more difficult to persuade to join the organization than boys? It is a well known fact, and one which was mentioned on the evening in question, that girls prefer to go to dancehalls. Comrade Lotte laid special emphasis on the point that correct methods must be found to attract girls away from the dancehalls; she thought it was not enough to detail girls for this task, but that boys too should be used for this purpose. We may be sure that Comrade Lotte made no mistake there. She has overcome the reluctance to recognize the sexual needs of youth for what they are and to take them into account when trying to enliven our political work.

We must ask: Why would girls rather go to dance-halls than to political groups? If we dismiss the whole question by calling the girls "bourgeois" or "unproletarian," we shall have achieved nothing. Still less if we regard them as backward or, worse still, if we despise them. Our failure until now has been due to our ignoring the fact that youth is more concerned with sexual worries than with political ones. We have made the mistake of pushing sexual matters aside as a "bourgeois affair." We have to learn to recognize that the sexual difficulties of youth are just as important to youth as are material difficulties. Both types of difficulty—the one directly, the other indirectly—are rooted in our capitalist society.

We must recognize that the lesser degree of political interest among girls is connected with the greater sexual oppression which they suffer from childhood as compared with boys. And we must draw the conclusion that sexual oppression is an important political issue. We must finally say out loud what every young comrade knows, namely, that an undetermined but large proportion of girls and boys join the youth organization for the same subjective reasons as those which take them to the dancehalls—that is to say, in search of a sexual partner and a sex life. The fact that, in the end, most of them are prevented from having such a life by external or internal causes does not alter the fact that they are seeking one. We must not look at this through bourgeois eyes, and we must not be shocked and talk about brothels. As revolutionaries, we must unhesitantly and unambiguously place ourselves on the side of facts. If it is true that sexuality is what preoccupies young people most and what sends them into the dancehalls, then, we must act accordingly and get them inside our organization, sexual preoccupations and all.

Young people often (much more often than we believe, because after all they don't tell us and it isn't talked about openly) join the organization as much because of their sexual needs as due to an inarticulate political urge. A general subject of complaint in the youth movement is that many young comrades drift away from the organizations because they do not find there what they were looking for in the personal sense. Comrade Lotte said that girls and boys between their eighteenth and twenty-second year are no longer to be found in the YCL.

"They aren't in the YCL, they aren't in the party. They are lost to us. We must find ways and means of holding their interest."

Other observations support this statement. Boys and girls come into the youth organization at fifteen or sixteen and drop out at eighteen or nineteen, and only a very small proportion reappear later in the party.

This is also connected with the way in which the day-to-day work of the YCL is done. The situation today is that a small number of party workers are overloaded with work almost to the point of collapse, while the majority only turn up for the May

Day demonstration and do very little otherwise. We know that these inactive comrades are afraid of being overloaded with work like the others—that, as many of them say, they don't want to be squeezed dry like lemons. Here we are faced with an organizational problem of far-reaching importance; for the question of a *correct distribution of functions* is involved. And on this we have just one thing to say. When there are roughly as many girls as boys in the organization, and when these girls and boys have achieved a good comradely and sexual relationship with one another, then all of them will want to join in the work and it will be more readily possible to distribute the functions among everybody, and in that way to lessen the load on some, and to get others more politically interested and involved. Official approval of sex life in the organization—that is to say, the opposite of the point of view which calls sexuality a private affair to be repressed wherever possible—can be helpful to us in a decisive way, even in the purely organizational sense.

If we do our work of political training energetically and fruitfully, we need no longer be afraid to offer recreation to the young comrades from time to time in forms which suit them. We still have to do a great deal of thinking about this. But we shall be successful only when we have completely eliminated mere hangers-on from our ranks.

There are two further things we must do. We must not only deliver our reports and lectures on economic, political and organizational matters in a livelier and more youthful way, as the comrade suggested. We must also take the essential problems of youth into account, and, as an integral part of our cultural discussions, we must schedule talks on sexual politics, starting from the purely personal questions that occupy youth and proceeding to the fundamental economic and social problems. In this way, we shall stop the majority of our young comrades from either being bored or having to force themselves to listen to the talks as is so often the case now. We shall then achieve what we are really aiming for: We shall create *an emotional and objective bond between youth and the cause of all the workers embodied in the Communist Party.* Young people—girls as well as boys, in all walks of life—will become deeply persuaded that the Communist youth movement and the Communist Party are the only ones really to understand their personal troubles, medically as well as socially; the only ones to offer them all possible assistance, by organizing sex counseling services for youth and by creating a freer, healthier atmosphere more naturally suited to youth; the only ones to show them a way out of their predicament. This way out may not lead directly into paradise, but to the young comrades it will mean real fulfillment and a recognition of their innermost nature. It will mean a struggle against the ruling class; against church and school, against the bourgeois parental home, and political reaction. A struggle for the material and sexual liberation not only of youth, but of all those suffering material and sexual oppression, of the oppressed masses in general.

We shall then see young people streaming into the

organization in masses. Our new worry then will be how to obtain the means and the organizational forces to organize these masses of young comrades properly, and to offer them the knowledge—political as well as sexual—for which they hunger.

But we shall solve that problem, too, provided we are not afraid of the attacks of the bourgeoisie and of the petty-bourgeois social-democratic leaders who are certain to reproach us with "running brothels."

Are we going to stop making our propaganda in favor of the abolition of factory, real-estate and land ownership—are we going to hesitate to carry through their expropriation when the time comes— just because the bourgeoisie call us a pack of thieves and robbers? Most certainly not! In the same way, we should not let the accusation of "running brothels" stop us from using every possible means to carry through the sexual liberation of all workers.

We must finally stop trying to prove to the bourgeoisie that we too are "moral" citizens. On the contrary, we must fight "morality" as they understand it with every means in our possession, we must unmask it as a brothel morality in the truest sense of the word. We must eradicate it and replace it with a morality of our own, which, as this paper explains, will be on the side of an ordered and satisfying sexual life.

Only then shall we find the right way out of our difficulties, only then shall we take the right steps to prepare for the sexual liberation of youth. We must learn to speak as openly as Comrade Fritz spoke on that evening:

We sometimes see in the organization that when there's only one or a few girls in a group, then they are completely isolated and, as it were, used for purely spiritual purposes. I think it's very important, especially for girls, that they aren't just given theoretical or even practical work to do; it's very stimulating, both for boys and for girls, to be friendly with one another. Of course there mustn't be any pressurizing, we'd have to take a very energetic stand against that, and we must also prevent the girls being hurt by the party workers thinking that, because they're doing important work and can only spare a few minutes for sex, they're entitled to be careless about personal matters. The fellow goes now with this girl, now with that, and that's all as far as he's concerned, he gives it no more thought. But a girl, especially if she's only just joined the group, may be marked for a long time by such an experience, and if a party worker she thought the world of at first has used her just to pass the time, she may suffer the same fate as Sanya in the book, and I believe that for many girls things have often gone the same way as for the "First Girl." We must make sure that the numerical ratio between boys and girls improves, so that there aren't just a few girls facing a large number of fellows. But when the number of girls and fellows in a cell is about the same, then we mustn't make bourgeois reproaches such as "he goes with one girl one day and with another the next." The girls stay in the cell, don't they? And so do the fellows, and it's purely a bourgeois prejudice if we insist that a fellow must absolutely continue to remain friendly with the same girl; we have a proletarian view of the world and for us such rules simply don't exist.

This comrade has posed the question and has answered it, too, in an absolutely correct way. The bourgeois demands "responsibility" from youth, and by that he means "sexual continence"; he says that sexuality must not be given "free rein," and by this he means extramarital sexual relations in general. Yet who, in reality, is more irresponsible—or more lecherous—than the bourgeois moralist? Who seduces girls, who uses them as objects, and who indulges in drinking and sex orgies? We do not want to seduce or force anybody; we do not want to reduce sex to the level of dirt. But we do want young men and girls to have a satisfying sex life; if you wish to call that "giving free rein to sexuality," then do.

Many of our young men and girls know exactly what is the difference between giving rein to a sick sexuality and to a healthy one. If in our cultural-political and sexual-political work we had taken more account of the views of boys and girls from the junior organizations, and less of the opinions of intellectual comrades with their much more complex sensibilities, we should long ago have found the right political approach to the sex problem of youth. This is certainly not to disparage the intellectual comrades. But we aren't the only ones to say it, and our intellectual comrades—students, ·doctors, teachers, lawyers, etc.—should be well aware themselves that they come from bourgeois homes. And often they bring along with them their sexual insecurity, bourgeois judgments, an overestimation of so-called platonic relations between the sexes, etc. As regards sexual ideology, they have suffered much greater deformation than simple workers. Many moral condemnations of the sexual life of young people have come precisely from those intellectual comrades who haven't succeeded in solving the problem for themselves.

To return to Comrade Fritz's remarks: he is right, as well, in the way he interprets the central problem of the book, *The First Girl*. Let us briefly discuss this question. What does the book describe, what are the problems it raises, and what solutions does it propose?

The First Girl is a brilliant description of the struggle of Russian youth against reaction and for the building of socialism. For this reason alone it deserves to be put in the hands of every young person. But it also treats centrally the problem of sex. It describes a Communist party cell which is extraordinarily enlivened by the first girl who joins it; it really blossoms for the first time. Although every line makes it clear that the cause of this "shot in the arm" is the sexual attraction that the girl radiates, this is not explicitly stated. But we may be sure that a sexually less attractive girl comrade, though she worked as well as Sanya, would not have played the same role. In the cell described in the book, as in our own organization, the problem is a generalized one: *one* girl to *seven* boys. That can only end in trouble. At first the cell blossoms, but then, when the girl makes friends among the boys, the disproportion begins to be disturbing. The girl starts leading what is called a "loose" sexual life. We can't prove it, but our medical experience tells us that her "sleeping around," her unselective acceptance of all sexual partners, is perhaps primarily due to a disturbance of her sexuality. The boy who has fallen particularly deeply in love with her becomes jealous. It would be quite wrong to try to ignore this fact: without being explicitly mentioned, it is clearly implicit in the whole relationship. It is no accident that it is precisely this boy that eventually shoots her. Other comrades in the cell are equally interested in the honor of the group, yet none of them—except just that one—picks up his gun to shoot her. Why did this unhappy ending have to come?

The boys in this particular cell were caught up in the bourgeois idea that venereal disease is a frightful disgrace and has to be treated in secret. They failed to see that the real harm done to the cell was due to the fact that there was only one girl and that many men were without a sexual partner, and to the fact that neither the men nor the girl dared to tackle the sex problem, which was so immensely important to them, as energetically as they tackled the problem of political desertion; and, lastly, the boy who shot the girl was completely unaware of his jealousy as the final link in a chain of causes—a particularly dangerous form of ignorance. It is absolutely against the spirit of Marxism and Leninism to ignore facts just because the fact of the class struggle comes first. The relative value of facts has to be assessed correctly. Beside and apart from the fact that Communists are bound together by the common goal of revolution, jealousy, too, has to be recognized as a fact of human life, and its importance in a given situation has to be properly judged. We must not simply say that jealousy is "unproletarian" and therefore does not exist among us. Had the question been openly raised and discussed in Sanya's cell; had not all members of the cell suffered from that highly dangerous legacy of capitalism: a fear of sexual matters? Had they not—and especially the girl—been sexually disturbed in some way; had they known how venereal disease can be avoided, then Sanya would not have had to die and the cell's party work would not have been wrecked.

We must try to the utmost to free ourselves from the peculiarly bourgeois notion of "loose living," which is still too common among us. The essential fact for us must not be how often and with which comrade a boy or a girl has sexual intercourse—but solely and exclusively whether they are causing personal unhappiness or damaging the political work. To say it straight out, and in the spirit of Comrade Fritz's remarks: If boys and girls "go now with this comrade, now with that" and if this does no harm to party work; if relationships among the comrades in the group are strengthened as a result; if girls and boys stay in the group because of it and the work prospers; if the personal development of both comrades is undamaged; then it would be reactionary to oppose it, just because we have a crazy petty bourgeois idea of morality. "Going now with one, now with another" can, in some cases, be a good thing. It can be harmful in many others. The only thing to be done is to make young people just as clear-headed and responsible in these matters as the tasks of revolutionary work demand.

To begin with: it would be a good idea to make a list of all the phrases that are used, in discussions on sexual questions, to conceal sexual prudery and, as a result, mystify things still further instead of making them clearer. Here are some of the phrases: "spiritual love," "comradeship," "the sexes coming to know one another," "progression from sensual to personal love," "understanding one another," etc.

Whenever anybody gets up and uses these words and phrases without making themselves clear, whenever we feel that somebody is just beating around the bush in regard to sexual intercourse, then we must tell him with our customary Communist frankness that he should either keep his mouth shut if he doesn't know what he's talking about, or, if he's got something to say, he should say it clearly. Otherwise we'll never get to the end of it.

When somebody comes along and says: "We need all our strength for the proletarian revolution," we agree with him a thousand per cent. But if he says "There's no such thing as private life" or "your private life is your private affair," then we must ask him if he maintains this as a general rule. We must talk to him and try to convince him that not only the sexual problem of youth but the question of sex as a whole is something quite different *before* the revolution, *during* the revolution and *after* the revolution.

We shall be able to prove to him that it is non-Marxist and bourgeois to generalize and to refuse to consider concrete facts.

Before the revolution, the task of class-conscious Communist youth is to mobilize the mass of all youth for the revolution. During this phase the sex problem of youth is part of the general front of the proletarian movement. Before the revolution we cannot do much to help the mass of young people in sexual matters, but we must politicize the issue, and transform the secret or open sexual rebellion of youth into revolutionary struggle against the capitalist social order.

In time of revolution, when the old order is shattered and everything outdated sinks into oblivion, when we are standing knee-deep in the debris of a corrupt, predatory, cruel, rotten social system, we must not moralize if the sexual contradictions among the young are at first intensified. We must see the sexual revolution in the context of general historical change, we must place ourselves alongside of youth, we must help youth so far as we are able, but more than anything else we must realize that we are living in a time of transition. To be put off by the confusions of such a transitional period, to take fright at the "crazy youngsters" and to fall back into bourgeois attitudes such as asceticism and moralizing attitudes which it is one of the tasks of the proletarian revolution to eradicate, means being left behind by historical events and standing in the way of progress.

After the revolution, when the people liberated

from their exploiters can at last begin to build socialism, to transform the economy into a socialist one and to destroy the rotten remains of capitalism in every sphere, the question is once again entirely different. The workers' society is then faced with the important task of thinking about the future order of sexual life and preparing for it. This future order cannot and will not be other than, as Lenin put it, a full love life yielding joy and strength. Little as we can say about the details of such a life, it is nevertheless certain that in the Communist society the sexual needs of human beings will once more come into their own. To the degree that working hours and working pressures are reduced as a result of socialist rationalization of work and increased productivity of labor, sexual life, side by side with cultural and sports activities, no longer corrupted by money and brutality, will once again take its place on a higher level in human society. And human beings will once again become capable of enjoying their sexuality, because private economy, which is the basis of sexual oppression and which makes people incapable of enjoyment and therefore sick or crazy in the true sense of the word, will drop away. We are not painting a picture of utopia.

We can clearly see developments taking place in that direction today, fourteen years after the proletarian revolution in the Soviet Union. Evidence that socialism alone can bring about sexual liberation is on our side. Therefore under capitalism we must use all our energies to convince the oppressed masses of this truth, too, and mobilize them for a merciless struggle against everything that impedes such liberation. And in this mobilization, precisely because of the great material and sexual oppression, the authoritarian bondage in which they are held today and which creates a link between them all, young people will march in the front rank. We shall win them over to the cause of the revolution, we shall be assured of their enthusiasm, to the extent that we understand their sexual plight and can get across to them the only message which is compatible with complete responsibility and truthfulness today. The message is this:

In capitalist society there can be no sexual liberation of youth, no healthy, satisfying sex life; if you want to be rid of your sexual troubles, fight for socialism. Only through socialism can you achieve sexual *joie de vivre*. Pay no attention to the opinions of people who don't know anything about sex. Socialism will put an end to the power of those who gaze up towards heaven as they speak of love whilst they crush and destroy the sexuality of youth.

11. Civilization and Its Dispossessed: Wilhelm Reich's Correlation of Sexual and Political Repression

PHIL BROWN

Currently the work of Wilhelm Reich is becoming very popular, especially *The Mass Psychology of Fascism,* of which three editions have been printed in the last year-and-a-half. The questions which Reich deals with for the most part are sexuality in "human nature," the possibilities of freedom in the context of human civilization, and authoritarianism (especially fascism) in light of sexual repression. Fascism is seen very much as the result of authoritarian patterns, primarily sexual, in society. The problem stems from Freud's work and Reich is not the only one to answer it—Fromm and Marcuse have dealt with the matter extensively.

From *The Radical Therapist,* vol. 2, no. 4 (Dec. 1971).

What is Freud's original theory which gives rise to these inquiries and critiques? After Freud had laid down a complete system of psychopathology he turned to socio-historical theorizing. Following up on *Totem and Taboo* with its primal horde, murder of the primal father, and the resultant repressive mores of civilization, Freud wrote *Civilization and Its Discontents,* a very bad translation of *Das Unbehagen in der Kultur* (discomfort or malaise in society). This was his definitive work on the nature of civilization and its requisite social control. For Freud, the pleasure principle, as enticing and pleasurable to the individual, is to be controlled by the reality principle which dictates correct social conformity so that society may "advance." This is a psychologization of the earlier *The Ego and the Id,* the ego mediating the "bad" id instincts with the aid of the moralistic superego. Freud asserts that civilization cannot progress if the instincts are not sublimated, channeled to another pathway. This means primarily the sublimation of Eros, sexuality. Civilization, for Freud, is nothing more than an institution "to protect men against nature and to adjust their mutual relations," a tool with which humanity can aspire to "higher psychical activities—scientific, artistic, or ideological."

Freud sees humanity as basically evil—he replaces original sin with instincts—and repression (especially sexual) is the way to control people. He invents Thanatos, the destructive, aggressive death instinct —as if Eros were not enough. Now, Freud sees the need to control this mystical aggressiveness as well as a "normal," "healthy" libido, control "like a

garrison in a conquered city." (Is this a revolutionary anti-Victorian or a Junker militarist?)

Sexuality was a great threat to Freud, and he
psychologized to such an extent that he demanded
authoritarian social control to guarantee the success
of familial sexual repression on a widespread societal
scale. In 1933 his wish came true, but the Nazis
were ungrateful and Freud was disappointed.[1]

Marcuse, in *Eros and Civilization,* wrote a "philosophical inquiry" supporting most of the beliefs of
Civilization and Its Discontents. Nearly the only
difference was the hope for a "nonrepressive reality
principle," but no idea is given of how that will be
brought about. Although Marcuse well understands
"repressive desublimation" (the fetishist sexualiza-
tion of nonsexual objects, as in advertising), he
doesn't give any indication of how to fight against it.
Marcuse is basically pessimistic about people's ability
to live lives which they themselves control. He tries
to get us to believe that Freud's view contains within
it the possibilities of liberation, that it contains hope
for a nonrepressive culture, but this is not the case
for either Freud or Marcuse—the latter picks out of
context to prove Freud's "humanism," and his
choice of pickings is not too attractive: mainly a
collection of Freud's parenthetical *mea culpas.*

1. "Freud was able to justify the renunciation of happiness on the part of humanity as splendidly as he defended
the fact of infantile sexuality. A few years later, a pathological genius—making the best of human ignorance and fear
of happiness—brought Europe to the verge of destruction
with the slogan of 'heroic renunciation' " (*Function of the
Orgasm*).

Even Marcuse's fantasy of a nonrepressive reality principle is distasteful, as mechanistic as Freud ever was: "The body in its entirety would become an object of cathexis. . . ." What does this mean? Do we hear even one word about the quality of people's lives, save that quality is important? No—Marcuse's system is in the realm of pure ideas: free, but useless.

Fromm switches back and forth from this pessimism to a halfhearted optimism, but he at least challenges Freud's mysticism concerning instincts. *Escape from Freedom* views humanity as afraid and somewhat unable to live in free relationships, but *The Sane Society* reverses that into some hope for social change, since Fromm sees society as the most important variable in determining the conditions of the psyche. Although he, along with Horney and Sullivan, led a direction within psychoanalytical circles which demanded a certain materialist basis, none of them offered a real radical outlook. Nevertheless, they were important, and Marcuse's attack on them as "neo-Freudian revisionists" is the worst kind of "lefter-than-thou" game, since Marcuse himself retreats into orthodox, conservative Freudianism.

The one person whom Marcuse did not have the courage, or capacity, to answer in such a manner was Wilhelm Reich, who had gone far beyond the neo-Freudians in search of an answer to the question of society and sexuality. Reich had begun a favorable association with Freud and the "inner circle" of psychoanalysis, but there was no way for it to last, especially upon Reich's publishing of *The Mass Psychology of Fascism*. This book followed his disagreement with Freud over *Civilization and Its Discontents,* and reasserted in more radical form the corellation of sexual and political repression discussed in *The Sexual Revolution*. He pressed the point that sexual repression is not instinctually based, but rather a result of socio-economic conditions.

Reich spends a good deal of time in *The Function of the Orgasm* refuting *Civilization and Its Discontents*. Concerning the reality principle, Reich states: "Freud neither questioned the irrational in this 'reality,' nor did he ask which kind of pleasure is compatible with sociality and which kind is not." The sexual sublimation required by civilization "dams up" sexual life-energy and causes psychic disturbances on both the individual and mass levels. Reich was very upset at the psychoanalytic position that all instincts must be sublimated or rejected, a position "based on a fundamental misconception of sexuality." Psychoanalysis was at a dead-end: its "psychologizing of sociology as well as of biology took away every prospect for a practical solution to these enormous problems." Reich saw Freud as never changing his views on the immutability of human structure and existence, and proposed to do Freud's unfinished work in a biological/sociological investigation.

Reich prefaces *Mass Psychology* by showing how the surface of society is a mask of perverse distortions of all "genuine expressions of life." But he not only opposes this function of society; he sees it as changeable:

> We, however, decline to accept the error of idealist philosophy, namely that this human structure is immutable to all eternity. After social conditions and changes have transmuted man's original biological demands and made them a part of his character structure, the latter reproduces the social structure of society in the form of ideology.

This mass sublimation, and idealist approaches to it, have been partly responsible for the development of fascism, the highest form of authoritarian social structure—"the organized political expression of the structure of the average man's character . . . the basic emotional attitude of the suppressed man of our machine civilization and its mechanistic-mystical conception of life."

This is, of course, the exact opposite of Freud's views: civilization and its requisite sublimation are an evil rather than a benefit in Reich's eyes. Where Freud blames the individual for not resisting sociosexual sublimation, Reich holds the person responsible *for* resisting it.

What method will Reich use to investigate the mass psychology of fascism? Not psychoanalysis, for his disagreement with it was too fundamental, although he maintained certain Freudian elements for many years thereafter. Marxism too he rejected— not because of a failure in Marx's thought, but because of the failure of the so-called Marxist parties to comprehend fascism on account of their vulgar orthodoxy and refusal to deal with repressed sexuality.[2] Also important is Reich's moving to a purist position in which class structure does not count: "There are no class distinctions when it comes to character." Marxism is, in fact, rejected more strongly than psychoanalytic theory. (Reich's earlier movement away from Marxism can be traced in the preceding essay.)

Reich turns to his own method of character-analytic vegetotherapy with a comprehension of the individual in a social environment, involving a loosening of the "armor" of the musculature and the genitals in order to liberate bound-up sexual energy.

Strongly fighting against economic determinism, Reich formulates the theory of ideology becoming a material force. This occurs as a continuation of actual social conditions which engendered certain human behavior, but this behavior is no longer practicable for new social conditions: "the psychic structures lag behind the rapid changes of the social conditions from which they derive, and later come into conflict with new forms of life."

Reich follows, generally, Marx's ideas of consciousness, but adds the Gramscian theory of cultural hegemony—the psychological oppression in advanced capitalist society in which ruling class ideology becomes the dominant ideology through the transmission of it by social institutions.

2. For an understanding of the failure of the Communist Party in Germany to grasp the importance of sexuality in the political struggle, see Reich's *What Is Class Consciousness?* in *Liberation* (Oct. 1971).

For Reich the most dangerous and omnipresent sublimation is that of sexuality, conducted mainly through the family. Sexual repression of the basic life/sexual energy in children leads to the masses of people accepting this nuclear kernel of authoritarian society, and makes them ripe for fascism.

Why is the family the conductor of this authoritarianism, and why is the family the nucleus of society? Using Engels's interpretation (*Origins of the Family, Private Property and the State*) of the social anthropology of Morgan and Bachofen, Reich traces patriarchy from its birth as guardian of surplus value and division of labor to the present when it functions to control the economic unity of the family in the path of the status quo. Sexuality, as the basic life energy, is repressed, this repression being the most effective means of control by the authoritarian patriarchy:

> The interlacing of the socio-economic structure with the sexual structure of society and the structural reproduction of society takes place in the first four or five years and in the authoritarian family. The church only continues this function later. Thus, the state gains an enormous interest in the authoritarian family: it becomes the factory in which the state's structure and ideology are molded.

Continuous sexual repression makes children fearful, shy, respectful of authority out of coercion and fear, docile, malleable, afraid of their own sexuality. Built up from the nuclear family, mass sexual repression lends itself to authoritarian statism. Reich sees militaristic personality coming out of dammed-up libido, coupled with fear of officers and other hierarchical persons as authoritarian father figures.

Thus, ideology, once a response to material force, becomes a material force itself. Reich did not clearly see how this could fit into a Marxist framework—this is why I stated earlier that Reich did not utilize a *conscious* Marxist methodology. Nevertheless, it fits to a certain extent, particularly when viewed in terms of Luxemburgian spontaneity (*Mass Strike*) and Gramscian cultural hegemony (*The Modern Prince and Other Writings*).

It may seem that Reich has replaced economic determinism with sexual determinism. But that is mainly relevant to his later years when he worked on orgone theory, after having ceased work on sociopolitical matters. What is important is that a thorough understanding of the role of the family in society, coupled with seeing sexual repression as the most intense form of family authoritarianism, leads to grasping the crucial role of sexuality in society.

Children for the most part are brought up in sterile atmospheres where anything sexual in nature is stifled, displaced, or perverted by the parents. Childhood masturbation is punished, and the child receives threats of the most dire consequences for giving himself pleasure. "Polymorphous perversity" is treated likewise including masturbation as mentioned above, but more as well: mutual sexuality, anal eroticism, etc. Parents' sexuality is mystified and hidden, often made to seem dirty to the children. From Freud comes the primacy of the "Oedipal" situation, reflecting society's fear of the liberating possibilities of childhood sexuality. The "Oedipal" myth is a psychologization of the concrete reality of the father-dominated, sexually repressive family in which the child rebels against abstract authority; the wide acceptance of this myth is a functional proof of the seriousness of the situation which engenders it.

Such a full-blown mystery cult is of great use to the fascists, especially since they realize that it is a part of the fascist background and mentality. The Nazis utilized pent-up sexual frustration and fears; they mystified the family even more than it was before. Sexual purity was raised to a pinnacle—only procreation was desired or tolerated. Religious mysticism was employed, with the nation replacing the church and the leader replacing God. In their invention of the Hellenistic origins of the "aryan" race, the Nazis embraced ascetic gods, shunning Dionysus who represented unbridled sexuality. Classism and sexism came together: fascism crushed the workers' movement and then equated the suppressed class with "alien races," with whom the fear of interbreeding is based on fear of the mythic sexuality of the masses. This is not uncommon in authoritarian systems—Cleaver's brilliant observations in *Soul on Ice* show how the oppressed blacks have been mystified by white sexuality anxiety inventing legends of black sexuality, a situation still very widespread in the U.S. The French held the same attitudes toward the Algerians—as Fanon points out (*The Wretched of the Earth* and *A Dying Colonialism*), the psychological make-up of the oppressor will be reflected in

that of the oppressed by identification and by social
conditioning. The sexual reality of societal oppression is a thousand times mirrored in the sexual
reality being distorted under the authoritarian rule.

Reich sees the "emotional plague" of sexual repression in the masses as ready to embrace the
führer as representative of the authoritarian sexual
suppression of society. But it need not be a Hitler—
the plagued people will also be similarly enslaved in
a society with a fine liberal veneer. Under that
veneer is the irrationality of authoritarianism, this
irrationality being inevitable since, "sexual inhibition
prevents the average adolescent from thinking and
feeling in a rational way." Irrationality becomes a
key concept in the Reichian critique: it plays the role
of blocking out logical thought processes with which
people could see beyond the given belief system.

Unfortunately Reich didn't seek to fight this irrationality with mass political actions. He wanted mass
practice of "sex-politics," widespread application of
"sex-economy" (natural regulation of biological sexuality) through free mental hygiene clinics.

Another sexist illness shows up in authoritarian
systems to a greater extent than in liberal ones: fear,
prohibition, and punishment of homosexuality. This
can be seen as resulting from a fear of pleasurable,
nonprocreative sexuality and the danger that such
sexuality presents to the nuclear family. It also involves people's fear of the abolition of sexual roles
into which they have been conditioned.

Male supremacy, as a major repressive factor in
civilization to date, is based on the sexual enslave-

ment (as the superstructure of an economic base) of the female sex. It is a basic feature of the nuclear family, and must be used to maintain that institution: "Sexually awakened women, affirmed as such, would mean the complete collapse of the authoritarian ideology." Women's use as "child-bearers" is pressed by the fascists in "battles for births" to propagate the "pure race" and in liberal nations it is always the most reactionary elements who oppose birth control and abortion. The oppression of women, economically and sexually based, involved seeing them as sex-objects to be used by men, thought incapable of pleasure, certainly not considered as equal sexual partners. The woman must concede to a sexuality which is penis-oriented, and of no relation to her own needs. Reich did not see through the myth of vaginal orgasm, but such insight is not impossible in a more revolutionary restatement of the Reichian model.

To protect the authoritarian family and society, homosexuality becomes a major political question: the night of the long knives progresses into the seemingly placid days of the bourgeois state, and gays bear the hardest brunt of the state's antisexuality. Reich, for all his brilliant insight into certain sexual matters, failed to understand the oppression of gays. He had a fanatic anti-gay attitude, never questioning this or seeing it as part of the emotional plague which he was always ascribing to others.

Pluralistic sociology and psychology attempt to separate sexual repression from the "outer" society, fearing the realization of a totalistic conception of society. Psychoanalytic theory is a party to this, substituting reductionist psychopathology for social criticism.

Reich fought such approaches, but unfortunately wound up placing most blame on the individual, having given up on the possibility of a mass movement. Had Reich continued to write about sexual politics, he might have ended up in the same camp as Marcuse and Fromm, seeing the individual as incapable of attaining freedom, either alone or in a mass movement. Thus, it is probably better that Reich stopped where he did, although it is unfortunate that such a brilliant person could not go further.

There are other faults with Reich. Of great importance is his reliance on the medical model, by which he sees the necessity of "curing" the masses. This is the typical elitist contradiction that we find in so many people who have good analysis, but are still bound by professionalism and distrust of the masses.

Beyond Reich's failures, he has left us some brilliant thought which can be of great use to our Movement. The present development of revolutionary politics in this country has been greatly influenced and advanced by the realization of sexual politics as a motive force. The message which Reich wished to bring to the German workers—a message of sexual awakening and antifascism—must come out in our approach to the masses here.

12. The So-Called Dependency Complex in Colonized Peoples

FRANTZ FANON

> *In the whole world no poor devil is lynched, no wretch is tortured, in whom I too am not degraded and murdered.*
> —*Aimé Césaire,* Et les chiens se taisent

When I embarked on this study, only a few essays by Mannoni, published in a magazine called *Psyché,* were available to me. I was thinking of writing to M. Mannoni to ask about the conclusions to which his investigations had led him. Later I learned that he had gathered his reflections in a forthcoming book. It has now been published: *Prospero and Caliban: Psychology of Colonization.* Let us examine it.

Before going into details, I should like to say that

From *Black Skins, White Masks* (New York: Grove Press, London: Granada, 1967), pp. 83–108. Copyright © 1967 by Grove Press, Inc. Reprinted by permission of the publishers.

its analytic thought is honest. Having lived under the extreme ambivalence inherent in the colonial situation, M. Mannoni has managed to achieve a grasp—unfortunately too exhaustive—of the psychological phenomena that govern the relations between the colonized and the colonizer.

The basic characteristic of current psychological research seems to be the achievement of a certain exhaustiveness. But one should not lose sight of the real.

I propose to show that, although he has devoted 225 pages to the study of the colonial situation, M. Mannoni has not understood its real coordinates.

When one approaches a problem as important as that of taking inventory of the possibilities for understanding between two different peoples, one should be doubly careful.

M. Mannoni deserves our thanks for having introduced into the procedure two elements whose importance can never again escape anyone.

A quick analysis had seemed to avoid subjectivity in this field. M. Mannoni's study is sincere in purpose, for it proposes to prove the impossibility of explaining man outside the limits of his capacity for accepting or denying a given situation. Thus the problem of colonialism includes not only the inter-relations of objective historical conditions but also human attitudes toward these conditions.

Similarly, I can subscribe to that part of M. Mannoni's work that tends to present the pathology of the conflict—that is, to show that the white colonial is motivated only by his desire to put an end to a feeling of unsatisfaction, on the level of Adlerian overcompensation.

At the same time, I find myself opposing him when I read a sentence like this: "The fact that when an *adult* Malagasy is isolated in a different environment he can become susceptible to the classical type of inferiority complex proves almost beyond doubt that the germ of the complex was latent in him from childhood."[1]

In reading this one feels something turn upside down, and the author's "objectivity" threatens to lead one into error.

Nevertheless, I have tried zealously to retrace his line of orientation, the fundamental theme of his book: "The central idea is that the confrontation of 'civilized' and 'primitive' men creates a special situation—the colonial situation—and brings about the *emergence* of a mass of illusions and misunderstandings that only a psychological analysis can place and define."[2]

Now, since this is M. Mannoni's point of departure, why does he try to make the inferiority complex something that antedates colonization? Here one perceives the mechanism of explanation that, in psychiatry, would give us this: There are latent forms of psychosis that become overt as the result of a traumatic experience. Or, in somatic medicine, this: The appearance of varicose veins in a patient does not arise out of his being compelled to spend

1. [Dominique] O. Mannoni, *Prospero and Caliban: The Psychology of Colonization* (New York: Praeger, 1964), p. 40.
2. My italics—F.F.

ten hours a day on his feet, but rather out of the
constitutional weakness of his vein walls; his working conditions are only a complicating factor. And
the insurance compensation expert to whom the case
is submitted will find the responsibility of the employer extremely limited.

Before taking up M. Mannoni's conclusions in
detail, I should like to make my position clear. Once
and for all I will state this principle: A given society
is racist or it is not. Until all the evidence is available, a great number of problems will have to be put
aside. Statements, for example, that the north of
France is more racist than the south, the racism is
the work of underlings and hence in no way involves
the ruling class, that France is one of the least racist
countries in the world are the product of men incapable of straight thinking.

In order to show us that racism does not reflect an
economic situation, M. Mannoni reminds us that "in
South Africa the white laborers are quite as racialist
as the employers and managers and very often a
good deal more so."[3]

I hope I may be forgiven for asking that those
who take it on themselves to describe colonialism
remember one thing: that it is utopian to try to
ascertain in what ways one kind of inhuman behavior differs from another kind of inhuman behavior. I
have no desire to add to the problems of the world,
but I should simply like to ask M. Mannoni whether
he does not think that for a Jew the differences

3. Mannoni, *Prospero and Caliban*, p. 24.

between the anti-Semitism of Maurras and that of Goebbels are imperceptible.

After a presentation of *The Respectful Prostitute* in North Africa, a general remarked to Sartre: "It would be a good thing if your play could be put on in black Africa. It shows how much happier the black man is on French soil than his fellow Negroes are in America."

I sincerely believe that a subjective experience can be understood by others; and it would give me no pleasure to announce that the black problem is my problem and mine alone and that it is up to me to study it. But it does seem to me that M. Mannoni has not tried to feel himself into the despair of the man of color confronting the white man. In this work I have made it a point to convey the misery of the black man. Physically and affectively. I have not wished to be objective. Besides, that would be dishonest: It is not possible for me to be objective.

Is there in truth any difference between one racism and another? Do not all of them show the same collapse, the same bankruptcy of man?

M. Mannoni believes that the contempt of the poor whites of South Africa for the Negro has nothing to do with economic factors. Aside from the fact that this attitude can be understood through the analogy of the anti-Semitic mentality—"Thus I would call anti-Semitism a poor man's snobbery. And in fact it would appear that the rich for the most part *exploit*[4] this passion for their own uses

4. My italics—F.F.

rather than abandon themselves to it—they have
better things to do. It is propagated mainly among
middle classes, because they possess neither land or
house nor castle. . . . By treating the Jew as an
inferior and pernicious being, I affirm at the same
time that I belong to the elite."[5]—we could point
out to M. Mannoni that the displacement of the
white proletariat's aggression on to the black proletariat is fundamentally a result of the economic
structure of South Africa.

What is South Africa? A boiler into which thirteen
million blacks are clubbed and penned in by two and
a half million whites. If the poor whites hate the
Negroes, it is not, as M. Mannoni would have us
believe, because "racialism is the work of petty officials, small traders, and colonials who have toiled
much without great success."[6] No; it is because the
structure of South Africa is a racist structure:

> *Negrophilism* and *philanthropy* are pejoratives in
> South Africa . . . what is proposed is the sepa-
> ration of the natives from the Europeans, terri-
> torially, economically, and on the political level,
> allowing the blacks to build their own civilization
> under the guidance and the authority of the
> whites, but with a minimum of contact between
> the races. It is understood that territorial reserva-
> tions would be set up for the blacks and that most
> of them have to live there. . . . Economic com-
> petition would be eliminated and the groundwork
> would be laid *for the rehabilitation of the "poor*

5. Jean-Paul Sartre, *Anti-Semite and Jew* (New York:
Grove Press, 1960), pp. 26–27. Originally, *Réflexions sur la
question juive* (Paris: Morihien, 1946).
6. Mannoni, *Prospero and Caliban,* p. 24.

*whites" who constitute 50 per cent of the Euro-
pean population. . . .*

It is no exaggeration to say that the majority
of South Africans feel an almost physical revul-
sion against anything that puts a native or a person of color on their level.[7]

To conclude our consideration of M. Mannoni's
thesis, let us remember that "economic exclusion
results from, among other things, the fear of competition and the desire both to protect the poor-white
class that forms half the European population and to
prevent it from sinking any lower."

M. Mannoni adds: "Colonial exploitation is not
the same as other forms of exploitation, and colonial
racialism is different from other kinds of racialism. . . ."[8] He speaks of phenomenology, of psychoanalysis, of human brotherhood, but we should
be happier if these terms had taken on a more
concrete quality for him. All forms of exploitation
resemble one another. They all seek the source of
their necessity in some edict of a Biblical nature. All
forms of exploitation are identical because all of
them are applied against the same "object": man.
When one tries to examine the structure of this or
that form of exploitation from an abstract point of
view, one simply turns one's back on the major,
basic problem, which is that of restoring man to his
proper place.

7. R. P. Oswin, Magrath of the Dominican Monastery of
St. Nicholas, Stallenbosch, Republic of South Africa,
L'homme de coleur, p. 140. My italics—F.F.
8. Mannoni, *Prospero and Caliban,* p. 27.

K

Colonial racism is no different from any other racism.

Anti-Semitism hits me head-on: I am enraged, I am bled white by an appalling battle, I am deprived of the possibility of being a man. I cannot disassociate myself from the future that is proposed for my brother. Every one of my acts commits me as a man. Every one of my silences, every one of my cowardices reveals me as a man.[9]

9. When I wrote this I had in mind Jaspers' concept of metaphysical guilt:

There exists among men, because they are men, a solidarity through which each shares responsibility for every injustice and every wrong committed in the world, and especially for crimes that are committed in his presence or of which he cannot be ignorant. If I do not do whatever I can to prevent them, I am an accomplice in them. If I have not risked my life in order to prevent the murder of other men, if I have stood silent, I feel guilty in a sense that cannot in any adequate fashion be understood juridically, or politically, or morally. . . . That I am still alive after such things have been done weighs on me as a guilt that cannot be expiated.

Somewhere in the heart of human relations an absolute command imposes itself: In case of criminal attack or of living conditions that threaten physical being, accept life only for all together, otherwise not at all. (Karl Jaspers, *La Culpabilité allemande*, Jeanne Hersch's French translation, pp. 60–61.)

Jaspers declares that this obligation stems from God. It is easy to see that God has no business here. Unless one chooses not to state the obligation as the explicit human reality of feeling oneself responsible for one's fellow man. Responsible in the sense that the least of my actions involves all mankind. Every action is an answer or a question. Perhaps both. When I express a specific manner in which my being can rise above itself, I am affirming the worth of my action for others. Conversely, the passivity that is to be seen in troubled periods of history is to be interpreted as a

I feel that I can still hear Césaire:

> When I turn on my radio, when I hear that Ne-
> groes have been lynched in America, I say that
> we have been lied to: Hitler is not dead; when I
> turn on my radio, when I learn that Jews have
> been insulted, mistreated, persecuted, I say that
> we have been lied to: Hitler is not dead; when, fi-
> nally, I turn on my radio and hear that in Africa
> forced labor has been inaugurated and legalized,
> I say that we have certainly been lied to: Hitler
> is not dead.[10]

Yes, European civilization and its best representatives are responsible for colonial racism;[11] and I
come back once more to Césaire:

> And then, one lovely day, the middle class is
> brought up short by a staggering blow: The Ges-
> tapos are busy again, the prisons are filling up, the
> torturers are once more inventing, perfecting,
> consulting over their workbenches.
>
> People are astounded, they are angry. They
> say: "How strange that is. But then it is only

---

default on that obligation. Jung, in *Aspects du drame con-
temporain,* says that, confronted by an Asiatic or a Hindu,
every European has equally to answer for the crimes perpetrated by Nazi savagery. Another writer, Mme. Maryse
Choisy, in *L'Anneau de Polycrate,* was able to describe the
guilt of those who remained "neutral" during the occupation of France. In a confused way they felt that they were
responsible for all the deaths and all the Buchenwalds.

10. Quoted from memory—*Discours politiques* of the
election campaign of 1945, Fort-de-France.

11. "European civilization and its best representatives
are not, for instance, responsible for colonial racialism;
that is the work of petty officials, small traders, and colonials who have toiled much without great success" (Mannoni, *Prospero and Caliban,* p. 24).

Nazism, it won't last." And they wait, and they
hope; and they hide the truth from themselves: It
is savagery, the supreme savagery, it crowns, it
epitomizes the day-to-day savageries; yes, it is
Nazism, but before they became its victims, they
were its accomplices; that Nazism they tolerated
before they succumbed to it, they exonerated it,
they closed their eyes to it, they legitimated it because until then it had been employed only against
non-European peoples; that Nazism they encouraged, they were responsible for it, and it drips, it
seeps, it wells from every crack in western Christian civilization until it engulfs that civilization in
a bloody sea.[12]

Whenever I see an Arab with his hunted look,
suspicious, on the run, wrapped in those long ragged
robes that seem to have been created especially for
him, I say to myself, "M. Mannoni was wrong."
Many times I have been stopped in broad daylight
by policemen who mistook me for an Arab; when
they discovered my origins, they were obsequious in
their apologies; "Of course we know that a Mar-
tinican is quite different from an Arab." I always
protested violently, but I was always told, "You
don't know them." Indeed, M. Mannoni, you are
wrong. For what is the meaning of this sentence:
"European civilization and its best representatives
are not responsible for colonial racialism"? What
does it mean except that colonialism is the business
of adventurers and politicians, the "best representatives" remaining well above the battle? But, Francis

12. Aimé Césaire, *Discours sur le colonialisme* (Paris:
Présence Africaine, 1956), pp. 14–15.

Jeanson says, every citizen of a nation is responsible for the actions committed in the name of that nation:

> Day after day, that system elaborates its evil projects in your presence, day after day its leaders betray you, pursuing, in the name of France, a policy as foreign as possible not only to your real interests but also to your deepest needs. . . . You pride yourselves on keeping your distance from realities of a certain kind: so you allow a free hand to those who are immune to the most unhealthy climates because they create these climates themselves through their own conduct. And if, apparently, you succeed in keeping yourselves unsullied, it is because others dirty themselves in your place. *You hire thugs,* and, balancing the accounts, it is you who are the real criminals: for without you, without your blind indifference, such men could never carry out deeds that damn you as much as they shame those men.[13]

I said just above that South Africa has a racist structure. Now I shall go farther and say that Europe has a racist structure. It is plain to see that M. Mannoni has no interest in this problem, for he says, "France is unquestionably one of the least racialist-minded countries in the world."[14] Be glad that you are French, my fine Negro friends, even if it is a little hard, for your counterparts in America are much worse off than you. . . . France is a racist country, for the myth of the bad nigger is part of the collec-

13. Francis Jeanson, "Cette Algérie conquise et pacifiée . . . ," *Esprit* (April 1950): 624.
14. Mannoni, *Prospero and Caliban,* p. 110.

tive unconscious. We shall demonstrate this presently (Chapter Six).

But let us proceed with M. Mannoni: "In practice, therefore, an inferiority complex connected with the color of the skin is found only among those who form a minority within a group of another color. In a fairly homogeneous community like that of the Malagasies, where the social framework is still fairly strong, an inferiority complex occurs only in very exceptional cases."[15]

Once again one asks the author to be somewhat more careful. A white man in a colony has never felt inferior in any respect; as M. Mannoni expresses it so well, "He will be deified or devoured." The colonial, even though he is "in the minority," does not feel that this makes him inferior. In Martinique there are two hundred whites who consider themselves superior to 300,000 people of color. In South Africa there are two million whites against almost thirteen million native people, and it has never occurred to a single black to consider himself superior to a member of the white minority.

While the discoveries of Adler and the no less interesting findings of Kuenkel explain certain kinds of neurotic behavior, one cannot infer from them laws that would apply to immeasurably complex problems. The feeling of inferiority of the colonized is the correlative to the European's feeling of superiority. Let us have the courage to say it outright: *It is the racist who creates his inferior*.

This conclusion brings us back to Sartre: "The

15. Ibid., p. 39.

Jew is one whom other men consider a Jew: that is the simple truth from which we must start. . . . It is the anti-Semite who *makes* the Jew."[16]

What becomes of the exceptional cases of which M. Mannoni tells us? Quite simply, they are the instances in which the educated Negro suddenly discovers that he is rejected by a civilization which he has none the less assimilated. So that the conclusion would come to this: To the extent to which M. Mannoni's real typical Malagasy takes on "dependent behavior," all is for the best; if, however, he forgets his place, if he takes it into his head to be the equal of the European, then the said European is indignant and casts out the upstart—who, in such circumstance, in this "exceptional case," pays for his own rejection of dependence with an inferiority complex.

Earlier, we uncovered in a certain of M. Mannoni's statements a mistake that is at the very least dangerous. In effect, he leaves the Malagasy no choice save between inferiority and dependence. These two solutions excepted, there is no salvation. "When he [the Malagasy] has succeeded in forming such relations [of dependence] with his superiors, his inferiority no longer troubles him: everything is all right. When he fails to establish them, when his feeling of insecurity is not assuaged in this way, he suffers a crisis."[17]

The primary concern of M. Mannoni was to criticize the methods hitherto employed by the various

16. Sartre, *Anti-Semite*, p. 69.
17. Mannoni, *Prospero and Caliban*, pp. 61–62.

ethnographers who had turned their attention to primitive peoples. But we see the criticism that must be made of his own work.

After having sealed the Malagasy into his own customs, after having evolved a unilateral analysis of his view of the world, after having described the Malagasy within a closed circle, after having noted that the Malagasy has a dependency relation toward his ancestors—a strong tribal characteristic—M. Mannoni, in defiance of all objectivity, applies his conclusions to a bilateral totality—deliberately ignoring the fact that, since Galliéni,[18] the Malagasy has ceased to exist.

What we wanted from M. Mannoni was an explanation of the colonial situation. He notably overlooked providing it. Nothing has been lost, nothing has been gained, we agree. Parodying Hegel, Georges Balandier said of the dynamics of the personality, in an essay[19] devoted to Kardiner and Linton: "The last of its stages is the result of all its preceding stages and should contain all their elements." It is whimsical, but it is the principle that

18. General Joseph-Simon Galliéni, "the hero of the Marne," played a major part in French colonial expansion. After his conquests in Africa and his service on Martinique, he was appointed resident-general of Madagascar in 1896, when it was made a French colony, and he later became governor-general. According to the Encyclopaedia Britannica (fourteenth edition), "He completed the subjugation of the island, which was in revolt against the French. . . . His policy was directed to the development of the economic resources of the island and was conciliatory toward the non-French *European* population." (Translator's note.)

19. Georges Balandier, "Où l'ethnologie retrouve l'unité de l'homme," *Esprit* (April 1950).

guides many scholars. The reactions and the behavior patterns to which the arrival of the European in Madagascar gave rise were not tacked on to a preexisting set. There was no addition to the earlier psychic whole. If, for instance, Martians undertook to colonize the earth men—not to initiate them into Martian culture but to *colonize* them—we should be doubtful of the persistence of any earth personality. Kardiner changed many opinions when he wrote: "To teach Christianity to the people of Alor would be a quixotic undertaking. . . . [It] would make no sense inasmuch as one would be dealing with personalities built out of elements that are in complete disaccord with Christian doctrine: It would certainly be starting out at the wrong end."[20] And if Negroes are impervious to the teachings of Christ, this is not at all because they are incapable of assimilating them. To understand something new requires that we make ourselves ready for it, that we prepare ourselves for it; it entails the shaping of a new form. It is utopian to expect the Negro or the Arab to exert the effort of embedding abstract values into his outlook on the world when he has barely enough food to keep alive. To ask a Negro of the Upper Niger to wear shoes, to say of him that he will never be a Schubert, is no less ridiculous than to be surprised that a worker in the Berlict truck factory does not spend his evenings studying lyricism in Hindu literature or to say that he will never be an Einstein.

Actually, in the absolute sense, nothing stands in the way of such things. Nothing—except that the people in question lack the opportunities.

20. Ibid., p. 610.

But they do not complain! Here is the proof:

> At the hour before dawn, on the far side of my
> father and my mother, the whole hut cracking
> and blistered, like a sinner punished with boils,
> and the weather-worn roof patched here and there
> with pieces of gasoline tins, and this leaves bogs
> of rust in the dirty gray stinking mud that holds
> the straw together, and, when the wind blows, all
> this patchwork makes strange sounds, first like
> something sizzling in a frying pan and then like
> a flaming board hurled into water in a shower of
> flying sparks. And the bed of planks from which
> my race has risen, all my race from this bed of
> planks on its feet of kerosene cases, as if the old
> bed had elephantiasis, covered with a goat skin,
> and its dried banana leaves and its rags, the ghost
> of a mattress that is my grandmother's bed (above
> the bed in a pot full of oil a candle-end whose
> flame looks like a fat turnip, and on the side of
> the pot, in letters of gold: MERCI).[21]

Wretchedly,

> this attitude, this behavior, this shackled life caught
> in the noose of shame and disaster rebels, hates it-
> self, struggles, howls, and, my God, others ask:
> "What can you do about it?"
>   "Start something!"
>   "Start what?"
>   "The only thing in the world that's worth the
> effort of starting: The end of the world, by
> God!"[22]

What M. Mannoni has forgotten is that the
Malagasy alone no longer exists; he has forgotten
that the Malagasy exists *with the European*. The

21. Aimé Césaire, *Cahier d'un retour au pays natal*
(Paris: Présence Africaine, 1956), p. 56.
22. Ibid.

arrival of the white man in Madagascar shattered not
only its horizons but its psychological mechanisms.
As everyone has pointed out, alterity for the black
man is not the black but the white man. An island
like Madagascar, invaded overnight by "pioneers of
civilization," even if those pioneers conducted themselves as well as they knew how, suffered the loss of
its basic structure. M. Mannoni himself, further-
more, says as much: "The petty kings were all very
anxious to get possession of a white man."[23] Explain that as one may in terms of magical-totemic
patterns, of a need for contact with an awesome
God, of its proof of a system of dependency, the fact
still remains that something new had come into being
on that island and that it had to be reckoned with—
otherwise the analysis is condemned to falsehood, to
absurdity, to nullity. A new element having been
introduced, it became mandatory to seek to understand the new relationships.

The landing of the white man on Madagascar
inflicted injury without measure. The consequences
of that irruption of Europeans onto Madagascar
were not psychological alone, since, as every authority has observed, there are inner relationships between consciousness and the social context.

And the economic consequences? Why, colonization itself must be brought to trial!

Let us go on with our study.

> In other words, the Malagasy can bear not be-
> ing a white man; what hurts him cruelly is to have
> discovered first (by identification) that he is a
> man and *later* that men are divided into whites

23. Mannoni, *Prospero and Caliban,* p. 80.

and blacks. If the "abandoned" or "betrayed" Malagasy continues his identification, he becomes clamorous; he begins to demand *equality* in a way he had never before found necessary. The equality he seeks would have been beneficial before he started asking for it, but afterwards it proves inadequate to remedy his ills—for every increase in equality makes the remaining differences seem the more intolerable, for they suddenly appear agonizingly irremovable. This is the road along which [the Malagasy] passes from psychological dependence to psychological inferiority.[24]

Here again we encounter the same misapprehension. It is of course obvious that the Malagasy can perfectly well tolerate the fact of not being a white man. A Malagasy is a Malagasy; or, rather, no, not he *is* a Malagasy but, rather, in an absolute sense he "lives" his Malagasyhood. If he is a Malagasy, it is because the white man has come, and if at a certain stage he has been led to ask himself whether he is indeed a man, it is because his reality as a man has been challenged. In other words, I begin to suffer from not being a white man to the degree that the white man imposes discrimination on me, makes me a colonized native, robs me of all worth, all individuality, tells me that I am a parasite on the world, that I must bring myself as quickly as possible into step with the white world, "that I am a brute beast, that my people and I are like a walking dung-heap that disgustingly fertilizes sweet sugar cane and silky cotton, that I have no use in the world."[25] Then I

24. Ibid., p. 84.
25. Césaire, *Cahier d'un retour*.

will quite simply try to make myself white: that is, I will compel the white man to acknowledge that I am human. But, M. Mannoni will counter, you cannot do it, because in your depths there is a dependency complex.

"Not all peoples can be colonized; only those who experience this need [for dependency]." And, a little later: "Wherever Europeans have founded colonies of the type we are considering, it can safely be said that their coming was unconsciously expected— even desired—by the future subject peoples. Everywhere there existed legends foretelling the arrival of strangers from the sea, bearing wondrous gifts with them.[26] It becomes obvious that the white man acts in obedience to an authority complex, a leadership complex, while the Malagasy obeys a dependency complex. Everyone is satisfied.

When the question arises of understanding why the European, the foreigner, was called *vazaha,* which means *honorable stranger;* when it is a matter of understanding why shipwrecked Europeans were welcomed with open arms; why the European, the foreigner, was never thought of as an enemy, instead of explaining these things in terms of humanity, of good will, of courtesy, basic characteristics of what Césaire calls "the old courtly civilizations," scholars tell us that it happened quite simply because, inscribed in "fateful hieroglyphics"—specifically, the unconscious—there exists something that makes the white man the awaited master. Yes, the unconscious —we have got to that. But one must not extrapolate.

26. Mannoni, *Prospero and Caliban,* pp. 85–86.

A Negro tells me his dream: "I had been walking for a long time, I was extremely exhausted, I had the impression that something was waiting for me, I climbed barricades and walls, I came into an empty hall, and from behind a door I heard noise. I hesitated before I went in, but finally I made up my mind and opened the door. In this second room there were white men, and I found that I too was white." When I try to understand this dream, to analyze it, knowing that my friend has had problems in his career, I conclude that this dream fulfills an unconscious wish. But when, outside my psychoanalytic office, I have to incorporate my conclusions into the context of the world, I will assert:

1. My patient is suffering from an inferiority complex. His psychic structure is in danger of disintegration. What has to be done is to save him from this and, little by little, to rid him of this unconscious desire.

2. If he is overwhelmed to such a degree by the wish to be white, it is because he lives in a society that makes his inferiority complex possible, in a society that derives its stability from the perpetuation of this complex, in a society that proclaims the superiority of one race; to the identical degree to which that society creates difficultes for him, he will find himself thrust into a neurotic situation.

What emerges then is the need for combined action on the individual and on the group. As a psychoanalyst, I should help my patient to become *conscious* of his unconscious and abandon his attempts at a hallucinatory whitening, but also to act in the direction of a change in the social structure.

In other words, the black man should no longer be confronted by the dilemma, *turn white or disappear;* but he should be able to take cognizance of a possibility of existence. In still other words, if society makes difficulties for him because of his color, if in his dreams I establish the expression of an unconscious desire to change color, my objective will not be that of dissuading him from it by advising him to "keep his place"; on the contrary, my objective, once his motivations have been brought into consciousness, will be to put him in a position to *choose* action (or passivity) with respect to the real source of the conflict—that is, toward the social structures.

Conscientious in his desire to examine the problem from every angle, M. Mannoni has not overlooked the investigation of the unconscious of the Malagasy. To this end he analyzes seven dreams: seven narratives that open the unconscious to us, and in six of them we find a dominant theme of terror. Six children and an adult tell us their dreams, and we see them trembling, seeking flight, unhappy.

> *The cook's dream.* "I was being chased by an angry *black*[27] bull. Terrified, I climbed up into a tree and stayed there till the danger was past. I came down again, trembling all over. . . ."
>
> *Dream of a thirteen-year-old boy, Rahevi.* "While going for a walk in the woods, I met two *black*[28] men. 'Oh,' I thought, 'I am done for!' I tried to run away but couldn't. They barred my way and began jabbering in a strange tongue. I thought they were saying, 'We'll show you what death is.' I shivered with fright and begged,

27. My italics—F.F.
28. My italics—F.F.

'Please, Sirs, let me go, I'm so frightened.' One of them understood French but in spite of that they said, 'We are going to take you to our chief.' As we set off they made me go in front and they showed me their rifles. I was more frightened than ever, but before reaching their camp we had to cross a river. I dived deep into the water and thanks to my presence of mind found a rocky cave where I hid. When the two men had gone I ran back to my parents' house. . . ."

Josette's dream. The dreamer, a young girl, got lost and sat down on a fallen tree-trunk. A woman in a white dress told her that she was in the midst of a band of robbers. The account goes on: " 'I am a schoolgirl,' I said, trembling, 'and I lost my way here when I was going home from school,' and she replied: 'Follow this path, child, and you will find your way home. . . .' "

Dream of a fourteen-year-old boy, Razafi. He is being chased by (Senegalese) soldiers who "make a noise like galloping horses as they run," and "show their rifles in front of them." The dreamer escapes by becoming invisible; he climbs a stairway and finds the door of his home. . . .

Dream of Elphine, a girl of thirteen or fourteen. "I dreamed that a fierce *black*[29] ox was chasing me. He was big and strong. On his head, which was almost mottled (*sic*) with white he had two long horns with sharp points. 'Oh how dreadful,' I thought. The path was getting narrower. What should I do? I perched myself in a mango tree, but the ox rent its trunk. Alas, I fell among the bushes. Then he pressed his horns into me; my stomach fell out and he devoured it. . . ."

Raza's dream. In his dream the boy heard someone say at school that the Senegalese were coming. "I went out of the school yard to see."

29. My italics—F.F.

The Senegalese were indeed coming. He ran home. "But our house had been dispersed by them too. . . ."

Dream of a fourteen-year-old boy, Si. "I was walking in the garden and felt like a shadow behind me. All around me the leaves were rustling and falling off, as if a robber was in hiding among them, waiting to catch me. Wherever I walked, up and down the alleys, the shadow still followed me. Suddenly I got frightened and started running, but the shadow took great strides and stretched out his huge hand to take hold of my clothes. I felt my shirt tearing, and screamed. My father jumped out of bed when he heard me scream and came over to look at me, but the big *shadow*[30] had disappeared and I was no longer afraid."[31]

Some ten years ago I was astonished to learn that the North African despised men of color. It was absolutely impossible for me to make any contact with the local population. I left Africa and went back to France without having fathomed the reason for this hostility. Meanwhile, certain facts had made me think. The Frenchman does not like the Jew, who does not like the Arab, who does not like the Negro. . . . The Arab is told: "If you are poor, it is because the Jew has bled you and taken everything from you." The Jew is told: "You are not of the same class as the Arab because you are really white and because you have Einstein and Bergson." The Negro is told: "You are the best soldiers in the French Empire; the Arabs think they are better than you, but they are wrong." But that is not true; the

30. My italics—F.F.
31. Mannoni, *Prospero and Caliban,* pp. 89–92.

Negro is told nothing because no one has anything to tell him, the Senegalese trooper is a trooper, the-good-soldier-under-command, the brave fellow-who-only-knows-how-to-obey.

"You no come in."

"Why not?"

"Me not know. You no come in."

Unable to stand up to all the demands, the white man sloughs off his responsibilities. I have a name for this procedure: the racial distribution of guilt.

I have remarked that certain things surprised me. Whenever there has been any attempt at insurrection, the military authorities have ordered only colored soldiers into action. They were "men of color" who nullified the liberation efforts of other "men of color," proof that there was no reason to universalize the procedure: If those good-for-nothings, the Arabs, took it into their heads to revolt, it was not in the name of any acceptable principle but purely and simply in order to get rid of their *"bicot"* unconscious.

From the African point of view, a colored student said at the Twenty-fifth Congress of Catholic Students during its discussion of Madagascar, "I wish to protest against the dispatch of Senegalese troops there and the misuse that is being made of them." We know from other sources that one of the torturers in the Tananarive police headquarters was a Senegalese. Therefore, since we know all this, since we know what the archetype of the Senegalese can represent for the Malagasy, the discoveries of Freud are of no use to us here. What must be done is to restore this dream *to its proper time,* and this time is the period during which eighty thousand natives were killed—that is to say, one of every fifty persons in the population; and *to its proper place,* and this place is an island of four million people, at the center of which no real relationship can be established, where dissension breaks out in every direction, where the only masters are lies and demagogy.[32]

32. We bring up in this connection the following testimony given at a trial in Tananarive.

(Session of August 9. Rakotovao states:)
M. Baron said to me, "Since you refuse to accept what I just told you, I'm sending you to the 'thinking room.' . . ." I was led into the adjoining chamber. The floor of the room in question was already covered with water. There was a pail full of dirty water, not to mention other things. M. Baron said to me, "Now you'll learn to agree to what I said you should declare." He gave an order to a Senegalese to "do the same to me as to the others." The Senegalese made me kneel with my wrists facing outward; then he took wooden tongs and squeezed my hands together; then, with me kneeling and my two hands pressed together, he put his foot on the back of my neck and forced my head down into the bucket. Seeing that I was on the point of fainting, he removed his foot so that I could get some air. And this was repeated again and again until I was completely exhausted. Then M. Baron said, "Take him away and beat him." The Senegalese thereupon used a bull-whip, but M. Baron came into the torture chamber and personally took part in the whipping. This went on for about fifteen minutes, I think, after which I said that I couldn't endure any more, because in spite of my youth it was unbearable. Then he said, "In that case you must agree to what I told you before!"

"No, *Monsieur le directeur,* it is not true."

Thereupon he sent me back into the first torture chamber and called in another Senegalese, since one was not enough, and he ordered them to hold me up by the feet and lower me into the bucket as far as my chest. This they did several times. Finally I told them, "It's too much! Let me talk to M. Baron," and to him I said, "I request at least that I be treated in a manner

One must concede that in some circumstances the *socius* is more important than the individual. I recall what Pierre Naville wrote:

> To speak of society's dreams as one speaks of the dreams of the individual, to discuss collective will to power as one discusses individual sexual drive, is to reverse the natural order of things once more, because, on the contrary, it is the economic and social conditions of class conflicts that explain and determine the real conditions in which individual sexuality expresses itself, and because the content of a human being's dreams de-

---

befitting France, *Monsieur le directeur*," to which he replied, "You're getting French treatment!"

Since I could stand no more, I said to him, "All right, I'll accept the first part of your statement." M. Baron replied, "No, I don't want the first part, I want it all." "Am I supposed to lie, then?" "Lie or no lie, you must agree to what I tell you. . . ."

(The testimony went on:)

Immediately M. Baron said, "Try some other method on him." I was then taken back into the adjoining room, where there was a small stone stairway. My arms were tied behind me. The two Senegalese again held me with my feet in the air and made me go up and down the stairs in this way. This was beginning to be unendurable, and, even if I had had any moral strength left, it was physically too much. I said to the Senegalese, "Tell your boss I'll agree to what he wants me to say." (In the session of August 11, Robert, a defendant, testified:)

The policeman took me by my shirt collar and kicked me in the behind and punched me in the face. Then he forced me to kneel, and M. Baron began hitting me again.

Without my knowing how he managed it, he got behind me and I felt hot irons against the back of my neck. I tried to protect myself with my hands and they were burned too. . . .

The third time I was knocked down I lost conscious-

pends also, in the last analysis, on the general conditions of the culture in which he lives.[33]

The engraged black bull is not the phallus. The two black men are not the two father figures—the one standing for the real father, the other for the primal ancestor. Here is what a thorough analysis could have found, on the same basis of M. Mannoni's conclusions in his section, "The Cult of the Dead and the Family."

The rifle of the Senegalese soldier is not a penis but a genuine rifle, model Lebel 1916. The black bull and the robber are not *lolos*—"reincarnated souls"—but actually the irruption of real fantasies into sleep. What does this stereotype, this central theme of the dreams, represent if not a return to the right road? Sometimes we have *black* soldiers, some-

---

ness and I don't know any more what happened. M. Baron told me to sign a paper that was all ready; I shook my head *no;* then the director called the Senegalese in again and he half-carried me into another torture chamber. "You better give in or you'll be dead," the Senegalese said. The director said, "That's his lookout, you have to get started, Jean." My arms were tied behind my back, I was forced down on my knees, and my head was pushed into a bucket full of water. Just as I was about to suffocate I was pulled out. Then they did the same thing over and over again until I passed out completely. . . .

Let us recall, so that no one may plead ignorance of the fact, that the witness Rakotovao was sentenced to death.

So, when one reads such things, it certainly seems that M. Mannoni allowed one aspect of the phenomena that he analyzes to escape him: The black bull and the black men are neither more nor less than the Senegalese police torturers.

33. Pierre Naville, *Psychologie, Marxisme, Matérialisme,* 2nd ed. (Paris: Marcel Rivière, 1948), p. 151.

times *black* bulls speckled with white at the head,
sometimes, outright, a white woman who is quite
kind. What do we find in all these dreams if not this
central idea: "To depart from routine is to wander in
pathless woods; there you will meet the bull who will
send you running helter-skelter home again."[34]

Settle down, Malagasies, and stay where you
belong.

After having described the Malagasy psychology,
M. Mannoni takes it upon himself to explain colonialism's reason for existence. In the process he adds
a new complex to the standing catalogue: the "Prospero complex." It is defined as the sum of those
unconscious neurotic tendencies that delineate at the
same time the "picture" of the paternalist colonial
and the portrait of "the racialist whose daughter has
suffered an [imaginary] attempted rape at the hands
of an inferior being."[35]

Prospero, as we know, is the main character of
Shakespeare's comedy, *The Tempest*. Opposite him
we have his daughter, Miranda, and Caliban. Toward Caliban, Prospero assumes an attitude that is
well known to Americans in the southern United
States. Are they not forever saying that the niggers
are just waiting for the chance to jump on white
women? In any case, what is interesting in this part
of his book is the intensity with which M. Mannoni
makes us feel the ill-resolved conflicts that seem to
be at the root of the colonial vocation. In effect, he
tells us:

34. Mannoni, *Prospero and Caliban*, p. 70.
35. Ibid., p. 110.

> What the colonial in common with Prospero lacks, is awareness of the world of Others, a world in which Others have to be respected. This is the world from which the colonial has fled because he cannot accept men as they are. Rejection of that world is combined with an urge to dominate, an urge which is infantile in origin and which social adaptation has failed to discipline. The reason the colonial himself gives for his flight—whether he says it was the desire to travel, or the desire to escape from the cradle or from the "ancient parapets," or whether he says that he simply wanted a freer life—is of no consequence. . . . It is always a question of compromising with the desire for a world without men.[36]

If one adds that many Europeans go to the colonies because it is possible for them to grow rich quickly there, that with rare exceptions the colonial is a merchant, or rather a trafficker, one will have grasped the psychology of the man who arouses in the autochthonous population "the feeling of inferiority." As for the Malagasy "dependency complex," at least in the only form in which we can reach it and analyze it, it too proceeds from the arrival of white colonizers on the island. From its other form, from this original complex in its pure state that supposedly characterized the Malagasy mentally throughout the whole precolonial period, it appears to me that M. Mannoni lacks the slightest basis on which to ground any conclusion applicable to the situation, the problems, or the potentialities of the Malagasy in the present time.

36. Ibid., p. 108.

13. Concerning Violence

FRANTZ FANON

National liberation, national renaissance, the restoration of nationhood to the people, commonwealth: whatever may be the headings used or the new formulas introduced, decolonization is always a violent phenonomen. At whatever level we study it—relationships between individuals, new names for sports clubs, the human admixture at cocktail parties, in the police, on the directing boards of national or private banks—decolonization is quite simply the replacing of a certain "species" of men by another "species" of men. Without any period of transition, there is a total, complete and absolute substitution. It is true that we could equally well stress the rise of a new nation, the setting up of a

From *The Wretched of the Earth* (New York: Grove Press, London: Granada, 1963), pp. 29–46. Copyright © 1963 by Présence Africain. Reprinted by permission of the publishers.

new State, its diplomatic relations, and its economic and political trends. But we have precisely chosen to speak of that kind of *tabula rasa* which *characterizes* at the outset all decolonization. Its unusual importance is that it constitutes, from the very first day, the minimum demands of the colonized. To tell the truth, the proof of success lies in a whole social structure being changed from the bottom up. The extraordinary importance of this change is that it is willed, called for, demanded. The need for this change exists in its crude state, impetuous and compelling, in the consciousness and in the lives of the men and women who are colonized. But the possibility of this change is equally experienced in the form of a terrifying future in the consciousness of another "species" of men and women: the colonizers.

Decolonization, which sets out to change the order of the world, is, obviously, a program of complete disorder. But it cannot come as a result of magical practices, nor of a natural shock, nor of a friendly understanding. Decolonization, as we know, is a historical process: that is to say that it cannot be understood, it cannot become intelligible nor clear to itself except in the exact measure that we can discern the movements which give it historical form and content. Decolonization is the meeting of two forces, opposed to each other by their very nature, which in fact owe their originality to that sort of substantification which results from and is nourished by the situation in the colonies. Their first encounter was marked by violence and their existence together— that is to say the exploitation of the native by the settler—was carried on by dint of a great array of bayonets and cannon. The settler and the native are old acquaintances. In fact, the settler is right when he speaks of knowing "them" well. For it is the settler who has brought the native into existence and who perpetuates his existence. The settler owes the fact of his very existence, that is to say his property, to the colonial system.

Decolonization never takes place unnoticed, for it influences individuals and modifies them fundamentally. It transforms spectators crushed with their inessentiality into privileged actors, with the grandiose glare of history's floodlights upon them. It brings a natural rhythm into existence, introduced by new men, and with it a new language and a new humanity. Decolonization is the veritable creation of new men. But this creation owes nothing of its legitimacy to any supernatural power; the "thing" which has been colonized becomes man during the same process by which it frees itself.

In decolonization, there is therefore the need of a complete calling in question of the colonial situation. If we wish to describe it precisely, we might find it in the well-known words: "The last shall be first and the first last." Decolonization is the putting into practice of this sentence. That is why, if we try to describe it, all decolonization is successful.

The naked truth of decolonization evokes for us the searing bullets and bloodstained knives which emanate from it. For if the last shall be first, this will only come to pass after a murderous and decisive struggle between the two protagonists. That affirmed intention to place the last at the head of things, and to make them climb at a pace (too quickly, some say) the well-known steps which characterize an organized society, can only triumph if we use all means to turn the scale, including, of course, that of violence.

You do not turn any society, however primitive it may be, upside-down with such a program if you are not decided from the very beginning, that is to say from the actual formulation of that program, to overcome all the obstacles that you will come across in so doing. The native who decides to put the program into practice, and to become its moving force, is ready for violence at all times. From birth it is clear to him that this narrow world, strewn with prohibitions, can only be called in question by absolute violence.

The colonial world is a world divided into compartments. It is probably unnecessary to recall the existence of native quarters and European quarters, of schools for natives and schools for Europeans; in the same way we need not recall Apartheid in South Africa. Yet, if we examine closely this system of compartments, we will at least be able to reveal the lines of force it implies. This approach to the colonial world, its ordering and its geographical lay-out will allow us to mark out the lines on which a decolonized society will be reorganized.

The colonial world is a world cut in two. The dividing line, the frontiers are shown by barracks and police stations. In the colonies it is the policeman and the soldier who are the official, instituted go-betweens, the spokesmen of the settler and his rule of oppression. In capitalist societies the educational system, whether lay or clerical, the structure of moral reflexes handed down from father to son, the exemplary honesty of workers who are given a medal after fifty years of good and loyal service, and the affection which springs from harmonious relations and good behavior—all these esthetic expressions of respect for the established order serve to create around the exploited person an atmosphere of submission and of inhibition which lightens the task of policing considerably. In the capitalist countries a multitude of moral teachers, counsellors and "bewilderers" separate the exploited from those in power. In the colonial countries, on the contrary, the policeman and the soldier, by their immediate presence and their frequent and direct action maintain contact with the native and advise him by means of rifle-butts and napalm not to budge. It is obvious here that the agents of government speak the language of pure force. The intermediary does not lighten the oppression, nor seek to hide the domination; he shows them up and puts them into practice with the clear conscience of an upholder of the peace; yet he is the bringer of violence into the home and into the mind of the native.

The zone where the natives live is not complementary to the zone inhabited by the settlers. The two zones are opposed, but not in the service of a higher unity. Obedient to the rules of pure Aristotelian logic, they both follow the principle of reciprocal exclusivity. No conciliation is possible, for of the two terms, one is superfluous. The settlers' town is a strongly-built town, all made of stone and steel. It is a brightly-lit town; the streets are covered with asphalt, and the garbage-cans swallow all the leavings, unseen, unknown and hardly thought about. The settler's feet are never visible, except perhaps in the sea; but there you're never close enough to see them. His feet are protected by strong shoes although the streets of his town are cleaned and even, with no holes or stones. The settler's town is a well-fed town, an easy-going town; its belly is always full of good things. The settler's town is a town of white people, of foreigners.

The town belonging to the colonized people, or at least the native town, the Negro village, the medina, the reservation, is a place of ill fame, peopled by men of evil repute. They are born there, it matters little where or how; they die there, it matters not where, nor how. It is a world without spaciousness; men live there on top of each other, and their huts are built one on top of the other. The native town is a hungry town, starved of bread, of meat, of shoes, of coal, of light. The native town is a crouching village, a town on its knees, a town wallowing in the mire. It is a town of niggers and dirty Arabs. The look that the native turns on the settler's town is a look of lust, a look of envy; it expresses his dreams of possession —all manner of possession: to sit at the settler's table, to sleep in the settler's bed, with his wife if possible. The colonized man is an envious man. And this the settler knows very well; when their glances meet he ascertains bitterly, always on the defensive "They want to take our place." It is true, for there is no

native who does not dream at least once a day of
setting himself up in the settler's place.

This world divided into compartments, this world
cut in two is inhabited by two different species. The
originality of the colonial context is that economic
reality, inequality and the immense difference of
ways of life never come to mask the human realities.
When you examine at close quarters the colonial
context, it is evident that what parcels out the world
is to begin with the fact of belonging to or not belonging to a given race, a given species. In the
colonies the economic substructure is also a superstructure. The cause is the consequence; you are rich
because you are white, you are white because you
are rich. This is why Marxist analysis should always
be slightly stretched every time we have to do with
the colonial problem.

Everything up to and including the very nature of
precapitalist society, so well explained by Marx,
must here be thought out again. The serf is in
essence different from the knight, but a reference to
divine right is necessary to legitimize this statutory
difference. In the colonies, the foreigner coming
from another country imposed his rule by means of
guns and machines. In defiance of his successful
transplantation, in spite of his appropriation, the
settler still remains a foreigner. It is neither the act
of owning factories, nor estates, nor a bank balance
which distinguishes the governing classes. The governing race is first and foremost those who come
from elsewhere, those who are unlike the original
inhabitants, "the others."

The violence which has ruled over the ordering of the colonial world, which has ceaselessly drummed the rhythm for the destruction of native social forms and broken up without reserve the systems of reference of the economy, the customs of dress and external life, that same violence will be claimed and taken over by the native at the moment when, deciding to embody history in his own person, he surges into the forbidden quarters. To wreck the colonial world is henceforward a mental picture of action which is very clear, very easy to understand and which may be assumed by each one of the individuals which constitute the colonized people. To break up the colonial world does not mean that after the frontiers have been abolished lines of communication will be set up between the two zones. The destruction of the colonial world is no more and no less than the abolition of one zone, its burial in the depths of the earth or its expulsion from the country.

The natives' challenge to the colonial world is not a rational confrontation of points of view. It is not a treatise on the universal, but the untidy affirmation of an original idea propounded as an absolute. The colonial world is a Manichean world. It is not enough for the settler to delimit physically, that is to say with the help of the army and the police force, the place of the native. As if to show the totalitarian character of colonial exploitation the settler paints the native as a sort of quintessence of evil.[1] Native society is not simply described as a society lacking in

1. We have demonstrated the mechanism of this Manichean world in *Black Skin, White Masks*.

values. It is not enough for the colonist to affirm that
those values have disappeared from, or still better
never existed in, the colonial world. The native is
declared insensible to ethics; he represents not only
the absence of values, but also the negation of
values. He is, let us dare to admit, the enemy of
values, and in this sense he is the absolute evil. He is
the corrosive element, destroying all that comes near
him; he is the deforming element, defiguring all that
has to do with beauty or morality; he is the deposi-
tory of maleficient powers, the unconscious and
irretrievable instrument of blind forces. Monsieur
Meyer could thus state seriously in the French
National Assembly that the Republic must not be
prostituted by allowing the Algerian people to become part of it. All values, in fact, are irrevocably
poisoned and diseased as soon as they are allowed in
contact with the colonized race. The customs of the
colonized people, their traditions, their myths—
above all, their myths—are the very sign of that
poverty of spirit and of their constitutional deprav-
ity. That is why we must put the DDT which destroys parasites, the bearers of disease, on the same
level as the Christian religion which wages war on
embryonic heresies and instincts, and on evil as yet
unborn. The recession of yellow fever and the advance of evangelization form part of the same balance sheet. But the triumphant *communiqués* from
the missions are in fact a source of information
concerning the implantation of foreign influences in
the core of the colonized people. I speak of the
Christian religion, and no one need be astonished.
The Church in the colonies is the white people's

Church, the foreigner's Church. She does not call the native to God's ways but to the ways of the white man, of the master, of the oppressor. And as we know, in this matter many are called but few chosen.

At times this Manicheism goes to its logical conclusion and dehumanizes the native, or to speak plainly it turns him into an animal. In fact, the terms the settler uses when he mentions the native are zoological terms. He speaks of the yellow man's reptilian motions, of the stink of the native quarter, of breeding swarms, of foulness, of spawn, of gesticulations. When the settler seeks to describe the native fully in exact terms he constantly refers to the bestiary. The European rarely hits on a picturesque style; but the native, who knows what is in the mind of the settler, guesses at once what he is thinking of. Those hordes of vital statistics, those hysterical masses, those faces bereft of all humanity, those distended bodies which are like nothing on earth, that mob without beginning or end, those children who seem to belong to nobody, that laziness stretched out in the sun, that vegetative rhythm of life—all this forms part of the colonial vocabulary. General de Gaulle speaks of "the yellow multitudes" and François Mauriac of the black, brown and yellow masses which soon will be unleashed. The native knows all this, and laughs to himself every time he spots an allusion to the animal world in the other's words. For he knows that he is not an animal; and it is precisely at the moment he realizes his humanity that he begins to sharpen the weapons with which he will secure its victory.

As soon as the native begins to pull on his moor-

L

ings, and to cause anxiety to the settler, he is handed over to well-meaning souls who in cultural congresses point out to him the specificity and wealth of Western values. But every time Western values are mentioned they produce in the native a sort of stiffening or muscular lockjaw. During the period of decolonization, the native's reason is appealed to. He is offered definite values, he is told frequently that decolonization need not mean regression, and that he must put his trust in qualities which are well-tried, solid and highly esteemed. But it so happens that when the native hears a speech about Western culture he pulls out his knife—or at least he makes sure it is within reach. The violence with which the supremacy of white values is affirmed and the aggressiveness which has permeated the victory of these values over the ways of life and of thought of the native mean that, in revenge, the native laughs in mockery when Western values are mentioned in front of him. In the colonial context the settler only ends his work of breaking in the native when the latter admits loudly and intelligibly the supremacy of the white man's values. In the period of decolonization, the colonized masses mock at these very values, insult them and vomit them up.

This phenomenon is ordinarily masked because, during the period of decolonization, certain colonized intellectuals have begun a dialogue with the bourgeoisie of the colonialist country. During this phase, the indigenous population is discerned only as an indistinct mass. The few native personalities whom the colonialist bourgeois have come to know here and there have not sufficient influence on that immediate discernment to give rise to nuances. On the other hand during the period of liberation, the colonialist bourgeoisie looks feverishly for contacts with the *élite,* and it is with these *élite* that the familiar dialogue concerning values is carried on. The colonialist bourgeoisie, when it realizes that it is impossible for it to maintain its domination over the colonial countries, decides to carry out a rear-guard action with regard to culture, values, techniques and so on. Now what we must never forget is that the immense majority of colonized peoples is oblivious of these problems. For a colonized people the most essential value, because the most concrete, is first and foremost the land: the land which will bring them bread and, above all, dignity. But this dignity has nothing to do with the dignity of the human individual: for that human individual has never heard tell of it. All that the native has seen in his country is that they can freely arrest him, beat him, starve him: and no professor of ethics, no priest has ever come to be beaten in his place, nor to share their bread with him. As far as the native is concerned, morality is very concrete; it is to silence the settler's defiance, to break his flaunting violence—in a word, to put him out of the picture. The well-known principle that all men are equal will be illustrated in the colonies from the moment that the native claims that he is the equal of the settler. One step more, and he is ready to fight to be more than the settler. In fact, he has already decided to eject him and to take his place; as we see it, it is a whole material and moral universe which is breaking up. The intellectual who for his part has followed the colonialist with regard to the universal abstract will fight in order that the settler and the native may live together in peace in a new world. But the thing he does not see, precisely because he is permeated by colonialism and all its ways of thinking is that the settler, from the moment that the colonial context disappears, has no longer any interest in remaining or in coexisting. It is not by chance that, even before any negotiation[2] between the Algerian and French governments has taken place, the European minority which calls itself "liberal" has already made its position clear: it demands nothing more or less than twofold citizenship. By setting themselves apart in an abstract manner, the liberals try to force the settler into taking a very concrete jump into the unknown. Let us admit it, the settler knows perfectly well that no phraseology can be a substitute for reality.

Thus the native discovers that his life, his breath, his beating heart are the same as those of the settler. He finds out that the settler's skin is not of any more value than a native's skin; and it must be said that this discovery shakes the world in a very necessary manner. All the new, revolutionary assurance of the native stems from it. For if, in fact, my life is worth as much as the settler's, his glance no longer shrivels me up nor freezes me, and his voice no longer turns me into stone. I am no longer on tenterhooks in his presence; in fact, I don't give a damn for him. Not

2. Fanon is writing in 1961. (Trans.)

only does his presence no longer trouble me, but I am already preparing such efficient ambushes for him that soon there will be no way out but that of flight.

We have said that the colonial context is characterized by the dichotomy which it imposes upon the whole people. Decolonization unifies that people by the radical decision to remove from it its heterogenity, and by unifying it on a national, sometimes a racial, basis. We know the fierce words of the Senegalese patriots, referring to the maneuvers of their president, Senghor: "We have demanded that the higher posts should be given to Africans; and now Senghor is Africanizing the Europeans." That is to say that the native can see clearly and immediately if decolonization has come to pass or no, for his minimum demands are simply that the last shall be first.

But the native intellectual brings variants to this petition, and, in fact, he seems to have good reasons: higher civil servants, technicians, specialists— all seem to be needed. Now, the ordinary native interprets these unfair promotions as so many acts of sabotage, and he is often heard to declare: "It wasn't worth while, then, our becoming independent. . . ."

In the colonial countries where a real struggle for freedom has taken place, where the blood of the people has flowed and where the length of the period of armed warfare has favored the backward surge of intellectuals towards bases grounded in the people, we can observe a genuine eradication of the superstructure built by these intellectuals from the bourgeois colonialist environment. The colonialist

bourgeoisie, in its narcissistic dialogue, expounded by
the members of its universities, had in fact deeply
implanted in the minds of the colonized intellectual
that the essential qualities remain eternal in spite of
all the blunders men may make: the essential qualities of the West, of course. The native intellectual
accepted the cogency of these ideas, and deep down
in his brain you could always find a vigilant sentinel
ready to defend the Greco-Latin pedestal. Now it so
happens that during the struggle for liberation, at the
moment that the native intellectual comes into touch
again with his people, this artificial sentinel is turned
into dust. All the Mediterranean values,—the triumph of the human individual, of clarity and of
beauty—become lifeless, colorless knickknacks. All
those speeches seem like collections of dead words;
those values which seemed to uplift the soul are revealed as worthless, simply because they have nothing to do with the concrete conflict in which the
people is engaged.

Individualism is the first to disappear. The native
intellectual had learned from his masters that the
individual ought to express himself fully. The colonialist bourgeoisie had hammered into the native's
mind the idea of a society of individuals where each
person shuts himself up in his own subjectivity, and
whose only wealth is individual thought. Now the
native who has the opportunity to return to the
people during the struggle for freedom will discover
the falseness of this theory. The very forms of organization of the struggle will suggest to him a different
vocabulary. Brother, sister, friend—these are words

outlawed by the colonialist bourgeoisie, because for them my brother is my purse, my friend is part of my scheme for getting on. The native intellectual takes part, in a sort of *auto-da-fé,* in the destruction of all his idols: egoism, recrimination that springs from pride, and the childish stupidity of those who always want to have the last word. Such a colonized intellectual, dusted over by colonial culture, will in the same way discover the substance of village assemblies, the cohesion of people's committees, and the extraordinary fruitfulness of local meetings and groupments. Henceforward, the interests of one will be the interests of all, for in concrete fact *everyone* will be discovered by the troops, *everyone* will be massacred —or *everyone* will be saved. The motto "look out for yourself," the atheist's method of salvation, is in this context forbidden.

Self-criticism has been much talked about of late, but few people realize that it is an African institution. Whether in the *djemaas*[3] of Northern Africa or in the meetings of Western Africa, tradition demands that the quarrels which occur in a village should be settled in public. It is communal self-criticism, of course, and with a note of humor, because everybody is relaxed, and because in the last resort we all want the same things. But the more the intellectual imbibes the atmosphere of the people, the more completely he abandons the habits of calculation, of unwonted silence, of mental reservations, and shakes off the spirit of concealment. And it is true that already at that level we can say that the community

3. Village assemblies. (Trans.)

triumphs, and that it spreads its own light and its own reason.

But it so happens sometimes that decolonization occurs in areas which have not been sufficiently shaken by the struggle for liberation, and there may be found those same know-all, smart, wily intellectuals. We find intact in them the manners and forms of thought picked up during their association with the colonialist bourgeoisie. Spoiled children of yesterday's colonialism and of today's national governments, they organize the loot of whatever national resources exist. Without pity, they use today's national distress as a means of getting on through scheming and legal robbery, by import-export combines, limited liability companies, gambling on the stock exchange, or unfair promotion. They are insistent in their demands for the nationalization of commerce, that is to say the reservation of markets and advantageous bargains for nationals only. As far as doctrine is concerned, they proclaim the pressing necessity of nationalizing the robbery of the nation. In this arid phase of national life, the so-called period of austerity, the success of their depredations is swift to call forth the violence and anger of the people. For this same people, poverty-stricken yet independent, comes very quickly to possess a social conscience in the African and international context of today; and this the petty individualists will quickly learn.

In order to assimilate and to experience the oppressor's culture, the native has had to leave certain of his intellectual possessions in pawn. These pledges include his adoption of the forms of thought of the colonialist bourgeoisie. This is very noticeable in the inaptitude of the native intellectual to carry on a two sided discussion; for he cannot eliminate himself when confronted with an object or an idea. On the other hand, when once he begins to militate among the people he is struck with wonder and amazement; he is literally disarmed by their good faith and honesty. The danger that will haunt him continually is that of becoming the uncritical mouthpiece of the masses; he becomes a kind of yes-man who nods assent at every word coming from the people, which he interprets as considered judgments. Now, the *fellah*, the unemployed man, the starving native do not lay a claim to the truth; they do not *say* that they represent the truth, for they *are* the truth.

Objectively, the intellectual behaves in this phase like a common opportunist. In fact he has not stopped maneuvering. There is never any question of his being either rejected or welcomed by the people. What they ask is simply that all resources should be pooled. The inclusion of the native intellectual in the upward surge of the masses will in this case be differentiated by a curious cult of detail. That is not to say that the people are hostile to analysis; on the contrary, they like having things explained to them, they are glad to understand a line of argument and they like to see where they are going. But at the beginning of his association with the people the native intellectual overstresses details and thereby comes to forget that the defeat of colonialism is the real object of the struggle. Carried away by the multitudinous aspects of the fight, he tends to concentrate on local tasks, performed with enthusiasm but almost always too solemnly. He fails to see the whole of the movement all the time. He introduces the idea of special disciplines, of specialized functions, of departments within the terrible stone crusher, the fierce mixing machine which a popular revolution is. He is occupied in action on a particular front, and it so happens that he loses sight of the unity of the movement. Thus, if a local defeat is inflicted, he may well be drawn into doubt, and from thence to despair. The people, on the other hand, take their stand from the start on the broad and inclusive positions of *Bread and the land:* how can we obtain the land, and bread to eat? And this obstinate point of view of the masses, which may seem shrunken and limited, is in the end the most worthwhile and the most efficient mode of procedure.

The problem of truth ought also to be considered. In every age, among the people, truth is the property of the national cause. No absolute verity, no discourse on the purity of the soul can shake this position. The native replies to the living lie of the colonial situation by an equal falsehood. His dealings with his fellow-nationals are open; they are strained and incomprehensible with regard to the settlers. Truth is that which hurries on the break-up of the colonialist regime; it is that which promotes the emergence of the nation; it is all that protects the natives, and ruins the foreigners. In this colonialist context there is no truthful behavior: and the good is quite simply that which is evil for *"them."*

Thus we see that the primary Manicheism which governed colonial society is preserved intact during the period of decolonization; that is to say that the settler never ceases to be the enemy, the opponent, the foe that must be overthrown. The oppressor, in his own sphere, starts the process, a process of domination, of exploitation and of pillage, and in the other sphere the coiled, plundered creature which is the native provides fodder for the process as best he can, the process which moves uninterruptedly from the banks of the colonial territory to the palaces and the docks of the mother country. In this becalmed zone the sea has a smooth surface, the palmtree stirs gently in the breeze, the waves lap against the pebbles, and raw materials are ceaselessly transported, justifying the presence of the settler: and all the while the native, bent double, more dead than alive, exists interminably in an unchanging dream. The settler makes history; his life is an epoch, an Odyssey. He is the absolute beginning: "This land was created by us"; he is the unceasing cause: "If we leave, all is lost, and the country will go back to the Middle Ages." Over against him torpid creatures, wasted by fevers, obsessed by ancestral customs, form an almost inorganic background for the innovating dynamism of colonial mercantilism.

The settler makes history and is conscious of making it. And because he constantly refers to the history of his mother country, he clearly indicates that he himself is the extension of that mother country. Thus the history which he writes is not the history of the country which he plunders but the history

of his own nation in regard to all that she skims off,
all that she violates and starves.

The immobility to which the native is condemned
can only be called in question if the native decides to
put an end to the history of colonization—the history of pillage—and to bring into existence the history of the nation—the history of decolonization.

A world divided into compartments, a motionless,
Manicheistic world, a world of statues: the statue of
the general who carried out the conquest, the statue
of the engineer who built the bridge; a world which
is sure of itself, which crushes with its stones the
backs flayed by whips: this is the colonial world.
The native is a being hemmed in; apartheid is simply
one form of the division into compartments of the
colonial world. The first thing which the native
learns is to stay in his place, and not to go beyond
certain limits. This is why the dreams of the native
are always of muscular prowess; his dreams are of
action and of aggression. I dream I am jumping,
swimming, running, climbing; I dream that I burst out
laughing, that I span a river in one stride, or that I
am followed by a flood of motorcars which never
catch up with me. During the period of colonization,
the native never stops achieving his freedom from
nine in the evening until six in the morning.

The colonized man will first manifest this aggressiveness which has been deposited in his bones
against his own people. This is the period when the
niggers beat each other up, and the police and
magistrates do not know which way to turn when
faced with the astonishing waves of crime in North

Africa. We shall see later how this phenomenon should be judged.[4] When the native is confronted with the colonial order of things, he finds he is in a state of permanent tension. The settler's world is a hostile world, which spurns the native, but at the same time it is a world of which he is envious. We have seen that the native never ceases to dream of putting himself in the place of the settler—not of becoming the settler but of substituting himself for the settler. This hostile world, ponderous and aggressive because it fends off the colonized masses with all the harshness it is capable of, represents not merely a hell from which the swiftest flight possible is desirable, but also a paradise close at hand which is guarded by terrible watchdogs.

The native is always on the alert, for since he can only make out with difficulty the many symbols of the colonial world, he is never sure whether or not he has crossed the frontier. Confronted with a world ruled by the settler, the native is always presumed guilty. But the native's guilt is never a guilt which he accepts; it is rather a kind of curse, a sort of sword of Damocles, for, in his innermost spirit, the native admits no accusation. He is overpowered but not tamed; he is treated as an inferior but he is not convinced of his inferiority. He is patiently waiting until the settler is off his guard to fly at him. The native's muscles are always tensed. You can't say that he is terrorized, or even apprehensive. He is in fact ready at a moment's notice to exchange the role of the

4. See Chapter V: *Colonial war and mental disorders.*

quarry for that of the hunter. The native is an oppressed person whose permanent dream is to become
the persecutor. The symbols of social order—the
police, the bugle calls in the barracks, military
parades and the waving flags—are at one and the
same time inhibitory and stimulating: for they do
not convey the message "Don't dare to budge";
rather, they cry out "Get ready to attack." And, in
fact, if the native had any tendency to fall asleep and
to forget, the settler's hauteur and the settler's anxiety to best the strength of the colonial system would
remind him at every turn that the great showdown
cannot be put off indefinitely. That impulse to take
the settler's place implies a tonicity of muscles the
whole time; and in fact we know that in certain
emotional conditions the presence of an obstacle
accentuates the tendency towards motion.

The settler-native relationship is a mass relationship. The settler pits brute force against the weight
of numbers. He is an exhibitionist. His preoccupation with security makes him remind the native out
loud that there he alone is master. The settler keeps
alive in the native an anger which he deprives of
outlet; the native is trapped in the tight links of the
chains of colonialism. But we have seen that in-
wardly the settler can only achieve a pseudo petrification. The native's muscular tension finds outlet
regularly in bloodthirsty explosions—in tribal warfare, in feuds between sects, and in quarrels between
individuals.

Where individuals are concerned, a positive negation of common sense is evident. While the settler or

the policeman has the right the livelong day to strike
the native, to insult him and to make him crawl to
them, you will see the native reaching for his knife at
the slightest hostile or aggressive glance cast on him
by another native; for the last resort of the native is
to defend his personality *vis-à-vis* his brother. Tribal
feuds only serve to perpetuate old grudges deep
buried in the memory. By throwing himself with all
his force into the *vendetta,* the native tries to persuade himself that colonialism does not exist, that
everything is going on as before, that history continues. Here on the level of communal organizations
we clearly discern the well-known behavior patterns
of avoidance. It is as if plunging into a fraternal
blood-bath allowed them to ignore the obstacle, and
to put off till later the choice, nevertheless inevitable,
which opens up the question of armed resistance to
colonialism. Thus collective autodestruction in a
very concrete form is one of the ways in which the
native's muscular tension is set free. All these patterns of conduct are those of the death reflex when
faced with danger, a suicidal behavior which proves
to the settler (whose existence and domination is by
them all the more justified) that these men are not
reasonable human beings. In the same way the
native manages to bypass the settler. A belief in
fatality removes all blame from the oppressor; the
cause of misfortunes and of poverty is attributed to
God; He is Fate. In this way the individual accepts
the disintegration ordained by God, bows down before the settler and his lot, and by a kind of interior
restabilization acquires a stony calm.

Meanwhile, however, life goes on, and the native will strengthen the inhibitions which contain his aggressiveness by drawing on the terrifying myths which are so frequently found in underdeveloped communities. There are maleficent spirits which intervene every time a step is taken in the wrong direction, leopard-men, serpent-men, six-legged dogs, zombies—a whole series of tiny animals or giants which create around the native a world of prohibitions, of barriers and of inhibitions far more terrifying than the world of the settler. This magical superstructure which permeates native society fulfills certain well-defined functions in the dynamism of the libido. One of the characteristics of underdeveloped societies is in fact that the libido is first and foremost the concern of a group, or of the family. The feature of communities whereby a man who dreams that he has sexual relations with a woman other than his own must confess it in public and pay a fine in kind or in working days to the injured husband or family is fully described by ethnologists. We may note in passing that this proves that the so-called prehistoric societies attach great importance to the unconscious.

The atmosphere of myth and magic frightens me and so takes on an undoubted reality. By terrifying me, it integrates me in the traditions and the history of my district or of my tribe, and at the same time it reassures me, it gives me a status, as it were an identification paper. In underdeveloped countries the occult sphere is a sphere belonging to the community which is entirely under magical jurisdiction. By entangling myself in this inextricable network where actions are repeated with crystalline inevitability, I find the everlasting world which belongs to me, and the perenniality which is thereby affirmed of the world belonging to us. Believe me, the zombies are more terrifying than the settlers; and in consequence the problem is no longer that of keeping oneself right with the colonial world and its barbed wire entanglements, but of considering three times before urinating, spitting or going out into the night.

The supernatural, magical powers reveal themselves as essentially personal; the settler's powers are infinitely shrunken, stamped with their alien origin. We no longer really need to fight against them since what counts is the frightening enemy created by myths. We perceive that all is settled by a permanent confrontation on the phantasmic plane.

It has always happened in the struggle for freedom that such a people, formerly lost in an imaginary maze, a prey to unspeakable terrors yet happy to lose themselves in a dreamlike torment, such a people becomes unhinged, reorganizes itself, and in blood and tears gives birth to very real and immediate action. Feeding the *moudjahidines,*[5] posting sentinels, coming to the help of families which lack the bare necessities, or taking the place of a husband who has been killed or imprisoned: such are the concrete tasks to which the people is called during the struggle for freedom.

In the colonial world, the emotional sensitivity of the native is kept on the surface of his skin like an

5. Highly-trained soldiers who are completely dedicated to the Moslem cause. (Trans.)

open sore which flinches from the caustic agent; and the psyche shrinks back, obliterates itself and finds outlet in muscular demonstrations which have caused certain very wise men to say that the native is a hysterical type. This sensitive emotionalism, watched by invisible keepers who are however in unbroken contact with the core of the personality, will find its fulfillment through eroticism in the driving forces behind the crisis' dissolution.

On another level we see the native's emotional sensibility exhausting itself in dances which are more or less ecstatic. This is why any study of the colonial world should take into consideration the phenomena of the dance and of possession. The native's relaxation takes precisely the form of a muscular orgy in which the most acute aggressivity and the most impelling violence are canalized, transformed and conjured away. The circle of the dance is a permissive circle: it protects and permits. At certain times on certain days, men and women come together at a given place, and there, under the solemn eye of the tribe, fling themselves into a seemingly unorganized pantomime, which is in reality extremely systematic, in which by various means—shakes of the head, bending of the spinal column, throwing of the whole body backwards—may be deciphered as in an open book the huge effort of a community to exorcise itself, to liberate itself, to explain itself. There are no limits—inside the circle. The hillock up which you have toiled as if to be nearer to the moon; the river bank down which you slip as if to show the connection between the dance and ablutions, cleansing and purification—these are sacred places. There are no limits—for in reality your purpose in coming together is to allow the accumulated libido, the hampered aggressivity to dissolve as in a volcanic eruption. Symbolical killings, fantastic rites, imaginary mass murders—all must be brought out. The evil humors are undammed, and flow away with a din as of molten lava.

One step further and you are completely possessed. In fact, these are actually organized *séances* of possession and exorcism; they include vampirism, possession by djinns, by zombies, and by Legba, the famous god of the Voodoo. This disintegrating of the personality, this splitting and dissolution, all this fulfills a primordial function in the organism of the colonial world. When they set out, the men and women were impatient, stamping their feet in a state of nervous excitement; when they return, peace has been restored to the village; it is once more calm and unmoved.

During the struggle for freedom, a marked alienation from these practices is observed. The native's back is to the wall, the knife is at his throat (or, more precisely, the electrode at his genitals): he will have no more call for his fancies. After centuries of unreality, after having wallowed in the most outlandish phantoms, at long last the native, gun in hand, stands face to face with the only forces which contend for his life—the forces of colonialism. And the youth of a colonized country, growing up in an atmosphere of shot and fire, may well make a mock of, and does not hesitate to pour scorn upon the zombies of his ancestors, the horses with two heads, the dead who rise again, and the djinns who rush into your body while you yawn. The native discovers reality and transforms it into the pattern of his customs, into the practice of violence and into his plan for freedom.

We have seen that this same violence, though kept very much on the surface all through the colonial period, yet turns in the void. We have also seen that it is canalized by the emotional outlets of dance and possession by spirits; we have seen how it is exhausted in fratricidal combats. Now the problem is to lay hold of this violence which is changing direction. When formerly it was appeased by myths and exercised its talents in finding fresh ways of committing mass suicide, now new conditions will make possible a completely new line of action.

14. Freudianism Is Not a Basis for a Marxist Psychology

KEITH BROOKS

Introduction

This essay will attempt to deal with some of the issues that have been raised in regard to the relationship between Marxism and Freudianism. The point of view expressed here is that the two are at fundamental odds with each other over the nature of human reality.

Due to the failure of Marxism to deal with those spheres of social life that have come to be the domain of psychology, many on the left have come to look toward Freud to fill in the gap. Thus the influence of Marcuse's interpretation of Freud and Marxism, and the resurgence of interest in Wilhelm Reich's Marxist period. Marcuse and Reich represent the view that Freudianism is capable of being integrated with Marxist social thought, and can serve as the basis of a Marxist psychology given a few adjustments. This essay is not intended as a critique of their efforts to make this synthesis, and due to lack of space, only parenthetical reference will be made to them.

Nor is this an attempt to recapitulate the excellent critiques that have come out of the woman's and gay liberation movements in regard to Freud's sexist formulations on women and homosexuality. It will be taken for granted that Freud's social views on these and other issues were reactionary.

But despite the growing awareness of Freud's sexism, many continue to see this as only a regrettable part to a theory that can otherwise provide many valuable concepts and insights into human behavior. The focus of this essay will be to examine what these other "contributions"—like the unconscious—actually say about human behavior. It will be seen that when placed back into the political contexts in which they function (therapy, family, mental institutions, everyday relations between whites and blacks, men and women, heterosexuals and homosexuals, etc.), the unconscious and other like concepts serve to mystify the *political dimensions* of these contexts. Far from being a "neutral" or "objective" scientific residue that can be extracted from Freud's reactionary social views, it will be seen that they comprise a fundamentally irrationalist anthropology. What is being called into question is the entire world that is both presupposed and set up by terms like the unconscious, transference, paranoia, etc. The world that these terms describe is a misrepresentation with *concrete political implications* for the human situations in which they are employed. By defining psychology as the study of the "psychodynamics" and "mental life" of individuals, as entities separate and outside of the world (which is usually referred to as an "external" factor) Freudianism is fundamentally opposed to a psychology founded upon the Marxist assumption that "Consciousness is from the beginning a social product, and remains so as long as men exist at all."[1]

It is Freud's microview—his theories and concepts as to how human beings "work," and what human beings "are"—that will be examined here. The point about Freudianism is that it is not only a reactionary social philosophy, *but that its so-called "scientific," "value free," "technical" concepts both already contain a social philosophy and are directly related to Freud's views on larger social issues.*

Freudianism as Ideology

The thrust of this essay is directed mainly to a certain group of people—university based student and teacher progressives, radicals, Marxists. But to think that the importance of Freudian psychology is limited to this group would be a mistake. It has become more and more apparent that the role that psychology plays in legitimizing the oppression of this society is by no means minor. Its effects go way

1. K. Marx, "German Ideology" in *Karl Marx, Selected Writings in Sociology and Social Philosophy,* ed. Bottomore and Rubel (New York: McGraw-Hill, 1964), p. 71.

beyond the relatively small number of people who in
one way or another are directly involved in it (and
that number is not so small considering all the
people who are imprisoned in mental institutions and
who are in therapy). One does not have to read
Freud to believe that women are inferior to men,
that men are by nature aggressive and competitive,
that homosexuals are sick, or that changing society
will not solve anything since people are basically the
same and unchangeable. In this sense, psychology
comes *after* the fact that women are oppressed and
subjugated by this society, that men do have to com-
pete in order to succeed under capitalism, or that
homosexuals do not agree with the way in which sex
roles are set up by heterosexuals. But one does need
an interpretation—through the family, schools, TV,
psychology—explaining that these things are so because they are *natural,* and that when people do not
do what is "natural" it is because of some sickness.
In part, then, the role of psychology in regard to the
masses of people is that of a *higher philosophy of
common sense,* where one can find "scientific confirmation" of the everyday beliefs that the other
sense-making institutions of this society provide as a
world view. It is no mistake that Jensen comes up
with a report that confirms that blacks are best
suited for unskilled manual labor as they do not have
the same abstractive capacities as whites demonstrate on IQ tests. Nor is it accidental that a recently
published study by Harlow, reported in the daily
newspapers, shows that female monkeys are more
passive than male monkeys, thus proving once again

that while the boys are out playing ball, the girls are out sitting under a tree. That more and more people are no longer willing to buy this same old bill of goods can be seen in the growing social movements of blacks, women, workers, gay people, political prisoners, who are no longer accepting the official definitions of their realities and the consequences of those definitions.

It is indicative of the extensiveness of the social upheaval in the U.S. that psychology, an important but relatively secondary ideological institution, should come under attack. People look to psychology when the other institutions of the society have failed to present a coherent world view that one can personally appropriate. As Chief Bromden in Kesey's *One Flew over the Cuckoo's Nest* puts it (specifically in reference to the role of mental institutions, but it can also be seen as referring to the failure of the other institutions of society and how psychology is a "repair shop"),

> The ward is a factory for the combine (society). It's for fixing up mistakes made in the neighborhood and in the schools and in the churches, the hospital is.[2]

That psychology itself has come under attack speaks to the general crisis of the ideological superstructure in its failure to generate new myths that could keep people from focusing on the political and economic realities of a capitalism in decline.

2. Ken Kesey, *One Flew over the Cuckoo's Nest* (New York: Viking, 1962).

With the demystification of the "science" of psychology as an ideology, the question arises whether or not there is anything worth salvaging in that ideology. This raises a vast question about the Marxist understanding of ideology, a question permeated with confusion. Part of the task of this essay is to understand the social weight of ideology, whether it be the belief in the unconscious as the source of human action or the belief in original sin as the source of evil in the world. To take a dialectical view of ideology is to see that ideology in its relationship to a real world of social relationships. On this assumption, all ideologies have their social intelligibility. Ideologies are not merely "false ideas" about reality; there must be something in that reality that sustains that belief and makes it credible for that person or class. A fundamental definition of consciousness for Marxism is that it is always in relationship to a world. Marxists must understand the relative truths of people's lives under capitalism.

But to progress from seeing the dialectical relationship between the way in which people make sense out of their lives and the economic base of society to stating a priori that all bourgeois ideologies have something to contribute to Marxism is not dialectics but *eclecticism*. If Marxism has certain consistent assumptions about the relationship of social existence to consciousness, then the assumptions of this relationship embodied in Freudian terms such as the unconscious, transference, or paranoia are simply in contradiction to Marxism. The relationship of any specific bourgeois ideology to Marxism necessarily depends on the concrete instance.

To say that upon examination Freudianism—technical terms, theory, social philosophy, etc.—has nothing to offer in the working out of a Marxist psychology is not to say that all bourgeois theories are useless. With some bourgeois theorists (*i.e.,* Hegel) the concepts do point beyond the context of the theory. This is true of that group that might loosely be described as the "antipsychiatrists" (*i.e.,* Laing, Cooper, Szasz, Goffman, Scheff). None of them have explicitly set out to develop a Marxist psychology, but they have provided a critique of contemporary psychology which can be part of a basis for developing a Marxist psychology.

While Marxism has certain basic assumptions about the world, it is not supposed that Marxism is a closed final set of truths. There are real gaps in Marxist social thought, perhaps most particularly in regard to psychology. For instance, what is being posed to Freudianism in this essay is not behaviorism, for that too is part of the problem (and also another essay). What is being attempted is to apply certain basic Marxist assumptions to those areas of social life that have come to be considered the province of the "science" of psychology, which is as much a further development of Marxism as it is a critique of psychology. One of the arguments of some Freudian Marxists is that Marxism as a macroview lacks a theory of individuals, or a microdimension. The macroview of Marxism will thus be integrated with Freudianism, a theory of psychodynamics whose social philosophy can be discarded as extraneous. But in further developing a Marxist view of individuals seen as the nexus of their social relations, Freudianism, as a microview that considers the "truth" of human beings to reside outside of their social relations, *does not even understand individuals*. From this point of view, the only contribution Freud made was in providing the basic concepts to be used in the *mystification and obfuscation of people's everyday lives*. *Freudianism is part of the problem*.

The Social Roots of the Freudianism of the Left

An examination of the social roots of "left Freudianism" is also an examination of certain trends in Marxist thought. The following is not intended as a thoroughgoing analysis of the attraction that Freud has had for leftists, but simply represents some observations.

Within the context of the universities in the 1950s and '60s, which is where most Marxist intellectuals have come from, Freud and Freudianism were typically seen as the "human" counterpart to cold sterile behaviorism. Added to this was a certain reputation for having been rejected by the academic psychology establishment for not meeting the criteria of a positivist science (not that Freudian psychologists do not try). Thus Freudianism was posed as the psychology that dealt with those problems that were not "scientific" enough for behaviorism to study—like love, hate, fear, anxiety, etc. It supposedly restored to the individual that "depth" which behaviorism took away. One was either Freudian-oriented or behaviorist-oriented. And few courses or books would point out that in restoring this depth to the individual (by way of the unconscious as the key factor in understanding human motivation), Freudianism obliterated the conscious human subject by reducing her or him to a metaphysical passivity at the sway of the forces of the mind. On this point, Freudianism coincided with behaviorism, rather than contradicted it. One had a choice of mechanical determinisms without any conception of an active subject. The real determinants of human life were not to be found in one's relationship to the world and other people, but either in the mechanics of the mind or, in the case of behaviorism, in some transcendent absolute objective laws.

The psychic determinism of Freud was seen as supporting the mechanical determinism of a vulgarized Marxism, a view that led to seeing people as totally acted upon objects. For these Marxists revolution would be the result of the objective unfolding of the laws of history, rather than the result of conscious human praxis within the context of historical realities and conditions. On a "psychological" level, this absence of a subject led to the ignoring of the very real way in which people fight back against the oppression in their lives, albeit on a spontaneous, unarticulated level—the very ground from which Marxist revolutionaries should work to bring these responses to a higher level. Both views, the Freudian subjectless determinism and vulgar Marxism, lead toward a view of people in their weakness and impotence, rather than in their anger and strength.

One of the key questions throughout the history of Marxism has been how to develop a materialism that does not reduce people to pure objects, but that understands how it is that people do make history, although under conditions they have not chosen.

Along with the view of Freudianism as a "subjective" psychology (which led some confusedly to Freud in search of the "subjective factor" that seemed to be missing from Marxism) was the other side of its "depth." In contrast to empiricist, positivist behaviorism, which takes things as they "appear," Freudianism sees all human reality as "mere appearance" in relationship to the true psychic reality, the unconscious. What Freudianism granted with one hand it took away with the other. Love? A mere reaction formation to deal with unacceptable hostility. Hate? A mere reaction formation to cover up one's unacceptable desires. There is clearly a close relationship between this view of human beings as not knowing at all what they are about and the brand of Marxism that sees all human realities under capitalism through arrogant onesided views of "false needs" and "false consciousness."

For someone like Marcuse, the synthesis of Marx and Freud can be seen as a justification or apology for the validity of socialism during a time when, from the point of view of his own analysis, the contradictions of capitalism were not to be found in everyday life. Marcuse uses the Freudian model as the repository of these contradictions, with the hope for revolution residing in the instinctual structure of the individual. If capitalism were bad, and nobody seemed to notice except Marcuse, then the world of libido, pleasure principle, and the unconscious would vindicate him. Unable to see the contradictions in everyday life during the '50s, as evidenced through despair, cynicism, alcoholism, the turn to psychoanalysis, and "juvenile delinquency," Marcuse turned to Freudianism to bail out his reified Marxism.[3]

With the growth of the student protest movements in the '60s (civil rights, Vietnam, student power) and the lack of a clear class position of the protestors, some people came to have a stake in seeing people as mentally ill or sick so that they could attest to both the cause and the effects of an oppressive (sick) society. Freudian psychology provided a language of psychopathology and mental illness that placed the source of irrationality in individuals. The moralism accompanying the lack of a class or social analysis of the student left during these years caused many leftists to denounce, through the covertly moralistic language of Freudianism, people in positions less privileged than those of students. But the problem is not that people are sick (irrational) and society is not, nor that both are, nor that capitalism "causes" mental illness, but that the entire concept of *oppression as an illness* fundamentally obscures an understanding of the impossible lives people are forced into in this society.

It should also be mentioned that many Freudian Marxists or leftists are also therapists; to question

3. On this point, see also Piccone and Delfini, "Marcuse's Heideggerian Marxism," *Telos* 6 (Fall 1970): 44–45.

Freudianism might be to question one of the chief
sources of income and social status of these
"Marxists."

A fundamental tenet of Freudianism is that anyone who questions its validity is either sick or acting
out of unconscious motives. Any disagreement with
a part of Freudian theory must be immediately balanced by paying homage to the brilliance of the rest
of the theory—lest one be deemed irrational. (An
interesting comment about R. D. Laing's work was
that he was simply saying about psychology what
"crazy" people had been saying all the time.) For
someone who has learned to make sense out of their
lives through Freudianism, rejecting it is akin to the
process of change one goes through from seeing oneself as the source of one's problems to seeing one's
problems in their relation to an oppressive reality.

There was also the total lack (referred to above)
of any Marxist psychology. One got either the crude
materialism associated with Soviet psychology, or
Freud. Because of the hegemony by both, many
basic theoretical questions on the relationship between Marxism and psychology were never raised—
these were not issues for either. Issues such as the
myth of mental illness, positivism, the definition of
psychology as a "science," reductionism, the meaning of Marxist materialism as applied to everyday
life and social relationships, etc., were picked up
more by progressives within the field of psychology
than by Marxists.

It should be mentioned that around the early '60s,
a group representing themselves as a "third force"

posed itself as an alternative to cold, sterile behaviorism and pessimistic, pathological Freudianism. If Freudianism held that the individual was totally under the control of "inner determinisms" such as the unconscious, that the best one could do was learn to be unhappy in a world of misery, then the humanistic existentialists said there could be ecstasy, total freedom, and creativity—precisely because the world did not count if one learned well enough to cultivate "inner strength" and "inner freedom." Despite its classically idealist slave ideology, humanistic psychology attracted many people by showing that Freudianism was just as dehumanizing and degrading as behaviorism. By emphasizing the supposedly free, active, and creative human being, it appeared as a real alternative to the total determinism of behaviorism and Freudianism. With the continued absence of a Marxist psychology[4] that could provide a view of the ongoing synthesis of determination and praxis that is human reality, this "active side was developed abstractly by idealism, which of course does not know real sense activity as such."[5]

None of the three—behaviorism, Freudianism, or humanism—took the question of the social order as crucial to its subject matter; one accepts it blindly, the other says it is only a projection of a more real world of inner psychic conflicts, and humanism takes

4. Or the ignoring of the few like Sartre who were trying to deal with the problem. See *Search for a Method*.
5. Marx, "Theses on Feuerbach," in Bottomore and Rubel, *Karl Marx,* p. 67.

you away from it on weekends. However, at about the same time as the humanists, the "antipsychiatrists" and sociologists of mental illness emerged. Despite their differences, they all held certain key assumptions: that what is referred to as mental illness is unequivocally a social myth that labels human problems as the result of an illness in order to obscure the real issues; that these issues and problems cannot be understood without understanding the social context and circumstances of the individual who lives them; that "psychiatric" problems are in the world and not in the mind (if mind is to be understood, as it is by psychology, as a place outside of what is meant by "world"); and that psychiatry and psychology have by and large played a basically oppressive role of social control. The radicalism of these people more or less ends on these crucial but relatively abstract points. Szasz is basically a moralist, Goffman an academic sociologist, and Laing is moving toward mysticism. But they have indicated how to give meaning to a Marxist materialism applied to everyday life—not as the "effect of matter on the brain," but as the *relationship of social context to human consciousness.*

The Practical Implications of Theory

The question whether human thinking can pretend to objective truth is not a theoretical but a practical question. Man must prove the truth, *i.e.,* the reality and power, the "this-sidedness" of his thinking in practice. The dispute over the reality or nonreality of thinking that is isolated from practice is a purely scholastic question.[6]

The primary question of a Marxist approach to theory is what that theory implies for social practice. All theories and concepts, whether bourgeois or revolutionary, have implications for practice. The fact that the bourgeois social sciences pretend to be "neutral" with regard to the reality they are "merely describing" only means that they offer a deceptive theory in the service of a deceptive practice. There are basically two stances one may take in refuting bourgeois theory. One may accept the terms and assumptions of the way the theory sets up the problem (*e.g.,* the bourgeois academic debates in regard to Jensen's findings on the role of heredity in IQ scores of blacks) and attempt to refute these empirically.[7] Or, one may pose as one's criteria the consistency or comprehensiveness of the theory as ends in themselves (for instance in the critique of the concept of the unconscious such as Sartre's, which demonstrates its own conceptual confusion and inconsistency).[8] While the original intention of this essay was to examine some of these critiques in regard to the existence or nonexistence of the unconscious, libido, Oedipal complex, etc., due to limitations of space, Freud's "scientific constructs" will be viewed in the context of their *implications for human*

6. Ibid.
7. See R. Bickley, "Race, Class and the IQ Controversy," *Radical Therapist,* vol. 2, no. 5.
8. J.-P. Sartre, *Being and Nothingness* (New York: Washington Square Press, 1966), pp. 56–66.

practice. What the criteria of empirical verification fail to admit is that its results are already contained in its structuring of reality. Thus, a theory that starts from an assumption that blacks are inferior usually "finds" data to support itself. Comprehensiveness or consistency are also false criteria—for instance, both astrology and religion are comprehensive and consistent, yet they are rejected as "unscientific."

The key point about the unconscious and other Freudian concepts is that rather than uncovering human social reality, they are a way of *obscuring* the issues of everyday life. By locating the source of human praxis in the unconscious of the Freudian-defined personality structure, Freudianism turns attention away from an examination of that behavior in terms of the process and praxis of human situations.

The Subject Matter of Marxist Psychology

One of the main assumptions that unites all bourgeois psychologies is the taking of the "individual" as both the *unit of study* and as the *unit of meaning.* Whether it is the mind, mental processes, or behavior that are defined as the subject of the science of psychology, the problem is situated in the individual, defined in his or her isolation. The solitary individual is defined not only as the unit of study, but also as the unit of meaning to the extent that attempts are made to eliminate the "variable" of the "environment" (of which the psychologist is a part) in order to get to the "real" truth of the individual. Thomas Scheff comments on this theme:

Genetic, biochemical, and psychological investigations seek different causal agents, but utilize similar models: dynamic systems that are located within the individual . . . social processes tend to be relegated to a subsidiary role . . . the basic model upon which psychoanalysis is constructed is the disease model, in that it portrays neurotic behavior as unfolding relentlessly out of a defective psychological system that is entirely contained within the body.[9]

Marxism from the start takes this conception to be part of the problem. The "psyche" or "mental life" of Freudianism are defined as things-in-themselves, and can only mechanically add on to the initial definition. The social is not something to be found outside of the individual; *the individual is a social being.* If people can only be found in situations, in relationships, if the isolated solitary monad exists nowhere but in the assumptions (and practice drawn from these assumptions) of psychology, then to treat the situation, the life setting that people are in, as either secondary, unimportant, peripheral, after the fact, or derived, is precisely to mutilate the nexus from which the intelligibility of all behavior comes. It is obvious and logical, given the premise that the world is an externality or is peripheral, that psychology should have to create a new context through which to understand behavior. That context becomes the mind, the unconscious, the inner world. One of the traditional dualisms that Marxism has to overcome is that of the "inner" and "outer" worlds, with

9. T. Scheff, *Being Mentally Ill* (Chicago: Aldine Publishing Company, 1966), p. 9.

Freudianism defined as the study of the inner world.
A Marxist psychology has to challenge the entire set
of problems upon which Freudianism is based, with
its dualisms of internal and external, mind and body,
individual and society. It is precisely *human praxis*
—behavior, but understood in a radically different
way than in traditional behaviorism—that can overcome these dichotomies and dualisms. As Merleau-
Ponty has put it:

> Classical psychology unquestioningly accepted the
> distinction between inner observation, or intro-
> spection, and outer observation. "Psychic facts"—
> anger or fear, for example—could be directly
> known only from the inside and by the person
> experiencing them. It was thought to be self-evi-
> dent that I can grasp only the corporal signs of
> anger or fear from the outside and that I have to
> resort to the anger or fear I know in myself
> through introspection in order to interpret these
> signs. . . . Young children understand gestures
> and facial expressions long before they can re-
> produce them on their own; the meaning must,
> so to speak, adhere to the behavior. We must re-
> ject that prejudice which makes "inner realities"
> out of love, hate, or anger, leaving them accessi-
> ble to one single witness: the person who feels
> them. *Anger, shame, hate, and love are not
> psychic facts hidden at the bottom of another's
> consciousness: they are types of behavior or styles
> of conduct which are visible from the outside.*
> They exist on this face or in these gestures, not
> *hidden behind them. . . . Emotion is not a
> psychic internal fact but rather a variation in our
> relations with others and the world which is ex-*

pressed in our bodily attitude . . .[10] (*emphasis added*).

What is needed then is a definition of the individual as a social being, as a "being-in-the-world." The individual does not "receive" her or his social nature from a world conceived as something separate and outside. Nor is it a matter of "dialectically relating" the individual and the world if the individual is still conceived of as a monad. The redefinition of the individual as a social being is part of what is meant by *"world":*

> The human subject, the body subject is simply mutual compenetration with a real world. No matter how profoundly we penetrate into the subject, we always find the world. . . .[11]

One of the tasks of a Marxist critique of Freudianism, then, is to *put back into the world what has been placed in the psychic structure of the individual.* That this is more than an academic matter can be seen in the growing politicization of oppressed and exploited people at all levels of this society. Part of that growing awareness has been in the understanding that this "misplacement" of problems—in the individual or in the social structure that individuals are forced to endure and suffer under—has served a quite definite political purpose.

10. M. Merleau-Ponty, "The Film and the New Psychology," in *Merleau-Ponty Sense and Non-Sense,* trans. H. Dreyfus and P. Dreyfus (Evanston, Ill.: Northwestern University Press, 1964), pp. 52–53.
11. R. Kwant, "Merleau-Ponty and Phenomenology," in *Phenomenology,* ed. J. Kockelmans (New York: Doubleday-Anchor, 1967), p. 387.

The Structures and Functioning
of the Freudian Mind

> He (the analyst) directs his attention equally and
> objectively to the unconscious elements in all
> three institutions . . . when he sets about his
> work of enlightenment he takes his stand equi-
> distant from the id, the ego, and the superego.[12]

In atomizing and depersonalizing the person,
Freudianism depicts human behavior as the manifestation of the play of forces of the unconscious and
id, ego, superego, rather than as a meaningful act revealing a world. The only subject to be found in
Freudian psychology is the Freudian psychologist.
Even the conflicts that are depicted intrapsychically
are ultimately reducible to conflicting quantities of
excitation. As Helen Merrell Lynd shows, in an excellent critique of the basic conceptions of bourgeois
psychology and Freudianism in particular, Freud's
entire conception of personality is founded upon the
assumptions of 19th-century physics and economics.
The wage-fund theory of bourgeois economics (that
Marx criticizes in *Value, Price and Profit*) is taken
over for Freud's theory of libido:

> The basic analogy of Freud's theory of personality
> is a quantitative analogy of economic distribution
> . . . in its classical model, the economics is an
> economics of scarcity. Freud constantly makes
> use of such terms as the economy of the person-
> ality and the quantity of energy that can be dis-

12. A. Freud, *The Ego and the Mechanisms of Defense*
(New York: International Universities Press, 1946), p. 30.

tributed. Basic to his thinking is a libido-fund theory analogous to the wage-fund theory. There is a limited amount of money, or of psychic energy to be distributed; it can be redistributed and obstacles to its maximum or optimum distribution can be removed, but it cannot be enhanced or enriched.[13]

It is often not realized how explicitly Freud looked to capitalism to help describe "mental life." For instance, there is Freud in *The Interpretation of Dreams* talking about the relationship of daytime life to dreams:

A daytime thought may very well play the part of entrepreneur for a dream; but the entrepreneur who, as people say, has the idea and the initiative to carry it out, can do nothing without capital; he needs a capitalist who can afford the outlay and the capitalist who provides the psychical outlay for the dream is invariably and indisputably, whatever may be the thoughts of the previous day, a wish from the unconscious.[14]

It is interesting to see how Freud took over the concepts of a historical economic system to explain and describe the functioning of an ahistorical psyche.

But Freud's positivist, mechanistic conception of the subject matter of psychology—which is amply documented by Lynd and numerous others,[15] is

13. H. M. Lynd, *On Shame and the Search for Identity* (Science Editions, 1958), p. 84.
14. S. Freud, *The Interpretation of Dreams* (New York: Avon, 1965), p. 600.
15. Lynd, *On Shame.* See also Sartre, *Being and Nothingness;* "Interview with Sartre," *New Left Review* 68 (November–December 1969): 43–50; R. S. Peters, *Concept of Mo-*

more than just bad theory. Its reduction of human problems, conflicts, confusions, and such to a mechanical maldistribution of psychic energy has provided the ideology for a social practice that has served to legitimize the social order by taking that social order for granted.

The Unconscious

> The unconscious is the true psychical reality; *in its inner nature is is just as unknown to us as is the reality of the outer world, and it is just as imperfectly communicated to us by the data of consciousness as is the outer world through the information reaching us from our sense organs*[16] (*emphasis in original*).

As Freud depicts it, the relationship of the person to both the unconscious and the "outer world" is one of a radical separation of subject and object. Both are essentially unknowable in their essence. The unconscious as the context of behavior acts without the knowledge, choice, or decision of the person, leaving the subject in a necessarily passive relationship to his or her own life. Both Freudianism and behaviorism share this definition of the human subject, and it renders their starting points insufficient for a Marxist psychology. It also makes it paradoxical that some Freudian Marxists should look to Freud for the subject that Marxism supposedly does not contain (unless, of course, one is content with an unconscious

---

tivation (London: Routledge & Kegan Paul, 1958), pp. 52–94.

16. Freud, *The Interpretation of Dreams*, p. 651.

subject). On the other hand, in a Marxist psychology, the subject must not be defined primarily as a knowing subject; rather knowing must be seen as a moment of doing, or practice.[17]

The unconscious is also an implicit restatement of Freud's explicit views on the question of whether people can achieve control over their lives. For instance, in *Civilization and Its Discontents* (in which can be found the epitome of the cynical realism that Marcuse celebrates in Freud, in opposition to the optimistic neo-Freudians), Freud makes clear his views on the struggles for liberation still going on today. At one point, Freud explicitly says that the abolition of private property, sexual inequality, and the family would in effect make no real difference in the lives of human beings since the human nature that Freud so "objectively" described in the book would still remain.[18]

Much of the point of Freud's work, and of Freudianism in general, can be seen within the context of demonstrating just how little control people have over their everyday lives.[19] But if human relations on an everyday level *are* carried out, as with history, behind the backs of individuals, this is neither an ahistorical necessity based upon human

17. Further on this point, see H. Lefebvre, *The Sociology of Marx* (New York: Vintage, 1969), pp. 30–31; Mao Tsetung, *On Practice* (Foreign Languages Press), *Selected Works,* 1: 297.

18. S. Freud, *Civilization and Its Discontents* (New York: Norton, 1961), pp. 59–61.

19. See for instance Freud's essay "One of the Difficulties of Psychoanalysis."

nature, nor is it due to the characteristics of the psyche as described by Freud.

For Marxism, this alienation arises from the social relations of capitalist society, which are organized in such a way that people neither have control over the product of their labor, nor over the institutions which are part of the reproduction of that society on an everyday level (for instance, the family and schools). If history is made behind the backs of the people under capitalism, that is due to the exigencies of capitalist production and the exigencies of the modes of social life that are mediately related to the social relation of production. Given the context of male dominance and its economic and social implications, the institution of marriage is not just some trick that women are fooled into. Even for women with a high degree of political consciousness, it would seem to be a hard institution to avoid, particularly in the absence of any real alternatives. Alienated institutions have to be overcome in the world, not only in the mind.

The separation of people's conscious intentions from actual results achieved, which is often pointed to as indicating the presence of unconscious motives, is due under capitalism to a *lack of power over social reality,* not to the irrepressible force of the unconscious. For Marxists, this is obvious when the example is that of a worker who is forced to increase productivity, thereby creating more commodities and glutting the market, with the final result of unemployment—a situation the worker had no intention of creating, let alone had any control over. In one sense the struggle for socialism is people making history for themselves, taking cognizance and control over their own life activities in order to establish a position to collectively size up consequences, to make more direct the relationship between human intentions and results. But the conscious praxis that achieves this is not developed through some therapy, nor is it due to the unconscious becoming conscious. Rather it is through a process of political education and struggle, whereby the "lacking" of the previous consciousness is not seen as rooted in the individual, but rather in the way that the person or class's position in society has been misrepresented to him by the institutions of that society. For the Marxist, the unconscious is nothing more than the fact that people have not come to see the meaning of their lives in society as the Marxist has; it should be remembered that the Marxist came to a class analysis and position through a process of struggle and education in the real world with other people.

People are born into certain social structures, and one aspect of these structures is how they present themselves as legitimate, rational, or natural. People live roles within that structure—as worker, as black, as woman, as child—*without being given the means to understand and know the full meanings of their actions within these roles.* This speaks not to an intrapsychic unconscious, but to a situation in which the original exploitation and oppression of these roles is doubled because its meaning is obscured for those who live them. People come to see their unhappiness and problems as everything but what they are. Freudianism tells a woman who is unhappy in her marriage that it is the result of unresolved unconscious feelings toward her father, outside of the world of real social relations. People do not have to be told by Marxists that they have problems—they know that. Marxism is a way of defining what the problem is and what has to be done about it.

The concept of the unconscious places the source of the problem outside the world. It denies that the world is the context of behavior, particularly when there does not seem to be any "obvious" reason for the behavior. But why should the lack of obviousness generate a concept that leads further away from that nonunderstood world?

Marxists have had a much harder time, though, in understanding that the mystification of social relationships under capitalism takes place at *all levels of social reality,* and not simply at the level of the fetishism of commodities. The opaqueness of human behavior that Freudianism ascribes to the unconscious can usually be seen as a function of two things—one's distance from that person's world, and the fact that people are often caught up in opaque, mystified situations, *whose opaque structure is an objective social reality,* and not the distortion of a diseased mind.

No one has described this mystified nature of reality as concretely as Laing and Esterson have done in *Sanity, Madness and the Family.*[20] Through the case histories of eleven women, they demonstrate

20. R. D. Laing and A. Esterson, *Sanity, Madness and the Family* (New York: Basic Books, 1964).

how the seemingly crazy, socially nonsensical behavior of women officially certified as psychotic, in fact constituted quite intelligible responses to a highly mystified family reality. They deal with people who have been labeled mentally ill, who have been publicly labeled as people who do not have "reasons," "purposes," "motives," when in fact these people came from situations in which to have intentions or reasons was to be destroyed. The invalidation that has systematically taken place in the families of these women has been further cemented by the higher articulation of the praxis and process of the families—the psychiatric institution and establishment. The function of this social act of invalidation is to *absent the social order*—here the power structure of the family—*in order to maintain it as legitimate*. Rather than exploring the basis in reality for a woman to make a half-attack on her mother with a knife, the action is seen as an id-process, an id-eruption; it is an "aggressive outburst."

One analysis leaves social reality intact: here the family by looking into the unconscious for the motivation—there is an *outside agitator* at work. The other analysis looks further *into reality* (and that must be further than Laing and Esterson go) to ask questions about the nature of the family, the role of father-husband, mother-wife, child-daughter, and the relationship of that family to its context of capitalist division of labor, sexist role structures, etc. Human behavior takes on intelligibility when placed back into the social context that Freudianism rips it out of. The unconscious comes to be seen as *in the*

*theory of the Freudian, with its rigorous ignor-ance
of the world* as the ground of human action. As can
be seen throughout the book, the Freudian terms for
supposedly understanding what is going on—the unconscious, paranoia, and so forth—are all part of
the problem.

To say that the lives of these people can be understood without resort to Freudian mythology, and
that this mythology is part of the very process of
mystification that these women have been the victims
of, is *not* to pose the social relations which they are a
part of as transparent to the actors within the setting.
It is not a matter of eclectically adding the two contexts together—the unconscious and social reality—
but of understanding that it is *the reality itself that is
mystified and opaque.* The women act on the basis
of *what they see and know,* in a situation such that
they themselves come to mistrust what they are
seeing. The mystification that is a characteristic of
the reality and not of the person's perception of it,
expresses itself in the confusion and disorientation of
these women. *They are in confusing and disorienting
situations,* and their behavior is an attempt to make
sense out of what is going on and what other people
are doing. As with the "false consciousness" and
"false interests," ascribed sometimes onesidedly by
Marxism to the behavior of individuals in spheres of
capitalist social life such as production and con-
sumption, the consciousness and behavior of the
people described in *Sanity, Madness and the Family*
are based upon a "false" reality. The tendency of
Marxists to see the lived realities of people under

capitalism as a "mere appearance" is discussed by Norman Geras in an article entitled *Fetishism in Marx's Capital:*

> If then the social agents experience capitalist society as something other than it really is, this is fundamentally because capitalist society *presents itself* as something other than it really is. As Maurice Godelier has put it: It is not the subject who deceives himself, but *reality* which deceives *him*.[21]

In the context of the family, the unconscious as used by Freudianism parallels on another level a Marxism that sees only false consciousness and that arrogantly dismisses people's perceptions of the realities surrounding them as "mere appearances" in no relation to the "real" world of the Marxist. It is obviously not a matter of giving total autonomy to the person's own view of his situation, but of understanding the *social basis and reality* of ideology. As Merleau-Ponty puts it,

> The bourgeois ideologies which contaminate all of bourgeois society including its proletariat, are not appearances; they mystify bourgeois society and present themselves to it in the guise of a stable world. They are exactly as "real" as the structures of capitalist economy, with which they form a single system. Both these ideologies and this economy are appearances with respect to socialist economy and life, which are already taking shape within them; but until these latter have been realized the bourgeois forms of production and life

21. *New Left Review*, no. 65, p. 79.

retain their weight, their effectiveness, and their reality.[22]

On another level, the unconscious is a way of obscuring the dialectic between how one sees the meaning of one's behavior and how others see it. In therapy, the unconscious of the patient can be seen in the theory of the analyst as to how the person *should* be seeing reality. For instance, putting the problem of "resistance" in therapy back into the social world, it can be seen not as the unconscious resisting of "probes" of the analyst, but as a *refusal* to accede to the definition of the situation provided by the analyst. "Overcoming the resistance" means that the person has taken over the view of the analyst—not that the "truth" of the unconscious has been made conscious. In both the therapeutic situation and in everyday life, *the unconscious is used to obscure the power relations between people by locating the dynamics and issues of intersubjective life inside of the individual.* The obscuring of the politics of therapy by the unconscious is made clear in the following quote:

> The analyst's one-up position becomes especially obvious whenever the concept of the unconscious is invoked. If the patient rejects an interpretation the analyst can always explain that he is pointing to something that the patient must by definition be unaware of, because it is unconscious. If, on the other hand, the patient tries to claim unconsciousness for something, the analyst can reject

22. Merleau-Ponty, "Marxism and Philosophy," in Dreyfus and Dreyfus, *Merleau-Ponty,* p. 132; see also Lefebvre, *Sociology of Marx* on this point.

this by saying that if it were unconscious the patient could not refer to it.[23]

It would be a mistake to assume, however, that one can separate the unconscious as a concept from the unconscious as a strategy for depoliticizing human relations. There is no "pure" theory of concept that is used to describe or explain human behavior; all theory is practical:

> Social Life is essentially practical. All mysteries which mislead theory into mysticism find their rational solution in human practice and in the understanding of this practice.[24]

The unconscious, then, is one of those mysticisms that lead astray, with a quite definite political end for the situations in which they are employed. A Marxist psychology solves the "mysteries" of human behavior by understanding human practice in its setting—social life.

Paranoia

It would be interesting to go over the case histories of Freud and others and try to retrace the social base of "symptoms." This might be difficult, as the social context is generally mentioned only to discredit it. There is Freud's essay on paranoia, for instance, in which he describes the case of a patient who was diagnosed as suffering from persecutory delusions in reference to his psychiatrist, among

23. Watzlawick, Beavin, and Jackson, *Pragmatics of Human Communication* (New York: Norton, 1967), p. 245.
24. Marx, "Thesis on Feuerbach."

others. While it might never be known what realities his other "symptoms" spoke to, Freud tells us in a comment that seems almost comical in light of the present growing understanding of the oppressive role that psychiatry plays that

> We should be glad to know to what conditions the relatively favorable issue of the present case is due; *for if we cannot willingly attribute the whole responsibility for the outcome to anything so casual as the "improvement due to change in residence" which set in after the patient's removal* from Prof. Fleischig's sanitorium[25] (*emphasis added*).

It would of course be too trivial or obvious if the issue involved here were what it seems to be. Freud's cynical realism turns out to be nothing more than *liberal optimism,* a view that reality is neutral or benign. This myth runs as a guiding assumption throughout Freudianism, whether it be paranoia, "defense mechanisms," or whatever.

The question of paranoia brings up a number of issues that are related to the task of understanding the social intelligibility of behavior. For instance, metaphor is an everyday part of speech, but in the views and assumptions of Freudianism, metaphors take on literal interpretations. When a person says "they're after me," the Freudian looks out the door, sees no one there, and assumes paranoia. (Similarly, a person who says he is dead must be suffering from

25. S. Freud, "On the Mechanism of Paranoia" in *Freud, General Psychological Theory* (New York: Collier, 1963), p. 47.

a delusion, because his heart is still beating.) Rather than trying to understand the meaning of the statements in reference to people's lives, the psychiatric understanding duplicates what was often the original situation of mystification, by locating the problem in the mind or by labeling it a mental illness. There is more to this problem than simply understanding that people have personal languages to describe their worlds. For instance, even Laing, who has contributed so much to understanding the social intelligibility of "psychotic" behavior, fails to understand that metaphor too unveils a social situation and political order. He says, for example, in his early work, *The Divided Self*:

> Julie in her psychosis called herself Mrs. Taylor. What does this mean? It means "I'm tailor made," "I'm a tailored maid; I was made, fed, clothed and tailored." Such statements are psychotic not because they may not be true but because they are cryptic; they are often impossible to fathom without the patient decoding them for us.[26]

This view expressed here is not so different from that of other psychiatrists who acknowledge that paranoids see the truth but in order to co-opt it; the real criteria being how they say the truth they are seeing. Julie is psychotic because she is cryptic; she is cryptic because she is psychotic. But in the same work, a few pages before, Laing himself gives an understanding of crypticity in terms of the situa-

26. R. D. Laing, *The Divided Self* (New York: Pantheon, 1970), p. 192.

tion.[27] There are real reasons why people have to disguise what they are saying when in a situation in which to comment directly on oppression is to incur further oppression for commenting on it. Not to see cryptic language as socially intelligible is to miss a further political structure of the situation—people who use this language are not allowed to be direct. Free speech in bourgeois society supposedly means the right to comment on one's oppression, as long as one does not move to change it. Part of the problem of people in the situations and families that Laing describes is that they do not even have basic bourgeois democratic rights. Oppressed people have long known and used this way of surviving while having to live in realities dominated by the rules of the oppressor. Cryptic language can be a way of commenting on one's circumscribed position while under that circumscription.

Another aspect of metaphor that Laing illustrates in *Sanity, Madness and the Family* is that what is at one time and place metaphorical comes to be everyday language in another. One of the woman's "paranoid delusions" was the belief that her parents were not her real parents, but were really business partners.[28] That this has come to be seen as roughly expressing one aspect of the reality of marriage in this society is due not to a massive cure of neuroses, but is the result of the political education carried on through the women's liberation movement (*i.e.*, marriage is a deal between unequal partners).

27. Laing, *Divided Self*, pp. 163–165.
28. Laing and Esterson, *Sanity*, p. 63.

To state that there is a social intelligibility to that "psychic process" known as paranoia, is not, on the other hand, to romanticize the perception of everyone who has ever been labeled paranoid. That too would miss the point that the situation in which people sometimes find themselves can be a highly confused one, in which it would be difficult for *anyone* to figure out what is going on. It is not assumed that all "paranoids" are "right"—but that they are socially intelligible, and further that when they are *"wrong,"* that too has social intelligibility.

There also seem to be recurrent metaphors in the language and beliefs of "paranoids." The Freudian view is that this expresses some common psychodynamic of the mentally ill. However, if attention is directed not to the psyche, but rather to the structures and characteristics of these situations, repetitive "symptoms" are seen as referring to repetitive, common *situations,* and not to a common pathology (as Goffman has demonstrated in regard to prisoners in mental institutions, or as Laing has demonstrated in the family).

Paranoia, like other Freudian concepts, has the primary effect of discrediting a person's life situation as the ground for behavior. The political purpose of this is much more obvious when it takes place on a larger level, such as when Bruno Bettleheim labeled people who were protesting the firing of Marlene Dixon from the University of Chicago as paranoids, or when Thomas Foran, who was the chief prosecutor of the Chicago Eight said that all talk about political repression in this country was paranoia(!).

In both instances, it is a clear strategy of dealing with the issues that are raised by saying they do not *really* exist. It would be too much to expect, of course, for Bettleheim to argue that women *should* be discriminated against, or for Foran to argue that political repression *is* a necessary and legitimate way for the government to deal with those who threaten the ruling order.

But what Marxists have by and large failed to see is how this operates on a microlevel like the family. A Marxist psychology must understand that political struggle takes place not only on the level of organized political movements, but also between people in their daily lives. That the ideology (and the power behind the ideology, incarceration) of mental illness is a key weapon in these microstruggles is clearly demonstrated by Laing in *Sanity, Madness and the Family.* While Laing does not make explicit the political context within which the social intelligibility of these women is nullified, he does show the process whereby a person's experience and perception of the world gets invalidated through the ideology of mental illness. One woman felt that her parents were conspiring against her, that they had a secret system of communication between them. Laing, interviewing the family together, found this delusion to be literally true—the mother and father were constantly exchanging nods, gestures, winks, and such like.[29] The patient was correct in her perception, and it was denied by the parents that this was true, as Laing

29. Ibid., p. 24.

found out when he mentioned it to them. The label of paranoid delusion made official the parents' definition of reality. But all this must be seen in its context—that what is being dealt with, and what psychology deals with, are the *political struggles over definitions of reality in everyday life. Sanity, Madness and the Family* documents eleven case histories of *political struggle,* waged between parents and their children, in which the ideology is low, the issues relatively undefined, but in which all revolve around questions of independence, autonomy, and self-definitions. In each case, the meaning of these issues for the women growing up runs counter to the parents' definition of who their children are or what they should be (from saying forbidden things to developing new, unapproved interests, friends, and so on). The women act in ways contrary to the reified definitions prevailing in the social and political order of the family, and the parents act to maintain their control. The ideology of psychopathology enables the struggle to go on without the issues ever being acknowledged. This type of struggle could only go in a society in which children are considered private property, where the sole worth of women as mothers resides in how "well" they can bring up their children (well as defined by that society), and where the family is offered to the man as the place to exercise a control he has nowhere else in society. That a full understanding of these microstruggles can only be achieved by placing them into their larger contexts, is a view that Laing articulates in his essay "The Obvious" (and which unfortunately he has failed to follow up on):

> As we begin from microsituations and work up to macrosituations we find that the apparent irrationality of behavior on a small scale takes on a certain form of intelligibility when one sees it in context. One moves, for example from the apparent irrationality of the single "psychotic" individual to the intelligibility of that irrationality within the context of the family. The irrationality of the family in its turn must be placed within the context of its encompassing networks. These further networks must be seen within the context of yet larger organizations and institutions. These larger contexts do not exist out there on some periphery of social space: they pervade the interstices of all that is comprised by them.[30]

The inconsistency of some Marxists who have not fully integrated their Marxist assumptions about the larger social order with their Freudian assumptions about microsituations can be seen in what is otherwise an excellent summing up of "paranoia" by Kupers, writing in *The Radical Therapist:*

> Interpretations and feedback compiled while examining *transference distortions* of *paranoid individuals* result in understanding as best as possible their experience and *paranoid stance* toward their environment something as follows: I am the center of something that is going on. I do not understand what is going on. Others out there not only understand what is going on but are in control and are the cause of it. They must be in control

30. R. D. Laing, "The Obvious" in *To Free a Generation,* ed. D. Cooper (New York: Collier, 1969), p. 15.

since I cannot control what happens to me. I am powerless. I can only guess what is expected of me and hope to discover it in time to avoid more punishment[31] (*emphasis added*).

Rather than a "paranoid fantasy" or "stance," this is a highly cogent statement describing the *reality* of the situation—that a person is in a situation in which in fact others are doing something to the person, while at the same time covering that action up, and the person labeled paranoid continues to act in reality along the same principles and assumptions that all people do. That is, people act on the basis of what they see and know, and in the case of this situation, *reality* is a fragmented and mystified reality, by the denials and collusions of others. Unfortunately, given Kupers's way of describing this, it is seen as a distortion of reality, that these phenomena do not go on in the world, that reality at this level is neutral. It is precisely this dichotomy between *macro-oppression as real* and *micro-oppression as unreal* that has stood in the way of the development of a psychology based on Marxism, and that has inhibited Marxist analysis of these other orders of social life under capitalism.

Transference

Transference is another of those "scientific" residues that can be rescued from Freudianism. As with

31. T. Kupers, "Radical Therapy Needs Revolutionary Theory," in *The Racial Therapist*. See also Lemert's essay on paranoia in Scheff, *Mental Illness and Social Processes*.

the unconscious and paranoia, the concept is part of
a whole set of assumptions as to the nature of
human social reality, and cannot be separated from
them without changing its meaning beyond recognition. As another key term for the invalidation of
experience, it is not surprising that with all the
modifications and revisions of Freud (*i.e.,* rejection
of death instinct, Oedipus complex, etc.) virtually
none have rejected transference. To do so would be
to relinquish one of the key weapons in the *political
struggle* of psychotherapy.

Basically, the concept of transference refers to the
transferring or projecting of feelings or thoughts onto
the therapist that supposedly have no basis in the
present, but are reflections of one's past relationship
with one's parents—usually, of course, unconscious.
Freud's concept of transference was based upon the
idea that if the patient is encouraged to regress to
earlier attitudes centering around one's parents,
along with the intentional "anonymity" of the therapist, the person will transfer onto the therapist feelings and attitudes which are not based upon anything
real in the situation. The person relates to the therapist not as he "is," but as he is unconsciously
imagined or fantasied to be. The fact that the therapist is "unknown" renders all of the patient's feelings
toward him (love, hate, fear, and so on) unwar-
ranted; hence, such feelings are the result of transference. The transference reaction, or neuroses, then
becomes the focus of attention and attempts are
made to bring "insight" to the patient about the
basis of his or her irrational projections. The cure of
analysis then hinges around a resolution of the trans-

ference, with the person advancing from a "distorted" view of reality based upon infantile wishes, fears, or whatever to a more accurate reading of "reality"—seeing the therapist and oneself as who they "really are."

These of course are precisely the issues that transference nullifies when used to explain some behavior in therapy—who is the therapist, what interests does he represent ("Why the patient's, of course"), who is the patient, what are the patient's interests and problems, who is to define them, what is going on in therapy between the therapist and the patient. This obfuscation of the real issues has been highlighted by the increasing attention focused on therapy as a socialization process reflecting the dominant ideologies of what, for instance, a woman or a homosexual is.[32] What has not been focused on as much is how one of its key concepts, that of transference, plays a role in the process.

What transference does within the context of therapy is to pose two metaphysically distinct beings, one, the therapist who has sole access to truth and who is in relationship with reality (he would not be a therapist if that were not the assumption) and the "patient" whose primary context is the world of the mind, of the past. To suggest that the concept of countertransference does nothing to alter this relationship is to ask the same question about the unconscious as it is used in therapy, cited above. When was the last time a patient was able to use it as the

32. See for instance, Phyllis Chesler, "Marriage and Psychotherapy," in *Radical Therapist* (New York: Ballantine, 1971), pp. 175–180.

therapist does? The therapist is not there to be remolded; that is the role of the "patient." Even if it was admitted, aside from the fact that it would probably be a tactical move, it would mystify *in reverse* the basis in reality the question of what had been going on.

By posing the unconscious past as the context for the patient's behavior, the concept of transference turns attention from any examination of what the therapist is doing to *encourage* certain behavior by the patient. In the same way that Freudian terms were used in the context of the family to ignore the process and praxis of the situation, so they are used in therapy. If the patient feels that the therapist hates him, this is seen as the projection by the patient of expected parental disapproval, rather than a perception of the subtle ways in which people communicate what is ostensibly not to be communicated. Or, if the patient says to the therapist "I hate you," transference again invalidates any reference and base in the reality of the situation for that hate.

On the other hand, as with the question of paranoia, to assume that there is a social intelligibility to behavior is not to assume that the person is always correct in his perception. If a patient says to a therapist "you hate me," and the therapist is quite sure of his feelings, this does not mean that this *difference in perception* is due to transference. Rather it is a matter of understanding that the meaning of human actions is neither given monolithically by the *subject* (the usual view of the analyst in regard to his own behavior) nor by the *other* (the usual view of the analyst toward the behavior of the patient). It means that the truth in interpersonal relationships can be problematic. It is to say that the patient can be *wrong,* can *misinterpret* the meaning of another's behavior, can misread the signs the actor intends to give. But to say that the patient can be wrong or mistaken, or unfair, or not understanding is to say that it is not the past people relate to in therapy, but what is going on between two people. And a key question of this whole analysis is to see how the stated intentions of analysts—that they are there to help—runs counter to the meaning their actions have in the realities of others—that they do not "heal," but oppress. Reducing these conflicts over reality to a process of transference prevents not only seeing how these differences are founded in the present situation, but also how class, race, sex and age are parts of and reflective of those differences— the very issues that are considered *irrelevant* to therapy.

One aspect, then, of seeing therapy as a relationship in the present between two people, each with a different defined and assumed role in that situation, is to see how the structures of therapy fosters the very irrationality that it then assigns to the patient as an inner emanation. For instance, there is the "dependency complex"[33] that arises in therapy. If in fact, a patient develops a dependency on the therapist, is this a socially nonsensical intrapsychic process, or is it due to the way in which the therapist sets up the situation for the person to respond to? The

33. See Fanon, *The So-Called Dependency Complex in Colonized Peoples* in which he demonstrates this psychiatric imperialism specifically applied to the question of racism.

therapist is set up and defined as one who knows how to deal with problems, therapy is widely publicized as the answer for basically white middle class people ("good clinical material") who have problems which they might be inclined to see as arising from their world but which really are all in their minds. The therapist cultivates silence, anonymity, and ambiguity while at the same time *discrediting* the patient's conscious view of himself, and then accuses the patient of being dependent. That the patient *cannot* win (is not supposed to) can be seen by the fact that not developing this dependency is also seen as a problem—resistance to the transference.[34] Dependency is cultivated, disclaimed, and then decried. (This is similar to the phenomena of certain rock stars who, after cultivating their own mystiques, then attack their "fans" for a mystification that originated with the "star.") That the mystification of therapy is breaking down, that people are seeing through this game can be seen in Nadine Miller's letter to her therapist:

> You, by virtue of your title, set yourself up as the source of knowledge. You have something that I want. As a woman, forced to accept the whole male structure, I accept the idea that I have a problem

34. On this entire conception of therapy as a continual process of one-upping and creation of "therapeutic paradoxes," see J. Haley, *Strategies of Psychotherapy* (New York: Grune and Stratton, 1963). Starting from the assumption that "symptoms" are a way for the person to exercise control over others, without any questioning of the objective power relations in the situations he describes, this book provides a view that both demystifies psychotherapy and reaches a new height of cynicism about the situation of people who have come to be labeled mentally ill or neurotic.

rather than realizing that I as a woman am forced
to function in a male supremacist structure and
that I cannot function as a human being when I
am being constantly knocked down, forced to
have meaningless relationships with men because
I am afraid of the consequences if I don't, forced
to submit to a life of educational tracking—and
then told I am sick when I refuse to put up with
any more of the shit. I am tired of being told I
have a basic insecurity, a mother complex, a
father complex. I am tired of thinking of myself
as Crazy—a nice way to make sure I never throw
off the oppression—a way to keep women dependent upon their oppressors.

Men make the definitions of crazy or not crazy,
they then set themselves up as the saviors. They
have the "answer." Of course they don't tell you
(the patient) what they know. How else could
they keep you dependent.[35]

The concept of transference, then, is contrary to a
Marxist view of human social life not only by the
fact that it is used to serve the dominant class, racial,
and sexual order, but that beyond the criticism of
misuse, it reflects an entire theory of the fundamental *irrationality* of human beings.[36]

There is a vulgarized Marxism that shares with
Freudianism that people's behavior is based upon
false ideas with no relation to reality. For the
Freudian, these false ideas are found in the unconscious, in the past. For vulgar Marxism, the false

35. See pp. 484–489 in this collection for entire letter.
36. Another key factor not mentioned here is the mystification of psychology that is a privileged knowledge, known
to a few, who study psychology as the physicist studies
physics.

ideas are those of ideology, as brought to people through the schools, TV, and advertising. It assumes that ideology creates false needs rather than reflecting and exploiting the *real needs* of people living in a "false" reality of capitalism. As does Freudianism, this Marxism assumes that the problem is one of recognizing the falseness of the ideas, of overcoming a brainwashing process. Both views assume that people are irrational, and that the basic context and determinations of behavior are not to be found in the present life situations of people with all its exigencies.[37] Coming from Freudianism, this is no surprise. That it should come from Marxists is indicative of the inconsistency that enables their views to remain undifferentiated from the irrationalism and elitism (which is just the other side at irrationalism) of Freudianism.

To start from the assumption that human practice is fundamentally socially intelligible is to search out the social context for behavior. It is also to declare that mental illness is a social myth, which through the language of Freudianism and psychopathology is used to discredit people in order to preserve specific social orders. At the same time, the myth of mental illness offers reaccreditation to these structures by incorporating the rules and roles of the family, therapist, state, or institution—the very roles and

37. For a more expanded presentation of this point, see the excellent articles by Ellen Willis on "consumerism" and women in Leslie Tanner, ed., *Voices from Women's Liberation* (New York: Signet Books, 1970). See also A Redstocking Sister, "Brainwashing and Women," in *The Radical Therapist;* and Paul Baran, *The Political Economy of Growth* (New York: Monthly Review, 1957), pp. xv–xvii.

rules that were the basis for the behavior that was originally discredited. *Except now they are not presented as roles and rules, but as a medical cure.*

The Social Psychology of Freudianism

Any psychology is, implicitly or explicitly, a theory of how people relate to and operate in society. The criticism that Freud is ahistorical is only partly true, as ahistoricism itself is a theory of what history is. For Freudianism, history is the mere backdrop for the drama of intrapsychic conflicts. Ego against id, reality against pleasure principles, secondary against primary process, consciousness against unconsciousness, and ultimately Eros against Thanatos— the social world is no more than the playing out of these internal dynamics. The world and other people are merely instrumental means to the end of instinctual gratifications. As Maurice Friedman has described it,

> Freud does not see the cathexis as an essential relation with another person, but as *an instinctual relation with oneself* through the other person. It is like a closed circuit in which the other person is the intermediate transmitter, but never really the initiator or receiver[38] (*emphasis added*).

Freud's individualistic concepts are not merely asocial, but define society as only a collection of atomized individuals connected by cathected libidos. That the social bonds tying people to each other should come to be seen as extraneous and in need of

38. M. Friedman, *To Deny Our Nothingness* (New York: Delta, 1967), pp. 193–194.

explanation is itself a historical phenomena, as Marx
demonstrates:

> The further we go back into history, the more
> the individual and therefore the producing indi-
> vidual seems to depend on and constitute a part of
> a larger whole: at first it is quite naturally the
> family and the clan, which is but an enlarged
> family; later on it is the community growing up in
> its different forms out of the clash and amalgama-
> tion of clans. It is but in the eighteenth century, in
> "bourgeois society," that the different forms of
> social union confront the individual as a *mere
> means to his private ends,* as an outward neces-
> sity. But the period in which this view of the
> isolated individual becomes prevalent, is the very
> one in which the interrelations of society . . .
> have reached the highest state of development.
> Man is in the most literal sense of the word a
> zoon politikon, not only a social animal, but an
> animal that can develop into an individual only
> in society[39] (*emphasis added*).

For Freudianism, then, the social is secondary and
is derived from the more basic instinctual biological
nature of human beings. But the very concept of
instinct is a reactionary one; people can be known
only in relationship to other people and the world.
There is no human nature outside of the social relations of people. The question of a human nature
repressed in the interests of civilization is a "purely
scholastic question,"[40] if "the essence of man is not

39. K. Marx, "Introduction to the Critique of Political
Economy," in *Marx and Modern Economics,* ed. D. Horo-
witz (New York: Monthly Review Press, 1968), pp. 22–23.
40. In the sense taken here that the debate over the existence or nonexistence is not the real issue, since human nature cannot be known outside of history; rather the real is-

an abstraction inherent in each particular individual. The real nature of man is the totality of social relations."[41]

It is often an embarrassment for left Freudians, who already have to apologize for Freud's reactionary social philosophy, to discover that not only did Freud place the essence of human beings in an instinctual biological energy system, but that he had resort to "archaic heritages" to explain the Oedipal complex as the foundation of civilization. When Freud cannot find a way to place the context of behavior outside of social relations, he manages to put it outside of history, which amounts to the same thing:

> In studying traumata we often find to our surpirse that they do not keep strictly to what the individual himself has experienced, but deviate from this in a way that would accord much better with their being reactions to genetic events and in general can be explained only through such an influence. The behavior of a neurotic child to his parents when under the influence of an Oedipus and castration complex is very rich in such reactions, which seem unreasonable in the individual and can only be understood phylogenetically. . . . The archaic heritage of mankind includes not only dispositions, but also ideational contents, memory traces of the experiences of former generations. . . . We have bridged the gap between individual and mass psychology and can treat peoples as we do the individual neurotic.[42]

---

sue is what it *means* to say there is a human nature in terms of its social implications.

41. Marx, "Theses on Feuerbach," in Bottomore and Rubel, *Karl Marx,* p. 68.

42. S. Freud, *Moses and Monotheism* (New York: Vintage, 1962), pp. 127–128; see also S. Freud, *Totem and*

Rather than tracing and examining the real power relations in the family and seeing the behavior of children in its social context, Freud's Oedipal complex operates like a thing inside the person. The guilt which is for Freud the foundation and sustenance of society is not even ultimately to be found in that society; it is to be found in an inherited collective mind.

In its inability to start from the fundamentally sociohistorical nature of human beings, Freudianism must take as given

> separate individual human atoms and then poses as a problem how they can be related in society . . . the separateness is assumed; the relationship is to be constructed.[43]

For Marxism, then,

> Society for man is not an accident he suffers but a dimension of his being: He is not in society as an object is in a box; rather he assumes it by what is innermost in him.[44]

It is these splits between society and the individual, the outer and the inner, the public and the private that is at the base of Freudianism. It is a

---

Taboo (New York: Norton, 1950), pp. 157–158. That Marcuse does not shy at all from this can be seen in his essay "Freedom and Freud's Theory of Instincts," in *Five Lectures* (Boston: Beacon Press, 1970), p. 26, and elsewhere where he ascribes the failure of the Russian Revolution to a "Psychic Thermidor."

43. Lynd, *On Shame,* p. 82.

44. Merleau-Ponty, "Marxism and Philosophy," in Dreyfus and Dreyfus, *Merleau-Ponty,* p. 128.

reified theory based on a reified society. These splits are real in the lives of people, but what is neeced is a theory that provides a way for *overcoming* them rather than *mirroring* them. That capitalist society is an obstacle to the lives of people should be seen as a historical problem in need of transformation, not an ontological problem in need of resignation.

It is interesting here to see how Marcuse has approached this problem. Marcuse's conception of the individual winds up closer to a utopian anarchist position than to a Marxist view. Marcuse takes over the concepts of the Freudian defined individual in order to show how capitalism is in conflict with this essence. Part of his argument is that in the era of the totalitarian state, the "private" individual is more and more absorbed by the demands of the society. Starting from the reified fiction of the private individual, Marcuse sees the merging of the private and the public as being bad, their separation good.[45] The "obsolescence of the Freudian concept of man" is just another indication of how bad things have gotten.[46] Starting from the premises of the "free individual" outside of society, there was an "autonomous and identifiable" private psychic being; there were somehow "individual needs and potentialities" outside of society, which have now been taken over by the demands of the dominant oppressive reality. But Marcuse's criticism of society misstates the prob-

45. H. Marcuse, *Eros and Civilization* (New York: Vintage, 1955), p. xvii.
46. Marcuse, "The Obsolescence of the Freudian Concept of Man," in *Five Lectures*.

lem, at least from a Marxist point of view. Marcuse *recapitulates* the splits of Freudianism, with the same splits now couched in Marxist terms. Marcuse's Freudianism is based upon alienated premises, especially in his formulation of the problem of individual and society. Thus, when he says that "the political needs of society become individual needs and aspirations"[47] as if that in itself was the problem, Marcuse misses the point that society will not act or should not act to make its political needs the political needs of individuals who live in it. The real question is what kind of society is it, what are its needs, who defines them, and what is the relationship politically and socially of the individual to the society? Is it a society ruled and defined by a small group of parasites or is that society the collective expression of the needs of the people, the same people who run it?

The residual individualism in Marcuse's thought leads him to imply that socialism is the struggle for the "private" person that never existed in the first place. That Marcuse's socialism is more of an "asocialism" can also be seen in an interview with him entitled "The End of Utopia." When asked a question about the attempt to create the "new person" in the third world, Marcuse was most impressed with the fact that in North Vietnam, a country that could not have defeated U.S. imperialism were it not for the tremendous unity and will of the Vietnamese people,

47. H. Marcuse, *One-Dimensional Man* (Boston: Beacon Press, 1964), p. ix.

they are building park benches that only seat two![48]

Marcuse takes over, then, the bourgeois conception of freedom as existing *outside* of society, whether it is placed in a human nature, or the private individual. The rejection of these premises, the rejection of human nature or the private individual is the other side of the demand *that freedom be established in the real world.*[49]

Conclusion

On the Meaning of Social Intelligibility for a Marxist Psychology

The concept of social intelligibility is obviously not new to Marxism. A class analysis assumes a real operative context for behavior, real interests and assumptions in conflict with other real interests and assumptions. A certain rationality of friend and foe alike is assumed. A Marxist philosophy would not label Nixon or Rockefeller mentally ill or paranoid. This would mean assuming that everything would be all right if people only got their heads straight, that the real problem is in their distorted views of reality. It would presuppose that the real world, devoid of distortion, is a place where all interests coincide.

It is not insanity or repressed wishes that guides Nixon or Rockefeller but their real class interests.

48. Marcuse, "The End of Utopia," in *Five Lectures,* p. 82.

49. See, *e.g., One-Dimensional Man,* p. 10: "The idea of 'inner freedom' has its reality in . . . the private space in which man may become and remain 'himself.'"

There might be other people who can better represent the interests of the ruling class of which they are a part, but that is a question of greater skill or better strategy, not fewer neuroses. If behavior is a function of a behavioral field structured by one's perceived interests and assumptions, it was certainly not insanity to invade Cambodia when the liberation forces of that country threatened the rule of imperialism. It was not some irrational "id eruption" that led Rockefeller in effect to murder forty-three people at Attica, but a decision, from his point of view, on how *best* to deal with the problem. If anything, his decision had the same basis that the Vietnam conflict is meant to have—to show people the consequences if they move for their freedom. Yes, it could have been dealt with differently, but again, this is a question of differences in opinion on how best to maintain "law and order."

Marxism looks to the world for the context of events at this level, then, and not to minds, the unconscious, or mental illness. But when it comes to understanding the actions of people on a different level, a certain Marxism gives up and adopts Freudian assumptions. Marxism holds that ideas do not occur in a vacuum, out of nowhere, but Marxism collapses when, for example, faced with a girl who says her parents are poisoning her, or who hears voices. These ideas do not refer to a social context, but to a "psyche." Rather than further investigating what type of *situation* someone has to be in so that ascribing one's actions to a voice that tells one what to do is a viable attempt to live in that situation, the context of the unconscious replaces that of the social world. Perhaps there are two metaphysics here: some people are in touch with reality, some are not. That is the standard approach. What it takes for granted, usually to someone's benefit, as has been seen, is the question of what *in fact is the reality* for the person so described? Freudianism assumes social intelligibility for one group (the normal, the sane) and social irrationality for another (the sick, the mentally ill). What is needed though is a conception that starts from the assumption of social intelligibility at all levels, micro and macro, and that looks to the world as its context.

It is also not a matter of turning concepts such as paranoia, or unconscious around. These concepts would still serve to mystify the problems and conflicts, albeit in a different direction. For instance, if paranoia is defined as seeing danger in the world where there is none, it has been suggested the creation of a new term "polyanoia" (from pollyanna) to indicate a pathological state where there is danger all around and the person does not see it. While this might have a certain polemical usefulness, it would continue to miss the point, for instance, about who Bettleheim or Foran is, if taken seriously as an explanation of their behavior. It is in their interest to defuse political issues through psychiatric terminology.

It is the task of a Marxist psychology to put back into the world what has been placed in the worldless mind through concepts like the unconscious or paranoia. But these are terms that are designed to describe precisely such a view of human behavior. One of the key reasons why Freudianism cannot be integrated with Marxism is that they have totally contradictory views of social reality. Freudian terminology is the manifold expression and location of that point *outside* of human social relations that controls people. One does not give social content to ahistorical, asocial, individualistic concepts; they already have a social content. Individualism is not just a Marxist curseword; it is a way of conceiving the world that has real implications. What is needed is a theory with a different social content, that starts from different assumptions. Elephants cannot fly, even if you give them wings.

Starting from this point of view, the subject matter of psychology can be defined on one level as the study of the mode of relatedness of this individual social being to his or her situation; more specifically as the study of the way in which people live the oppression and exploitation of capitalist society— how class, race, sex, and age are lived on an everyday level and how people can move against this context so as to change it. With this definition, there is no longer the mechanistic positivist conception of psychology as a distinct and separate science. It includes in its definition the concept that one cannot understand individuals without understanding the world they live in and the meaning it has for them. This definition of psychology also allows a way of systematizing and seeing how the most seemingly depoliticized "symptoms" fall within the context of a power struggle over the defining of situations, and how those microsituations involve questions of class, race, sex, and age.

The understanding that the "personal" refers to an order of social reality is summed up in the phrase "the personal is political."[50] Without intending to exhaust all of the meanings this phrase has, it is important to understand at least this aspect of it— that some people now believe that problems they were taught to see as "in them" were really problems in the world. So-called personal problems are really a part of a social-political context, and it was in the interest of this context to have people seeing the problems in their lives as separated and isolated from any common, shared world. Many of the difficulties people would (and sometimes did) go to see a therapist about—such as hating one's parents, hating school, hating one's sex role, loving people of the same sex, having no desire to succeed, or not understanding why no matter how hard one tried, success never came—came to have a social intelligibility when put back into their political context. Hence, people turned not to therapy, but to political action.

Simultaneously came the understanding that one of the main sense-making institutions that this society offers—psychology—had a *political* function in separating the personal from the *political*. Because of this role, psychology, and Freudianism in particu-

50. For other writings on the topic, see Roy Money, "The Personal and the Political," *Radical Therapist* vol. 2, no. 2; Carol Hanish, "The Personal Is Political," in *The Radical Therapist;* John Judis, "The Personal and the Political," *Social Revolution* 7 (January–February 1971): 9–29.

lar, can be seen as an intricate theory of self-hatred that itself is part of the over-all problem. And looking backward to the biographical past, by reintegrating the personal with the political, people see that even if their counterparts did not know then who the enemy was, they certainly knew there was an enemy. That was what all the misbehavior, "self-destructiveness," or passivity was about—trying to live in oppressive situations in the only ways people knew how. As with the "mentally ill," children too are socially intelligible; and as with "mental illness," Freudianism is a mystification of childhood.

The analysis offered in this essay of the relationship between the ideology (the way in which people come, through society, to make sense of their lives) and the social structure of society by no means presents a picture of people locked into their own oppression and exploitation by the very real demands of reality under capitalism. It is simply an attempt to work out a context for psychology that does not lapse into idealism. The concept of social intelligibility looks to the structures of the social realities people find themselves in, and also presents a view of an active subject trying to deal with reality at the level at which he understands it. The other side of the mechanical determinism that does not recognize conscious human praxis is the elitism that "forgets that circumstances are changed by men and that the educator must himself be educated."[51] In distinction to this mechanical determinism, which

51. Marx, "Theses on Feuerbach," in Bottomore and Rubel, *Karl Marx,* p. 67.

has to go outside its own analysis to find freedom, the concept of social intelligibility states that all human action, behavior, thought, and so on, refer to a structured social world, and that the moment of freedom is a part of that world, as human praxis.

This view then, is not an objectivism, but sees struggle, conflict, and contradiction at all levels of capitalist society—whether on an organized level, or on the spontaneous everyday level of the job, family, and school. The question of social intelligibility in relationship to a Marxist psychology is one of seeing human behavior *dialectically,* of seeing the contradictory and mystified realities that this behavior is a response to, while also understanding how one can combat those realities by bringing those responses to a higher level.

> It is only in a social context that subjectivism and objectivism, spiritualism and materialism, activity and passivity, cease to be antinomies, and thus cease to exist as such antinomies. The resolution of theoretical contradictions is possible only through practical means, only through the practical energy of man. Their resolution is by no means, therefore, the task only of the understanding, but it is a *real task of life,* a task which philosophy was unable to accomplish precisely because it saw there a purely theoretical problem.[52]

The overcoming of the splits described in this essay—between the inner and the outer, the private and the public, the personal and the political, consciousness and unconsciousness, the individual and

52. K. Marx, "Economic and Philosophic Manuscripts," in ibid., p. 72.

the society, the "sane" and the "insane," is not just a theoretical problem, these are not just illusions; they refer to real social realities. A Marxist psychology, then, can only be part of a revolutionary social movement that seeks to transform these social realities.

15. Synthesis or Science?

TERRY KUPERS

From Marx we inherit a scientific method (dialectical and historical materialism) along with important applications of this method to an understanding of man and society. From Freud we inherit a theory of mental functioning and psychopathology based on concepts and abstractions (*e.g.*, metapsychology and the Unconscious) derived from a technical practice (psychoanalysis). We would like to increase the depth of this inheritance by combining the two approaches. There are any number of ways of doing this. We can, with Erich Fromm, hear Freud's concepts emerge from a discriminating choice of Marx's early words. We can, with Reuben Osborne, fit together the Marxist "objective" social piece and the Freudian "subjective" personal piece to complete the human puzzle. We can, with Wilhelm Reich, apply the glue of sexual energy to a fragile but all inclusive model. We can, with Herbert Marcuse, add speculations about Marx to speculations from Freud to total a dialectical mythology. In fact, any number of such "syntheses" have been created. However, the paucity of real advances in our scientific knowledge about the real world resulting from these combinations belies the seemingly profound nature of the intricate theoretical systems. Here we will examine this problem and the context in which these "syntheses" are developed with a few necessarily sketchy examples and schematic thoughts about the difficulties encountered.

It is a gap more than any developed contradiction which first motivates the search for synthesis. Actually, the term synthesis should be discarded altogether in this context. If the models of Freud and Marx were comparable in intent, scope, subject matter, or method; and if there were identifiable contradictions between the two models (there actually are plenty—but very few have been elucidated beyond critiques of Freud's metapsychology and peripheral speculations about social issues); and if the resolution was to be sought in a third, superior model; then the use of the term synthesis would still imply a rather mechanical oversimplification of the dialectical process. In fact, each of the above "ifs" is problematical in itself. Let us begin by looking at what gaps encourage Marxists to look to psychoanalysis and psychoanalysts to look to Marxism for the gap-filling "synthesis."

From Marxism

The gap that leads many Marxists to look into psychoanalysis has to do with the difficulty of ex-

plaining in classical Marxist terms the concrete experience of the individual, whether this experience is
described as subjective, internal, intrapsychic, or personality. There are at least three easily identifiable
roots for this problem. One has to do with the fact
that Marx did not develop a psychological theory.
Another has to do with twentieth-century mechanical
distortions of Marx's ideas. The third is related to
the battle of ideologies in which the entire question
finds itself enmeshed. We can only briefly examine
these factors and some of their interactions.

Though Marx never worked out a comprehensive
psychology, it is possible to situate a space for such
a study in his theoretical framework just as it is
possible to identify the object in the real world that
this study is to investigate. Lucien Sève, the French
Marxist philosopher, has impressively attempted
this.[1] Space permits only the comment that such a
task requires a tremendous rigor in the application of
dialectical and historical materialism. It is not this
method nor Marx's application of this method to the
study of specific objects which creates a gap. Marxism was never meant to dictate the technique nor
predict the empirical findings of specific branches of
science. Rather, the findings of each science must be
incorporated into and provide the impetus for an
ever expanding Marxist perspective. This perspective
can guide the development, uses, and organization of
science while waging a battle against the ideologies
(false consciousness) which inhibit a scientific
understanding of the real world. So it is with psy-

1. Lucien Sève, *Marxisme et Theorie de la Personalité*
(Paris: Editions Sociales, 1969).

chology, one of those specific areas of science which Marx did not develop fully. Scientists working independently or Marxists working in this specific area will develop a theory adequate to psychology's specific object and eventually find their work articulating dialectically within the framework of dialectical and historical materialism.

The potential importance of psychoanalysis in supplying the scientific technique and data which might be part of the investigation of this area has not been overlooked. Reuben Osborne has suggested that while Marxism is perfectly adequate to explain objective social facts, our knowledge of man must be supplemented by the psychoanalytic explanation of subjective personal facts.[2] Of course, this is a crude distortion of the entire Marxist view of subject and object. Additionally, he fails to develop either theory to the point of coming into contact with the other. Thus, he applies one theory to one set of facts and another to another set of facts without considering possible contradictions. This approach is more eclectic than it is scientific. Georges Politzer articulated a more sophisticated critique of psychoanalysis in showing how, unlike physiology or classical psychology, it was able to begin to explore the concrete life drama of the individual.[3] Rather than describing the mechanism of dreams in general, psychoanalysis describes the meaning of the particular dream as a

2. Reuben Osborne, *Marxism and Psychoanalysis* (London: Barrie and Rockcliff, 1965).
3. Georges Politzer, *Critique des Fondements de la Psychologie* (Paris: Presses Universitaires de France, 1968).

concrete event in the individual's life. Politzer's weakness was that he failed to differentiate between the legitimate and the idealist employment of abstraction. Our concepts of concrete objects are formed by a process of *abstraction* which Marx claimed should progress toward successively closer and closer approximations to a proper reflection of the concrete object.[4] This is not the same as forming concepts *of abstractions* like a "universal human essence." Politzer rejected Freud's concept of the unconscious as "abstract" as if any mention of the term becomes taboo. The attempts by Osborne and Politzer to supply a concrete psychology were weakened by their eclecticism and failure to understand abstraction, respectively. However, they did suggest the possibility that some part of psychoanalysis at least might be incorporated into the development of a scientific psychology.

Not only the lack of a psychology in Marx's work, but also the failure of a mechanical form of Marxism to deal with questions like those concerning the individual, cause many who seek answers to turn away from Marxism toward such philosophies as existentialism or phenomenology. Psychoanalysis then also becomes viewed as an alternative rather than a potential contributor to science and thus to Marxism. The popularity of Marcuse and Ron Laing must be in part related to this phenomenon. They are able to put into flowing words what many people are thinking and feeling. When Marxism becomes

4. See K. Marx, "Introduction" to *Critique of Political Economy*, 1857.

mechanical and claims to be in itself the truth rather than the theory most helpful in our discovering more and more about reality, it cannot relate to the real experiences of those who are then turned away. Marcuse speculates about consciousness, technology, and the proper form of sexuality for the future.[5] Laing, who approaches Marxism closest in its Sartrean existential version, is unable to anchor his very valuable conceptualization of intersubjectivity and "mapping" to any concrete analysis of material reality or concrete social relations beyond the family. His well formulated attack on insane capitalist society is lost in relativities about who is projecting what. Concomitantly, the potential contribution of Marxism in those areas is blunted because of a rejection of mechanical Marxism by those seeking answers without a more thorough look at the depths of Marx's and Marxism's works.

Breaches in the understanding of Marxism quickly become issues in the battle of ideologies. Lenin wrote about the fate of contributions from "great revolutionaries" like Marx in such a battle: "After their death, attempts are made to convert them into harmless icons, to canonize them, so to say, and to hallow their *names* to a certain extent for the 'consolation' of the oppressed classes and with the object of duping the latter, while at the same time robbing the revolutionary theory of its *substance,* blunting its revolutionary edge and vulgarizing it."[6] This was

5. H. Marcuse, *Eros and Civilization* (New York: Vintage, 1955).

6. V. I. Lenin, *The State and Revolution, Collected Works,* vol. 26, p. 1.

certainly the fate of Marx's early works after they became generally available in the 1930s. The "humanism" of the early Marx became the basis for attacks on the "antihumanism" of the mature Marx and the "inhumanity" of Marx's successors who represent the "Red menace."

Unfortunately, this kind of sophisticated ideology becomes a part of the attempt to merge Marxism and psychoanalysis. Erich Fromm seeks in Marx's early works references to psychological phenomena as if to attribute to Marx a psychology not too unlike Freud's.[7] He seems more interested in speculations the young Marx made about personal events than in the scientific theories of the mature Marx where such speculations are left aside. Supplying a scientific psychology to be articulated with the historical materialism of Marx's later work seems to be less of a priority for Fromm than attacking the "distorted and degraded Marxism preached in almost one third of the world." Thus, his work contributes to the ideological battle against Marxism whether or not he considers himself a Marxist.

From Psychoanalysis

When psychoanalysts attempt to fill in the gaps and inconsistencies in Freud's statements about social events, they often turn to Marxism. These attempts to merge Marxism with psychoanalysis frequently fall into inconsistencies and dead ends of

7. Erich Fromm, *Beyond the Chains of Illusion* (New York: Trident Press, 1962).

their own. It is difficult to generalize about why this is the case, but let us offer here one possible but much oversimplified reason. Until he began to speculate about larger social issues in the 1920s, Freud based his theories on his observations of individuals. Thus, in his search to discover the "motor" that drives individuals to act, he looked within and decided it was the instincts. Later, when he discussed social issues, he carried the instinctual motor he had formulated within the individual over to his studies of society. Thus, war is directly related to a Death Instinct. The psychoanalysts who disagree with Freud about social factors never entirely correct this psychologization of Freud's. Reich and Marcuse exemplify this difficulty. Wilhelm Reich's ideas about sexual libido and social repression never quite escape basing social relations on instinctual and biological factors.[8] Marcuse pretends to alter the ahistorical aspects of instinct theory by historicizing the Oedipus complex or describing as "surplus repression" that social component of otherwise intrapsychic phenomena required for class domination. However, his attempt fails because he is too insistent on using Freud's nearly intact metapsychology as a springboard for his overly speculative assumptions about technological society. Thus, neither Reich nor Marcuse are able to reject certain ideological distortions in Freud to develop their critiques at a more basic scientific level.

All of these criticisms of Marcuse, Laing, Fromm,

8. Wilhelm Reich, *The Sexual Revolution* (New York: Orgone Institute Press, 1945).

and Reich must be balanced by a recognition of their contributions. For instance, Laing's work on dialectics, though tending toward idealism and though not very accurate in its examination of Marx, is an important stance against dogmatism.[9] Marcuse's "repressive desublimation," Fromm's "social character," and Reich's "repressed sexuality" are all concepts that contribute to our understanding of the mediations between individual, economic base, and ideological superstructure. Generally, though, their attempts to merge and manipulate theoretical models are isolated from any depth investigation of the objects these theories were developed to explain. This results in their revising both Marx and Freud.

Science

Perhaps the filling in of the gaps in Marx's and Freud's work is not really the important task. What we are seeking is to develop a theory which allows us to know more and more accurately about the real situation of the individual and society in order to alter that situation in a meaningful way. Here we are talking about science. Our goal should not be to synthesize two theories, however compatible or contradictory they may be. Rather, we would like to develop our scientific knowledge of the real world.

Certainly, the work of Marx cannot be criticized for a lack of scientific rigor. The fact that he did not undertake the investigation of certain psychological

9. R. D. Laing and D. G. Cooper, *Reason and Violence* (London: Tavistock, 1964).

facts does not mean he did not provide a theoretical framework in which these facts can be developed. The mechanical distortions of Marx's work prevalent in the twentieth century are just starting to be overcome with the publication of more of his writings (*e.g.,* the *Grundrisse*), the general availability in English of important Marxist texts (*e.g.,* Antonio Gramsci, Georg Lukacs), and the work of contemporary Marxists to clarify and take stands in debates on science and ideology (*e.g.,* Louis Althusser[10] and Lucien Sève).

Where does Freud fit into this picture? It is very likely that the part of Freud's work that does accurately reflect the reality of psychological experience can be incorporated into such a scientific psychology if only the ideological distortions in Freud's writings and in the practice of psychoanalysis can be identified and discarded. Many revolutionaries would disagree with this view and reject all of Freud's work as "reactionary ideology." Too often this approach is related to a failure to distinguish properly between Freud's real discoveries and his speculations about these discoveries or between the reactionary social implications of the private practice of psychoanalysis and the scientific value of its findings.

10. Louis Althusser's discussion of "Freud and Lacan," in *New Left Review* 455 (May–June 1969) stresses the scientific status of psychoanalysis and its object, the Unconscious. He refers to the re-reading of Freud by the French psychoanalyst, Jacques Lacan. Lacan brings social determinants into the very core of this theory via language. This approach potentially offers more of scientific value than the stress on social environment which appears as an afterthought in the revisions of Freud by Fromm and others.

Wilhelm Reich has claimed that psychoanalysis is compatible with dialectical materialism.[11] His argument is weakened by some of his examples. Nevertheless it would not be surprising if many components of psychoanalysis were compatible with dialectical materialism. If dialectical materialism is the best theoretical reflection we have of the real world and if psychoanalysis is in part scientific (*i.e.*, accurately reflects the real world), then we might expect parts of psychoanalysis to be consistent with dialectical materialism independent of any awareness on Freud's part about this.

Our task should not be to "synthesize Freud and Marx." Rather, it should be to distinguish science from ideology in Freud and use the scientific aspects to expand Marxism and our knowledge of the real world.

11. Wilhelm Reich, *Dialectical Materialism and Psychoanalysis,* trans. Anna Bostock (Copenhagen: Verlag für Sexualpolitik, 1934). U.S. Copyright 1966 by Lee Baxandall.

IV

Sex Roles

Introduction

Sexuality and sex roles have been a fundamental area of concern for radical psychology. Along with the women's and gay movements, radical psychology has come to understand the great importance of sexuality and sex roles in terms of society as a whole. That women and homosexuals are oppressed because they are members of particular sexual groups is no new insight. And, the psychological oppression of these groups is also nothing new. It has become increasingly clear that the psychological and related professions have been probably the most vicious attackers of women and gays.

Oppression of women by psychology comes from many sources. Social psychologists, child psychologists, clinicians, personality theorists, and many others have attempted to "prove" inherent female inferiority. They theorize that women are instinctively incapable of analytic thought, that women are weak and dependent. They hold women responsible for their men's failures, claiming that these women did not play supportive roles for their men. They claim that women are largely incapable of sexual autonomy—part of this is the long history of near-total acceptance of vaginal orgasm since the admission of clitoral orgasm would be a step in ending the oppression of male-oriented sexuality. Of course, recent changes have been apparent in this attitude, but only due to the women's movement, not to a change in psychological theory. The psychology professions tells us that women are instinctively qualified mainly to bear children, keep a home, and be satisfied by their men's successes. When women object and fight back, they are labeled as mentally ill. Therapy is then recommended, in order that women may "adjust" to their appropriate roles. If this fails, commitment to a mental hospital is often prescribed.

The psychology professions, for the most part, claim that only heterosexual behavior is normal. Homosexuality is, in their eyes, an emotional disturbance. For "causes" of these problems, they often point to people's failure to accept socially correct sexual roles at an early age; or they blame people's mothers. For "cures" these professionals offer hospitalization and behavior modification. One particularly abhorrent type of behavior modification consists of placing electrodes on a gay man, showing him pictures of naked men, and shocking him for becoming excited. When the man is finally broken and worn down from the shocks, and learns to stop becoming excited, he is considered cured. Of course, psychologists often prefer to save all that trouble by devising tests to screen out homosexuals when they apply for jobs.

Then, of course, there are the "hip" psychologists who rant about a sexual revolution in which women become "common property" and in which an occasional gay experience is permissible. Such psychologists clearly show themselves to be little less repressive than their traditional counterparts. Sexual freedom for them is simply sexual experimentation and exploitation.

Sexuality has been at the root of the majority of emotional problems, but has always been covered up by mainstream psychology. Even those like Wilhelm Reich who took socialist paths in attempting to free up sexuality, were not able to provide real alternatives. Reich was very oppressive toward his several wives, and severely attacked homosexuality as abnormal. Sexuality and sex roles still present radicals with the many problems of fighting sexism in themselves and in institutions, and in casting off their own repressed sexuality. Women's and gay consciousness-raising groups have done more in the last few years than even a truly radical psychology could have expected. Men's groups, where they have formed, have also begun to make dents in the armor of sexual oppression. Radical psychology must delve deeply into the problems of sexual oppression and repression, seeing the basis of social fear of women's and gay liberation, two connected movements which have already begun to upset the social control of sexuality and personal freedom.

Naomi Weisstein's "Psychology Constructs the Female, or the Fantasy Life of the Male Psychologists" is a revised edition of her classic article, one of the most widely reprinted in the left press. It surveys the oppressive theories concerning women which male psychologists have formulated, seeing those efforts as attempts to rationalize the existing oppression of women. Nancy Henley's "The Politics of Touch" deals with the sexual hierarchy set up by interpersonal touching. My article, "Male Supremacy in Freud," reviews Freud's sexism throughout his career, including its relation to Freud's generally reactionary social theory. Carl Wittman's "Gay Liberation Manifesto" and Radicalesbians' "Woman-Identified Woman," also very popular articles, are important in providing a general framework for understanding the oppression of gays in this society.

16. Psychology Constructs the Female: or, the Fantasy Life of the Male Psychologist

NAOMI WEISSTEIN

It is an implicit assumption that the area of psychology which concerns itself with personality has the onerous but necessary task of describing the limits of human possibility. Thus when we are about to consider the liberation of women, we naturally look to psychology to tell us what "true" liberation would mean: what would give women the freedom to fulfill their own intrinsic natures.

Psychologists have set about describing the true natures of women with a certainty and a sense of their own infallibility rarely found in the secular world. Bruno Bettelheim, of the University of Chicago, tells us that

We must start with the realization that, as much
as women want to be good scientists or engineers,
they want first and foremost to be womanly com-
panions of men and to be mothers.[1]

Erik Erikson of Harvard University, upon noting
that young women often ask whether they can "have
an identity before they know whom they will marry,
and for whom they will make a home," explains
somewhat elegiacally that

Much of a young woman's identity is already defined in her kind of attractiveness and in the se-
lectivity of her search for the man (or men) by
whom she wishes to be sought. . . .[2]

Mature womanly fulfillment, for Erikson, rests on
the fact that a woman's

. . . somatic design harbors an "inner space"
destined to bear the offspring of chosen men, and
with it, a biological, psychological, and ethical
commitment to take care of human infancy.[3]

Some psychiatrists even see the acceptance of
woman's role by women as a solution to societal
problems. "Woman is nurturance . . . ," writes
Joseph Rheingold, a psychiatrist at Harvard Medical School,

. . . anatomy decrees the life of a woman. . . .
When women grow up without dread of their

1. B. Bettelheim, "The Commitment Required of a
Woman Entering a Scientific Profession in Present Day
American Society," *Woman and the Scientific Professions,*
the MIT symposium on American Women in Science and
Engineering, 1965.
2. E. Erikson, "Inner and Outer Space: Reflections on
Womanhood," *Daedalus* 93 (1964): 582–606.
3. Ibid.

o

biological functions and without subversion by feminist doctrine, and therefore enter upon motherhood with a sense of fulfillment and altruistic sentiment, we shall attain the goal of a good life and a secure world in which to live it.[4]

These views from men who are assumed to be experts reflect, in a surprisingly transparent way, the cultural consensus. They not only assert that a woman is defined by her ability to attract men, they see no alternative definitions. They think that the definition of a woman in terms of a man is the way it should be; and they back it up with psychosexual incantation and biological ritual curses. A woman has an identity if she is attractive enough to obtain a man, and thus, a home; for this will allow her to set about her life's task of "joyful altruism and nurturance."

Business certainly does not disagree. If views such as Bettelheim's and Erikson's do indeed have something to do with real liberation for women, then seldom in human history has so much money and effort been spent on helping a group of people realize their true potential. Clothing, cosmetics, home furnishings, are multi-million dollar businesses; if you don't like investing in firms that make weaponry and flaming gasoline, then there's a lot of hard cash in "inner space." Sheet and pillowcase manufacturers are concerned to fill this inner space:

> Mother, for a while this morning, I thought I wasn't cut out for married life. Hank was late for

4. J. Rheingold, *The Fear of Being a Woman* (New York: Grune & Stratton, 1964), p. 714.

work and forgot his apricot juice and walked out
without kissing me, and when I was all alone I
started crying. But then the postman came with
the sheets and towels you sent, that look like big
bandana handkerchiefs, and you know what I
thought? That those big red and blue handkerchiefs are for girls like me to dry their tears on
so they can get busy and do what a housewife
has to do. Throw open the windows and start
getting the house ready, and the dinner, maybe
clean the silver and put new geraniums in the box.
*Everything to be ready for him when he walks
through that door*[5] (*emphasis added*).

Of course, it is not only the sheet and pillowcase
manufacturers, the cosmetics industry, the home
furnishings salesmen who profit from and make use
of the cultural definitions of man and woman. The
example above is blatantly and overtly pitched to a
particular kind of sexist stereotype: the child nymph.
But almost all aspects of the media are normative,
that is, they have to do with the ways in which beautiful people, or just folks, or ordinary Americans,
should live their lives. They define the possible; and
the possibilities are usually in terms of what is male
and what is female. Men and women alike are waiting for Hank, the Silva Thins man, to walk back
through that door.

It is an interesting but limited exercise to show
that psychologists and psychiatrists embrace these
sexist norms of our culture, that they do not see
beyond the most superficial and stultifying media
conceptions of female nature, and that their ideas of

5. Fieldcrest—Advertisement in the *New Yorker*, 1965.

female nature serve industry and commerce so well. Just because it's good for business doesn't mean it's wrong. What I will show is that it *is wrong;* that there isn't the tiniest shred of evidence that these fantasies of servitude and childish dependence have anything to do with women's true potential; that the idea of the nature of human possibility which rests on the accidents of individual development of genitalia, on what is possible today because of what happened yesterday, on the fundamentalist myth of sex organ casuality, has strangled and deflected psychology so that it is relatively useless in describing, explaining, or predicting humans and their behavior.

It then goes without saying that present psychology is less than worthless in contributing to a vision which could truly liberate—men as well as women.

The central argument of my paper, then, is this: Psychology has nothing to say about what women are really like, what they need and what they want, essentially because psychology does not know. I want to stress that this failure is not limited to women; rather, the kind of psychology which has addressed itself to how people act and who they are has failed to understand, in the first place, why people act the way they do, and certainly failed to understand what might make them act differently.

The kind of psychology which has addressed itself to these questions divides into two professional areas: academic personality research, and clinical psychology and psychiatry. The basic reason for failure is the same in both these areas: the central assumption for most psychologists of human personality has been that human behavior rests on an individual and inner dynamic, perhaps fixed in infancy, perhaps fixed by genitalia, perhaps simply arranged in a rather immovable cognitive network. But this assumption is rapidly losing ground as personality psychologists fail again and again to get consistency in the assumed personalities of their subjects.[6] Meanwhile, the evidence is collecting that what a person does and who she believes herself to be, will in general be a function of what people around her expect her to be, and what the overall situation in which she is acting implies that she is. Compared to the influence of the social context within which a person lives, his or her history and "traits," as well as biological makeup, may simply be random variations, "noise" superimposed on the true signal which can predict behavior.

Some academic personality psychologists are at least looking at the counterevidence and questioning their theories; no such corrective is occurring in clinical psychology and psychiatry: Freudians and neo-Freudians, nudie-marathonists and touchy-feelies, classicists and swingers, clinicians and psychiatrists, simply refuse to look at the evidence against their theory and practice. And they support their theory and practice with stuff so transparently biased as to have absolutely no standing as empirical evidence.

To summarize: the first reason for psychology's

6. J. Block, "Some Reasons for the Apparent Inconsistency of Personality," *Psychological Bulletin* 70 (1968): 210–212.

failure to understand what people are and how they act is that psychology has looked for inner traits when it should have been looking for social context; the second reason for psychology's failure is that the theoreticians of personality have generally been clinicians and psychiatrists, and they have never considered it necessary to have evidence in support of their theories.

Theory without Evidence

Let us turn to this latter cause of failure first: the acceptance by psychiatrists and clinical psychologists of theory without evidence. If we inspect the literature of personality, it is immediately obvious that the bulk of it is written by clinicians and psychiatrists, and that the major support for their theories is "years of intensive clinical experience." This is a tradition started by Freud. His "insights" occurred during the course of his work with his patients. Now there is nothing wrong with such an approach to theory *formulation;* a person is free to make up theories with any inspiration that works: divine revelation, intensive clinical practice, a random numbers table. But he/she is not free to claim any validity for his/her theory until it has been tested and confirmed. But theories are treated in no such tentative way in ordinary clinical practice. Consider Freud. What he thought constituted evidence violated the most minimal conditions of scientific rigor. In *The Sexual Enlightenment of Children,*[7] the clas-

7. S. Freud, *The Sexual Enlightenment of Children* (New York: Collier, 1963).

sic document which is supposed to demonstrate empirically the existence of a castration complex and its connection to a phobia, Freud based his analysis on the reports of the father of the little boy, himself in therapy, and a devotee of Freudian theory. I really don't have to comment further on the contamination in this kind of evidence. It is remarkable that only recently has Freud's classic theory on the sexuality of women—the notion of the double orgasm—been actually tested physiologically and found just plain wrong. Now those who claim that fifty years of psychoanalytic experience constitute evidence enough of the essential truths of Freud's theory should ponder the robust health of the double orgasm. Did women, until Masters and Johnson,[8] believe they were having two different kinds of orgasm? Did their psychiatrists badger them into reporting something that was not true? If so, were there other things they reported that were also not true? Did psychiatrists ever learn anything different than their theories had led them to believe? If clinical experience means anything at all, surely we should have been done with the double orgasm myth long before the Masters and Johnson studies.

But certainly, you may object, "years of intensive clinical experience" is the only reliable measure in a discipline which rests for its findings on insight, sensitivity, and intuition. The problem with insight, sensitivity, and intuition, is that they can confirm for all time the biases that one started with. People used

8. W. H. Masters and V. E. Johnson, *Human Sexual Response* (Boston: Little Brown, 1966).

to be absolutely convinced of their ability to tell which of their number were engaging in witchcraft. All it required was some sensitivity to the workings of the devil.

Years of intensive clinical experience is not the same thing as empirical evidence. The first thing an experimenter learns in any kind of experiment which involves humans is the concept of the "double blind." The term is taken from medical experiments, where one group is given a drug which is presumably supposed to change behavior in a certain way, and a control group is given a placebo. If the observers or the subjects know which group took which drug, the result invariably comes out on the positive side for the new drug. Only when it is not known which subject took which pill, is validity remotely approximated. In addition, with judgments of human behavior, it is so difficult to precisely tie down just what behavior is going on, let alone what behavior should be expected, that one must test again and again the reliability of judgments. How many judges, blind, will agree in their observations? Can they replicate their own judgments at some later time? When, in actual practice, these judgment criteria are tested for clinical judgments, then we find that the judges cannot judge reliably, nor can they judge consistently: they do no better than chance in identifying which of a certain set of stories were written by men and which by women; which of a whole battery of clinical test results are the products of homosexuals and which are the products of heterosexuals,[9] and which,

9. E. Hooker, "Male Homosexuality in the Rorschach," *Journal of Projective Techniques* 21 (1957): 18–31.

of a battery of clinical test results *and* interviews
(where questions are asked such as "Do you have
delusions?")[10] are products of psychotics, neurotics,
psychosomatics, or normals. Lest this summary
escape your notice, let me stress the implications of
these findings. The ability of judges, chosen for their
clinical expertise, to distinguish male heterosexuals
from male homosexuals on the basis of three widely
used clinical projective tests—the Rorschach, the
TAT, and the MAP—was *no better than chance*.
The reason this is such devastating news, of course,
is that sexuality is supposed to be of fundamental
importance in the deep dynamic of personality; if
what is considered gross sexual deviance cannot be
caught, then what are psychologists talking about
when they, for example, claim that at the basis of
paranoid psychosis is "latent homosexual panic"?
They can't even identify what homosexual anything
is, let alone "latent homosexual panic."[11] More
frightening, expert clinicians cannot be consistent on
what diagnostic category to assign to a person, again
on the basis of both tests and interviews; a number
of normals in the Little and Schneidman study were

10. K. B. Little, and E. S. Schneidman, "Congruences
among Interpretations of Psychologica and Anamestic
Data, *Psychological Monographs* 73 (1959): 1–42.
    11. It should be noted that psychologists have been as
quick to assert absolute truths about the nature of homosexuality as they have about the nature of women. The
arguments presented in this paper apply equally to the
nature of homosexuality; psychologists know nothing about
it; there is no more evidence for the "naturalness" of heterosexuality. Psychology has functioned as a pseudo-scien-
tific buttress for patriarchal ideology and patriarchal social
organization: women's liberation and gay liberation fight
against a common victimization.

described as psychotic, in such categories as "schizo-phrenic with homosexual tendencies" or "schizoid character with depressive trends." But most dis-heartening, when the judges were asked to rejudge the test protocols some weeks later, their diagnoses of the same subjects on the basis of the same proto-col differed markedly from their initial judgments. It is obvious that even simple descriptive conventions in clinical psychology cannot be consistently applied; if clinicians were as faulty in recognizing food from nonfood, they'd poison themselves and starve to death. That their descriptive conventions have any explanatory significance is therefore, of course, out of the question.

As a graduate student at Harvard some years ago, I was a member of a seminar which was asked to identify which of two piles of a clinical test, the TAT, had been written by males and which by females. Only four students out of twenty identified the piles correctly, and this was after one and a half months of intensively studying the differences be-tween men and women. Since this result is below chance—that is, the result would occur by chance about four out of a thousand times—we may con-clude that there *is* finally a consistency here; students are judging knowledgeably within the context of psychological teaching about the differences between men and women; the teachings themselves are simply erroneous.

You may argue that the theory may be scientifi-cally "unsound" but at least it cures people. There is no evidence that it does. In 1952, Eysenck[12] reported the results of what is called an "outcome of therapy" study of neurotics which showed that, of the patients who received psychoanalysis the improvement rate was 44%; of the patients who received psychotherapy the improvement rate was 64%; and of the patients who received no treatment at all the improvement rate was 72%. These findings have never been refuted; subsequently, later studies have confirmed the negative results of the Eysenck study.[13] How can clinicians and psychiatrists, then, in all good conscience, continue to practice? Largely by ignoring these results and being careful not to do outcome-of-therapy studies. The attitude is nicely summarized by Rotter[14] (quoted in Astin[15]): "Research studies in psychotherapy tend to be con-

12. H. J. Eysenck, "The Effects of Psychotherapy: An Evaluation," *Journal of Consulting Psychology* 16 (1952): 319–324.

13. F. Barron, and T. Leary, "Changes in Psychoneurotic Patients with and without Psychotherapy," *Journal of Consulting Psychology* 19 (1955): 239–245. A. E. Bergin, "The Effects of Psychotherapy: Negative Results Revisited," *Journal of Consulting Psychology* 10 (1963): 244–250. R. D. Cartwright and J. L. Vogel, "A Comparison of Changes in Psychoneurotic Patients during Matched Periods of Therapy and No-therapy," *Journal of Consulting Psychology* 24 (1960): 121–127. C. B. Truax, "Effective Ingredients in Psychotherapy: An Approach to Unraveling the Patient-Therapist Interaction," *Journal of Counseling Psychology* 10 (1963): 256–263. E. Powers and H. Witmer, *An Experiment in the Prevention of Delinquency* (New York: Columbia University Press, 1951).

14. J. B. Rotter, "Psychotherapy," *Annual Review of Psychology* 11 (1960): 381–414.

15. A. W. Astin, "The Functional Autonomy of Psychotherapy," *American Psychologist* 16 (1961): 75–78.

cerned more with psychotherapeutic procedure and less with outcome. . . . To some extent, it reflects an interest in the psychotherapy situation as a kind of personality laboratory." Some laboratory.

The Social Context

Thus, since we can conclude that since clinical experience and tools can be shown to be worse than useless when tested for consistency, efficacy, agreement, and reliability, we can safely conclude that theories of a clinical nature advanced about women are also worse than useless. I want to turn now to the second major point in my paper, which is that, even when psychological theory is constructed so that it may be tested, and rigorous standards of evidence are used, it has become increasingly clear that in order to understand why people do what they do, and certainly in order to change what people do, psychologists must turn away from the theory of the causal nature of the inner dynamic and look to the social context within which individuals live.

Before examining the relevance of this approach for the question of women, let me first sketch the groundwork for this assertion.

In the first place, it is clear[16] that personality tests never yield consistent predictions; a rigid authoritarian on one measure will be an unauthoritarian on the next. But the reason for this inconsistency is only now becoming clear, and it seems overwhelmingly to have much more to do with the

16. Block, "Some Reasons."

social situation in which the subject finds him/herself than with the subject him/herself.

In a series of brilliant experiments, Rosenthal and his co-workers[17] have shown that if one group of experimenters has one hypothesis about what they expect to find, and another group of experimenters has the opposite hypothesis, both groups will obtain results in accord with their hypotheses. The results obtained are not due to mishandling of data by biased experimenters; rather, somehow, the bias of the experimenter creates a changed environment in which subjects actually act differently. For instance, in one experiment, subjects were to assign numbers to pictures of men's faces, with high numbers representing the subject's judgment that the man in the picture was a successful person, and low numbers representing the subject's judgment tht the man in the picture was an unsuccessful person. Prior to running the subjects, one group of experimenters was told that the subjects tended to rate the faces high; another group of experimenters was told that the subjects tended to rate the faces low. Each group of experimenters was instructed to follow precisely the same procedure: they were required to read to subjects a set of instructions, and to *say nothing else*. For the 375 subjects run, the results showed clearly that those subjects who performed the task with experimenters who expected high ratings gave high

17. R. Rosenthal and L. Jacobson, *Pygmalion in the Classroom: Teacher Expectation and Pupil's Intellectual Development* (New York: Holt, Rinehart & Winston, 1968). R. Rosenthal, *Experimenter Effects in Behavioral Research* (New York: Appleton-Century-Crofts, 1966).

ratings, and those subjects who performed the task with experimenters who expected low ratings gave low ratings. How did this happen? The experimenters all used the same words; it was something in their conduct which made one group of subjects do one thing, and another group of subjects do another thing.[18]

The concreteness of the changed conditions produced by expectation is a fact, a reality: even with animal subjects, in two separate studies,[19] those experimenters who were told that rats learning mazes had been especially bred for brightness obtained better learning from their rats than did experimenters believing their rats to have been bred for dullness. In a very recent study, Rosenthal and Jacobson[20] extended their analysis to the natural classroom situation. Here, they tested a group of students and reported to the teachers that some among the students tested "showed great promise." Actually, the students so named had been selected on a random basis. Some time later, the experimenters retested the group of students: those students whose teachers had been told that they were "promising" showed real and dramatic increments in

18. I am indebted to Jesse Lemisch for his valuable suggestions in the interpretation of these studies.

19. R. Rosenthal and K. L. Fode, "The Effect of Experimenter Bias on the Performance of the Albino Rat." Unpublished manuscript, Harvard University, 1960. R. Rosenthal and R. Lawson, "A Longitudinal Study of the Effects of Experimenter Bias on the Operant Learning of Laboratory Rats." Unpublished manuscript, Harvard University, 1961.

20. Rosenthal and Jacobson, *Pygmalion in the Classroom*.

their IQs as compared to the rest of the students. Something in the conduct of the teachers toward those whom the teachers believed to be the "bright" students, made those students brighter.

Thus, even in carefully controlled experiments, and with no outward or conscious difference in behavior, the hypotheses we start with will influence enormously the behavior of another organism. These studies are extremely important when assessing the validity of psychological studies of women. Since it is beyond doubt that most of us start with notions as to the nature of men and women, the validity of a number of observations of sex differences is questionable, even when these observations have been made under carefully controlled conditions. Second, and more important, the Rosenthal experiments point quite clearly to the influence of social expectation. In some extremely important ways, people are what you expect them to be, or at least they behave as you expect them to behave. Thus, if women, according to Bettelheim, want first and foremost to be good wives and mothers, it is extremely likely that this is what Bruno Bettelheim, and the rest of society, want them to be.

There is another series of brilliant social psychological experiments which point to the overwhelming effect of social context. These are the obedience experiments of Stanley Milgram[21] in which subjects

21. S. Milgram, "Some Conditions of Obedience and Disobedience to Authority," *Human Relations* 18 (1965): 57–76. S. Milgram, "Liberating Effects of Group Pressures," *Journal of Personality and Social Psychology* 1 (1965): 127–134.

are asked to obey the orders of unknown experimenters, orders which carry with them the distinct possibility that the subject is killing somebody.

In Milgram's experiments, a subject is told that he/she is administering a learning experiment, and that he/she is to deal out shocks each time the other "subject" (in reality, a confederate of the experimenter) answers incorrectly. The equipment appears to provide graduated shocks ranging upwards from 15 volts through 450 volts; for each of four consecutive voltages there are verbal descriptions such as "mild shock, danger, severe shock," and, finally, for the 435 and 450 volt switches, a red XXX marked over the switches. Each time the stooge answers incorrectly, the subject is supposed to increase the voltage. As the voltage increases, the stooge begins to cry in pain; he/she demands that the experiment stop; finally, he/she refuses to answer at all. When he/she stops responding, the experimenter instructs the subject to continue increasing the voltage; for each shock administered the stooge shrieks in agony. Under these conditions, about 62½ % of the subjects administered shocks that they believed to be possibly lethal.

No tested individual differences between subjects predicted how many would continue to obey, and which would break off the experiment. When forty psychiatrists predicted how many of a group of 100 subjects would go on to give the lethal shock, their predictions were orders of magnitude below the actual percentages; most expected only one-tenth of one per cent of the subjects to obey to the end.

But even though *psychiatrists* have no idea how people will behave in this situation, and even though individual differences do not predict which subjects will obey and which will not, it is easy to predict when subjects will be obedient and when they will be defiant. All the experimenter has to do is change the social situation. In a variant of Milgram's experiment, two stooges were present in addition to the "victim"; these worked along with the subject in administering electric shocks. When these two stooges refused to go on with the experiment, only ten per cent of the subjects continued to the maximum voltage. This is critical for personality theory. It says that behavior is predicted from the social situation, not from the individual history.

Finally, an ingenious experiment by Schachter and Singer[22] showed that subjects injected with adrenalin, which produces a state of physiological arousal in all but minor respects identical to that which occurs when subjects are extremely afraid, became euphoric when they were in a room with a stooge who was acting euphoric, and became extremely angry when they were placed in a room with a stooge who was acting extremely angry.

To summarize: if subjects under quite innocuous and noncoercive social conditions can be made to kill other subjects and under other types of social conditions will positively refuse to do so; if subjects can react to a state of physiological fear by becom-

22. S. Schachter and J. E. Singer, "Cognitive, Social and Physiological Determinants of Emotional State," *Psychological Review* 63 (1962): 379–399.

ing euphoric because there is somebody else around who is euphoric, or angry because there is somebody else around who is angry; if students become intelligent because teachers expect them to be intelligent, and rats run mazes better because experimenters are told the rats are bright, then it is obvious that a study of human behavior requires, first and foremost, a study of the social contexts within which people move, the expectations as to how they will behave, and the authority which tells them who they are and what they are supposed to do.

Biologically Based Theories

Biologists also have at times assumed they could describe the limits of human potential from their observations not of human, but of animal behavior. Here, as in psychology, there has been no end of theorizing about the sexes, again with a sense of absolute certainty surprising in "science." These theories fall into two major categories.

One category of theory argues that since females and males differ in their sex hormones, and sex hormones enter the brain,[23] there must be innate behavioral differences. But the only thing this argument tells us is that there are differences in physiological state. The problem is whether these differences are at all relevant to behavior.

23. D. A. Hamburg and D. T. Lunde, "Sex Hormones in the Development of Sex Differences in Human Behavior," in *The Development of Sex Differences,* ed. E. Maccoby (Stanford, Calif: Stanford University Press, 1966), pp. 1–24.

Consider, for example, differences in levels of the sex hormone testosterone. A man who calls himself Tiger[24] has recently argued[25] that the greater quantities of testosterone found in human males as compared with human females (of a certain age group) determines innate differences in aggressiveness, competitiveness, dominance, ability to hunt, ability to hold public office, and so forth. But Tiger demonstrates in this argument the same manly and courageous refusal to be intimidated by evidence which we have already seen in our consideration of the clinical and psychiatric tradition. The evidence does not support his argument, and in most cases, directly contradicts it. Testosterone level does not seem to be related to hunting ability, dominance, aggression, or competitiveness. As Storch has pointed out,[26] all normal *male mammals* in the reproductive age group produce much greater quantities of testosterone than females; yet many of these males are neither hunters nor are they aggressive (*e.g.,* rabbits). And, among some hunting mammals, such as the large cats, it turns out that more hunting is done by the female than the male. And there exist primate species where the female is clearly more aggressive, competitive, and dominant than the male[27] (see below). Thus,

24. Schwarz-Belkin (1914) claims that the name was originally Mouse, but this may be a reference to an earlier L. Tiger (putative).
25. L. Tiger, "Male dominance? Yes. A Sexist plot? No," *New York Times Magazine,* Section N, October 25, 1970.
26. M. Storch, "Reply to Tiger," Unpublished manuscript, 1970.
27. G. D. Mitchell, "Paternalistic Behavior in Primates," *Psychological Bulletin* 71 (1969): 399–417.

for some species, being female, and therefore, having less testosterone than the male of that species means hunting more, or being more aggressive, or being more dominant. Nor does having *more* testosterone preclude behavior commonly thought of as "female": there exist primate species where females do not touch infants except to feed them; the males care for the infants at all times[28] (see fuller discussion below). So it is not clear what testosterone or any other sex-hormonal difference means for differences in nature, or sex-role behavior.

In other words, one can observe identical types of behavior which have been associated with sex (*e.g.*, "mothering") in males and females, despite known differences in physiological state, *i.e.*, sex hormones, genitalia, etc. What about the converse to this? That is, can one obtain differences in behavior given a single physiological state? The answer is overwhelmingly yes, not only as regards non-sex-specific hormones (as in the Schachter and Singer 1962 experiment cited above), but also as regards gender itself. Studies of hermaphrodites with the same diagnosis (the genetic, gonadal, homonal sex, the internal reproductive organs, and the ambiguous appearances of the external genitalia were identical) have shown that one will consider oneself male or female depending simply on whether one was defined and raised as male or female:

> There is no more convincing evidence of the power of social interaction on gender-identity differentiation than in the case of congenital her-

28. Ibid.

maphrodites who are of the same diagnosis and
similar degree of hermaphroditism but are differently assigned and with a different postnatal medical and life history.[29]

Thus, for example, if out of two individuals diagnosed as having the adrenogenital syndrome of
female hermaphroditism, one is raised as a girl and
one as a boy, each will act and identify her/himself
accordingly. The one raised as a girl will consider
herself a girl; the one raised as a boy will consider
himself a boy; and each will conduct her/himself
successfully in accord with that self-definition.

So, identical behavior occurs given different
physiological states; and different behavior occurs
given an identical physiological starting point. So it
is not clear that differences in sex hormones are at
all relevant to behavior.

The other category of theory based on biology, a
reductionist theory, goes like this. Sex-role behavior
in some primate species is described, and it is con-
cluded that this is the "natural" behavior for humans. Putting aside the not insignificant problem of
observer bias (for instance, Harlow[30] of the University of Wisconsin, after observing differences
between male and female rhesus monkeys, quotes

29. J. Money, "Sexual Dimorphism and Homosexual
Gender Identity," *Psychological Bulletin* 6 (1970): 425–
440.
See also J. L. Hampton, and J. C. Hampton, "The Onto-
genesis of Sexual Behavior in Man," *Sex and Internal Se-
cretions*, ed. W. C. Young (1966), pp. 1401–1432.
30. H. F. Harlow, "The Heterosexual Affectional System
in Monkeys," *The American Psychologist* 17 (1962): 1–9.

Laurence Sterne to the effect that women are silly and trivial, and concludes that "men and women have differed in the past and they will differ in the future"), there are a number of problems with this approach.

The most general and serious problem is that there are no grounds to assume that anything primates do is necessary, natural, or desirable in humans, for the simple reason that humans are not nonhumans. For instance, it is found that male chimpanzees placed alone with infants will not "mother" them. Jumping from hard data to ideological speculation, researchers conclude from this information that *human* females are necessary for the safe growth of human infants. It would be reasonable to conclude, following this logic, that it is quite useless to teach human infants to speak, since it has been tried with chimpanzees and it does not work.

One strategy that has been used is to extrapolate from primate behavior to "innate" human preference by noticing certain trends in primate behavior as one moves phylogenetically closer to humans. But there are great difficulties with this approach. When behaviors of lower primates are directly opposite to those of higher primates, or to those one expects of humans, they can be dismissed on evolutionary grounds—higher primates and/or humans grew out of that kid stuff. On the other hand, if the behavior of higher primates is counter to the behavior considered natural for humans, while the behavior of some lower primate is considered the natural one for humans, the higher primate behavior can be dismissed also, on the grounds that it has diverged from an older, prototypical pattern. So either way, one can select those behaviors one wants to prove as innate for humans. In addition, one does not know whether the sex-role behavior exhibited is dependent on the phylogenetic rank, or on the environmental conditions (both physical and social) under which different species live.

Is there then any value at all in primate observations as they relate to human females and males? There is a value but it is limited: its function can be no more than to show some extant examples of diverse sex-role behavior. It must be stressed, however, that this is an extremely limited function. The extant behavior does not begin to suggest all the possibilities, either for non-human primates or for humans. Bearing these caveats in mind, it is nonetheless interesting that if one inspects the limited set of observations of existing nonhuman primate sex-role behaviors, one finds, in fact, a much larger range of sex-role behavior than is commonly believed to exist. "Biology" appears to limit very little; the fact that a female gives birth does not mean, even in non-humans, that she necessarily cares for the infant (in marmosets, for instance, the male carries the infant at all times except when the infant is feeding[31]); "natural" female and male behavior varies all the way from females who are much more aggressive and competitive than males (*e.g.,* Tamarins) and male "mothers" (*e.g.,* Titi monkeys, night monkeys,

31. Mitchell, "Paternalistic Behavior in Primates."

and marmosets)[32] to submissive and passive females and male antagonists (*e.g.,* rhesus monkeys).

But even for the limited function that primate arguments serve, the evidence has been misused. Invariably, one of those primates has been cited which exhibits exactly the kind of behavior that the proponents of the biological fixedness of human female behavior wish were true for humans. Thus, baboons and rhesus monkeys are generally cited: males in these groups exhibit some of the most irritable and aggressive behavior found in primates, and if one wishes to argue that females are naturally passive and submissive, these groups provide vivid examples. There are abundant counterexamples, such as those mentioned above[33]; in fact, in general, a counterexample can be found for every sex-role behavior cited, including, as mentioned in the case of marmosets, male "mothers."

But the presence of counterexamples has not stopped florid and overarching theories of the natural or biological basis of male privilege from proliferating. For instance there have been a number of theories dealing with the innate incapacity in human males for monogamy. Here, as in most of this type of theorizing, baboons are a favorite example, probably because of their fantasy value: the family unit of the hamadryas baboon, for instance, consists of a highly constant pattern of one male and a number of

32. All these are lower-order primates, which makes their behavior with reference to humans unnatural, or more natural; take your choice.
33. Mitchell, "Paternalistic Behavior in Primates."

females and their young. And again, the counter-examples, such as the invariably monogamous gibbon, are ignored.

An extreme example of this maiming and selective truncation of the evidence in the service of a plea for the maintenance of male privilege is a recent book, *Men in Groups* by Tiger. The central claim of this book is that females are incapable of "bonding" as in "male bonding." What is "male bonding"? Its surface definition is simple: ". . . a particular relationship between two or more males such that they react differently to members of their bonding units as compared to individuals outside of it."[34] If one deletes the word male, the definition, on its face, would seem to include all organisms that have any kind of social organization. But this is not what Tiger means. For instance, Tiger asserts that females are incapable of bonding; and this alleged incapacity indicates to Tiger that females should be restricted from public life. Why is bonding an exclusively male behavior? Because, says Tiger, it is seen in male primates. All male primates? No, very few male primates. Tiger cites two examples where male bonding is seen: rhesus monkeys and baboons. Surprise, surprise. But not even all baboons: as mentioned above, the hamadryas social organization consists of one-male units; so does that of the Gelada baboon.[35] And the great apes do not go in for male bonding much either. The "male bond" is hardly a serious

34. L. Tiger, *Men in Groups* (New York: Random House, 1969), pp. 19–20.
35. Mitchell, "Paternalistic Behavior in Primates."

contribution to scholarship; one reviewer for *Science* has observed that the book ". . . shows basically more resemblance to a partisan political tract than to a work of objective social science," with male bonding being ". . . some kind of behavioral phlogiston."[36]

In short, primate arguments have generally misused the evidence; primate studies themselves have, in any case, only the very limited function of describing some possible sex-role behavior; and at present, primate observations have been sufficiently limited so that even the range of possible sex-role behavior for nonhuman primates is not known. This range is not known since there is only minimal observation of what happens to behavior if the physical or social environment is changed. In one study,[37] different troops of Japanese macaques were observed. Here, there appeared to be cultural differences: males in three out of the eighteen troops observed differed in their amount of aggressiveness and infant-caring behavior. There could be no possibility of differential evolution here; the differences seemed largely transmitted by infant socialization. Thus, the very limited evidence points to some plasticity in the sex-role behavior of nonhuman primates; if we can figure out experiments which massively change the social organization of primate groups, it is possible that we might observe great changes in behavior. At present, however, we must

36. M. H. Fried, "Mankind excluding woman," review of Tiger's *Men in Groups, Science* 165 (1969): 883–884.
37. J. Itani, "Paternal Care in the Wild Japanese Monkeys, *Macaca fuscata*," in *Primate Social Behavior,* ed. C. H. Southwick (Princeton: Van Nostrand, 1963).

conclude that given a constant physical environment, non-human primates do not change their social conditions by themselves very much and thus the "innateness" and fixedness of their behavior is simply not known. Thus, even if there were some way, which there isn't, to settle on the behavior of a particular primate species as being the "natural" way for humans, we would not know whether or not this were simply some function of the present social organization of that species. And finally, once again it must be stressed that even if nonhuman primate behavior turned out to be relatively fixed, this would say little about our behavior. More immediate and relevant evidence, *e.g.*, the evidence from social psychology, points to the enormous plasticity in human behavior, not only from one culture to the next, but from one experimental group to the next. One of the most salient features of human social organization is its variety; there are a number of cultures where there is at least a rough equality between men and women.[38] In summary, primate arguments can tell us very little about our "innate" sex-role behavior; if they tell us anything at all, they tell us that there is no one biologically "natural" female or male behavior, and that sex-role behavior in nonhuman primates is much more varied than has previously been thought.

Conclusion

In brief, the uselessness of present psychology (and biology) with regard to women is simply a

38. M. Mead, *Male and Female: A Study of the Sexes in a Changing World* (New York: William Morrow, 1949).

special case of the general conclusion: one must understand the social conditions under which humans live if one is going to attempt to explain their behavior. And, to understand the social conditions under which women live, one must understand the social expectations about women.

How are women characterized in our culture, and in psychology? They are inconsistent, emotionally unstable, lacking in a strong conscience or superego, weaker, "nuturant" rather than productive, "intuitive" rather than intelligent, and, if they are at all "normal," suited to the home and the family. In short, the list adds up to a typical minority group stereotype of inferiority[39]: if they know their place, which is in the home, they are really quite lovable, happy, childlike, loving creatures. In a review of the intellectual differences between little boys and little girls, Eleanor Maccoby[40] has shown that there are no intellectual differences until about high school, or, if there are, girls are slightly ahead of boys. At high school, girls begin to do worse on a few intellectual tasks, such as arithmetic reasoning, and beyond high school, the achievement of women now measured in terms of productivity and accomplishment drops off even more rapidly. There are a number of other, nonintellectual tests which show sex differences; I choose the intellectual differences since it is seen

39. H. M. Hacker, "Women as a minority group," *Social Forces* 30 (1951): 60–69.
40. Eleanor E. Maccoby, "Sex differences in intellectual functioning," in *The Development of Sex Differences*, pp. 25–55.

clearly that women start becoming inferior. It is no use to talk about women being different but equal; all of the tests I can think of have a "good" outcome and a "bad" outcome. Women usually end up at the "bad" outcome. In light of social expectations about women, what is surprising is that little girls don't get the message that they are supposed to be stupid until high school; and what is even more remarkable is that some women resist this message even after high school, college, and graduate school.

My paper began with remarks on the task of the discovery of the limits of human potential. Psychologists must realize that it is they who are limiting discovery of human potential. They refuse to accept evidence, if they are clinical psychologists, or, if they are rigorous, they assume that people move in a context-free ether, with only their innate dispositions and their individual traits determining what they will do. Until psychologists begin to respect evidence, and until they begin looking at the social context within which people move, psychology will have nothing of substance to offer in this task of discovery. I don't know what immutable differences exist between men and women apart from differences in their genitals; perhaps there are some other unchangeable differences; probably there are a number of irrelevant differences. But it is clear that until social expectation for men and women are equal, until we provide equal respect for both men and women, our answers to this question will simply reflect our prejudices.

Additional References:

A. P. Goldstein and S. J. Dean, *The Investigation of Psychotherapy: Commentaries and Readings* (New York: John Wiley, 1966).

R. Rosenthal, "On the Social Psychology of the Psychological Experiment: the Experimenter's Hypothesis as Unintended Determinants of Experimental Results," *American Scientist* 51 (1963): 268–283.

Schwarz-Belkin, "Les Fleurs de Mal" in *Festschrift for Piltdown* (New York: Ponzi Press, 1911).

17. The Politics of Touch

NANCY M. HENLEY

Social interaction is the battlefield where the war between the sexes is fought daily, minute by minute; or, perhaps better said, the arena where women are continually being chewed up (as one of my students is fond of saying, "Lions 10, Christians 0"). Women are constantly being put down when they act uppity, or reminded to stay down even when they don't, by many "little" reminders of their inferior status. These status reminders are the same ones used to control other one-down groups by psychological means, but they are probably more readily applied to women, since women are more amenable to such control. In addition, it is probable that different reminders are used to varying extents with different groups.

Examples of the status reminders I'm referring to

From Know Press.

are nonhuman environmental cues, noncontent aspects of language, and movement and gesture in interaction. Every woman as she walks through her environment sees, whether aware of it or not, the pictures showing a boss dictating while the secretary writes, head bent; or the doctor operating with the nurse assisting him; or sees the difference between her office and that of the man she works for; she sees the restaurants populated with waitresses serving men, and banks with women behind, men in front; the ads don't let her forget that care of the house and the children are her responsibilities, not her husband's, or that she is first and foremost a sexual object and has an obligation to nurture that image of herself. In the noncontent aspects of language, I refer to such reminders as terms of address, which, as Brown and others have shown us, indicate status when used nonreciprocally, and to dialect differences which indicate status (women's distinctive vocabulary has not been studied enough, though it is well known that they are barred from using a good deal of the lexicon available to men). In the realm of social interaction with respect to language, there is the phenomenon of interruption: while it is often assumed that interrupting is a personality characteristic perhaps associated with dominance, it is nevertheless true that members of a dominant social group use it to assert themselves over subordinate groups. Interrupting, and refusing to allow interruption from others, are indicators of status and are used frequently in conversation groups when men and women are talking.

Of course, in interaction there are indicators of self-confidence, security, and self-esteem which are more likely to be found in members of the dominant culture—less hesitation in speech and movement, for instance. Though tendencies to hesitate and to apologize may seem to proceed more from personality differences than direct power plays, their more likely presence in members of the subordinate culture is a reminder of relative power, and they are often shown in situations where power is being asserted by someone else. Because of this, such actions, *i.e.,* hesitation and apologizing, may be considered submissive gestures. Some typical dominant gestures which may evoke submissive ones are staring directly at a person, pointing at a person, and touching a person. Corresponding gestures of submission, all of them common to women, include lowering the eyes, shutting up or not even beginning to speak when pointed at, and cuddling to the touch.

When the content of language is considered we find straightforward put-downs, frequently disguised as humor or compliments, but they are intended to distract a woman from serious purpose and remind her of her sexual role. ("How can someone as pretty as you come on so intellectual?" "You're beautiful when you're mad.") Watch a man losing an argument with a woman, and you will often find either comments like these (one male professor told a female instructor, "I can't hear a word you're saying, because you're wearing a skirt") or reminders of physical strength, subtle or not so subtle. Veiled physical threats may be seen in the playful and

P

casual lifting and tossing around that is often done
with women—in a park where hippies hang out
recently one evening, I saw one girl placed over a
guy's knee and spanked, another more or less thrown
in the water. At a country square dance a month
ago, I saw an offensive game between two men on
opposite sides of a square, to see who could swing
the women hardest and highest off the ground; what
started out pleasantly enough soon degenerated into
a brutal competition that left the women of the
square staggering dizzily from place to place, completely unable to keep up with what was going on in
the dance, and certainly getting no pleasure from it.
What woman would not be reminded of her inferior
physical abilities by such a display?

The act of touching, when nonreciprocal, is, I believe, an even more subtle physical threat used to
remind persons of their status, and is particularly
used by men against women. To support the argument that touching is a sign of power, I would like to
ask you to consider interactions of various pairs of
persons that I will name, and to picture who would
be more likely to touch the other (*e.g.*, putting an
arm around the shoulder, hand on the back, tapping
the chest, holding the wrist, etc.): teacher and student, master and servant, policeman and accused,
doctor and patient, minister and parishioner, adviser
and advisee, foreman and worker, businessman and
secretary. If you have had the usual enculturation, I
think you will find the typical picture to be that of
the superior-status person touching the inferior-
status one. In fact, it is often considered an affront,

insubordination, for a person of lower status to touch one of higher status. Did you ever see a family portrait made with the wife standing resting her hand on the husband's shoulder rather than the other way around?

Other considerations that have led me to consider touching in this light are some stories told me by other women, and I'd like to share them with you. One woman friend of mine told me that when she worked in an Italian grocery there was, among the persons working in the store, a hierarchy of who touched whom, from the owner down. A woman student who works as a waitress tells me that where she works she is being touched all the time by men customers—these men do not touch the waiters, nor do women customers. What happens when women do touch men, if, as I say, they are not supposed to? Another woman student tells me she freaks out her male friends constantly by initiating and reciprocating their touch—they don't know how to deal with it. An older woman told me of an incident in which, at a party one evening, a male friend of her and her husband sat often with his arm around her in what she took to be a friendly gesture. When she reciprocated the gesture, with only friendly intent, he soon got her alone and suggested sleeping together; she showed surprise at the suggestion, but he said, "Wasn't that what you were trying to tell me all evening?" In other words, women do not interpret a man's touch as necessarily implying sexual intent, but men interpret a woman's touch in that way. I will consider later the hypothesis that touching is a sexual gesture, and my own analysis of the difference in implications of touching for men and women. My favorite anecdote involves myself, the Vice Chancellor, and Chancellor of my own university. After a large meeting last spring, the Vice Chancellor came over to me and took my upper arms in his two hands, saying he wanted to tell me something; he continued holding me in this restrictive fashion as he proceeded to talk with me. After he finished, and he had finally let go, I grabbed him back (something I try to do now whenever men lay their hands on me—really scares them), then remarked that I would have to tell him sometime about my thesis which is the subject of this paper. He expressed interest, so I began telling him about it, and since he is an intelligent man he saw some truth in it; at this moment the Chancellor approached, the only man on campus in higher authority, laid his hand on the arm of the Vice Chancellor, and urged him to accompany him to their next meeting. The Vice Chancellor and I were both struck by the aptness of this action, and I think I made my point.

There is also some empirical evidence in support of the thesis that females are touched by others more than males are. Goldberg and Lewis (1969) report that six-month-old girls are already being touched more often by their mothers than are infant boys. Among older subjects, Jourard has done two studies, the second with Rubin, which investigate the amount of touching done among certain members of the family and among friends of college age. Young unmarried students of both sexes filled out a question-

naire in which they indicated on which of a number
of body regions they had touched or been touched by
their mother, father, closest same-sex friend, or
closest opposite-sex friend. Jourard writes in his first
study, "When it comes to physical contact within the
family, it is the daughters who are the favored
ones," presumably referring to the finding that
daughters both touch their mothers and fathers
more, and are touched more by their fathers, than
are sons. The second study shows a more pro-
nounced pattern of sexual interaction within the
family: mothers touch their sons more than do
fathers, and fathers touch their daughters more than
they do their sons; daughters touch their fathers
more than sons do, and sons touch their mothers
more than they touch their fathers. At first sight this
may look like a pattern of opposite-sex tactual interaction within the family; however, the pattern may
be succinctly, and more accurately, described by
saying that fathers and sons refrain from touching
each other; other tactual interaction within the family group (between parents and children) is about
equal. When we examine the percentage of subjects
reporting touching and being touched in the different
body regions, we find mothers touch daughters in
more regions than they do sons; fathers touch
daughters in more regions than they do sons (and
are touched by their daughters in more regions than
sons touch them in); and males touch their opposite-
sexed best friends in more regions than females
report doing to their opposite-sexed friends. In other
words, in three of the four significant comparisons,

females are begin touched more. The women's mean
total "being-touched" score, reported only in the
second study, is indeed higher than the men's. Inter-
correlations among scores of being touched by
different persons show first of all, higher r's among
women than men, suggesting, in Jourard's words,
"more consistency in attitude and behavior regarding
body contact, or perhaps less discrimination than the
males in accepting or spurning the extended hands of
others." Jourard and Rubin take the view that
"touching is equated with sexual intent, either consciously, or at a less-conscious level."

I turn now to my own research. A male research
assistant, naive to the thesis of this paper, has spent
fifty-odd hours observing incidents of touching in
public. In the ninety-nine incidents he recorded, sex,
age, race, approximate social class, and occupational
status were recorded for both toucher and touchee.
Nine observations were discarded either because the
initiation of touching was not observed or because
one of the demographic variables could not be recorded. Summary statistics for incidence of touching
between persons differing in the various categories
support the thesis that touch indicates a status difference: for both socioeconomic status and age, the
differences in touch initiations by higher status and
lower status persons have a probability of .05 or
less. There were only three cases of interracial touching, so no conclusions can be drawn about the use of
touch in this status category. For sex, there were
forty-one cases of men touching women, compared
with twenty-one of women touching men; touching

within the sexes was about equal, fifteen for women and thirteen for men. The differences in this distribution are significant, $p < .001$, by the chi square one-sample test (with expectancies for interactions calculated from the percentages of males and females in the population). Moreover, when we look only at cases in which all other recorded demographic data are equal, the only difference being in sex, we find an even more striking difference: for males touching females, twenty-three cases; for all other categories, five each. In other words, all other things equal, men touch women at an even greater rate; when other things are unequal, as for instance when women have other status advantages in the absence of the sex one, there is more chance of women initiating touching incidents. It is also interesting to look at some data detailing more closely the combined or conflicting influences of sex and age on tendency to touch another: of the forty-two cases having age differences, thirty involved children. Even here, where age status sometimes conflicted with sex status, there is a tendency toward the adult distribution, with more cases of males touching females than any other. Of only four cases in which a child was observed to initiate touch with an older person, all were touching females; and of only three cases observed of children touching each other, all were touching females. I interpret these data as support for my theses that touch indicates higher status, and especially, that men touch women more than vice versa.

There is not necessarily conflict in the alternative hypothesis that touch represents intimacy. Rather, the two hypotheses are complementary, in the same way that hypotheses that first-naming someone indicates superior status or indicates intimacy. There is no question that persons who are psychologically close to one another exchange touch more; touch may be regarded as a nonverbal equivalent of calling another by first name: used reciprocally, it indicates solidarity; when nonreciprocal, it indicates status. Even when there is solidarity, however, we may note that there is some indication of status difference when we consider who, over the course of dating by a couple, initiates touching: usually the male is the first to place his arm around the female, rather than vice versa.

Another hypothesis that may be advanced is that touching indicates no more than sexual attraction when it involves the two sexes; this hypothesis is sometimes offered as a complete explanation of why men touch women more. But the question must be asked why, if it is a matter of sex, women don't also touch men just as frequently. Would anyone argue that women are less sexually motivated than are men? If not that, if women are equally motivated, then we must say that women are inhibited from displaying their sexual interest in this manner, and the question becomes why this is so. At this point we are back where we started, asking why one sex group feels free to express its motivation tactually and another does not. We are left with the status difference, which becomes all the more worthy of our consideration when we recall that it is a common variable to the other situations of status difference examined in which touch frequencies differed. If status may be accepted as a basis for the explanation in all other cases, why when sex status is considered must we look for another explanation? The law of parsimony tells us to base our explanations on as few common variables as possible. The question of why a man's touch is not interpreted as sexual while a woman's is, may be seen then in this light: because touch is an indication of power, it is acceptable when done by a man; when by a woman, the implication of power is unacceptable and must be denied.

In summary, I take the findings of more frequent initiation of touching by males as indicative that touching is one more tool used by a male supremacist society to keep women in their place, another reminder that women's bodies are free property for everyone's use. One is appalled to consider that something so human, so natural, as touching should be perverted into a symbol of status and power. But a moment's thought reminds us that this is the story of other simple facts of our being unrelated to status, such as clothing, shelter, and food. Acceptance of the thesis of my paper has certain implications for men and women who wish to change the male-dominant nature of our society. Men should become conscious of their tactual interactions with women especially, and guard against using touch to assert authority; they should be careful not to teach their sons to do so; at the same time, men should monitor their reactions to being touched by women, correcting and reversing negative feelings based purely on receiving touch. Women similarly have a responsibility to themselves to refuse to accept tactual assertion of authority—they should remove their hands from the grasp of men who hold them too long, and remove men's hands from their person when such a touch is unsolicited and unwanted; they should train themselves, at the same time, not to submit to another's will because of the subtle implication of his touch, and—why not?—start touching men, if the situation is appropriate, in order to break through the sexist pattern of tactual interaction. (I happen to favor forcefully applied tactual interaction when the situation calls for it.)

Finally, I would like to point out vehemently that all the correctives I have just listed are mere stop-gaps which cannot begin to alter the male chauvinist nature of male-female interactions; I doubt, in fact, that they *can* be applied in the present nature of things. Only when these power relations themselves are destroyed, not just their indicators, will we strip the indicators of their power symbolism.

References

R. Brown, *Social Psychology* (Glencoe, Illinois: Free Press, 1965).

R. Brown and M. Ford, "Address in American English," *Journal of Abnormal and Social Psychology* 62 (1961): 375–385.

R. Brown and A. Gilman, "The Pronouns of Power and Solidarity," in *Style in Language,* ed. T. A. Sebeok (Cambridge: Technology Press, 1960).

S. Goldberg and M. Lewis, "Play Behavior in the

Year-Old Infant: Early Sex Differences," *Child Development* 40 (1969): 21–31.

S. M. Jourard, "An Exploratory Study of Body-Accessibility," *British Journal of Social and Clinical Psychology* 5 (1966): 221–231.

S. M. Jourard and J. E. Rubin, "Self-Disclosure and Touching: A Study of Two Modes of Interpersonal Encounter and Their Interreaction," *Journal of Humanistic Psychology* 8 (1968): 39–48.

18. Male Supremacy in Freud

PHIL BROWN

Introduction

The intent of this paper is to set forth a critique of
Sigmund Freud's ideology of male supremacy, a
necessary critique since the Freudian framework has
been of tremendous influence in Western culture for
the greater part of this century. The context in which
I am setting this down is one of attempting to
destroy certain mythologies about women. My position as a man makes this task rather difficult, although I am not attempting to create a definitive
work on this subject. Rather, I am working as a man
in fighting male supremacy, and this paper is a part
of that. I take for granted a basic understanding
among readers that male supremacy is a major form
of oppression in our nation, and that it is not only a

From *The Radical Therapist*, vol. 2, no. 2 (September
1971).

socioeconomic formation. Rather, like most oppression in advanced industrial nations of the West, the
oppression of women takes psychological roots
within the masses of people by socialization into sex-
roles and accompanying life-styles. Since Freud is
the major figure in this crusade against 51 per cent
of the population, it is imperative that his mythologies be cast aside.

The classic picture of Freud is of an anti-Victorian, struggling against sexual repression. This is,
of course, a false picture—Freud codified the prevalent attitudes toward sex rather than oppose them.
His work was not part of a "sexual revolution," but
of a counterrevolution, as Kate Millett points out,[1]
an attempt which succeeded in molding many of the
psychological and lay opinions about women which
are held to date.

Part of Freud's male supremacist views were more
than codifications of prevailing beliefs—these were
the new myths he invented, especially penis envy,
vaginal orgasm, and masculinity complex. It is amazing that he would not admit to this speculative
nature—Freud claimed that his views on women
were based on "nothing but observed facts, with
hardly any speculative additions."[2] But Freud's
patients were mainly adult males, and it is known
that a good deal of his theorizing on sexuality is

1. Kate Millett, *Sexual Politics* (New York: Doubleday,
1970).
2. S. Freud, *New Introductory Lectures on Psychoanalysis*, trans. W. J. H. Sprott (New York: Norton, 1933), p.
154.

composed of hypothetical thoughts for which his
main source was the young son of a patient, and a
few admissions by a very small number of female
patients. If Freud's theories in general were misinter-
pretations of clinical observations (they rarely were
that close, even), those on women were fabrications
with no real basis whatsoever.

In 1885, Freud's first major work was published,
Studies on Hysteria[3] with Josef Breuer. It is full of
cases of female hysterics (Freud saw hysteria as
mainly a female neurosis) who are clearly victims of
sexually repressed upbringings with sharply defined
sex-typing, but Freud takes this for granted, and it is
the women who must adjust to their social conditions. Throughout the book, conversion symptoms
are presumed by Freud to be based on sexual fears,
traumatically based; and these fears, very real ones,
are stated by Freud to be neurotic. Even were
Freud's interpretations of the symptoms correct, his
approach to the problem as one of adjustment is an
implicit statement in support of male-dominated
sexuality.

The active and passive human activities, associated by Freud respectively with men and women, is
begun in *Hysteria*, but is picked up more in *The
Interpretation of Dreams*,[4] a book which in fact
prefigures much of the later theories on women.
There are constant references to the woman as the

3. S. Freud and Josef Breuer, *Studies on Hysteria*, trans.
James Strachey (New York: Basic Books, 1957).
4. S. Freud, *The Interpretation of Dreams* in *Basic Writings of Sigmund Freud*, ed. and trans. A. Brill (New York:
Random House, 1938).

passive sex in her role as housewife, male-seeker, suckler of babies, and physically clumsy. This is carried on into dream-symbolism:

> All elongated objects, sticks, tree trunks, umbrellas, all sharp and elongated weapons, knives, daggers, and pikes, represent the male member. . . . Small boxes, chests, cupboards, and ovens correspond to the female organ; also cavities, ships, and all kinds of vessels.[5]

The basic assumption behind this is the penetration of the male penis into the female vagina as the only acceptable mode of sexuality, but this view is expanded to include all forms of human endeavor; persons in dreams are taken to symbolize the penis, and landscapes to represent the vagina,[6] the logic of this being that men are active persons within an environment, passive women being the background for male achievement.

Freud sees dreams as wish-fulfillments, nearly always sexually oriented, and within that framework he attributes women's dreams as desires to be penetrated by men, or other desires which he equates with passive femininity. Interpreting a woman's dream of putting a candle into a holder, the candle breaking as she tried to perform the task, Freud speaks of the candle as "an object which excites the female genitals" and the breaking of it as representing the woman's frigidity due to masturbation. Similar is the view that when a woman dreams of a man masturbating, that is a vicarious act of penetration

5. Ibid., p. 371.
6. Ibid., p. 379.

by him into her.[7] Women's dream symbolism, because of Freud's presumed weakness of women, is always representative of the worst: "When a person of the female sex dreams of falling, this almost always has a sexual significance; she becomes a fallen woman." Also due to female weakness, a woman's dream of carrying a man is an infantile fantasy because that is not the proper arrangement of things.[8]

The Oedipus complex, one of psychoanalysis's most warped myths, is mentioned substantially for the first time in *Interpretation of Dreams*. It brings with it the fallacy of penis envy. I will take this up at this time, rather than continue chronologically, for most of the basic points of the Freudian psychology of women are at least in embryonic form by this time, to be nearly fully codified five years later in the infamous *Three Contributions to the Theory of Sexuality*.[9]

Freud would have us believe that the young girl, upon finding out that little boys have a penis, envies this organ, and feels that she has the castrated, blaming her mother for this. We are further led to believe that the larger part of the female psyche is based on the missing penis and the female wish for it.[10] Freud assumes that the little girl is tremendously threatened by the lack of a penis, feeling "herself at a great

7. Ibid., pp. 253–254, 388.
8. Ibid., pp. 264, 327.
9. S. Freud, *Three Contributions to the Theory of Sexuality*, in Brill, *Basic Writings*.
10. Freud, *Interpretation of Dreams*, pp. 306–309, 377–378.

disadvantage . . . she clings for a long time to the desire to get something like it. . . ." She will then search, through the rest of her life, for surrogates, converting this search into other human activities:

> The desire after all to obtain the penis for which she so much longs may even contribute to the motives that impel a grown-up woman to come to analysis; and what she quite reasonably expects to get from analysis, such as the capacity to pursue an intellectual career, can often be recognized as a sublimated modification of this repressed wish.[11]

The young girl's discovery of her "castration" leads to her Oedipal stage, in the opposite order of the male Oedipal situation. Penis envy and its corresponding reverse Oedipal complex will have many consequences for her, including the performance of erroneous acts,[12] seduction fantasies, narcissism, and masochism. These "perversions" are attributed to the female passivity theory of Freud—narcissism since "for them to be loved is a stronger need than to love," and masochism since it is "constitutional" in the weak feminine psyche.[13]

In terms of general development after puberty, the female child has three choices left to her by Freud: ". . . one leads to sexual inhibition or to neurosis, the second to a modification of character in the sense of masculinity complex, and the third to formal femininity."[14] Freud has already dealt with the first

11. Freud, *New Introductory Lectures*, p. 171.
12. S. Freud, *The Psychopathology of Everyday Life*, in Brill, *Basic Writings*, p. 122.
13. Freud, *New Introductory Lectures*, pp. 158, 164, 180.
14. Ibid., p. 172.

alternative to some extent in *Hysteria,* but the "masculinity complex" is a new turn. It involves "clinging" to clitoral activity through masturbation and retaining clitoral sensitivity; Freud sees the clitoris as not good enough for sexual pleasure, and additionally as a male activity since the clitoris is a "stunted penis."[15] In the Freudian view, the woman must transfer sensitivity to the vagina in order to be normal:

> In the transformation to womanhood very much depends upon the early and complete relegation of this sensitivity from the clitoris over to the vaginal orifice. In those women who are sexually anaesthetic, as it is called, the clitoris has stubbornly retained this sensitivity.[16]

This is the Freudian biology which is aimed at making the woman the property of the man by defining correct sexuality as penetration, thus giving the woman no pleasure in sexual intercourse. Vaginal orgasm has, of course, been completely discredited by scientific research and personal experience of women.

The only role that Freud will allow to the clitoris is that of conducting pleasure to the vagina, but even this is minimized. Failure to adjust to this type of sexuality leads, in Freud's mind, to neurosis (especially hysteria) and perversions, like foot fetishism.[17]

15. Ibid., pp. 93, 172, 177.
16. S. Freud, *A General Introduction to Psychoanalysis,* trans. Joan Riviere (New York: Permabook, 1953), p. 327.
17. Freud, *Three Contributions to the Theory of Sex,* p. 592.

On hysteria, Freud had this to say:

> One may often observe that it is just those girls
> who in the years before puberty showed a boyish
> character and inclinations who had become hys-
> terical at puberty. In a whole series of cases the
> hysterical neuroses are nothing but an over-
> accentuation of the typical wave of repression
> through which the masculine type of sexuality is
> removed and the woman emerges.[18]

Masculine sexuality in the woman means, for Freud,
the refusal to give up the real seat of sexual pleasure.

Another possibility, according to Freud, if the
woman does not conform is homosexuality, which he
sees as bad,[19] and continued infantile "polymorphous perversity." Freud, in fact, sees women as
naturally inclined to take part in the so-called perversions at the slightest suggestion by any man.[20]

What, then, is normal female sexuality for Freud?
Since clitoral sensitivity is supposed to shift to the
vagina, then it is logical in the Freudian weltan-
schauung to assert the penetration of the vagina by
the penis is the one correct sexual mode. But Freud
goes far beyond this, sanctifying this oppression with
biological fulfillment: ". . . the achievement of the
biological aim is entrusted to the aggressive male,
and is to some extent independent of the cooperation

18. S. Freud, *Dora—An Analysis of a Case of Hysteria*, trans. Philip Rieff (New York: Collier, 1963), p.
157.
19. Freud, *New Introductory Lectures*, p. 177.
20. Freud, *Three Contributions to the Theory of Sex*,
p. 592.

of the female."[21] This is related to the male aggressive/female passive approach that exists throughout Freud's writings, based in his eyes at the supposed anal stage where active and passive modes of behavior prefigure what will be the later masculine and feminine sexual modes. Freud sticks to the Victorian idea of sexual activity as correct only for procreation, although he attempts to make it seem not so. For him, the culmination of human sexual activity is the discharge of semen by the male into the female.[22] The only attempt at explanation is within the scope of biological determinism:

> The male sexual cell is active and mobile; it seeks out the female one while the latter, the ovum, is stationary, and waits passively. This behavior of the elementary organisms of sex is more or less a model of the behavior of the individual of each sex in sexual intercourse.[23]

It is, by far, a weak analogy, but Freud's procreative bent is not the only fault in his theory; also important is that for Freud, sexuality precludes anything but penile/vaginal sex, and classifies exceptions as pathological: To be raped is normal, to have pleasure is crazy—this is the master's dictum.

Another important part of Freud's male supremacy is found in his theories concerning the nature of civilization, and families within it. He sees the authoritarian father of the primal horde who keeps all the women for himself being slain by the sons, who

21. Freud, *New Introductory Lectures,* p. 180.
22. Freud, *Three Contributions to the Theory of Sex,* pp. 597–598, 604.
23. Freud, *New Introductory Lectures,* p. 156.

then set up a sexually repressive society to prevent a similar occurrence from happening in the future. This is Freud's original Oedipal situation, and agrees with the correctness of the sons setting up a sexually repressive society not only to contain the "aggressive" male sexuality, but also because he sees women as an incitement to sex because of their "peculiar helplessness."[24] The modern parallel to this is the male claim that rape is the fault of the woman for putting out certain psychological feelers and inducements, and certainly shows in what low esteem Freud holds women. The mythical primal horde is the basis for all future male supremacist society, and for Freud this is a positive step in the progress of history.

Based on his conception that sublimation of instincts is necessary for civilization, Freud sees the family as an important nexus of this, although one wonders how much sublimation is required of the male:

> One may suppose that the founding of families was connected with the fact that a moment came when the need for genital satisfaction no longer made its appearance like a guest who drops in suddenly, and, after his departure, is heard of no more for a long time, but instead took up its quarter as a permanent lodger. When this happened, the male acquired a motive for keeping the female, or speaking more generally, his sexual object, near him; while the female who did not want to be separated from her helpless young, was

24. S. Freud, *Totem and Taboo*, in Brill, *Basic Writings*, pp. 832, 915.

obliged, in her interests, to remain with the stronger male.[25]

This seems more like legalized rape than "civilization," but Freud consistently equated the oppression of women with the sublimation of instincts and the progress of society:

> The communal life of human beings has, therefore, a two-fold foundation: the compulsion to work, which is created by external necessity, and the power of love, which made the man unwilling to be deprived of his sexual object—the woman—and made the woman unwilling to be deprived of the part of herself which had been separated off from her—her child.[26]

Now we come to the role of the woman in the family—she is no more than one who bears children and then takes care of them; moreover, that is the fulfillment of all her needs, psychologically and socially.[27] The progress of civilization is the enslavement of women:

> Women increasingly represent the interests of the family and of the sexual life. The work of civilization has become increasingly the business of men, it confronts them with the ever more difficult tasks and compels them to carry out instinctual sublimations of which women are little capable.[28]

The only truth that might be hidden here is that the authoritarian sublimation demanded by Freud hits women harder than it does men because of the

25. S. Freud, *Civilization and Its Discontents*, trans. James Strachey (New York: Norton, 1961), p. 46.
26. Ibid., p. 48.
27. Freud, *Totem and Taboo*, p. 818.
28. Freud, *Civilization and Its Discontents*, p. 50.

formers' socio-sexual enslavement. One of the attempts at hiding female sexuality, in Freud's imagination, is the invention by women of weaving and plaiting as an attempt to replicate their pubic hair whose purpose it is to hide their "inferior" genitalia.[29]

Female "weakness," based on the infantile penis envy, is found by Freud in every aspect of human endeavor—women have weak libido which may be all used up on the first child and thus lead to a bad marriage; but the marriage was fated to fail anyway because all women wish to play the role of mother to their husbands.[30] The woman is damned from the first, and nothing she does will satisfy the Freudian construct of society, but she is again blamed for her own damnation: ". . . the woman finds herself forced into the background by the claims of civilization and she adopts a hostile attitude towards it."[31] If, in fact, all women were engaged in active rebellion against such a society, it would be only the most human reaction to the oppression of such a system.

In the Freudian outlook, women are naturally vain as a "further effect of penis envy,"[32] they have a "conventional reticence and insincerity," and a constitutionally-based excessive need for affection.[33] Women's intelligence, like their other Freudian attributes is based on sexual determinism:

> You know, too, that women in general are said to suffer from "physiological feeble-mindedness"—

29. Freud, *New Introductory Lectures*, p. 181.
30. Ibid., pp. 182–183.
31. Freud, *Civilization and Its Discontents*, p. 50.
32. Freud, *New Introductory Lectures*, p. 180.
33. Freud, *Three Contributions*, pp. 565, 618.

that is, from a lesser intelligence than men. The fact itself is disputable and its interpretation doubtful, but one argument in favor of this intellectual atrophy being of a secondary nature is that women labor under the harshness of an early prohibition against turning their thoughts to what would most have interested them—namely, the problem of sexual life.[34]

Again Freud is blaming women for their being oppressed by male society, and he posits as the explanation the fact the women are basically only interested in sexuality and nothing more.

Of justice and social interest, Freud has this to say:

It must be admitted that women have but little sense of justice, and this is no doubt connected with the preponderance of envy in their mental life; for the demands of justice are a modification of envy; they lay down the conditions under which one is willing to part with it. We also say of women that their social interests are weaker than those of men, and that their capacity for the sublimation of their instincts is less.[35]

All in all, there is no hope for women in the psychoanalytic framework. Where Freud sees a thirty-year-old man as youthful with many possibilities ahead, a woman of the same age displays, as he puts it, ". . . psychological rigidity and unchangeability. Her libido has taken up its final positions, and seems

34. S. Freud, *The Future of an Illusion,* trans. W. D. Robson-Scott (Garden City, N.Y.: Doubleday, 1964), p. 79.

35. Freud, *New Introductory Lectures,* p. 183.

powerless to leave them for others."[36] But the classic dehumanizing statement is the last few lines of the lecture on "The Psychology of Women" in the *New Introductory Lectures,* one of his most sexist works:

> You must not forget, however, that we have only described women in so far as their nature is determined by their sexual function. The influence of this factor is, of course, very far-reaching, but we must remember that *an individual woman may be a human being apart from this.* If you want to know more about femininity, you must interrogate your own experience, or turn to the poets, or else wait until Science can give you more profound and more coherent information[37] (*my emphasis*).

What Freud called the riddle of femininity was a situation for him, as the master of psychoanalysis, to delve into—knowing that he could not understand it; and no one else was to touch the subject, especially the women in the feminist movement whom he reproached for not understanding the immutability of the Oedipal stage and penis envy.[38]

The remarkable thing about Freudianism (in the original) is that single parts of it neither stand alone nor can be refuted alone. One either accepts the whole, or rejects it. If one attempts to disprove it, the problem is presented of how exactly to do it. Mere presentation of its male supremacist ideology, explicit and implicit, is not enough to convince psychoanalysts and others utilizing some type of

36. Ibid., p. 184.
37. Ibid., p. 184.
38. Ibid., p. 177.

psychoanalytic framework, for they have taken the ideology deep inside and feel it rather than only think it, so far has it reached. Some neo-Freudians have attempted to correct the sexist deficiencies in Freud's work, but they basically do this within the psychoanalytic tradition. This is not the answer.

Rationalist thought of the Western tradition relies on faulty empiricism as well as outright speculation, and its basically metaphysical foundations are constructed to ward off such attacks. In Freudian theory, a metapsychology has been created, and there is always that foundation for it to fall back on. This metapsychology is not the result of male supremacy alone, nor is an attack on male supremacy alone enough to puncture it. Its intellectual background is composed of very fallible logic—one aspect of this is its reductionism by which the metapsychology seeks to reduce complex human thought and behavior to a lowest common denominator, based on the supposition that the whole is composed of individual parts which can be mathematically tied together with no pretence of grasping complex human interaction.

This is tied in with the positivism of the Freudian metapsychology which posits an absolute world with definite (and thus unchanging) structures. Freud's modern positivism does not dwell on an empyrean universe, but instead fixates on a universe of immutable human nature. Given this novel form of original sin, people are not to be trusted; and given the mythic Eve, women especially are not to be trusted. There is a real continuity between the oppression of women and the basic distrust of people in general in the Freudian viewpoint, an outlook which for all its anti-clericalism, is dependent upon Judaeo-Christian traditions of renunciation of pleasure, and of family-based male supremacy. Stripped of its pseudo-biology, Freudianism could be found for the greater part, in different language, in the holy books of Western culture.

But Freudianism has taken root in the United States more than in any advanced Western nation. Why is this, given the U.S. as the least religious of these countries? Psychoanalysis, as the new religion, fits into an American framework, for it demands less actual ritual than a traditional religion and requires analyst/technicians rather than priest/counsellors to administer it, quite a drawing card in a nation of technicians.

One aspect of religion is the fixation of guilt on a certain group in order to exculpate the mass of believers; this is based on the early church's mythologizing of the "heathens" as the "natural" enemy of the faithful, quite one-sided in light of the conquering stance of the "Church Militant." Women were always a convenient scapegoat; in the Middle Ages, rebellious women—that is, those who distributed contraceptive information, performed abortions, and criticized the church as a repressive and male-dominated authoritarian institution—were called "witches" and burned in order to preserve the sanctity of the rest. Freud pioneered in shifting the blame and guilt of society onto women, and the new religion thus recapitulated its predecessors.

Also, the mystification of sexuality is fitting in a nation where sexuality has been turned around and used in nongenital ways to sell consumer products. This holds true to a greater extent in terms of women, for it is their sexuality that is usually thus mystified. This blends in with the U.S. giving women more opportunities in a superficial sense than other Western countries, but in turn repressing their sexuality even more. Additionally, psychopathology, as the new star chamber, has been utilized in this country more than anywhere in the interests of social control, and psychoanalysis presents the most comprehensive system of psychopathology known or possible (everyone is crazy, and the cause is in their heads rather than in their environment).

For women, this is even more dangerous since in order to keep them tied to societally determined roles, they bear the brunt of psychopathological classification—not only in terms of being more relatively diagnosed (and mis-treated) as "mentally ill," but also in terms of special illnesses being invented just for them; *e.g.,* puerperal (childbirth) and menopausal neuroses and psychoses.

Having earlier mentioned Millett's idea of Freud as a major force in the counterrevolution against the sexual revolution, I would like to pick up on this. Coming as a protest against Victorian moralism (and to some extent emerging from its underground lair inhabited during the Victorian period) a sort of sexual revolution grew up. It protested procreative-oriented sexuality and thus undermined the repressive sexual mores, but it was not complete enough to emancipate the masses, especially the women. Nonetheless, society felt threatened and had to begin a counterattack—Millett clarifies this very well:

> The real causes of the counterrevolution appear to lie in the fact that the sexual revolution had perhaps necessarily, even inevitably, concentrated on the superstructure of patriarchal policy, changing its legal forms, its more flagrant abuses, altering its formal educational patterns, but leaving the socialization processes of temperament and role differentiation intact. Basic attitudes, values, emotions—all that constituted the psychic structure several millennia of patriarchal society had built up—remained insufficiently affected, if not completely untouched. Moreover, the major institutions of the old traditions, patriarchal marriage and the family, were never or rarely challenged.[39]

As to the question of psychoanalytic theory taking root in the U.S. so strongly, Millett states that this nation was the center of the sexual revolution and therefore very much needed Freud.[40]

The rapidly growing women's liberation movement in this country has become very aware of the oppressive Freudian mythology and begun to expose it, not only in scholarly papers and movement periodicals, but in personal understanding and criticism and the development of counterinstitutions as well. Probably one of the most definitive acts by women against Freudianism is leaving therapy guided by

39. Millett, *Sexual Politics,* pp. 176–177.
40. Ibid., p. 178.

Freudians as well as other forms which reflect the male supremacist psychology of women begun by Freud. The final end to Freudian male supremacy will come from the women who have been oppressed by it.

19. Gay Liberation Manifesto

CARL WITTMAN

On Orientation

1. What Homosexuality Is

Nature leaves undefined the object of sexual desire. The gender of that object is imposed socially. Humans originally made homosexuality taboo because they needed every bit of energy to produce and raise children: survival of species was a priority. With overpopulation and technological change, that taboo continues only to exploit us and enslave us.

As kids we refused to capitulate to demands that we ignore our feelings toward each other. Somewhere we found the strength to resist being indoctrinated, and we should count that among our assets. We have to realize that our loving each other is a good thing, not an unfortunate thing, and that we

From *Chicago Seed* with some help from Miller Francis.

have a lot to teach straights about sex, love, strength, and resistance.

Homosexuality is *not* a lot of things. It is not a makeshift in the absence of the opposite sex; it is not hatred or rejection of the opposite sex, it is not genetic; it is not the result of broken homes except inasmuch as we could see the sham of Amerikan marriage. *Homosexuality is the capacity to love someone of the same sex.*

2. Bisexuality

Bisexuality is good; it is the capacity to love people of either sex. The reason so few of us are bisexual is because society made such a big stink about homosexuality that we got forced into seeing ourselves as either straight or nonstraight. Also, many gays got turned off to the ways men are supposed to act with women and vice versa, which is pretty messed up. Gays will begin to turn on to women when 1) it's something that we do because we want to, and not because we should; and 2) when women's liberation changes the nature of heterosexual relationships.

We continue to call ourselves homosexual, not bisexual, even if we do make it with the opposite sex also, because saying "Oh, I'm bi" is a cop-out for a gay. We get told it's OK to sleep with guys as long as we sleep with women, too, and that's still putting homosexuality down. We'll be gay until everyone has forgotten that it's an issue. Then we'll begin to be complete.

3. Heterosexuality

Exclusive heterosexuality is messed up. It reflects a fear of people of the same sex, it's antihomosexual, and it is fraught with frustration. Heterosexual sex is messed up, too: ask women's liberation about what straight guys are like in bed. Sex is aggression for the male chauvinist; sex is obligation for the traditional woman. And among the young, the modern, the hip, it's only a subtle version of the same. For us to become heterosexual in the sense that our straight brothers and sisters are is not a cure, it is a disease.

On Women

1. Lesbianism

It's been a male-dominated society for too long, and that has warped both men and women. So gay women are going to see things differently from gay men; they are going to feel put down as women, too. Their liberation is tied up with both gay liberation and women's liberation.

This paper speaks from the gay male viewpoint. And although some of the ideas in it may be equally relevant to gay women, it would be arrogant to presume this to be a manifesto for lesbians.

2. Male Chauvinism

All men are infected with male chauvinism—we are brought up that way. It means we assume that

Q

women play subordinate roles and are less human than ourselves. (At an early gay liberation meeting, one guy said, "Why don't we invite women's liberation—they can bring sandwiches and coffee.") It is no wonder that so few gay women have become active in our groups.

Male chauvinism, however, is not central to us. We can junk it much more easily than straight men can. For we understand oppression. We have largely opted out of a system which oppresses women daily—our egos are not built on putting women down and having them build us up. Also, living in a mostly male world we have become used to playing different roles, doing our own shitwork. And, finally, we have a common enemy: the big male chauvinists are also the big antigays.

But we need to purge male chauvinism, both in behavior and in thought among us. "Chick" equals "nigger" equals "queer." Think it over.

3. Women's Liberation

They are assuming their equality and dignity and in doing so are challenging the same things we are: the roles, the exploitations of minorities by capitalism, the arrogant smugness of straight white middle-class Amerika. They are our sisters in struggle.

Problems and differences will become clearer when we begin to work together. One major problem is our own male chauvinism. Another is uptightness and hostility to homosexuality that many women have—that is the straight in them. A third problem is differing views on sex: sex for them has meant oppression, while for us it has been a symbol of our freedom. We must come to know and understand each other's style, jargon, and humor.

On Roles

1. Mimicry of Straight Society

We are children of straight society. We still think straight; that is part of our oppression. One of the worst of straight concepts is inequality. Straight (also white, English, male, capitalist) thinking views things in terms of order and comparison. A is before B, B is after A; one is below two is below three; there is no room for equality. This idea gets extended to male/female, on top/on bottom, spouse/not spouse, heterosexual/homosexual, boss/worker, white/black, and rich/poor. Our social institutions cause and reflect this verbal hierarchy. This is Amerika.

We've lived in these institutions all our lives. Naturally we mimic the roles. For too long we mimicked these roles to protect ourselves—a survival mechanism. Now we are becoming free enough to shed the roles which we've picked up from the institutions which have imprisoned us.

"Stop mimicking straights, stop censoring ourselves!"

2. Marriage

Marriage is a prime example of a straight institution fraught with role playing. Traditional marriage is a rotten, oppressive institution. Those of us who have been in heterosexual marriages too often have blamed our gayness on the breakup of the marriage. No. They broke up because marriage is a contract which smothers both people, denies needs, and places impossible demands on both people. And we had the strength, again, to refuse to capitulate to the roles which were demanded of us.

Gay people must stop gauging their self-respect by how well they mimic straight marriages. Gay marriages will have the same problems as straight ones except in burlesque. For the usual legitimacy and pressures which keep straight marriages together are absent, *e.g.,* kids, what parents think, what neighbors say, property inheritance, etc.

To accept that happiness comes through finding a groovy spouse and settling down, showing the world that "we're just the same as you," is avoiding the real issues and is an expression of self-hatred.

3. Alternatives to Marriage

People want to get married for lots of good reasons, although marriage won't often meet those needs or desires. We're all looking for security, a flow of love, and a feeling of belonging and being needed.

These needs can be met through a number of

social relationships and living situations. Things we want to get away from are: 1. exclusiveness, propertied attitudes toward each other, a mutual pact against the rest of the world; 2. promises about the future, which we have no right to make and which prevent us from, or make us feel guilty about, growing; 3. inflexible roles, roles which do not reflect us at the moment but are inherited through mimicry and inability to define equalitarian relationships.

We have to define for ourselves a new pluralistic, role-free social structure. It must contain both the freedom and physical space for people to live alone, live together for a while, live together for a long time, either as couples or in larger numbers; and the ability to flow easily from one of these states to another as our needs change.

Liberation for gay people is defining for ourselves how and with whom we live, instead of measuring our relationships in comparison to straight ones, with straight values.

4. Gay Stereotypes

The straights' image of the gay world is defined largely by those of us who have violated straight roles. There is a tendency among "homophile" groups to deplore gays who play visible roles—the queens and the nellies. As liberated gays, we must take a clear stand. 1. Gays who stand out have become our first martyrs. They came out and withstood disapproval before the rest of us did. 2. If they have suffered from being open, it is straight society whom we must indict, not the queen.

5. Closet Queens

This phrase is becoming analogous to "Uncle Tom." To pretend to be straight sexually, or to pretend to be straight socially, is probably the most harmful pattern of behavior in the ghetto. The married guy who makes it on the side secretly; the guy who will go to bed once but who won't develop any gay relationships; the pretender at work or school who changes the gender of the friend he's talking about; the guy who'll suck cock in the bushes but who won't go to bed.

If we are liberated, we are open with our sexuality. Closet queenery must end. *Come out*.

But: in saying come out, we have to have our heads clear about a few things: 1) closet queens are our brothers, and must be defended against attacks by straight people; 2) the fear of coming out is not paranoia; the stakes are high: loss of family ties, loss of job, loss of straight friends—these are all reminders that the oppression is not just in our heads. It's real. Each of us must make the steps toward openness at our own speed and on our own impulses. Being open is the foundation of freedom: it has to be built solidly; 3) "closet queen" is a broad term covering a multitude of forms of defense, self-hatred, lack of strength, and habit. We are all closet queens in some ways, and all of us had to come out—very few of us were "flagrant" at the age of seven! We must afford our brothers and sisters the same patience we afforded ourselves. And while their closet queenery is part of our oppression, it's more a part of theirs. They alone can decide when and how.

On Oppression

It is important to catalog and understand the different facets of our oppression. There is no future in arguing about degrees of oppression. A lot of "movement" types come on with a line of shit about homosexuals not being oppressed as much as blacks or Vietnamese or workers or women. We don't happen to fit into their ideas of class or caste. Bull! When people feel oppressed, they act on that feeling. We feel oppressed. Talk about the priority of black liberation or ending imperialism over and above gay liberation is just antigay propaganda.

1. Physical Attacks

We are attacked, beaten, castrated, and left dead time and time again. "Punks," often of minority groups who look around for someone under them socially, feel encouraged to beat up on "queens" and cops look the other way. That used to be called lynching.

Cops in most cities have harassed our meeting places: bars and baths and parks. They set up entrapment squads. A Berkeley brother was slain by a cop when he tried to split after finding out that the trick who was making advances to him was a cop. Cities set up "pervert" registration, which if nothing else scares our brothers deeper into the closet.

One of the most vicious slurs on us is the blame

for prison "gang rapes." These rapes are invariably done by people who consider themselves straight. The victims of these rapes are us and straights who can't defend themselves. The press campaign to link prison rapes with homosexuality is an attempt to make straights fear and despise us, so they can oppress us more. It's typical of the fucked-up straight mind to think that homosexual sex involves tying a guy down and fucking him. That's aggression, not sex. If that's what sex is for a lot of straight people, that's a problem they have to solve, not us.

2. Psychological Warfare

Right from the beginning we have been subjected to a barrage of straight propaganda. Since our parents don't know any homosexuals, we grow up thinking that we're alone and different and perverted. Our school friends identify "queer" with any nonconformist or bad behavior. Our elementary school teachers tell us not to talk to strangers or accept rides. Television, billboards, and magazines put forth a false idealization of male/female relationships, and make us wish we were different, wish we were "in." In family-living class we're taught how we're supposed to turn out. And all along, the best we hear if anything about homosexuality is that it's an unfortunate problem.

3. Self-Oppression

As gay liberation grows, we will find our uptight brothers and sisters, particularly those who are making a buck off our ghettos, coming on strong to defend the status quo. This is self-oppression: "Don't rock the boat"; "things in San Francisco [or Atlanta] are OK"; "Gay people just aren't together"; "I'm not oppressed." These lines are right out of the mouths of the straight establishment. A large part of our oppression would end if we would stop putting ourselves and our pride down.

4. Institutional

Discrimination against gays is blatant, if we open our eyes. Homosexual relationships are illegal, and even if these laws are not regularly enforced, they encourage and enforce closet queenery. The bulk of the social work/psychiatric field looks upon homosexuality as a problem, and treats us as sick. Employers let it be known that our skills are acceptable only as long as our sexuality is hidden. Big business and government are particularly notorious offenders.

The U.S. Army stands dead center in a culture founded on male supremacy and antihomosexualism, and no homosexual should be required to serve. But the Pentagon wants to have it both ways: officially it excludes a homosexual categorically if he is willing to publicly declare his "sickness," but in the last three years, as any number of gay men know, the army has drafted homosexuals even if they checked the box (obtaining not only another inductee but also useful information about him that might further his exploitation and oppression). For gay men to concern themselves about exclusion from the military is comparable to black people worrying about being denied entrance to the KKK. Once in, homosexuals are oppressed in every conceivable way, and many even have to carry some of these official forms of discrimination and harassment with them when they return to civilian life.

On Sex

1. What Sex Is

It is both creative expression and communication: good when it is either, and better when it is both. Sex can also be aggression, and usually is when those involved do not see each other as equals; and it can also be perfunctory, when we are distracted or preoccupied. These uses spoil what is good about it.

I like to think of good sex in terms of playing musical instruments: with both people on one level seeing the other body as an object capable of creating beauty when they play it well; and on a second level the players communicating through their mutual production and appreciation of beauty. As in good music, you get totally into it—and coming back out of that state of consciousness is like finishing a work of art or coming back from an episode of an acid or mescaline trip. And to press the analogy further: the variety of music is infinite and varied, depending on the capabilities of the players, both as subjects and as objects. Solos, duets, quartets (symphonies, even, if you happen to dig romantic music!), classical, folk, jazz, soul, country, rock and roll, electric or acoustic—got live if you want it, and everything is permitted! The variations in gender, response, and bodies are like different instruments. And perhaps what we have called sexual orientation probably just means that we have not yet learned to turn on to the total range of musical expression.

2. Objectification

In this scheme, people are sexual objects, but they are also subjects, and are human beings who appreciate themselves as object and subject. This use of human bodies as objects is legitimate (not harmful) only when it is reciprocal. If one person is always object and the other subject, it stifles the human being in both of them. Objectification must also be open and frank. By silence we often assume that sex means commitments: if it does, OK; but if not, say it. (Of course, it's not all that simple: our capabilities for manipulation are unfathomed—all we can do is try.)

Gay liberation people must understand that women have been treated exclusively and dishonestly as sexual objects. A major part of their liberation is to play down sexual objectification and to develop other aspects of themselves which have been smothered so long. We respect this. We also understand that a few liberated women will be appalled or disgusted at the open and prominent place that we put sex in our lives; and while this is a natural response from their experience, they must learn what it means for us.

For us, sexual objectification is a focus of our quest for freedom. It is precisely that which we are not supposed to share with each other. Learning how to be open and good with each other sexually is part of our liberation. And one obvious distinction: objectification of sex for us is something we choose to do among ourselves, while for women it is imposed by their oppressors.

3. On Positions and Roles

Much of our sexuality has been perverted through mimicry of straights and warped from self-hatred. These sexual perversions are basically antigay:

"I like to make it with straight guys."
"I'm not gay, but I like to be 'done.' "

This is role playing at its worst; we must transcend these roles. We strive for democratic, mutual, reciprocal sex. This does not mean that we are all mirror images of each other in bed, but that we break away from roles that enslave us. We already do better in bed than straights do, and we can be better to each other than we have been.

A note on exploitation of children: kids can take care of themselves, and are sexual beings way earlier than we'd like to admit. Those of us who began cruising in early adolescence know this, and we were doing the cruising, not being debauched by dirty old men. Scandals such as the one in Boise, Idaho— blaming a "ring" of homosexuals for perverting their youth—are the fabrications of press and police and

politicians. And as for child molesting, the overwhelming amount is done by straight guys on little
girls: it is not particularly a gay problem, and is
caused by the frustrations resulting from antisex
puritanism.

On Coalition

Right now the bulk of our work has to be among
ourselves—self-educating, fending off attacks, and
building free territory. Thus basically we have to
have a gay/straight vision of the world until the oppression of gays is ended.

But not every straight is our enemy. Many of us
have mixed identities, and have tics with other
liberation movements: women, blacks, other minority groups; we may also have taken on an identity
which is vital to us; ecology, dope, ideology. And
face it: we can't change Amerika alone:

Who do we look to for coalition?

1. Women's Liberation

Summarizing earlier statements, 1) they are our
closest ally; we must try hard to get together with
them; 2) a lesbian caucus is probably the best way
to attack gay guys' male chauvinism, and challenge
the straightness of women's liberation; 3) as males
we must be sensitive to their developing identities as
women, and respect that; if *we* know what *our* freedom is about, *they* certainly know what's best for
them.

2. Black Liberation

See Huey P. Newton's statement to the men of the
Black Panther Party on Gay Liberation and
Women's Liberation (*Bird,* vol. 3, no. 40). It
would be impossible to overestimate the significance
of this vanguard position on the potential solidarity
between third world liberation and the struggle
against male supremacy and sexism by women and
gay people. We must support black liberation, particularly when black people are under attack from
the system; we must show our black sisters and
brothers that we mean business, and we must figure
out which our common enemies are: police, city
hall, capitalism.

3. Chicanos

Basically the same situation—trying to overcome
mutual animosity and fear, and finding ways to
support them. The extra problem of super uptightness and machismo among Latin cultures, and the
traditional pattern of Mexicans beating up "queers,"
can be overcome: we're both oppressed, and by the
same people at the top.

4. White Radicals and Ideologues

No country or political/economic system has
treated gay people as anything other than non grata
so far. We know that we are radical, that we are

revolutionaries since we know the system we're under now is a direct source of oppression, and it's not a question of getting our share of the pie. The pie is rotten.

We can look forward to coalition and mutual support with radical groups if they are able to transcend their antigay and male chauvinist patterns. We support radical and militant demands when they arise, but only as a group; we can't compromise or soft-pedal our gay identity.

Perhaps most fruitful would be to broach with radicals their stifled homosexuality and the issues which arise from challenging sexual roles. Gay people also have a vanguard role to play in defining, establishing, and operating child-care centers.

5. *Hip and Street People*

A major dynamic of rising gay liberation sentiment is the hip revolution within the gay community. Emphasis on love, dropping out, being honest, expressing yourself through hair and clothes, and smoking dope are all attributes of this. The gays who are the least vulnerable to attack by the establishment have been the freest to express themselves on gay liberation.

The hip/street culture has led people into a lot of freeing activities: encounter/sensitivity, the quest for reality, freeing territory for the people, ecological consciousness, communes. These are real points of agreement and probably will make it easier for them to get their heads straight about homosexuality, too.

6. Homophile Organizations

1) Reformist or pokey as they sometimes are, they are our brothers. They'll grow as we have grown and grow. Do not attack them in straight or mixed company. 2) Ignore their attack on us. 3) Cooperate where cooperation is possible without essential compromise of our identity.

20. Woman-Identified Woman

RADICALESBIANS

What is a lesbian? A lesbian is the rage of all women condensed to the point of explosion. She is the woman who, often beginning at an extremely early age, acts in accordance with her inner compulsion to be a more complete and freer human being than her society—perhaps then, but certainly later— cares to allow her. These needs and actions over a period of years, bring her into painful conflict with people, situations, the accepted ways of thinking, feeling, and behaving, until she is in a state of continual war with everything around her, and usually with herself. She may not be fully conscious of the political implications of what for her began as personal necessity, but on some level she has not been able to accept the limitations and oppression laid on her by the most basic role of her society—the female role.

From *Come Out,* a New York gay liberation newspaper.

The turmoil she experiences tends to induce guilt proportional to the degree to which she feels she is not meeting social expectations, and/or eventually drives her to question and analyze what the rest of her society more or less accepts. She is forced to evolve her own life pattern, often living much of her life alone, learning usually much earlier than her "straight" (heterosexual) sisters about the essential aloneness of life (which the myth of marriage obscures) and about the reality of illusions. To the extent that she cannot expel the heavy socialization that goes with being female, she can never truly find peace with herself. For she is caught somewhere between accepting society's view of her—in which case she cannot accept herself—and coming to understand what this sexist society has done to her and why it is functional and necessary for it to do so. Those of us who work that through find ourselves on the other side of a tortuous journey through a night that may have been decades long. The perspective gained from that journey, the liberation of self, the inner peace, the real love of self and of all women, is something to be shared with all women—because we are all women.

It should first be understood that lesbianism, like male homosexuality, is a category of behavior possible only in a sexist society characterized by rigid sex roles and dominated by male supremacy. Those sex roles dehumanize women by defining us as a supportive/serving caste *in relation to* the master caste of men, and emotionally cripple men by demanding that they be alienated from their own bodies and emotions in order to perform their economic/political/military functions effectively. Homosexuality is a by-product of a particular way of setting up roles (or approved patterns of behavior) on the basis of sex; as such it is an inauthentic (not consonant with "reality") category. In a society in which men do not oppress women, and sexual expression is allowed to follow feelings, the categories of homosexuality and heterosexuality would disappear.

But lesbianism is also different from male homosexuality, and serves a different function in the society. "Dyke" is a different kind of put-down from "faggot," although both imply you are not playing your socially assigned sex role; are not therefore a "real woman" or a "real man." The grudging admiration felt for the tomboy, and the queasiness felt around a sissy boy point to the same thing: the contempt in which women—or those who play a female role—are held. And the investment in keeping women in that contemptuous role is very great. "Lesbian" is the word, the label, the condition that holds women in line. When a woman hears this word tossed her way, she knows she is stepping out of line. She knows that she has crossed the terrible boundary of her sex role. She recoils, she protests, she reshapes her actions to gain approval. "Lesbian" is a label invented by the Man to throw at any woman who dares to be his equal, who dares to challenge his prerogatives (including that of all women as part of the exchange medium among men), who dares to assert the primacy of her own needs. To have the

label applied to people active in women's liberation
is just the most recent instance of a long history;
older women will recall that not so long ago, any
woman who was successful, independent, not orient-
ing her whole life about a man, would hear this
word. For in this sexist society, for a woman to be
independent means she *can't* be a *woman*—she *must*
be a *dyke*. That in itself should tell us where women
are at. It says as clearly as can be said: woman and
person are contradictory terms. For a lesbian is not
considered a "real woman." And yet, in popular
thinking, there is really only one essential difference
between a lesbian and other women; that of sexual
orientation—which is to say, when you strip off all
the packaging, you must finally realize that the
essence of being a "woman" is to get fucked by men.

"Lesbian," is one of the sexual categories by
which men have divided up humanity. While all
women are dehumanized as sex objects, as the objects of men they are given certain compensations;
identification with his power, his ego, his status, his
protection (from other males), feeling like a "real
woman," finding social acceptance by adhering to
her role, etc. Should a woman confront herself by
confronting another woman, there are fewer rational-
izations, fewer buffers by which to avoid the stark
horror of her dehumanized condition. Herein we find
the overriding fear of many women toward exploring intimate relationships with other women: the fear
of being used as a sexual object by a woman, which
not only will bring her no male-connected compensations, but also will reveal the void which is woman's

real situation. This dehumanization is expressed when a straight woman learns that a sister is a lesbian; she begins to relate to her lesbian sister as her potential sex object, laying a surrogate male role on the lesbian. This reveals her heterosexual conditioning to make herself into an object when sex is potentially involved in a relationship, and it denies the lesbian her full humanity. For women, especially those in the movement, to perceive their lesbian sisters through this male grid of role definitions is to accept this male cultural conditioning and to oppress their sisters much as they themselves have been oppressed by men. Are we going to continue the male classification system of defining all females in *sexual relation* to some *other* category of people? Affixing the label "lesbian" not only to a woman who aspires to be a person, but also to any situation of real love, real solidarity, real primacy among women is a primary form of divisiveness among women: it is the condition which keeps women within the confines of the feminine role, and it is the debunking/scare term that keeps women from forming any primary attachments, groups, or associations among ourselves.

Women in the movement have in most cases gone to great lengths to avoid discussion and confrontation with the issue of lesbianism. It puts people uptight. They arc hostile, evasive, or try to incorporate it into some "broader issue." They would rather not talk about it. If they have to, they try to dismiss it as a "lavender herring." But it is no side issue. It is absolutely essential to the success and fulfillment of the women's liberation movement that this issue be dealt with. As long as the label "dyke" can be used to frighten women into a less militant stand, keep her separate from her sisters, keep her from giving primacy to anything other than men and family— then to that extent she is controlled by the male culture. Until women see in each other the possibility of a primal commitment which includes sexual love, they will be denying themselves the love and value they readily accord to men, thus affirming their second-class status. As long as male acceptability is primary—both to individual women and to the movement as a whole—the term "lesbian" will be used effectively against women. Insofar as women want only more privileges within the system, they do not want to antagonize male power. They instead seek acceptability for women's liberation, and the most crucial aspect of the acceptability is to deny lesbianism—*i.e.,* deny any fundamental challenge to the basis of the female role.

It should also be said that some younger, more radical women have honestly begun to discuss lesbianism, but so far it has been primarily as a sexual "alternative" to men. This, however, is still giving primacy to men, both because the idea of relating more completely to women occurs as a *negative reaction to men,* and because the lesbian relationship is being characterized simply by sex which is divisive and sexist. On one level, which is both personal and political, women may withdraw emotional and sexual energies from men, and work out various alternatives for those energies in their own lives. On a different political/psychological level, it must be understood that what is crucial is that women begin disengaging from male-defined response patterns. In the privacy of our own psyches, we must cut those cords to the core. For irrespective of where our love and sexual energies flow, if we are male-identified in our heads, we cannot realize our autonomy as human beings.

But why is it that women have related to and through men? By virtue of having been brought up in a male society, we have internalized the male culture's definition of ourselves. That definition views us as relative beings who exist not for ourselves, but for the servicing, maintenance, and comfort of men. That definition consigns us to sexual and family functions, and excludes us from defining and shaping the terms of our lives. In exchange for our psychic servicing and for performing society's non-profit-making functions, the man confers on us just one thing: the slave status which makes us legitimate in the eyes of the society in which we live.

This is called "femininity" or "being a real woman" in our cultural lingo. We are authentic, legitimate, real to the extent that we are the property of some man whose name we bear. To be a woman who belongs to no man is to be invisible, pathetic, inauthentic, unreal. He confirms his image of us—of what we have to be in order to be acceptable by him—but not our real selves; he confirms our womanhood—as he defines it, in relation to him—but cannot confirm our personhood, our own selves as absolutes. As long as we are dependent on the male culture for this definition, for this approval, we cannot be free.

The consequence of internalizing this role is an enormous reservoir of self-hate. This is not to say the self-hate is recognized or accepted as such, indeed most women would deny it. It may be experienced as discomfort with her role, as feeling empty, as numbness, as restlessness, a paralyzing anxiety at the center. Alternatively, it may be expressed in shrill defensiveness of the glory and destiny of her role. But it does exist, often beneath the edge of her consciousness, poisoning her existence, keeping her alienated from herself, her own needs, and rendering her a stranger to other women. They try to escape by identifying with the oppressor, living through him, gaining status and identity from his ego, his power, his accomplishments. And by not identifying with other "empty vessels" like themselves. Women resist relating on all levels to other women who will reflect their own oppression, their own secondary status, their own self-hate. For to confront another woman is finally to confront one's self—the self we have gone to such lengths to avoid. And in that mirror we know we cannot really respect and love that which we have been made to be.

As the source of self-hate and the lack of real self are rooted in our male-given identity, we must create a new sense of self. As long as we cling to the idea of "being a woman," we will sense some conflict with that incipient self, that sense of I, that sense of a whole person. It is very difficult to realize and accept that being "feminine" and being a whole person are irreconcilable. Only women can give each other a new sense of self. That identity we have to develop with reference to ourselves, and not in relation to men. This consciousness is the revolutionary force from which all else will follow, for ours is an organic revolution. For this we must be available and supportive to one another, give our commitment and our love, give the emotional support necessary to sustain this movement. Our energies must flow toward our sisters, not backwards toward our oppressors. As long as women's liberation tries to free women without facing the basic heterosexual structure that binds us in one-to-one relationship with our own oppressors, tremendous energies will continue to flow into trying to straighten up each particular relationship with a man, how to get better sex, how to turn his head around—into trying to make the "new man" out of him, in the delusion that this will allow us to be the "new woman." This obviously splits our energies and commitments, leaving us unable to be committed to the construction of the new patterns which will liberate us.

It is the primacy of women relating to women, of women creating a new consciousness of and with each other which is at the heart of women's liberation, and the basis for the cultural revolution. Together we must find, reinforce, and validate our authentic selves. As we do this, we confirm in each other that struggling incipient sense of pride and strength, the divisive barriers begin to melt, we feel this growing solidarity with our sisters. We see ourselves as prime, find our centers inside of ourselves.

We find receding the sense of alienation, of being cut off, of being behind a locked window, of being unable to get out what we know is inside. We feel a real-ness, feel at last we are coinciding with ourselves. With that real self, with that consciousness, we begin a revolution to end the imposition of all coercive identifications, and to achieve maximum autonomy in human expression.

V

The Therapy Rip-Off

Introduction

Therapy has been the area of psychology in which people have most frequently been oppressed. It has also been the major area criticized. With the advent of community mental health centers, new group techniques, nondegree training institutes, and easy entry into doing or getting therapy, more people than ever have begun going to therapists. The traditional stigma attached to going to a therapist is gone, but that is about the extent of it. "New" forms of therapy differ little from older ones, except in that they are more publicly known, and often appear as innovative and "open."

As a whole, therapy continues to maintain the traditional view that emotional problems are internal to the person, or at best are a function of interpersonal relationships, but that they are hardly ever based on social living. With such a view, therapy could deal with emotional problems in a nonsocial, "therapeutic" situation. This, of course, denies the real foundations of personal problems. From psychoanalysis to less traditional modes, therapy demands the filial subordination of the patient, as well as acceptance of the therapist's values, which are usually similar to accepted societal values. Therapy offers adjustment rather than liberation even if this distinction is not so clearly apparent. Today, in the shadow of supposedly liberated attempts at growth and encounter, the traditional implications of therapy are disclaimed, but in fact continue beneath the subterfuge. Places like Esalen, Janov's primal scream institute, and many others are financially available only to people with a lot of money. They offer the culture of false freedom which the wealthy assume they can buy with money. Businessmen, uptight over daily lives spent pushing workers around, go away for a weekend to "get in touch with their inner selves." What is happening is that a separate structure is set up—the person does not change his/her life, but simply lives in another partial life for short periods of time. This sort of compartmentalization is exactly what society accepts as therapeutic, for the results do not threaten the normal activities of American life. It is no wonder that Schutz, author of *Joy* and founder of Esalen, comes from a background of counterinsurgency work for the federal government.

Critiques of therapy have been raised in other sections of this book. In this section, we have four very personal accounts, rather than theoretical or descriptive pieces. Nadine Miller's "Letter to Her Psychiatrist," Nancy C.'s "Psychotherapy as a Rip-Off," James Coleman's "Surviving Psychotherapy," and Alice Mailhot's "Communication" are four beautiful statements by people who have suffered at the hands of therapists and have fought back, gaining a better understanding of what therapy was doing to them and a better feeling of how they could go further in their liberation by other means.

21. Letter to Her Psychiatrist

NADINE MILLER

Taking this vacation was the best thing that I could have done, and should have done a long time ago. It is not only the change of location that has been helpful, but also the change of routine, the time and space to think without pressure, and being with people I trust. The past week has been a really new high—a whole different perspective is visible to me. Whereas, before I could only think that the city and all that goes with it was destroying much of my feeling for life, and distorting my ability to think, I now know that it is true. I feel that so many more things enter the area of the possible. I know that it is against my survival instinct to live amongst the daily perversions which one has in the city. For the second time in my life, I feel in touch with my body. I have spent many hours thinking about decisions I had to

From *The Radical Therapist*, vol. 1, no. 3 (August–September 1970).

make before I go back to the city, and this letter is
only part of a number of positions I have made.

I know that I have made the decision to stop
therapy a number of times, and each time I was not
really sure of the reason, but was led by a feeling—a
feeling that said therapy was not in my best interest,
and might even be working against me. At those
times I could not articulate the reason, although I
used certain situations as the excuse for ending
therapy. What I realize now is that it is true I could
not discuss certain things with you; how could I trust
you? I tried to force myself to think of you as un-
touched or unaffected by your position, sex, class,
privileges, and prejudices. I was operating under a
false premise, namely that we could have an honest,
open exchange of ideas. Instead I have had to guess
where you stand from things you imply, rather than
have real feedback on which to defend my accusations. I also see that there are very real reasons why
you would want to withhold information from me,
and also channel things into a direction which would
and did work against me as a woman.

Therapy acts to enforce the whole male structure,
and ultimately forces women into dependence upon
an area which, founded and dominated by men, has
been used against women. Let me explain. You, by
virtue of your title, set yourself up as the source of
knowledge. You have something that I want. As a
woman, forced to accept the whole male structure, I
accept the idea that I have a problem, rather than
realizing that I as a woman am forced to function in
a male supremacist structure and that I cannot func-

tion as a human being when I am constantly being
knocked down, forced to have meaningless relationships with men because I am afraid of the consequences if I don't, forced to submit to a life of
educational tracking—and then told I am sick when
I refuse to put up with any more of the shit. I am
tired of being told I have a basic insecurity, a mother
complex, a father complex. I am tired of thinking of
myself as Crazy—a nice way to make sure I never
throw off the oppression—a way to keep women
dependent upon the oppressors.

Men make the definitions of crazy or not crazy,
they then set themselves up as the saviors. They have
the "answer." Of course they don't tell you (the
patient) what they know. How else could they keep
you dependent. Let's get down to the real facts. You
have said that my involvement with Women's Liberation was an outlet for my hostility against men. I
was made to feel that it was just another part of
therapy. Instead of hitting a punching bag, I joined
Women's Liberation. If I did not share the pain of
many women, I would begin to feel that I have a
unique problem. I read books (written by men) in
which I am told that I am maladjusted, cannot
accept authority, sexually deviant, etc., etc.

I was lucky enough to realize that my hostility
toward men was real, and was not an individual
problem. You bet I had reasons to hate men—you
not being the least. From age three I was dragged to
shrink after shrink because I was "too aggressive."
Meaning I was not acting as a little girl should. I hit
boys and talked back. I hated my father for treating

my mother so badly, and hated my mother for not defending herself (at the time I thought she had a choice). When I talked to you about the Collective, you made me feel it was an "escape," whatever that means. I mean, why should I live alone, work nine to five, five days a week? You call wanting to live with others, wanting to share living responsibilities, an escape. You think I am running away from my problems. Well, God damn it—I am tired of thinking that it is MY problem, rather than a political problem.

When I accuse you of using your maleness, and class against me, you say I am hostile—as if there is no basis for my feeling that way. You refuse to accept the fact that I prefer a relationship with a woman than with a man. You insist that there are "good" men around. If you use yourself as an example, well I am even more convinced that there are none. When we talked about me wanting to keep my baby, all you could say was how difficult it would be for me to get married, continue my schooling, meet other people (men). Did you ever think that maybe I didn't want to get married? Did you ever think that a Collective could be an alternative? Did you ever think of how I could do it, or did you only say, "I have a patient who tried and has a messed-up kid."

You see, there are very real reasons why you would want me to think certain things. I mean, what would happen if all women began to realize that they were not sick or crazy but reacting to very real problems, shared by many other women. Sure I hate sex with men. It has never been good. I don't come because I am made numb, used as a machine. You

R

have said that I pick these kinds of men. What shit!
There aren't any others around. I mean it takes a
long time to raise a man's consciousness—and I
have given up. I have been wrong in thinking that
you know more about me than I know about myself.
That is the same line men always use. "You're too
emotional."

Even a female psychiatrist falls into the same
trap. She also accepts the male structure (and there
are many reasons why she does), so that I would not
go to a female psychiatrist. The whole psychological
thing is based on the premise that there are INDI-
VIDUAL problems rather than a social problem
which is political.

I have reached the point where I know there is
only one solution for me as a woman—unity with
other women and ultimately a revolution. I have also
identified my oppressors. No, it is not society (that is
too general). My oppressors are not institutions. My
oppressors are MEN—and all the superstructures
which are set up by men: I refuse to allow MEN TO
DEFINE me anymore. I refuse to support a system
which works against me and my sisters.

One other thing. The $28.00 which I owe you will
be given to the Women's Center as a donation. Since
you used your privileges to exploit me, I feel it is
only fair (if there is such a thing) for me to take
your money and give it to the same people you have
made money from.

Let it also be understood, that when I have done
things like this which were in my best interest, you
resorted to calling me crazy rather than dealing with

my feeling. By thinking of me as crazy, you exempted yourself from all responsibility. Well, this time it won't work. If you cannot call me crazy then you will just be angry. I really don't care what you do. I know where things are at. For once I have told it like it is. . . .

All Power to Women.

22. Psychotherapy as a Rip-Off

NANCY C.

I had been in therapy with Phineas for two and a half years when he offered to have an affair with me!

This being my first experience in therapy, I was quite vulnerable—as most patients are. Using this vulnerability, he had subtly and not so subtly encouraged me to depend on him and invest him with a great deal of power. In this context, my sexual thoughts and fantasies were probed. He asked me often about my sexual feelings for him, and if I said that I didn't think I had any, it was suggested that I was repressing them. As a result, I was led to feel that not spending time fantasizing about being with him in bed indicated something wrong with me.

. . . And then the suggestion of an affair. My initial reaction was great confusion.

From *The Radical Therapist,* vol. 2, no. 4 (December 1971).

Looking back, I see that there were prior warnings. At one group session, two group members—one female, the other male—expressed a desire to see each other outside the group. Phineas quietly suggested that they fantasize about what would happen for the group. I thought that was "peeping tom" bullshit, and said so.—I felt that they should go do it and then come back and talk about it.

At that point, Phineas turned to me and said, "Maybe, you're the exception to the rule?"

"What rule?" I asked.

"The rule that therapists shouldn't sleep with their patients," he answered. "You might benefit from it . . . but I'm not ready yet," he added.

In a way, I guess that was fair warning to get out. But I didn't.

At a time when I was feeling particularly depressed and confused about leaving graduate school and other things, Phineas, one day, gave me the choice of continuing therapy with him or "making it" together. I was struck numb and unable to reply with much of anything. He tried to make it sound inviting, laughingly adding something about keeping sado-masochistic pleasures within the confines of the bedroom. When I walked out of his office, I was somewhat elated, thinking, "Wow! He knows how messed up I am and still he's attracted to me!" But, that feeling of elation was based on the old bullshit of "You're OK if you get approval from a man!" And approval meant that I was attractive to him in some way.

It didn't last long. I got more and more confused

as the week wore on. When I went for my next appointment, I asked him rather feebly why he was working out his own screwed up feelings on me. He smiled, shrugged and said that he was "only testing my motivation for therapy." I imagine that the expression on my face must have appeared strange to him, because he asked if I thought that his comment was a rejection.

It wasn't a rejection at all—it was a total betrayal!

Now I was fully confused. I felt that he was playing with my mind, and I knew then that I couldn't put myself in his hands again.

I canceled our next appointment. I felt that there was nowhere to turn for clarification and that I could make no sense out of any of it. The next two months were perhaps the worst I'd ever gone through. I really can't describe the agony. I felt totally powerless—there seemed nothing I could do. *After all, he was the therapist, with all the letters after his name; I was merely the patient.* Who would believe *me?*

I received a bill from him for $20.50 which I ignored. He gave it to a collection agency and they continued sending me letters threatening to take me to court. I began getting angrier and angrier at the whole situation.

It was then that I started thinking of suing him for malpractice!

Initially, the idea seemed doubtful. It seemed unlikely that I could win the case. But, I had to do something with the rage. At a Women's Conference on Rape, I attended a workshop on "Psychiatry and Rape." People told me that this was a fairly common thing, but it didn't hit home until I discovered that there were at least two other women in that workshop who had had similar but more devastating experiences, having actually been raped by their therapists.[1]

It really blew my mind to find out that the man who had referred me to Phineas, through a central referral agency in New York, was now being sued for raping one of his patients—and then another woman rose at the workshop to tell of the same experience with this same man six years earlier!

A woman at the workshop suggested that I go back to the therapy group and tell them where Phineas was at. The idea was inviting but terrifying. She offered to go with me as I couldn't imagine doing it alone. It took two weeks for me to summon up the nerve to call her and set it up. I asked another friend to join us.

The night before, the three of us got together to "talk tactics." Since we had no idea of what might happen, or even if the people in the group would be the ones I knew, we decided to play it by ear. What frightened me most was that I would repeat an old pattern when I got in touch with my anger: I would turn it in on myself and start crying.

The worst part was waiting outside his building for the group to begin. I was nervous and afraid. But, once I walked into his office and found that I knew all the group members, I felt better. I just

1. I consider it *rape* even when women consent at the time. I see it as a power relationship, with the extreme vulnerability of women involved, making it even more so.

faced my friends and told my story. When I finished, I turned to Phineas and asked if he manipulated all his female patients in this way. All he was able to say was that since he and I no longer had a therapeutic contract, he had no comment to make and would offer no explanations. But, it was clear that he was angry, because he then brought up the "unpaid bill." I told him that I had no intention of paying to get my head fucked over. At that point, he threw it back to the group and asked if *they* were inviting *us* to stay. I said that we were asking nothing and needed no invitation. At which point he said nothing, but continued looking very angry.

In general, the group felt the need to defend Phineas. One man got extremely angry, commenting, "No Women's Liberation is allowed in here . . . so why don't you all get the fuck out of here!" He had rationalized it all so that in his mind I was just uptight because *I* wanted to fuck Phineas who would have none of it. While another man seemed interested and thought that I should be heard out, the two women in the group seemed threatened by our show of sisterhood. Finally, the group decided to continue talking with me but not in the presence of the two women whom they didn't know. So, my friends left to wait for me.

The most common response was, "You must have misunderstood. I know you misunderstood." I could really relate to these feelings. After all, I, too, had trusted this man, had invested him with power and thought him a god who could do no wrong. I said that I thought it was important that they realize he was as human as the rest of us, and quite capable of taking out his hangups on his patients.

My strongest feelings were for the two women. Particularly when one said that she too had felt manipulated by Phineas. She related that he had also asked her about her sexual feelings for him, and offered to have an affair with her when therapy was finished. She kept adding, however. that she thought it was a "therapeutic manipulation" which she had worked out with him and now understood—and that I should have done the same. When I asked if his investment in her treatment wasn't now biased and not truly objective, she seemed to shut me off, unable to let what I was saying really hit home.

But, I hope what will eventually hit her is that his interest makes her in no way special, and that she is not alone in "turning him on." (Indeed, this "special" feeling seems essential to the whole game Phineas is playing.)

Finally, the group said that I was abusing their time to express feelings really directed at Phineas. I agreed and left to wait for the group's conclusion so as to confront Phineas directly. When they came out, I could tell that he had rationalized away his responsibilities by talking about my problems, not his. They all treated me as if I were very fragile or on the verge of hysteria. This bothered me for a moment, but I realized how much they all had at stake, having all invested their souls with this man. And paying him fees for it besides! But I knew that I had at least planted a small seed which they will all have to think on and deal with at some point in their therapy.

When I returned to Phineas' office to confront him, he said that he was just too angry at the moment, and couldn't talk to me. Again, he copped out with "and it's not in my contract." I asked him why, if he was a therapist, he couldn't deal with his feelings. He just kept asking us to leave his office. He seemed not only angry but incredibly shaken. It was as if he couldn't trust himself to say anything. It surprised me because I had expected him to remain very cool and do the "shrink thing" of putting it all back on my head.

My first feelings afterwards were sort of anticlimactic. I had really psyched myself up for a confrontation with him. Then I became enraged that he had waited until I was out of the room, unable to defend myself, to explain his position to the group. Now, I just feel really pleased that I did what I did, and I'm still somewhat high off the experience. Perhaps the best effect for me was to clarify that Phineas no longer has power over me. I see him very differently now. He's no longer god and certainly not powerful. But, he is very dangerous, and I feel badly that he, and others like him, can continue to abuse this very one-sided power relationship for their own ends.

23. Surviving Psychotherapy

JAMES COLEMAN

Through such actions as the disruption of last sum-
mer's American Psychiatric Association convention,
the Gay Liberation movement has focused attention
on psychiatrists' treatment of homosexuality. Some
writers have criticized Freudian and neo-Freudian
theories of homosexuality; others have exposed bar-
baric clinical practices such as the use of electroshock "therapy." Little has been written, however,
about the experience of psychotherapy.

My own experiences were not dramatic: I never
had shock treatment, I never even encountered the
gay analogue of the hair-raisingly male-chauvinist
statements reported by some Women's Liberation
activists who have had psychotherapy.

My therapists—there were three over the years—
were all intelligent, somewhat sensitive men. I can-

From *The Radical Therapist*, vol. 2, no. 2 (September
1971). Reprinted by permission of the author.

not even claim that they tried to convince me that homosexuality was an illness: product of an orthodox upbringing, I was convinced before I ever consulted them. All I can claim is that their treatment contributed nothing to my awareness of myself and even retarded it; that this was connected to their view of homosexuality as an illness; that my self-understanding eventually grew from quite different sources.

I first applied the term "homosexual" to myself when I was fourteen. If I wasn't then an irreversible homosexual, I was fast becoming one: almost all my sexual inclinations were toward males, virtually none toward females. I sought psychotherapy when I was seventeen, basically because I desperately wanted to be heterosexual. I was in therapy in my last year in high school and for four years in college. Nothing changed—though I did gain insight into various personal and especially family relationships. For two years after college I was a teacher; then I was fired for a homosexual affair with a student. Beginning graduate school, I began therapy again and continued for five years on a once-weekly basis.

In my teens I tried actively not to be homosexual. Even when I stopped trying, at twenty-two, I didn't accept being gay—I merely decided to express it *until something changed,* because I realized that in trying not to love men, I was losing the ability to love at all. Not until I was twenty-five did I begin to see homosexuality as something that shouldn't be despised, and not until I was twenty-eight—only one year ago—did I "come out" in the sense of beginning to live openly as a homosexual. Only then, moreover, did I actively step into gay life and begin to meet other gay people. During those fourteen years, I had almost no sexual contacts and was, naturally, unhappy, frustrated, and confused. If my entry into gay life seems unusually late, I am convinced this isn't so: while manning a Gay Liberation telephone in recent months, I have talked to many more like myself.

During those fourteen years of waste and unnecessary grief, my psychotherapists exposed none of what was really wrong. Please note: this means *what I now believe was really wrong*. Biased, yes—but true in my experience; I will stand on my judgment and on that standard so regularly invoked by psychotherapists themselves, success. In my opinion, I am healthier now.

I was not the happy homosexual who doesn't enter Dr. Socarides' office (and doesn't enter his statistics). There I was—in my teens, guilty about masturbation (my only form of sexual expression) and about homosexuality; occasionally thinking of suicide; drawn into passionate friendships with "straight" males and either guilty about the sexual element or blind to it; infrequently but regularly revealing the truth (in conversation, in the most nonsexual way) and sometimes, very infrequently, making tentative sexual advances—usually rejected. In later years, fewer self-revelations (I had control of myself now, achieved with the aid of my therapists: I never told anyone unless it was necessary) and more frequent advances.

In therapy, I looked for the factors which had
caused my homosexuality. It did not occur to me
that no one asked what caused heterosexuality, or
that the two questions stood on a par. None of my
psychotherapists ever pointed this out. When discussing my urge to self-revelation, my therapists and I
explored the dynamics of this "Dostoevskian" manifestation—guilt, eagerness for punishment combined
with eagerness for acceptance, etc. All of this, I must
make clear, was true—I *was* guilty, eager for punishment, and eager for acceptance. But while exploring this (and, as I mentioned, helping me master the
urge) *none of my therapists exposed to me the
simple, blinding, underlying truth that in a society
which condemns homosexuality and hence forces it
to be secret, the homosexual will wish to break out
of the secrecy by telling someone, and hence, that
the urge itself was not sick at all.* I had to figure this
out for myself, at twenty-eight. Still less did any of
my therapists ask why I *told* my friends rather than
making sexual advances, or explore with me the
question why I didn't seek gay society where I could
make advances without risk.

My other psychotherapeutic experiences, or non-
experiences, were like this. Twice while in therapy, I
met homosexual acquaintances with whom the possibility of a real relationship existed, and shunned
them. A therapist might usefully have explored why
I was so guilty, even urged me to overcome this
guilt; instead, these occurrences became evidence
that I did not really want to be homosexual (which
we already knew) and *since my not wanting to be
gay was implicitly a sign (perhaps my only sign) of*

*health, these occurrences were not examined criti-
cally.* Similarly, my therapists spent much time trying to discover why my relationships with straight
friends were so passionate—rather than asking me
why I formed these passionate relationships *with
straights*. Similarly, after the homosexual affair
which lost me my teaching job—a very warm relationship which continues, intermittently, to this
day—I brought to my next therapist the datum that
while in bed with my lover, I felt completely harmonious and "natural," not "sick" at all and not
even guilty. Although this contradicted the very basis
of the feeling which led me to psychotherapy, my
therapist never took the initiative in exploring this
contradiction.

This all might be thought to result from the "non-
directive" quality of psychotherapy, or some psychotherapy. But elsewhere, my therapists *were* "directive." Very late, actually while I was "coming out"
through Gay Liberation, I had a sexual affair with a
woman (also, a warm one, interrupted only by circumstances). To this my therapist's response was
positive: with a little smile, "Well, I see *something*
has 'come out.'" The therapist's cues revealed
clearly enough the idea of a repressed heterosexuality which *should* be "brought out," and though
Freudian theory assumes an inborn bisexuality (an
assumption I don't share, not regarding *any* particular form of sexuality as inborn), this theory assumes
that repressed *homo*sexuality *shouldn't* be brought
out, but should be sublimated. Thus psychotherapy,
in my case, was directive indeed.

Rather than from "nondirection," the omissions

of my therapists seem to me to have resulted from their assumption that I was, by definition, sick—that homosexuality (but not heterosexuality) is a pathology. It did not occur to them to "direct" me in ways which might raise in my mind the idea that I was *not* sick. But how can I complain of this? Didn't I know this was their theory, and didn't I myself share the assumption?

The point is simply that the therapists *failed to help me understand my situation*—to overcome my own *lack* of understanding. Even from a viewpoint assuming homosexuality to be a pathology, it would remain true, I think, that my urge to self-revelation was *in fact* related to my *social* isolation as a homosexual. But my therapists never helped me to understand this. Even from the viewpoint that homosexuality if "incurable" should be accepted, it might have made sense for me to explore the possible relationships with my two gay college friends. But my therapists never tried to make me focus on this. Similarly, if I hadn't already been moving away from psychotherapy, after my heterosexual affair (if it had occurred at all) my therapist would have encouraged me to mull over that experience, to try to cultivate my heterosexual impulses, and to waste another ten years on top of the fourteen I had wasted already.

Basically, the therapists' theory made them incapable of viewing my situation as I now view it. If I understand it, their view was that the conflicts in my mind about accepting homosexuality indicated a very strong heterosexual impulse being checked subconsciously. In my view today, they indicated a very strong socially-conditioned rejection of being gay, combined with certain patterns—such as the tendency to be attracted to straight men—which were related to the inability to think of myself as gay and which created impossible (and, I would not add, unnecessary) conflicts between my sexual impulses and my need for ordinary friendship. (Only in the last year has this conflict become unnecessary: until now, gay people have had either to repress their gay nature while with straight friends, or to make their entire social life among gay people. I wonder how many therapists, exploring this conflict with thousands of gay patients, have tried to expose the *socially-conditioned* nature of this conflict.) In short, psychotherapy could not help me to understand my situation because it did not—and given its theoretical basis, *could* not—encourage me to think of my conflicts as resulting from social conditions.

How did I come to do so? Although therapy helped me understand many side issues, my understanding of being gay comes from social movements. My first step toward health—oh yes, I was sick: I was unable to view myself as I was—came when I was twenty-two, in my determination to find love where I could. This step of simple self-preservation, never suggested by any psychotherapist, left me still viewing myself as an inferior creature. The first suggestion that homosexuals were unhappy not because we were sick but because we were oppressed, came from an acquaintance, who *not* coincidentally was a revolutionary socialist, who influenced me as I got deeply into the student radical movement at the late and lucky age of twenty-five.

My first real understanding of my oppression, however, came as the women's liberation movement grew. Some of my closest acquaintances were very active in it. The critique of the social stigmas attached to being a woman, of the myths of female personality type, of the role of social factors in producing the *real* personality disfigurations women suffered—and most of all, of the treatment of all this by psychiatry as personal neurosis demanding personal therapy rather than as social oppression demanding a collective struggle—all this seemed true of myself as well. Further, my fear and dislike of women, which my therapists and I had spent much time discussing, began to change as I saw—from the movement, not from my therapists—that I was *not* expected (any longer) to relate to women primarily sexually, something I had always felt unable to do. Simultaneously I began seeing women and myself as human beings.

Finally Gay Liberation . . . but it shouldn't be necessary to describe how this changed my view of myself. It did, however, change the direction and content of my life.

My break with psychotherapy came gradually. Women's liberation made me take seriously the critique of psychiatric theory as regards women, but this was tangential to my own therapy. Very late, relations with my therapist became strained when, discussing my mother and her ambitions for me, he referred to her using me as "her penis." I saw that what women's liberationists had been saying was true: my mother's ambitious and successful life, in which she had always had to struggle against the limits placed on her as a woman, was to my therapist a manifestation of the desire for a penis rather than a rebellion against constraints which warred against her great abilities. Had it not been for the women's movement, I might have accepted this view—and found a new, apparently analytical way to despise my mother, rather than coming to understand her.

Instead, I asked myself how this theory, which regarded women so barbarically, regarded me. And I asked my therapist. His reply, which covered several sessions and touched on both women and homosexuals, was roughly that homosexuality could be regarded as a pathology (and heterosexuality could not) because in this society (he said "culture") the norm for the family was that of a male occupying a dominant position, a female in a subordinate position, and the reproduction of these roles in the young. We agreed that in terms of these roles both an "aggressive" woman, such as my mother, and a homosexual child were deviant cases. We differed in that he insisted that this deviance be viewed simply in terms of its psychic determinants, a position which I maintained, and he denied, was equivalent to refusing to question the psychic costs of the dominant pattern. I insisted that if no positive value were placed on the dominant pattern, then the deviant manifestation had to be viewed not as a psychopathology, but as a manifestation of a pattern which might in the absence of social pressures, be as fulfilling or more fulfilling than the dominant one, but which was socially disapproved. Thus a woman or a homosexual should be encouraged to see social norms *as part of his or her "problem."* This my therapist denied.

In the midst of this argument I travelled to another city. Since I was now active in Gay Liberation, I asked the person I was going to see to ask around if a Gay Liberation group existed there. None did, but as a result of his queries, I was telephoned at his house by a man who said he was gay, asked about Gay Liberation, but refused to come to see us. He also refused to give his last name, but he told me his profession—psychologist.

It was clear to me that a profession whose homosexual members had to conceal themselves could not adequately counsel homosexuals. Returning home, I related the incident to my therapist. His reply was that my caller had been a psychologist, not a psychoanalyst. Suppose he had been a psychoanalyst? My therapist replied that there were no homosexual psychoanalysts. In fact, he repeated this three times, as I literally could not believe he had said it. Some psychoanalysts occasionally "decompensated" and became active homosexuals, he said—but they "stopped being psychoanalysts."

You and I both know, dear reader, that this isn't true. At most, it may be true that psychoanalysts publicly identified as gay are forced to give up practice. But my therapist had claimed much more, and the conclusion I was forced to draw was that *his theoretical outlook had so stereotyped his percep-*

tions that he was incapable of correctly perceiving reality.

This particular incident made me terminate therapy, but in fact I had been moving in that direction for years—every step I took toward living my life as a homosexual, toward being less concealing, toward being, finally, openly and proudly gay, was a step toward ending a "therapy" which encouraged none of this. Even during the few weeks in which I was making the decision to contact Gay Liberation, my therapist, while not actively discouraging this step, cautioned me about it—it was another of my comrades in the revolutionary movement who, viewing my condition as one of oppression, urged me toward this step.

I, of course, chose on the basis of my inclinations, and I have only my life to offer as evidence that my choice was correct. The last year has been, not just one of the happiest of my life, but one of the *few* happy years of my life. I do not mean I have found bliss—quite the contrary: I have enough problems to convince me that my happiness is not founded on thin ice. I do not believe that this happiness would have been predicted by my therapists. (Similarly the experience of several Gay Liberation activists, who "came out" as homosexuals for the first time *after* several years of well-adjusted heterosexual life, would not have been predicted by psychoanalytic theory.) And all over the United States there are thousands in psychotherapy, and millions more under the pervasive social influence of psychiatric dogma, who never will make this step until they are reached, not by doctors, but by the winds of social protest. As Trotsky said of his comrade Adolf Yoffe, several years in analysis and later an outstanding Bolshevik diplomat, "The revolution healed Yoffe better than psychoanalysis of all his complexes."

24. Communication

ALICE MAILHOT

Problem

He returned from his first visit to the marriage counselor prescribed by the health service for headaches. He dropped his books on the couch, tossed his coat on top of them, lay down, put his feet up on the pile, pulled out a magazine and, opening it to the middle, began to read.

"Hi," I greeted him tentatively. "How did it go?"

"Hmmm. Well, he said. . . ." He turned the page and began to hum.

"Do you think it'll help?" More humming.

I waited a minute or two; then, since the conversation was obviously over, I went into the kitchen to finish the dishes.

"He agrees that it's you giving me headaches," he

From *The Radical Therapist,* vol. 2, no. 2 (September 1971). Reprinted by permission of the author.

told me as I pulled on the second glove. "Hey! What're you doing in the kitchen? Don't you even care?"

I peeled off the gloves, returned them to the sink. It depressed me to think that the marriage counselor and the health service both thought I was giving my husband headaches; but, I told myself, that is the sort of thing you have to face up to in marriage, face and overcome. So I went back out to hear the awful truth.

"What am I doing wrong?" I asked, relieved that it was all going to open up and we were going to solve the problem.

"You can talk to him about that. You'll have to go in twice a week. You're not to miss any appointments. No excuses. You can't just lie there and not see him and say you're sick like the night I had to get my own supper."

"I was sick!" I protested. "My temperature was over 103. I was afraid if I moved, I'd throw up."

"Save your excuses. He'll tell you." He lay back and rubbed a tired hand across his forehead. He sighed. His eyes closed. I turned to go.

"You have to learn to communicate," he ordered, suddenly awake. "It's most important in marriage. There has to be communication."

"Well!" I blurted, taken aback. "I do communicate. Sometimes it seems to me you don't really communicate with me."

"There you go!" he accused, raising up on one elbow and pointing between my eyes, "making accusations! What are you trying to imply?"

"I . . . that's not an accusation, and I'm not trying to imply anything. I just don't feel communicated with. I tell you exactly what I feel and what I'd most like to do or what seems most reasonable to me to do and what my thinking is and, when I try to find out what you think and how you feel, I can't seem to, somehow."

"That's what I mean," he sneered, dropping heavily back, turning his head away, and firmly closing his eyes.

"Mean? Mean by what?" I heard my voice creep up with an increasing sense of exasperation; but I took a couple of deep breaths and asked, "When am I supposed to go in?"

But he slept on, the very picture of disdain.

Therapy

"You see," the counselor reasoned with me, "there must be a flow of communication between husband and wife. When communication breaks down, the marriage is in trouble." He beamed inquiringly into my eyes, obviously wondering how much of his message was registering.

"Yes," I agreed, leaning forward in my eagerness to hear how this might be done. "I wish I knew how."

"Oh, you'll have to do much better than wish," he admonished me, instantly stern. "Much, much better. Your marriage demands it. This is a very serious matter. You must work at it." He glanced at his watch and straightened his tie.

"But. . . ."

"Perhaps this would be a good place to stop for today," he suggested. "Now, you think it over. Communication is the lifeblood of a marriage."

Problem

"Language is for fooling people," he assured me again.

"Oh, no!" I countered. "It isn't. What's the use of talking if all you're going to do is lie?"

"Oh. If you're smart you won't have to lie. Much. At least, you won't get caught. No one will know. And if you're smart, you just let them think something that isn't true. People are fools."

"Mostly honest, more likely." Shifting into high, I tackled the subject. "The function of language is to help people get along together; civilization is based on it. In any society, there *has* to be a coherence between word and meaning. Why do you think the concept of a man's word being good has been so important to people? Like the Indians, for instance?"

"Look what happened to them!"

"OK," I agreed, "but they got along with each other; without a man's word being his bond, a society falls apart inside itself."

"So?" he retorted angrily. "What's society to force me to do anything? Why should I do what society says I should do? I'll say what I like. If people are fool enough to believe it, that's *their* fault."

"But . . ." I looked at him, wondering if he was merely trying to upset me; he seemed extremely pleased with himself. "You corrupt the very meaning of language."

"That's your version. You don't know what you're talking about. Language is just another weapon. You use it. If you're smart." He thought a moment, turned on me with the clincher:

"You don't want people to *know* what you think, do you?"

Therapy

"Perhaps," the counselor suggested gently, interrupting my replay of our arguments about language, "perhaps we should not waste our time on intellectualized debates and abstract philosophies. Let's talk about the real problems in your marriage."

Problem

"Oh, there you are," he said in the sort of tone a person might use on a child caught eating peanut butter by hand. "I want to talk to you. If you'd stop stirring that mess a minute."

I did.

"We need a new car," he said. "There'll be some men calling. Now, don't you lose their messages. And get them straight. I think the transmission is going. What do you think about getting a wagon?"

I stared out the window at the old car, digesting these various thoughts.

"Well," I answered slowly, "I guess. . . ." The kitchen door slammed. He was gone.

Later, having thought the matter over and having realized that a great many of our conversations came to the same abrupt conclusion, I asked him if we might, every now and again, arrange to hold a complete conversation; there were some things I would like to talk with him about.

"Talk!" he snorted. "That's all you want to do. What's there to talk about?"

"When you have the time, I'd be glad to tell you."

"That's the trouble," he retorted. "That's just what I mean. If you wouldn't talk, we could be happy." The door slammed.

Therapy

"I can never tell what we are going to be doing, or arrive at an agreement on what sort of limits we're setting for the children, or even make *any* kind of agreement with him, actually, or have a just-for-fun type conversation. He acts like I was trying to steal his teeth. I'm human. I need to be able to talk with the person I live with."

The social worker considered. "But if he doesn't like you to talk to him . . . maybe . . . do you *have* to talk to him?" She thought a little more and, visibly brightening, offered, "you can talk to me."

Friend of the Court

"My attorney advised me to call you about making sure the travel arrangements I sign for are what really happens, this time," I told her.

"Why don't you discuss it with the children's father," she asked. "Come to an agreement with him about it."

"But—if he was the kind of person you could come to agreements with. . . ."

"You'll have to communicate with him," she advised, her temper audibly shortening.

"Communicate with him? There *isn't* any communicating with him! He won't *be* communicated with. I tried for years. I've *never* been able to communicate with him."

"Well!" Crisply disposing of the problem, she snapped, "It's about time you learned."

VI

Fighting Back

Introduction

People all over have begun to fight back. The established power of the psychiatric/psychological professions is in imminent danger. Fighting back takes many forms. One of those forms has been shown in the previous section. Another form, on the institutional level, is the theme of this section.

"On Practice," an editorial from the first year of *The Radical Therapist,* speaks to the point of unifying theory and practice of radical therapy in a way most useful to serving the needs of people. The "Statement" from the New York Mental Patients' Liberation Project (one of a growing number of such groups across the country) sets forth a Bill of Rights for mental patients which serves as a guideline for much of their organizing work. Hernán Kesselman's "Psychoanalysis and Imperialism," while still operating somewhat in the left psychoanalytic framework, represents an important group, *Plataforma,* an international grouping in opposition to traditional psychoanalysis. The *Plataforma* people in Argentina, including Kesselman, are part of a general current of socialist approaches to psychoanalysis and other forms of therapy in that country. "Radical Psychiatry in Italy: 'Love Is Not Enough,'" by Donata Mebane-Francescato and Susan Jones, speaks of the radical therapeutic community set up in an Italian mental hospital under the guidance of Franco Basaglia. Basaglia's own writing of the project, *L'Instituzione Negata* (*The Institution Denied*) is, unfortunately, not yet available in English.

25. On Practice

An Editorial from *The Radical Therapist*

"Where do correct ideas come from? Do they fall from the sky? No. Do they spring innately from our minds? No. They come from social practice and from it alone."—Mao.

We can talk about radical therapy until we are blue in the face. But until we translate our talk into action, we are just mouth droolers. What kind of action depends on our situation and our goals. But that we must act is imperative.

People keep asking us, "What is radical therapy?" They want to know our tenets and techniques, as if they could then "learn" them. It doesn't work that way. Radical therapy isn't some other "kind" of therapy. We don't present ourselves at the left end of the serving table, a radical radish between the olives and canapes, for people to sample and taste. Radical therapy is a life style. It's not just what a therapist *does;* it's who and what she/he is and how she/he lives.

Life style is crucial.

Radical therapy is any of the following: organizing a community to seize control of the way it's run; helping a brother or sister through a crisis; rooting out our own chauvinism and mercilessly exposing it in others; focusing on the social dimensions of oppression and not on "intrapsychic" depression, fear, anger, and so on; organizing against the war, against polluting industries, against racist practice; developing a political/therapy center for young people; teaching students psychology like it is; refusing to be manipulated and co-opted by the sweet sucky pigs who heap praise on your head like garbage while they root their snouts in your guts.

Life style is crucial.

What kind of radical therapist sits in a private office and rakes in $50,000 a year from well-to-do patients? No kind.

What kind of radical therapist talks radical politics but remains ensconced in a university setting? That question is harder to answer.

It becomes a matter of risk and commitment.

Everyone needs money for food and shelter, for satisfying basic needs, and for smokes and music. Of course. Yet we begin to wonder if "radical" professors have any effect in a university, if their own lives stay bound by research, publishing "scholarly" articles, and being dominated by university administrators. Certainly, if teacher/therapists can radicalize students, show them alternatives, open their minds, and help them through crises, then they are doing good work. But we sometimes wonder if teacher/therapists are not socially sanctioned clowns

s

at times. They entertain the students for a while: and then the students go on into nice jobs in the system.

If the therapist who stays in a university is not engaged in radical action, then she/he is a fraud. Without participating in radical social action, she/he cannot feel the texture, nor the taste, nor the smarting of social practices.

Liberate the universities, yes. Let's see it. But let's *see* it.

We encourage the growth of free universities everywhere. We encourage the liberation of universities everywhere. But liberated universities without liberated teachers—liberated in the very ways they live—will be nothing new.

The challenge of becoming involved in action projects faces each of us.

26. Statement

MENTAL PATIENTS'
LIBERATION PROJECT

We, of the Mental Patents' Liberation Project, are
former mental patients. We've all been labeled
schizophrenic, manic-depressive, psychotic, and neurotic—labels that have degraded us, made us feel
inferior. Now we're beginning to get together—beginning to see that these labels are not true but have
been thrown at us because we have refused to conform—refused to adjust to a society where to be
normal is to be an unquestioning robot, without
emotion and creativity. As ex-mental patients we
know what it's like to be locked up in mental
institutions for this refusal; we know what it's like to
be treated as an object—to be made to feel less of a
person than "normal" people on the outside. We've
all felt the boredom, the regimentation, the inhu-

From *The Radical Therapist,* vol. 2, no. 4 (December
1971). Reprinted by permission of Mental Patients'
Liberation Project.

mane physical and psychological abuses of institutional life—life on the inside. We are now beginning to realize that we are no longer alone in these feelings—that we are all brothers and sisters. Now for the first time we're beginning to fight for ourselves—fight for our personal liberty. We, of the Mental Patients' Liberation Project, want to work to change the conditions we have experienced. We have drawn up a Bill of Rights for Mental Patients—rights that we unquestioningly should have but rights that have been refused to us. Because these rights are not now legally ours we are now going to fight to make them a reality.

Mental Patients' Bill of Rights

We are ex-mental patients. We have been subjected to brutalization in mental hospitals and by the psychiatric profession. In almost every state of the union, a mental patient has fewer *de facto* rights than a murderer condemned to die or to life imprisonment. As human beings, you are entitled to basic human rights that are taken for granted by the general population. You are entitled to protection by and recourse to the law. The purpose of the Mental Patients' Liberation Project is to help those who are still institutionalized. This Bill of Rights was prepared by those at the first meeting of MPLP held on June 13, 1971 at the Washington Square Methodist Church. If you know someone in a mental hospital, give him/her a copy of these rights. If you are in a hospital and need legal help, try to find someone to call the Dolphin Center

1. You are a human being and are entitled to be treated as such with as much decency and respect as is accorded to any other human being.

2. You are an American citizen and are entitled to every right established by the Declaration of Independence and guaranteed by the Constitution of the United States of America.

3. You have the right to the integrity of your own mind and the integrity of your own body.

4. Treatment and medication can be administered only with your consent, you have the right to demand to know all relevant information regarding said treatment and/or medication.

5. You have the right to have access to your own legal and medical counsel.

6. You have the right to refuse to work in a mental hospital and/or to choose what work you shall do and you have the right to receive the minimum wage for such work as is set by the state labor laws.

7. You have the right to decent medical attention when you feel you need it just as any other human being has that right.

8. You have the right to uncensored communication by phone, letter, and in person with whomever you wish and at any time you wish.

9. You have the right not to be treated like a criminal; not to be locked up against your will; not to be committed involuntarily; not to be fingerprinted or "mugged" (photographed).

10. You have the right to decent living conditions. You're paying for it and the taxpayers are paying for it.

11. You have the right to retain your own personal property. No one has the right to confiscate what is legally yours, no matter what reason is given. That is commonly known as theft.

12. You have the right to bring grievance against those who have mistreated you and the right to counsel and a court hearing. You are entitled to protection by the law against retaliation.

13. You have the right to refuse to be a guinea pig for experimental drugs and treatments and to refuse to be used as learning material for students. You have the right to demand reimbursement if you are so used.

14. You have the right not to have your character questioned or defamed.

15. You have the right to request an alternative to legal commitment or incarceration in a mental hospital.

The Mental Patients' Liberation Project plans to set up neighborhood crisis centers as alternatives to incarceration and voluntary and involuntary commitment to hospitals. We plan to set up a legal aid society for those whose rights are taken away and/or abused. Although our immediate aim is to help those currently in hospitals, we are also interested in helping those who are suffering from job discrimination, discriminatory school admissions policies and discrimination and abuse at the hands of the psychiatric profession. Call the number listed below if you are interested in our group or if you need legal assistance.

Please contact us if there is any specific condition you would like us to work against.

Mental Patients' Liberation Project
c/o Dolphin Center
56 East 4th Street
New York, N.Y. 10003
254-4270

27. Psychoanalysis and Imperialism

HERNAN KESSELMAN

1968 was a big year for the student and workers' movements in several European countries. The struggle of the exploited took the form of antiauthoritarian generational struggle; that is to say, a rebellion of youth against the paternalistic tyranny of the old and their traditional values (order, property, privacy, etc.).

At the same time in Latin America, where civilian and military governments exercise an *overt* systematic oppression on the people, revolutionary activity was flaring up also. Cordobazo and Rosariazo were examples of popular counterviolence in response to fifteen years of repression and subjugation in Argentina.

Opportunities to enrich revolutionary theories arose as new alternatives presented themselves in the

From *The Radical Therapist*, vol. 2, no. 5 (February 1972). Translated by Phil Brown.

different processes of national and social liberation.

In 1969, the International Psychoanalytic Association (IPA) decided to open its forthcoming twenty-sixth International Congress with an attractive theme and one of great currency: "Protest and Revolution." All would have gone *pro forma* on the luxurious carpeting of the Rome Hilton, had not a group of young European psychoanalysts gotten together under the name of "International Platform" and decided to conduct a countercongress in a nearby hall.

These young people proposed a discussion of four fundamental points ignored by the official congress:

1) Formation of the psychoanalyst. Critique of methods on the part of future analysts in selecting candidates for personal analysis on the basis of their "disturbed character."

2) Significance, structure, and function of the psychoanalytic societies, which seem preoccupied mainly with protecting the official papers of their members, and little or not at all with the social-scientific development of psychoanalysis.

3) The social role of the psychoanalyst and the social image of psychoanalysis. The hierarchical structure of psychoanalytic societies favors regressive relationships among the members, stimulating them toward the acceptance of a submissive (weak) role on the one hand, and a thirst for power on the other. The groups thus become insular and tend to idealize themselves in order to mystify outsiders as to their true function.

4) Relations between psychoanalysis and institutions. The aforesaid structure impedes the psychoanalyst from discussing his own role in contemporary society. Paradoxically, psychoanalytic societies have ignored profound changes in contemporary society.

The enthusiastic discussion of these themes resulted in setting up an international commission to function as clearing house for the various foci of work: a mobile, noninstitutionalized international scientific group free from the hierarchical connections and compromises with the system that characterize the "scientific" international organization known as IPA.

The South American group, especially the Argentine one, has been pointed out as one of the most productive among those which comprise "Platform." It is recognized in Europe on account of the profound antiimperialist and anticapitalist aptness that characterizes the methods of struggle of "Third World" people. Thus the title of the latest encounter celebrated by "Platform" in Vienna in July of 1971: "Psychoanalytic Theory and Practice in the Light of Different Paths to Socialism."

In the time since the Rome congress, the IPA (read: "the yanquis"), as a new policy, had decided to invite all the young candidates approved by or eligible for the official associations to meet together in a separate caucus under its auspices. It was probably thought that a precongress of this nature, taking place within the confines of the University of

Vienna, would leave satisfied the egalitarian demands of the "terrible children of Rome" and the IPA would be able to incorporate and neutralize some youthful, revolutionary seasoning.

The theme of its 1971 Congress taking place in the sumptuous salons of the Hoffburg palace in Vienna as homage to Sigmund Freud, was "Violence and Aggression." However, things did not proceed peacefully. For one thing, many young candidates were turned off at the precongress mentioned above because of its low scientific level and the infantile behavior they were subjected to. In addition, presentations of work by the great European and North American figures in psychoanalysis tended to reveal the great mystification that's been created around these persons. Finally, when a Latin American group was put in charge of introducing the problems of social and political conjunction in psychoanalytic theory and practice, the opposition within the IPA itself became unchained. Whether or not they knew it or liked it, psychoanalysts registered their views in line with the rules of the game that mark human relations in dependent societies. They left out an opposition position paper and denounced and struck down the possibility of participation in the creation of the New Person.

The opposition "Platform" group met at the Albert Schweitzer home, a student center. Three work groups were formed. They were composed of psychoanalysts, psychoanalytic society candidates, social workers, doctors, psychologists, and sociologists, as well as students in various fields at the University of Vienna. These were the themes:

1) Reconsiderations of psychoanalytic theory and its ideological bases.

2) Social intervention of the analyst as professional: Is a psychoanalytic practice contradictory to political struggle?

3) Is the crisis of psychoanalysis in the psychoanalytic world a crisis of the psychoanalyst as intellectual or one of psychoanalytic intellectualism?

General conclusions or recommendations in the style of the official IPA congress were not made, but several matters were clarified.

It was felt that intellectualism in psychoanalysis will overcome itself only as much as it is capable of integrating other struggling intellectuals, as well as assessing what is found in the most exploited sectors of world population in order to carry out the struggle to its end, together with the oppressed people of those sectors.

Amidst wall drawings done by the students and with promises to carry out the work of the revolution, the "Platform" meeting informally closed. On the other side of the plaza, in front of the Hoffburg palace, the silent wanderings of IPA Congress participants foretold the inevitable end of an old international congress and of the old psychoanalysis.

28. Radical Psychiatry in Italy: "Love Is Not Enough"

DONATA MEBANE-FRANCESCATO
AND SUSAN JONES

An oriental fable tells of a man who was entered by a serpent while he was asleep. The serpent settled in the man's stomach and took over control of his life so that the man no longer belonged to himself. One day, after a long period of domination, the serpent finally left; but the man no longer knew what to do with his freedom. He had become so used to submitting his will to that of the serpent, his wishes and impulses to those of the beast, that he had lost the capacity to wish, to strive, or to act autonomously. Instead of freedom he found only the "emptiness of the void," for the departure of the serpent had taken with it the man's new essence—the adapative fruit of

From *The Radical Therapist*, vol. 2, no. 5 (February 1972). Reprinted by permission of the authors.

his occupation. He was left with the awesome task of reclaiming, little by little, the former human content of his life.

It is hardly surprising that a sensitive psychiatrist would see in this fable a parable of the condition of the mentally ill. What is impressive is that Dr. Franco Basaglia, an Italian psychiatrist and author of *L'Instituzione Negata* ("The Institution Denied"), should see in the insidious serpent an analogy with the entire institutional, oppressive, political fabric of Western society: through the same actions of prevarication and violence by which the serpent destroyed the man, our system breeds "mental illness" by forcing the unwary individual to incorporate and submit to the very enemy who destroys him. And, warns Basaglia, *all* of us who participate in society are slaves of the serpent, and if we do not struggle to destroy or vomit it, we will lose all hope of regaining our human dignity.

Although Italy is far from being in the *avant-garde* of the mental health revolution, *L'Instituzione Negata* documents an exemplary attempt by its radical author not only to reverse the conventional pattern of institutional treatment of the mentally ill, but even more significantly, to see beyond the preliminary internal changes to a global, critical awareness of our social situation.

Basaglia's convictions grew out of his personal experience as director of the Provincial Psychiatric Hospital of Gorizia, a large, state institution located on the border between Italy and Yugoslavia. When he took over the directorship in 1961, he was con-

fronted with the typical atmosphere of a lower class,
custodial institution: locked wards; a rigid daily
schedule constructed more for the benefit of the
attendants than for the patients; a bedtime hour of
six o'clock; and such customary procedures as tying
the patients to their beds at night. One of the long-
term inmates explained, "When someone died, a bell
would ring; and we all used to wish the bell would
toll for us, for life held no hope."

Faced with what he termed a "tragic nuthouse
reality," Basaglia started by questioning all the institutional givens; and "depsychiatrization" became his
leitmotif. By depsychiatrization he meant a single-
minded attempt to eschew any preconceived system
of thinking or acting and to begin instead on undefined, uncoded terrain. Not only did he refuse to
accept that his patients were irretrievably sick
people and that his psychiatric role was that of a
paternalistic custodian, but he defied as well the
mandate of society which had put them both in their
positions. He felt that the institutionalized mentally
ill were ill first of all because they were deprived of
their human rights and then excluded and abandoned
by everybody.

In Basaglia's eyes, the level of dehumanization
attained by his patients was not so much a symptom
of their illness but rather the brutal consequence of
the continual violence and humiliation that institutional life had heaped upon them. He saw them as
victims of the same power imbalance which had
made them the refuse of society outside the institution walls. Violence, said Basaglia, is the preroga-

tive exercised by those who hold the knife againt those who are irrevocably without power—in every institution, be it the family, the school, the factory, the university, or the hospital, there is a neat division of roles between those who hold power and those who don't; and this leads to the exclusion and humiliation of the powerless.

Basaglia felt that mental illness could not begin to be understood until these environmental conditions were entirely changed. Having defined the problem as one of the unequal and oppressive power relationship, he set out to change the oppressive conditions in his own institution. And more important, he began a determined campaign to make the patients aware of their oppression, both within the hospital and in the society outside from which they had come. There were simple physical changes: opening up the nine wards; eliminating all uniforms both for the more than 150 doctors, nurses, and social workers and for the 500 patients; replacing the "Warning—Do Not Enter" sign at the entrance with an invitation to visitors to feel welcome at any time; and permanently opening the gates to the park which housed the hospital wards, church, and factory.

He then tossed out the use of all psychiatric labels, encouraging people to relate to one another as human beings rather than as disease prototypes. All forms of traditional therapy were replaced by a series of group meetings at a variety of levels, from intimate groups to plenary community meetings of patients and staff. In none of these groups was there a traditional therapy emphasis; rather they were a focus for "consciousness raising" much in the manner of the meetings of the Women's movement. An effort was made to involve the patients in planning and decisions on the daily operation, programs, and activities of the hospital; and more significant, there was a continuous push toward politicizing the situation—making the patients aware of their oppressed position, of the wrongs perpetrated on them outside the hospital walls.

Basaglia has compared his work to that being done by Maxwell Jones in England: the techniques of the two therapeutic communities are very similar, but the goals are quite different. He feels that in England there is less conscious effort being aimed at drawing political parallels from within the institution to the outside world, less attention given to promoting awareness of the power structure of society. And to Basaglia, political awareness is the central issue—awareness that the mentally ill are the objects of social violence. The violence directed against them is twofold: first, violence used to remove the patient forcibly from social contact, and the more subtle violence used before institutionalization, when the patient was a person without social or economic power, a failure in a system that seeks to remove its contradictions from the public eye.

In Basaglia's view, psychiatrists have been used by the system as technicians—its hirelings, whose job it is to take care of the rejects, deviants and failures, keeping them out of sight so that the system would not have to confront the injustices and inequities which promote these deviancies. Psychia-

trists, sociologists, psychologists, and social workers
have become the new administrators of the violence
of the power structure. In the measure that they
soothe conflicts, break down resistance, and "solve"
the problems created by situational realities, they
perpetuate the global violence by convincing the
individual to accommodate to the oppressive conditions.

Basaglia's solution is to refuse to administer the
therapeutic act when it serves only to mitigate the
reaction of the excluded against the excluder. And to
do this, therapists have to become aware of their
own exclusion from real power, even when they
serve as the technicians of this power. In his mind,
therapy is an encounter between equals, and the less
equal the power distribution, the less possibility
there is of a therapeutic encounter. Thus he makes
an important distinction between private therapy,
where the client has a modicum of power in that he
can freely enter into or terminate the relationship,
and the situation of the institutionalized patient who
has no freedom of choice in either his treatment or
its administrator.

Ideally, therapy is a political act; and it becomes
so to the degree that it tends to integrate an ongoing
crisis back into the roots from which the crisis
sprang, giving the individual an awareness of the
personal and social conditions which provoked his
crisis. The first step toward liberation is to help the
patient regain his sense of existential freedom and
responsibility, his right to a full human life. To
accomplish this monumental task, the therapeutic

community is the preferred vehicle; but it, too, runs the risk of becoming just another tool in the hands of the power structure, another gimmick for controlling the deviants and victims of the system. For this reason the therapeutic community must be only a transitional step toward the full assumption of political awareness and personal responsibility. Changing the traditional authority and power structure and experimenting with new roles within the institution can throw into dazzling relief the difference between this new reality and the oppression awaiting the patient in the world outside. Unless this new awareness can be carried beyond the hospital walls to greater engagement against the oppressive elements of the society at large, its efforts are to no avail. "Love" in the sense of therapeutic isolation and protection is not enough—it is necessary to change the basic social institutions which give rise to the need for therapy.

Unfortunately the next, global step to take is not clear to Basaglia; Italy, especially, is not ready for a social, political revolution. He concludes, somewhat pessimistically, that all radical therapists can do is to resist being co-opted and to keep alive, in themselves and in their patients, the vital awareness of the oppression and violence to which we all fall prey.

The path Basaglia indicates is certainly an uneasy and torturous one. On one hand, there is the continual danger of becoming involuted in our change efforts, of becoming sold on one technique or approach through which we have experienced some success; and to be tempted to repeat this same pattern at the expense of exploring new flexible pathways with a wider impact on society at large.

On the other hand we are faced with a more subtle and insidious problem: the "so what" syndrome, those feelings of disillusionment and defeat which arise when we contemplate the paucity of our resources and the magnitude of the task. The serpent within and without is so powerful as to make the struggle toward a more humane, loving, just society seem hopeless.

Basaglia's conclusions seem to illustrate this second crisis point. He has achieved a great deal within a limited setting (he has rehabilitated 50 per cent of so-called hopeless cases) and now the possibilities of his having a great influence on the rest of Italian society look dismal, so confusion and the temptation to despair grow powerful. It would be a big waste if this feeling of impotence were to keep Basaglia and the rest of us from continuing the search.

In our lifetime, we will probably not see the total personal, social, and political changes we want; however, to go on struggling we must have the hope that small contributions do have a cumulative effect, that we together as people can have a voice in shaping a better future. In the words of Camus:

> I know that the great tragedies of history often fascinate men with approaching horror. Paralyzed, they cannot make up their minds to do anything but wait. So they wait, and one day the Gorgon devours them. But I should like to convince you that the spell can be broken, that there

is only an ILLUSION OF IMPOTENCE, that strength of heart, intelligence and courage are enough to stop fate and sometimes reverse it. One has merely to will this, not blindly, but with a firm and reasoned will.

Bibliography

This list is incomplete since not all the works of every person are listed. Nor, generally, are magazines and newspapers. Strongly recommended are *The Radical Therapist* (New York: Ballantine, 1971) and *The Radical Therapist II* (New York: Ballantine, 1972), anthologies of articles from the first two years of *The Radical Therapist* magazine.

General and Sociological

Clark, Ted and Jaffee, Dennis. *Toward a Radical Therapy: Alternate Service for Personal and Social Change.* Forthcoming.

Foucault, Michel. *Madness and Civilization: A History of Insanity in the Age of Reason.* Translated by R. Howard. New York: Pantheon, 1965.

Friedman, Neil. *Social Nature of Psychological Research: The Psychological Experiment as a Social Interaction.* New York: Basic Books, 1967.

Goffman, Erving. *Asylums: Essays on the Social Situation of Mental Patients and Other Inmates.* Chicago: Aldine, 1961.

―――. *Behavior in Public Places: Notes on the Social Organization of Gatherings.* New York: Free Press, 1963.

―――. *Interaction Ritual: Essays on Face-to-Face Behavior.* Chicago: Aldine, 1967.

―――. *Presentation of Self in Everyday Life.* New York: Doubleday, 1959.

―――. *Stigma: Notes on the Management of Spoiled Identity.* Englewood Cliffs, N.J.: Prentice-Hall, 1963.

Haley, Jay. *Strategies of Psychotherapy.* New York: Grune & Stratton, 1963.

Lynd, Helen M. *On Shame and the Search for Identity.* New York: Harcourt, 1958.

Scheff, Thomas J. *Being Mentally Ill: A Sociological Identity.* Chicago: Aline, 1966.

Scheff, Thomas J., ed. *Mental Illness and Social Processes.* New York: Harper, 1967.

Szasz, Thomas S. *Ideology and Insanity: Essays on the Psychiatric Dehumanization of Man.* New York: Doubleday, 1970.

―――. *Law, Liberty, and Psychiatry.* New York: Macmillan, 1963.

―――. *The Manufacture of Madness: A Comparative Study of the Inquisition and the Mental Health Movement.* New York: Harper, 1970.

―――. *The Myth of Mental Illness.* New York: Harper, 1961.

Antipsychiatry

Barnes, Mary and Berke, Joe. *Mary Barnes: Two Accounts of a Journey through Madness.* New York: Harcourt, 1972.

Berke, Joe. *Counter-Culture.* New York: Hillary, 1971.

Cooper, David. *The Death of the Family.* New York: Pantheon, 1970.

———. *Psychiatry and Anti-Psychiatry.* New York: Ballantine, 1967.

Cooper, David, ed. *To Free a Generation.* New York: Macmillan, 1969.

Esterson, Aaron. *The Leaves of Spring.* London: Tavistock, 1971.

Laing, R. D. *The Divided Self.* New York: Pantheon, 1970.

———. *Knots.* New York: Pantheon, 1970.

———. *The Politics of Experience.* New York: Pantheon, 1967.

———. *The Politics of the Family.* Toronto: CBC Publications, 1969.

———. *The Self and Others.* New York: Pantheon, 1970.

Laing, R. D., Phillipson, H. and Lee, A. R. *Interpersonal Perception.* New York: Springer, 1966.

Laing, R. D. and Cooper, David. *Reason and Violence: A Decade of Sartre's Philosophy.* New York: Barnes & Noble, 1964.

Laing, R. D. and Esterson, Aaron. *Sanity, Madness and the Family.* vol. 1. *Families of Schizophrenics.* New York: Basic Books, 1965.

Left Freudians

Fromm, Erich. *Beyond the Chains of Illusion*. New York: Simon & Schuster, 1967.

―――. *Escape from Freedom*. New York: Holt, 1941.

―――. *The Sane Society*. New York: Holt, 1955.

Marcuse, Herbert. *Eros and Civilization: A Philosophical Inquiry into Freud*. Boston: Beacon Press, 1955.

―――. *Essay on Liberation*. Boston: Beacon Press, 1969.

―――. *Five Lectures*. Translated by Jeremy Shapiro and Sherry Weber. Boston: Beacon Press, 1970.

―――. *One Dimensional Man*. Boston: Beacon Press, 1964.

Reich, Wilhelm. *The Function of the Orgasm*. New York: Farrar, Straus & Giroux, 1961.

―――. *The Mass Psychology of Fascism*. Translated by Vincent Carfagno. New York: Farrar, Straus & Giroux, 1970.

―――. *The Sexual Revolution*. New York: Farrar, Straus & Giroux, 1963.

―――. "What Is Class Consciousness?" *Liberation*. October 1971.

Reiche, Reimut. *Sexuality and Class Struggle*. London: New Left Books, 1971.

Robinson, Paul A. *The Freudian Left: Wilhelm Reich, Geza Roheim, and Herbert Marcuse*. New York: Harper, 1969.

Marxism

Engels, Friedrich. *Origin of the Family, Private Property, and the State*. New York: International Publishers.

Fanon, Frantz. *A Dying Colonialism*. Translated by Haakon Chevalier. New York: Grove Press, 1967.

————. *Black Skin, White Masks*. Translated by Charles L. Markmann. New York: Grove Press, 1967.

————. *Toward the African Revolution*. New York: Grove Press, 1968.

————. *The Wretched of the Earth*. Translated by Constance Farrington. New York: Grove Press, 1965.

Gramsci, Antonio. *The Modern Prince and Other Writings*. New York: International Publishers, 1959.

————. *Prison Notebooks*. New York: International Publishers, 1971.

Marx, Karl. *Economic and Philosophical Manuscripts of 1844*. Edited by Dirk J. Struik, translated by Martin Milligan. New York: International Publishers, 1964.

————. *The Grundrisse*. Edited and translated by David McLellan. New York: Harper, 1970.

————. *The Poverty of Philosophy*. New York: International Publishers, 1963.

Merleau-Ponty, Maurice. *Sense and Non-Sense*. Translated by Hubert L. and Patricia A. Dreyfus.

Evanston, Ill.: Northwestern University Press, 1964.

Racism

Cleaver, Eldridge. *Post-Prison Writing and Speeches*. Edited by Robert Sheer. New York: Random House, 1969.
————. *Soul on Ice*. New York: McGraw-Hill, 1968.
Hernton, Calvin C. *Sex and Racism in America*. New York: Grove Press, 1966.
Jackson, George. *Soledad Brother*. New York: Coward, 1971.

Sex Roles

Babcox, Deborah and Belkin, Madeline. *Liberation Now!*
de Beauvoir, Simone. *The Second Sex*. Translated by H. M. Parshley. New York: Knopf, 1953.
Come Out. (Times Change Press).
Firestone, Shulamith. *The Dialectic of Sex: The Case for Feminist Revolution*. New York: Morrow, 1970.
Garskof, Michelle. *Roles Women Play*. Belmont, Calif.: Brooks Cole, 1971.
Greer, Germaine. *The Female Eunuch*. New York: McGraw-Hill, 1971.
Millett, Kate. *Sexual Politics*. New York: Doubleday, 1970.
Mitchell, Juliet. *Women's Estate*. New York: Pantheon, 1971.

Morgan, Robin, ed. *Sisterhood Is Powerful: An Anthology of Writings from the Women's Liberation Movement*. New York: Random House, 1970.

Roszak, Betty and Theodore, eds. *Masculine/Feminine: Readings in Sexual Mythology and the Liberation of Women*. New York: Harper, 1969.

Existentialism and Phenomenology

Binswanger, Ludwig. *Being-In-The-World*. Translated by Jacob Needleman. New York: Basic Books, 1963.

May, Rollo et al., ed. *Existence: A New Dimension in Psychiatry and Psychology*. New York: Basic Books, 1958.

Merleau-Ponty, Maurice. *Primacy of Perception*. Edited by James M. Edie. Evanston, Ill.: Northwestern University Press, 1964.

————. *Structure of Behavior*. Boston: Beacon Press, 1963.

Ruitenbeek, Hendrik M., ed. *Psychoanalysis and Existential Philosophy*. New York: Dutton, 1962.

Sartre, Jean-Paul. *Existential Psychoanalysis*. Chicago: Regnery, 1962.

————. *Search for a Method*. Translated by Hazel E. Barnes. New York: Knopf, 1963.

Fiction

Green, Hannah. *I Never Promised You a Rose Garden*. New York: Holt, 1964.

Kesey, Ken. *One Flew over the Cuckoo's Nest*. New York: Viking, 1962.

Keyes, Daniel. *Flowers for Algernon.* New York: Harcourt, 1966. (Made into the movie, *Charlie.*)

Lessing, Doris. *The Golden Notebook.* New York: Simon & Schuster, 1962.